STATESMEN of the LOST CAUSE

JEFFERSON DAVIS
And His Cabinet

By BURTON J. HENDRICK
Author of *The Lees of Virginia* and *Bulwark of the Republic*

WITH ILLUSTRATIONS

The Literary Guild of America, Inc.
NEW YORK

THE STARTING POINT OF THE GREAT WAR BETWEEN THE STATES
INAUGURATION OF JEFFERSON DAVIS

CONTENTS

PROLOGUE 3

I JEFFERSON DAVIS, SOUTHERN NATIONALIST
   1. A Miscellaneous Education 12
   2. The Early Tragedy 19
   3. Scholastic Recluse 24
   4. Varina Howell 34
   5. State Rights 40
   6. Leader of Secession 44
   7. Secretary of War 51

II THE GREAT GEORGIA TRIUMVIRATE
   1. Alexander H. Stephens 57
   2. The Man Within 65
   3. The Toombs-Stephens Coalition . . . 69
   4. Robert Toombs, Unionist 71
   5. Howell Cobb 75

III THE COTTON BELT SETS UP A CONFEDERACY
   1. The Montgomery Convention . . . 85
   2. Davis Elected President Accidentally . 95
   3. The Constitution for Secession . . . 100
   4. The First Cabinet 104

IV DIPLOMACY ON THE MEXICAN FRONT
   1. Recognition by Europe 107
   2. Colonel John Pickett 117
   3. Señor Corwin 125
   4. Farce in Mexico City 129

V A DIPLOMATIC DEBUT IN ENGLAND AND FRANCE
   1. The Quest for Recognition 139
   2. Lord Russell's Compliments 150

VI "THE BRAINS OF THE CONFEDERACY"
   1. Judah P. Benjamin 153
   2. Creole Marriage 164
   3. "Smiling As Usual" 169
   4. Benjamin in the War Office 181

CONTENTS

- **VII CONFEDERATE FINANCE**
  1. CHRISTOPHER MEMMINGER 188
  2. WHITE GOLD 194
  3. WHITE GOLD, CONTINUED 201
  4. THE COTTON FAMINE 208

- **VIII FRENCH BANKERS FLEECE THE CONFEDERACY**
  1. THE ERLANGER LOAN 216
  2. SLIDELL AND BENJAMIN 222
  3. INTERNATIONAL FINANCE 227

- **IX JAMES MURRAY MASON**
  1. A VIRGINIAN IN THE MAKING 233
  2. THE VIRGINIA CLAIM TO SUPERIORITY . . . 240
  3. ENGLAND AND THE UNITED STATES . . . 247

- **X QUEEN VICTORIA'S "TWO BAD BOYS"**
  1. LORD PALMERSTON 258
  2. LORD JOHN RUSSELL 262
  3. LONDON SOCIETY 267
  4. THE BLOCKADE 270
  5. THE MOVEMENT FOR RECOGNITION . . . 277

- **XI FRIENDS OF THE SECOND EMPIRE**
  1. JOHN SLIDELL 283
  2. EXILE IN NEW ORLEANS 289
  3. INTRIGUE IN PARIS 294

- **XII NAPOLEON III AND THE CONFEDERACY**
  1. A CAUTIOUS FRIEND 302
  2. A LARGE BRIBE OFFERED FRANCE . . . 309
  3. THE COLD SHOULDER 314

- **XIII THE DISCORD OF THE GOVERNORS**
  1. SECRETARY SEDDON 324
  2. PRO-UNIONISM IN THE SOUTH 330
  3. JOSEPH EMERSON BROWN 336
  4. ZEBULON B. VANCE 342

- **XIV "SECESSION" WITHIN THE CONFEDERACY**
  1. AN ARMY FOR GEORGIA 350
  2. JOE BROWN NULLIFIES CONSCRIPTION . . . 352
  3. JOE BROWN'S TEN THOUSAND 358

CONTENTS

XV MALLORY'S FIGHT ON THE BLOCKADE
  1. Stephen R. Mallory 363
  2. Men But No Ships 369
  3. The Ironclads 375

XVI COMIC RELIEF
  1. The Post Office 387
  2. The Propaganda of the Confederacy . . 389
  3. The Mission to the Vatican 399

XVII END OF THE "DESPOT" DAVIS
  1. The Inevitable Schism 409
  2. Hostility within the Cabinet . . . 414
  3. A Union Man at Heart 422
  4. The Failure of State Sovereignty . . . 429

BIBLIOGRAPHY 433

INDEX 441

ILLUSTRATIONS

THE STARTING POINT OF THE GREAT WAR BETWEEN THE
STATES . . . . *Frontispiece*
Inauguration of Jefferson Davis as Provisional President of the
Confederate States, February 18, 1861, at the state capitol,
Montgomery, Alabama

JEFFERSON DAVIS OF MISSISSIPPI (1808–1889) 14
Provisional and Permanent President of the Confederate States
of America

BIRTHPLACE OF JEFFERSON DAVIS IN KENTUCKY . . . 15
The log cabin in Christian (now Todd) County, Kentucky, in
which Jefferson Davis was born June 3, 1808

THE "WHITE HOUSE" OF THE CONFEDERACY, RICHMOND,
VIRGINIA 15
Official residence of Mr. and Mrs. Davis during the Civil War

ALEXANDER H. STEPHENS OF GEORGIA (1812–1883) . . . 76
Vice President of the Confederate States of America

ROBERT TOOMBS OF GEORGIA (1810–1885) 76
First Secretary of State of the Confederacy

HOWELL COBB (1815–1868) 77
United States Senator, Secretary of the Treasury under President Buchanan and afterward a leading Secessionist in Georgia

ROBERT M. T. HUNTER OF VIRGINIA (1809–1887) . . . 77
Secretary of State of the Confederacy from July, 1861, to
February, 1862

BENITO JUÁREZ (1806–1872) 120
The Indian who was President of Mexico at the outbreak of the
American Civil War

THOMAS CORWIN (1794–1865) 120
Senator from Ohio. Secretary of the Treasury under Fillmore,
and United States Minister to Mexico 1861–1864

WILLIAM LOWNDES YANCEY OF ALABAMA (1814–1863) . . 121
First Confederate Commissioner to European countries

ILLUSTRATIONS

JOHN T. PICKETT OF KENTUCKY 121
Confederate Commissioner to Mexico, 1861–1862. The daguerreotype shows him in his uniform as colonel of the Lopez filibustering expedition to Cuba in 1851

JUDAH PHILIP BENJAMIN (1811–1884) 188
Attorney General of the Confederacy, Secretary of War, and, from February, 1862, to the end, Secretary of State

GEORGE W. RANDOLPH OF VIRGINIA (1818–1867) . . . 189
Grandson of Thomas Jefferson. Secretary of War from March to November, 1862

CHRISTOPHER GUSTAVUS MEMMINGER OF SOUTH CAROLINA
(1803–1888) 189
Confederate Secretary of the Treasury

JAMES MURRAY MASON OF VIRGINIA (1798–1871) . . . 258
Confederate Commissioner to Great Britain

JOHN SLIDELL (1793–1871) 258
Son of New York City who became Confederate Commissioner to France

VISCOUNT PALMERSTON (1784–1865) 259
Prime Minister of Great Britain during the American Civil War

LORD JOHN RUSSELL (1792–1878) 259
Foreign Secretary of Great Britain during the Civil War

CHARLES LOUIS NAPOLEON BONAPARTE (1808–1873) . . 320
Emperor of the French, 1852–1870, as Napoleon III

EUGÉNIE DE MONTIJO (1826–1920) 320
Empress of the French by her marriage to Napoleon III, in 1853. Her maternal grandfather was an American

MAXIMILIAN (1832–1867) 321
Archduke of Austria, "Emperor" of Mexico

JOSEPH EMERSON BROWN (1821–1894) 362
Governor of Georgia, 1857–1885

ZEBULON BAIRD VANCE (1830–1894) 362
Governor of North Carolina, 1862–1865, afterward United States Senator

ILLUSTRATIONS

JAMES A. SEDDON OF VIRGINIA (1815–1880) 363
Secretary of War from November, 1862, to March, 1865

STEPHEN R. MALLORY OF FLORIDA (c. 1813–1873) . . . 363
Secretary of the Confederate Navy for the whole period of the war

BRIEF CHRONOLOGY OF THE CIVIL WAR

1860

November 6. Abraham Lincoln elected President of the United States.
December 20. South Carolina secedes from the Union.

1861

January 5. The Senators from Mississippi, Texas, Arkansas, Louisiana, Alabama, Florida, Georgia, hold a meeting in the Capitol at Washington. They recommend that these states secede from the Union and organize a Southern Confederacy. Advise that a Convention for this purpose be held at Montgomery, Alabama, not later than February 15 A committee, consisting of Davis, Slidell, and Mallory, appointed to supervise the execution of this programme.
January 9. Mississippi secedes.
January 10. Florida secedes.
January 11. Alabama secedes.
January 19. Georgia secedes. Alexander H. Stephens, Linton Stephens, and Herschel V. Johnson vote against Secession.
January 26. Louisiana secedes.
February 1. Texas secedes.
February 4. Confederate Convention organizes at Montgomery, Alabama, electing Howell Cobb President.
February 9. The Convention at Montgomery adopts a Constitution of the Confederate States of America, modeled on that of the United States. It establishes a provisional government with Jefferson Davis President and Alexander H. Stephens Vice President.
February 18. Jefferson Davis inaugurated President of the Confederate States of America.
March 4. Abraham Lincoln inaugurated President of the United States.
April 12. Fort Sumter fired upon.
April 15. President Lincoln issues a proclamation, calling for 75,000 volunteers to suppress insurrectionary "combinations."
April 17. Virginia secedes.
April 18. President Lincoln issues a proclamation, announcing the blockade of Southern ports.

April 29. The Legislature of Maryland passes resolutions refusing to secede.

May 21. North Carolina secedes.

May 26. The Confederate Congress at Montgomery, Alabama, adjourns to meet at Richmond, Virginia, on July 20.

June 8. Tennessee secedes.

July 21. Battle of Bull Run. The Federal army, routed, retreats to Washington.

July 26. Robert Toombs, Secretary of State, resigns. Robert M. T. Hunter appointed in his place.

November 8. Captain Wilkes removes Mason and Slidell, Confederate Commissioners to Great Britain and France, from the British merchant ship *Trent* and deposits them as prisoners in Fort Warren, Boston Harbor.

December 28. President Lincoln agrees to surrender Mason and Slidell to the British Government.

1862

January 19. Battle of Mill Springs, Kentucky. Federal victory. General Zollicoffer, Confederate commander, killed.

February 6. A fleet of Federal gunboats, under Flag Officer A. H. Foote, captures Fort Henry on the Tennessee River.

February 8. Roanoke Island, North Carolina, captured by a combined Federal military and naval expedition under General Burnside.

February 16. Fort Donelson, on the Cumberland River, Kentucky, surrenders to the Federal forces under General Grant.

February 22. Jefferson Davis, at Richmond, Virginia, inaugurated President of the Confederate States and Alexander H. Stephens Vice President, for terms of six years. On this day the permanent government of the Confederate States goes into effect.

February 26. Nashville, Tennessee, occupied by the Federals.

March 8. The Confederate ironclad *Merrimac* sails out of Norfolk Harbor and destroys the Federal warships *Cumberland* and *Congress,* lying at the mouth of the James River. The *Minnesota,* Federal warship, runs aground at Newport News.

March 9. The new Federal turreted warship, the *Monitor,* arrives at Hampton Roads and engages the *Merrimac.* After four hours of fighting, the *Merrimac* retires to Norfolk, having sustained serious injuries. It never fights again.

March 14. Federals, under General Burnside, capture New Bern, North Carolina.

BRIEF CHRONOLOGY OF THE CIVIL WAR xv

April 6 and 7. The Battle of Shiloh, Tennessee. Federals under Grant, Confederates under Albert Sidney Johnston and Beauregard. The first day the Confederates have the better of the struggle, but on the second reenforcements strengthen the Federals and the Confederates are forced to retreat to Corinth, Mississippi. Confederate Commander, Albert Sidney Johnston, killed on first day's battle and succeeded by Beauregard.

April 8. Federals capture Island No. 10, strategic point on the Mississippi River.

April 12. Fort Pulaski, Savannah, surrenders to the Federals.

April 16. President Lincoln signs the bill emancipating slaves in the District of Columbia.

April 24. Flag Officer Farragut passes the fortifications defending New Orleans.

April 25. New Orleans surrenders.

May 1. New Orleans taken possession of by Federal forces, under command of General Benjamin F. Butler.

May 3. Confederates evacuate Yorktown, Virginia.

May 5. Confederates defeated at Williamsburg, Virginia.

May 11. Confederates sink the *Merrimac* at her anchorage at Craney Island, Virginia, to prevent the ship from falling into the hands of the Federals.

May 24. Federals defeated by General (Stonewall) Jackson at Winchester, Virginia.

June 6. City of Memphis, Tennessee, surrenders to the Federals.

June 26–July 2. Seven days' battles before Richmond. General Joseph E. Johnston having been wounded, General Robert E. Lee succeeds to the command of the Confederates. The result of the battles is a triumph for the Confederate cause. The Federal Peninsular campaign a complete failure. General McClellan and the Union army forced to retreat to the James River, under the protection of Federal gunboats.

August 29, 30. Second Battle of Bull Run. Federals, under Pope, routed.

September 6. General Lee begins his invasion of Maryland.

September 17. Battle of Antietam, Maryland. Lee's army is repulsed, and forced to retreat to Virginia. His attempted invasion of the North a failure.

September 22. Lincoln issues his preliminary Emancipation Proclamation.

December 13. Battle of Fredericksburg, Virginia. The Federals, under General Burnside, repulsed and forced to retreat.

December 31. Battle of Murfreesboro, Tennessee, Rosecrans commanding Federals and Braxton Bragg the Confederates. Confederates at first successful; but three days later Bragg attacks again, is defeated and compelled to retreat.

1863

January 1. Lincoln issues his Emancipation Proclamation declaring free all slaves in states and parts of states then in "rebellion" against the Federal Government.
May 2–4. Battle of Chancellorsville. Federals defeated. Stonewall Jackson killed.
July 3. End of three-day battle of Gettysburg. Federal victory.
July 4. Vicksburg surrenders to General Grant.
July 9. Port Hudson, on the Mississippi, surrenders to the Federals. This gives the Union complete control of the Mississippi and splits the Confederacy in two.
September 19–21. Battle of Chickamauga. Confederate victory.
November 23–25. Battle of Chattanooga. Federal victory.

1864

March 1. Grant becomes Lieutenant General, in command of all the armies of the United States.
May 5–6. Battle of the Wilderness, Virginia. Grant starts his campaign against Lee. The result indecisive.
May 11–12. The "Bloody Angle" of Spottsylvania.
June 3. Battle of Cold Harbor. Federals, under Grant, repulsed with great loss.
June 13–18. Grant crosses the James, taking up headquarters at City Point.
June 18. Grant begins siege of Petersburg, Virginia.
June 27. Battle of Kenesaw Mountain. Sherman fails to carry Johnston's position. On July 2, however, Johnston abandons Kenesaw and retreats to the Chattahoochee.
July 18. Sherman crosses the Chattahoochee and begins his movement against Atlanta. President Davis removes Johnston and appoints General J. B. Hood in his place.
August 5. Farragut reduces the forts in Mobile Bay, Alabama.
September 2. Sherman captures Atlanta, Georgia, and starts on his March to the Sea.

November 8. Lincoln reëlected President.

December 20. Sherman captures Savannah, Georgia.

1865

February 18. Sherman captures Charleston, South Carolina.

March 23. Sherman captures Goldsborough, North Carolina, and forms a junction with Schofield.

April 1. Federals, under Sheridan, fight battle of Five Forks. A Confederate disaster.

April 2. Grant breaks through Lee's defenses at Petersburg. Confederates in flight, with Federals pursuing.

April 3. Federals enter Richmond and find the city in flames, the work of Confederate mobs. Davis and his Cabinet in flight.

April 9. Lee surrenders to Grant at Appomattox Court House, Virginia.

April 14. Assassination of Abraham Lincoln.

April 26. General Johnston surrenders his army to General Sherman at Durham, North Carolina. The war at an end.

STATESMEN OF THE LOST CAUSE

PROLOGUE

THIS volume on the Southern effort in the Civil War has at least one novel feature. It says practically nothing about military leaders. Lee, Stonewall Jackson, Jeb Stuart, Joseph E. Johnston — these, the usually dominating characters in books on the Confederacy, appear only occasionally in the following pages. The fact is commonly forgotten that the South possessed civic as well as military figures. It had a government as well as an army. Yet the civilian side has so far attracted little attention from historians. Perhaps the South itself is to blame for this neglect. Significantly its hero of that conflict to-day is Robert E. Lee, not Jefferson Davis. Just as significantly the hero of the North is Abraham Lincoln and not Grant or Sherman. Probably few Americans at the present time could name more than two or three of the seventeen Southerners who served in the Davis Cabinet, while Seward, Stanton, Chase, Welles, and other political captains of the Union are among the most familiar portraits in our national gallery.

Thus does the popular mind, working instinctively, perhaps subconsciously, arrive at a great historic truth. For the fact that the North emphasizes statesmanship in the Civil War and the South military achievement goes far to interpreting the events of 1861–1865. In particular, it may answer a question much debated in that era and since. Why did the South lose the war? Historians on both sides have had a ready explanation for this failure. There is now general agreement that the Southern cause was doomed from the start. The Union's superiority in population and wealth is the commonly accepted reason for its success. In view of the virtual consensus on this point, it is interesting to glance back at opinion contemporary with the Civil War, especially that of Europe. In 1861 and for at least the two succeeding years, European observers also regarded the end as foreordained. Only the judgment of England and the Continent differed from the one almost generally held to-day. In the eyes of Europe in 1861-1863, the North was the side destined inevitably to defeat. Not only military experts, but statesmen, held this conviction. On it the whole diplomatic policy of Europe on "the American question" was constructed. The Federal Union of the fathers was at an end. Two republics at least would occupy the area formerly ruled by one; not improbably, four, five, or even more independent nations would rise on the ruins of the Federal Union, thus creating a political system in the northern half of the Western Hemisphere not unlike that which for fifty years had raised havoc in South America.

What was the reason that the statesmen, diplomats, journalists, and historians of England and the Continent took this portentous view of the American Civil War? Why did they regard a Confederate triumph as inherent in the nature of the case? Merely because, as they interpreted history, Uncle Sam had undertaken an impossible military task. Many nations had assumed such problems in the past, and almost all had failed. The circumstance that the North outnumbered the South in population, the fact that its domestic wealth and commerce exceeded those of the Confederacy, did not seem to these experienced observers the ultimate considerations. Indeed, in face of the respective problems confronting the two parties, it was not certain that Northern power so greatly surpassed that of the South. In an absolute sense, of course, the Federal Government unquestionably counted more men, and commanded more resources, than its adversary. But surface ratios like these did not necessarily determine events. The military problems of the two sides were very different, and would have to be weighed in estimating their relative physical might. The

PROLOGUE

fight was an unequal one, if considered merely from the standpoint of men and materials; here the North clearly possessed the advantage. It was similarly unequal, from the standpoint of military strategy, and here the South just as unmistakably wielded the upper hand.

No one knows, and probably never will know, just how many men fought in the Civil War. The Confederacy kept no statistics of any value, and those of the Federal Government, superficially more precise, involve many repetitions. Reliable figures on the population of the two sections exist, and these usually do unwarranted service in attempts to arrive at their respective military strength. In 1860, the states that afterward formed the Confederacy had roughly 9,000,000 souls; those that remained loyal to the Union and contributed to its man power — Maryland, Kentucky, and Missouri, must be eliminated from the calculation — 19,000,000. The figures for the South, it is true, comprise 4,000,000 negroes, but these, from the first, increased its military power, for they could provide a service as teamsters, cooks, workers on entrenchments and fortifications — labor that white recruits performed in the Federal army. Negroes also gave the South its supply of laborers and farmers at home, thus freeing the Anglo-Saxon population for military service. Moreover, the blacks comprised a reserve for possible soldiers at the front; the idea of using them for this purpose, naturally revolting to Southern instincts, appealed from the first to many farseeing leaders. In the last two years, General Lee favored the enlistment of colored troops, and in March, 1865, Jefferson Davis himself advocated a bill for such enlistments. The Confederate Congress passed this measure in March, 1865, a few weeks before Lee's surrender.

It is therefore fair to say that the proportion of Northern to Southern men available for war service stood at about two to one. In view of the military problems confronting the two sides, this indicates a proportion rather in favor of the Davis

Government. The point is that the North was fighting on the offensive, the South on the defensive. The North was the invader; the South was engaged in repelling its invasion. Abraham Lincoln was waging a war of conquest, and Jefferson Davis was struggling to repel the attack. One side was encroaching on an unfamiliar country, comprising a vast territorial extent and a hostile people, and the other was standing firmly on its own friendly soil, could fight on positions of its own selection, and was engaged in no real effort to subdue the enemy, but merely to beat him off. It is a truism of the military art that success in offensive warfare requires a great superiority in men. The usual estimate places this at three to one. "The numerical preponderance of the North," says a leading English authority, Sir Frederick Maurice, in his book on Robert E. Lee, "was for the purposes of war far less than would appear from an examination of the election returns." The same authority places the proportion of North to South at five to three — somewhat under the two to one estimate above, and considerably inferior to the three to one usually regarded as necessary in offensive warfare.

The performance of the South which the world so greatly admired — that of holding, with half the population, the North at bay for two years — was no new phenomenon. Such exploits are found in all ages. Illustrations in plenty spring at once to mind. One thinks of the Greeks against the Persians; the little island of Queen Elizabeth against the mighty realm of Philip II; the Netherlands against Spain; Frederick the Great in the eighteenth century against the combined powers of Europe; the American colonies in 1776 against Great Britain. A striking case was that of 1792, when the ragamuffin soldiers of the French Revolution defeated and dispersed the finely equipped forces of Prussia and Austria, far outnumbering them. The battle of Valmy bears a certain resemblance to Bull Run, and it was the first step in that conquest of most of Europe ultimately achieved by Napoleon. Perhaps our own time supplies the most astounding instance, that of the two Boer republics of South Africa, with a population of 200,000, resisting the might of Great Britain (45,000,000) and its world empire for four years, from 1898 to 1902. All these powers, like the United States in 1861–1865, were invaders, engaged in conquest, fighting a people numerically weaker, but brave and determined, fiercely employed in the desperate task of defending their own firesides.

The courage and ability of the Southern armies aroused the admiration of their foes; that Southern generalship, at least in the first two years, surpassed that of the North, stands upon the surface; other facts than an inferiority in military strength must therefore hold the secret of Confederate failure. We shall probably find it rather in civil than in military affairs. Had statesmen ruled its domestic and foreign policies with the same skill that Lee and other generals guided its armies, the result might have easily been very different. In one respect this assertion may look like a reversal of history. Statesmanship was a quality on which the South had always prided itself. Its political thinkers had played a leading rôle in framing the Constitution. For nearly forty years following 1789 it gave the Union its Presidents. For most of the thirty years preceding the Civil War the South had governed the nation in all three departments. It seems strange, therefore, that at the supreme test of 1861–1865 this region should so disastrously fail in that statesmanship which it had always regarded as almost its exclusive possession. But perhaps there is a solution to the mystery. It may be found in the particular South that organized the Confederacy and plunged the nation into war. The fact to be kept always in mind is that the South which started the Confederacy, and dominated its government for four years, was not the South that wrote the Declaration of Independence, played so important a rôle in framing the Constitution, and provided so much leadership for the United States in its earliest days.

There is still too great a tendency to romanticize the "lost cause," to picture it as an uprising of the "chivalry of the South," and to regard its leaders as a gathering of traditional "Southern aristocrats." Really, the Confederate States of America rose in a region as recently frontier in character as the West that produced Abraham Lincoln. Of the seven states that formed the Montgomery Government, only two — South Carolina and Georgia — had existed in 1787. The soil of Florida, Louisiana, Arkansas, Texas, and a considerable section of Mississippi at that time were still parts of the Spanish empire. The Southern commonwealth chiefly famous for statesmen — Virginia — had no hand in organizing the Confederacy. Neither had North Carolina or Tennessee, other states distinguished for political leadership in the Union. These older states came in three months afterward, for particular reasons; they had no part in framing the Southern constitution, in organizing the government, and had little to do in the civil department for four years of war. Thus old-fashioned "Southern chivalry," and old-time "Southern aristocrats" were scarcely represented in the civic empire of Jefferson Davis at the outset. It was the creation of a new South that, in social amenities and in political wisdom, hardly resembled the South of history and legend. The new-rich Southwest contributed the political leaders, the old traditional South the military captains. Of the five Confederate generals who won world-wide fame — Lee, Jackson, Stuart, Joseph E. Johnston, Longstreet — four most suggestively were sons of Virginia; Longstreet came from Georgia, also a state of the old South. That is to say the leaders who gave the Confederacy prestige were mostly Virginians of superior breed, while the cotton belt was the region that provided the politicians who failed.

Probably the critic completely imbued with the spirit of the ancient southland would find little difficulty in solving the mystery. His explanation would be tinged with a snobbishness offensive to a democratic age. He would be thinking of "family"

PROLOGUE 9

and "tradition," and insisting on the right of certain wellborn classes to serve the state. Such an old James River patrician, looking upon the company of public men who dominated the Confederacy, would have found little to recall the ancient regime. The kind of Southern leadership that had gained the upper hand by 1861 hardly resembled that of tobacco-growing Virginia and Carolina; it was, to use a word made familiar in recent years, bourgeois, even Philistine. It was a land of newly acquired wealth, not particularly well-mannered or cultured, but pushing, self-assertive, and arrogant. Nor was this new country exclusively Southern, for the hordes that had rushed into the cotton El Dorado of the Southwest were composed not only of quick-fortune-hunting sons of Dixie Land, but of adventurers from the North and New England. These were the elements that gave rise to the Confederacy and provided its civic leaders. Merely to catalogue the most important of these chieftains shows how the insurgent South, in its social and economic aspects, differed from the land of Washington and Jefferson. The President of the Confederate States of America was born in a log cabin. The Vice President spent his early days as "corn dropper" on his father's slaveless farm and chore boy in tasks ordinarily assigned to negroes. The Secretary of State — at least the one who filled that office for most of the war — was the son of the keeper of a driedfish shop in London. The Secretary of the Treasury, born in Germany, spent his childhood in a Charleston orphanage. The Secretary of the Navy, son of a Connecticut Yankee, started life as assistant to his widowed mother in running a sailor's boardinghouse in Key West, Florida. The Postmaster General, son of a tanner, had for a time engaged in an occupation that made any man a social outcast in the South — that of plantation overseer. The Confederacy's ablest diplomat was not Southern in origin; born in New York City, he was the son of a tallow chandler, and had in his early days followed that trade himself. If the cabinet occasionally enlisted men of more pretentious stock, all of these recruits, with one exception — Seddon of Virginia — occupied their posts for very brief periods, and all were failures.

As intimated above, a democratic generation does not look upon beginnings of this kind as disqualifying men for eminent careers and high-minded service to the state. The only reason the point is insisted on in this place is to show that a new South, displacing the old in political dominance, had risen in the forty years preceding the Civil War and that the Confederacy was its creation. Probably the political philosopher would find an even more significant study in the effect exercised upon the Davis experiment by the constitutional ideas that formed its reason for existence. State Sovereignty, the Right of Secession — these were the foundation stones on which this new nation was built. They had provided the theme of impassioned argument for seventy-five years. Now at last Southern statesmen had before them the opportunity of testing the worth of these principles in the practical conduct of a government. Was a nation possible composed of independent units, each claiming to be a "sovereign state," joined to a central power only by the loosest ties? Could a Confederacy assert the authority necessary to vital existence in which each "sovereign republic" asserted the right to withdraw at will? The Federalists and Hamiltonians had always objected to Jeffersonism on pragmatic grounds; such theories were preposterous simply because they would not work. They could produce no orderly society — only chaos. The failure of Davis and his colleagues has an important bearing on this point. It seems to prove that the "consolidationists" had the practical argument on their side. Southern students of the Civil War are coming, more and more, to accept this point of view. One of the most scholarly of these, Professor Frank L. Owsley, of Vanderbilt University, has probably said the final word on the subject. "There is an old saying that the seeds of death are sown at our birth. This was true of the Southern Confederacy, and the seeds of death were state rights. The principle on which the South based its actions before 1861 and on which it hoped to base its future government was its chief weakness. If a monument is ever erected as a symbolical gravestone over the 'lost cause' it should have engraved upon it these words: 'Died of State Rights.' "

Thus the Confederacy failed for two reasons. It produced no statesmen, such as the South had produced in the revolutionary crisis of 1776 and afterward. It was also founded on a principle that made impossible the orderly conduct of public affairs. The purpose of the present volume is to study the statesmanship and diplomacy of this new Southern generation and to study it in the biographies of the characters who reigned in the time of America's most tragic crisis.

I

JEFFERSON DAVIS, SOUTHERN NATIONALIST

1

A Miscellaneous Education

ONE of the several paradoxes in the career of Jefferson Davis is that he should have passed into history as the typical "Southern aristocrat," the appropriate successor, in founding a new Southern nation, to the Virginians who played so great a rôle in establishing the American Union. The truth is that in birth and early environment Davis was as much of a frontiersman as Abraham Lincoln. The Northern President, in fact, had a much longer background of rough-and-ready Americanism than had his Southern rival. In 1861 the Lincolns had been Americans for seven generations, the Davises for only four. Father Abraham came of an English family that had settled in Hingham, Massachusetts, in 1637, while Jefferson Davis was the grandson of a Welshman who emigrated to Philadelphia in the first year of the eighteenth century. Both families, it will be observed, began their American existence in the North, and, after wanderings that extended over a century and a half, set up domiciles in the new state of Kentucky. The Davis gens started in Pennsylvania, paused for a generation in Georgia, then passed on to Christian County — now Todd — in the land of Daniel Boone, and built the log cabin at Fairview in which the future Confederate President was born, June 3, 1808. The Lincolns advanced by slower stages from Massachusetts to Pennsylvania, to Virginia, and then to the neighborhood of Hodgenville, Kentucky, and erected the log cabin in which, on February 12, 1809, the Emancipator first saw light. These two primitive structures were about one hundred and twenty miles apart. It is not likely, in view of the system of transportation existing at this time, that the Davis and the

Lincoln families ever met, but there was nothing in their circumstances which would have made neighborly relations impossible.

Mrs. Davis prefixes to the *Memoir*[1] of her husband a picture of his birthplace — a homestead that hardly suggests a Stratford Hall, a Westover, a Mount Vernon, or any of the other famous memorials of the aristocratic South. It is frankly a log cabin, slightly larger and more pretentious than Lincoln's, but still redolent of the forest. To present-day Americans a log cabin is a log cabin, but, in reality, there were as many varieties in this pioneer form of American architecture as in more ambitious orders. Lincoln's place of nativity had advanced beyond the three walls — the fourth side open to the winds — without door or other flooring than that of mother earth, which represented the beginning in a noble type of residence; it was completely closed, its logs were chinked with clay, it possessed a regular hinged opening and possibly a glazed window, to say nothing of a stick chimney. The house of Samuel Davis, Jefferson's father, had advanced one degree beyond the Lincolnian model. It consisted of two rooms; it was, in fact, two separate log cabins, each with its own outside chimney, connected by a passageway, the whole enclosed under a common roof. To what extent this symbolized a loftier scale of living, experts in such discriminations must decide. There is another sign of a slightly higher social plane in favor of Davis, for his father, in addition to unprofitable tobacco planting, engaged in breeding horses — and blooded racing animals at that. But, in the leveling gaze of contemporaries, there would probably have been no distinctions drawn between the two families. The fathers of Lincoln and Davis were unsuccessful men; both had the habit of pulling up stakes and tempting fortune in new situations. The biographers of Abraham Lincoln have discovered far more about his progenitor than

[1] *Jefferson Davis, Ex-President of The Confederate States of America; a Memoir*, by his wife. 2 vols. 1890.

have students of Jefferson Davis about his father Samuel, but it is safe to say that in circumstances, in standing, in the general tenor of their lives, they represented about the same stage of progress. Both were sober-living, honest, industrious — if not overthrifty — yeomen, and neither would have impressed his neighbors as likely to produce a son destined to play a great rôle in his country's history.

While in origin Jefferson Davis and Abraham Lincoln started on fairly even terms, circumstances, in childhood and youth, became far more favorable for the Southerner. Life bestowed on him one gift that Lincoln had been denied. That was an ambitious and successful older brother. Moreover, the difference in age between Jefferson and Joseph Emory Davis was so great — twenty-four years — that the position this elder brother occupied was practically that of a father. And it was Joseph Davis who lifted the family from obscurity and made it one of the foremost in Mississippi. Thus Jefferson Davis remembered little of the hardships that formed the lot of the pioneer. Of the early Kentucky log cabin he had no recollection. The family abandoned this home when the future statesman was still an infant, and started, with the usual apparatus of early American travel, — wagons, horses, cattle, a negro or two, and a family of ten children, Jefferson being the youngest, — through previously unpenetrated forests and swamps, on a six-month trek, crossing Kentucky, Tennessee, Mississippi, — at that time almost unsettled, and not yet a state, — until it finally came to a halt in Bayou Têche, southeastern Louisiana. Of this home, notable for its absence of prosperity and the constant menace of "chills and fever," Davis also had no remembrance, for, after a year or two, the family again struck camp, and crossed the great river into southwest Mississippi. Here, at Woodville, the elder Davis at last found his home, and it is here that Jefferson Davis's childhood consciousness begins. But here again, his memories are not extensive or deep-seated. The Davis family itself had

From a Photograph by Brady

JEFFERSON DAVIS OF MISSISSIPPI (1808–1889)

Brown Bros

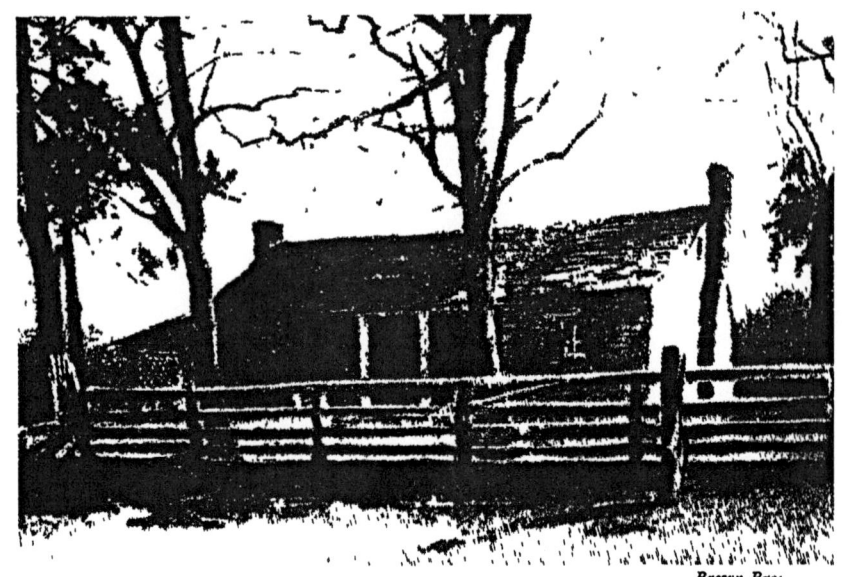

BIRTHPLACE OF JEFFERSON DAVIS IN KENTUCKY

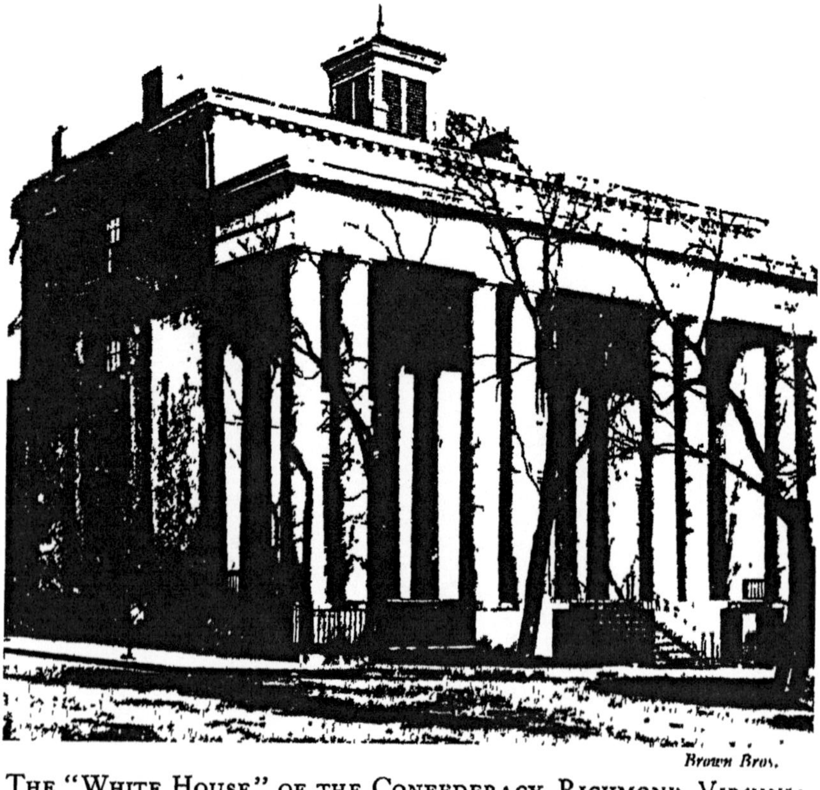

Brown Bros.

THE "WHITE HOUSE" OF THE CONFEDERACY, RICHMOND, VIRGINIA

found a permanent resting place, but the youngest child had not. He remained until his seventh year, obtaining such rudimentary instruction as was possible in a log-cabin school.

This section of the Mississippi delta is one in which such sanitary forces as the Rockefeller Board have recently been active. From time immemorial it has been the breeding ground of contagious disease — malaria, yellow fever, dysentery, hookworm. That the boy Jefferson was a sickly child is therefore not surprising. Here he laid the basis of that ill-health which pursued him to the end. This may have been the reason why he was sent back to his native Kentucky for his education. Not improbably he had also begun to display mental qualities that were deemed worthy of better cultivation than the Mississippi backwoods could provide. Unquestionably the determining influence was Joseph Davis, who had already begun to display pride in his "little Jeff." From all accounts that have come down of Davis at this time and for several years afterward, he was precisely the kind of boy in whom an elder brother of benevolent character would take delight. Jefferson was handsome and intelligent; his large blue eyes, thick brown hair, and finely shaped forehead, his erect, manly carriage, winning manners, amiability of temper, and honorable conduct, as well as an early manifested interest in study, held forth the promise, if not of a distinguished career, at least of a worthy one. Fortunately for the boy, his brother's success came at exactly the right moment. After a preparatory law course in Kentucky, Joseph Davis moved to Natchez, opened a law office, and secured a sufficiently gainful practice to lay the foundation of his real career as cotton planter. He acquired a large estate on the Mississippi, about twenty miles south of Vicksburg, which rapidly yielded a substantial fortune. The elevation of the Davis family now became an ambition as keenly pursued as the heaping up of wealth, and in realizing this programme the training of "little brother" was an essential detail. Thus Jefferson Davis, in his opportunities, his equipment of ideas, and political and constitutional convictions, was the achievement of this masterful and successful brother, generally esteemed the richest man in Mississippi, and in many ways the state's leading citizen.

The result was that Jefferson received a far better education than his brothers and sisters; far better, indeed, than fell to the lot of most boys in that undeveloped country. He certainly enjoyed far greater chances than fell to the lot of Abraham Lincoln. In consequence he grew up to be a polished gentleman, whereas Lincoln, in outward bearing at least, always carried the rustic quality with which he started life. Still, there was a haphazard character in Davis's scholastic career, and this is important in explaining the man's political views and allegiances. It was not the kind of experience that focused the boy's interest in any one Southern state; it made him rather a devotee of the South as a whole. It took him, at the most impressionable period, into several commonwealths, and brought him under a variety of influences. There was a log-cabin school in Mississippi until his seventh birthday; two years were spent in an academy in Lexington, Kentucky, maintained by the Dominican fathers; four years again in Mississippi, part of the time in a log-cabin school and part at a local institution kept by a clergyman from Boston; then two years at Transylvania College in Kentucky, followed by four years at West Point — a variety of residences, and a variety of instructors, ranging from old-fashioned schoolmasters to Catholic priests, New England scholars, and the miscellaneous staff at the Military establishment. All this might be expected to exercise a cosmopolitan influence on a receptive mind. Just how much learning Jefferson picked up in these wanderings is not clear. According to Mrs. Davis, the young man emerged from the experience with the ability "to read Latin well," some knowledge of Greek, and the traditional training in mathematics and "natural philosophy"; it was the routine education of the day, and though Davis made no reputation as a scholar, he probably acquired more culture than most young Americans of the time. In the matter of general literature his reading does not seem to have been extensive; at least, his writings show no familiarity with great authors, though they do indicate more than a cursory knowledge of American history, especially in its economic and constitutional departments. Davis's real education was not acquired under the lamp; it came afterward, as will appear — and again as a gift from the ever-attentive brother. But these early experiences left other traces than the purely mental. They gave the young man a wider acquaintance with the American nation than the average Southerner of his period received. In his last days Davis dictated an account of his itinerant preparation for life.[2] Significantly he recalls not so vividly his schools and teachers as the journeys that gave the background of the educational process. Greek and algebra did not leave such a lasting image as the trips, on pony back, from Mississippi, through Tennessee to Kentucky and return; trips that took several weeks, and included first-hand inspection of the wilderness, with its forests, it rivers, its Indians, its white pioneers, its camps in the open, its glimpses of flatboats on the Mississippi — the one way of river transportation. Several weeks spent with Andrew Jackson at the Hermitage — Jackson then famous for the battle of New Orleans, with his Presidency still nearly fifteen years ahead — left more permanent marks than did the schoolroom. Of chief importance, in its influence on Davis's life, was the varying picture which these early days gave him of the South. Significantly, the young man continued those Southern pilgrimages that had marked his father's existence. The elder Davis had lived in four Southern states — Georgia, Kentucky, Louisiana, and Mississippi; the young man became as familiar with Tennessee and Kentucky as with Mississippi. Thus it was the South as

---

[2] Published in Mrs. Davis's *Memoir*, Vol. I, Chapters I–IV There is also a brief autobiography in Dunbar Rowland's *Jefferson Davis, Constitutionalist*, Vol. I, pp. xx–xxxi.

a region rather than any particular state that formed his Southern background. Jefferson Davis, indeed, reached his thirtieth year before he became identified with any one community; the man who prided himself on being the most conspicuous spokesman of State rights had well advanced into manhood before he could claim any single state as his own. Quite different this, from the experience of the typical Virginian or Carolinian, to both of whom concentration on a definite commonwealth, or "country," as they called it, was the rule of being.

From the day that he left Kentucky, in 1824, to his return as a mature man to Mississippi in 1835, Davis continued this far from provincial career. Four years at West Point, on the Hudson, seven as an army officer in Wisconsin, Iowa, Illinois, and Missouri — here again the experience was national in its tendencies rather than particular. The first time Davis appears in the story as a well-defined character is the period spent at West Point. The picture on the whole is a pleasing one, though it does contain a few shadows — the very traits that warped the man's outlook as a statesman. Again we have reminiscences of the erect, handsome figure, with its springy step, its soldierlike bearing; of the finely shaped head, the meditative blue eyes, the sharp but symmetrical features; and there are references in plenty to the courtesy, the cheerfulness, the ever-present dignity that embellished the young man's daily life. It is also true that he was a little remote, not given to participating in sports — except dancing and riding, for his absorption in horses was worthy of his Kentucky birth. Neither are there many indications of a sense of humor or of lightheartedness; his companions afterward recalled that Davis was at times "taciturn," and there are early suggestions of that "arrogance" and "hauteur," that complete self-confidence and satisfaction with his own opinions which assumed greater prominence as the years wore on. He was not easily companionable and his bearing, on the whole, was serious. So far as official records indicate, Davis made no great success in scholarship; he was graduated twenty-third out of a class of thirty-three; and in deportment he did not achieve the impeccable rank of his fellow student, Robert E. Lee, who weathered the four years without a single demerit. Davis indeed acquired many black marks — a few more would have ruined his army career. Certain episodes give a more fallible portrait than the generalizations of his associates. His behavior on one or two occasions almost resulted in dismissal. An undue fondness for "Benny's Tavern," a drinking place surreptitiously favored by cadets, led to a court-martial, Davis escaping expulsion only on the ground of his previous good behavior. West Point was the scene of his first quarrel with Joseph E. Johnston, afterward general in the Confederate Army. This early altercation rose, not over military strategy, but romance, for Davis and Johnston became rivals for the affections of a "tavern keeper's daughter," finally settling their disagreement with their fists. According to legend Johnston proved the better man, and thus Davis, at an early age, suffered one of those "mental wounds" which, according to the modern psychologist, can so profoundly affect a man's whole life and even influence history. If this was indeed the germ of that hatred with which Davis pursued Johnston in after life, the "tavern keeper's daughter" at West Point may be one of those obscure characters who determine great events, for Davis's hostility to Johnston is usually regarded as one of the causes that led the Confederacy to destruction.

2

THE EARLY TRAGEDY

The seven years from 1828 to 1835 Davis spent as a lieutenant in the army of the United States. The story of this period, so far as exploits are concerned, is the familiar one of life at Western military posts; there was the usual amount of Indian fighting, fort building, scouting, simple social existence, that made up life in the undeveloped country. The Black Hawk War, in which the young officer played a creditable part, — to him was assigned the honor of conducting this celebrated Indian fighter, as war prisoner, from his native soil to Jefferson Barracks, Saint Louis, — was the one event of the time that cuts much figure in the history books. But probably the routine of army existence had a greater influence on Davis's character than on the average graduate of West Point. Most commentators make much of his confidence in himself as a military expert; some trace the military decline of the Confederacy to his constant interference with his generals, his tendency to accept literally the Presidential duty as commander in chief. But not improbably his field service under Uncle Sam influenced his character in more subtle fashion. It tended to strengthen a natural rigidity of will and thought. Davis was always more concerned with the formalities of life than with its flexibilities. Thinking and living by rote handicapped him as a politician and statesman. He adopted certain principles and certain rules of conduct, and sought to make all his opinions and acts fit into these patterns. This human difference between Davis and his future adversary is illustrated by their attitude towards this Black Hawk War. Abraham Lincoln served as captain of a kind of Mulligan's guard in this not particularly heroic struggle; in after life he seemed to retain memories only of its ridiculous aspects; he liked to describe the blood he had sacrificed for his country — most of it abstracted by huge swarms of mosquitoes — and his fierce onslaughts on wildonion beds. But all the comments of Davis are serious. And his attitude toward the army was similarly respectful, fairly reverential. Something in the experience harmonized with his own nature. Davis loved routine, definite organization, obedience, deference to superiors, authority, gradation in position; he liked to frame premises and draw from them the logical consequences. Army life stimulated these tendencies and really caked the man's mind into fixed habits. To give orders and have them obeyed; to look up to superiors and to keep those of lower rank in their appropriate place; to have ideas and deeds follow each other in precise regulation — such was his natural disposition, and army experience did much to intensify it.

Not that his service was empty of more "humane" experiences. In fact, it included the episode that formed nearly the most tragic chapter in a life that was full of tragedies. And nothing sheds more light upon the man's personal side than his romance with Sarah Knox Taylor. It reveals Davis in his several phases — his loyalty, his devotion, his capacity for giving and inspiring affection, as well as his tenacity, his fierceness of temper, and his capacity for arousing antagonisms in others. Those inclined to regard the man as all austerity and fixations should study his relations with Miss Taylor and her stormy sire. She was the petite, blue-eyed, brown-haired daughter of old "rough and ready" Zachary — the same gentleman who, fifteen years afterward, became twelfth President of the United States. In 1832 this future hero of Buena Vista was colonel of the First Infantry, and, as such, in command of Fort Crawford, near Prairie du Chien, Wisconsin, where one of his subordinate officers was the twenty-four-year-old Lieutenant Davis. Naturally the home of the commandant was the social centre of a community that offered little chance for diversion; and inevitably Taylor's three sprightly daughters — Anne, Sarah Knox, and Betty — became the lodestars of the junior officers. That Knox Taylor — she was always called by her middle name, given her, strangely enough, in honor of Washington's first Secretary of War — and Jefferson Davis should promptly fall in love caused some surprise, for the girl was as gay and witty and carefree as the Mississippian was matter of fact and thoughtful; but of the intensity of the emotion, on both sides, there were plenty of evidences.

Ordinarily the affair should have gone pleasantly enough. To most Southern parents, Jefferson Davis would have seemed an eminently acceptable son-in-law. He was handsome, his manners were highbred, his life was correct, he was well-educated, he had all the prudential qualities that make a responsible husband; besides, Jefferson's brother Joseph had already lifted the Davis family to front rank in Mississippi. But Taylor displayed a most unreasoning and implacable hostility to the match. All the arguments of daughter, wife, and brother officers at the Fort could not reconcile him to the marriage. Several explanations have been offered for this opposition, but none are satisfactory. The one on which most emphasis has been laid is Zachary's own — that he did not propose to have his daughter marry into army life. Yet his older daughter Anne was already the wife of an army officer, with her father's full consent; his youngest daughter subsequently made the same kind of an alliance, with parental approval. Moreover, in anticipation of marriage, Davis had already made his plans to retire from the service and set up as cotton planter. But the prospective father-in-law fought the wedding as bitterly as before. For two years the painful situation continued. Taylor would not permit Davis to enter his door, and the lovers were forced to meet in the homes of friends; everybody in the region took their side, harshly criticizing Taylor for unfriendliness to so desirable a bridegroom. In 1835, two years after plighting herself to Jefferson, Knox Taylor took the boat from Prairie du Chien for Louisville, Kentucky, where, at her aunt's home, she planned to marry the lieutenant. Just before sailing time, her father came aboard; the girl, it is said, literally fell upon her knees, beseeching forgiveness and consent to the marriage. Zachary proved adamant as ever. The wedding took place June 17, 1835, in the approving presence of many members of the Taylor family. "The estrangement between Lieutenant Davis and Colonel Taylor," says the second Mrs. Davis,[3] "was not healed in the lifetime of Mrs. Davis."

[3] *Memoir*, Vol. I, p. 162.

What is the reason for Taylor's behavior? Many years afterward the two men met on the battlefield of Buena Vista, in the Mexican War. Military experts, then and since, have given a large measure of credit for the success of this critical engagement to Jefferson Davis. So did Zachary Taylor at the time. According to the story, he congratulated his former adversary on his tactics and heroism, adding, "My daughter was a better judge of men than I was." This would imply that his opposition had been personal. And that was undoubtedly the fact. He did not like Davis; the man aroused in him an irrational antagonism; he turned from him for no reason that could be analyzed. And Davis returned this hostility in full measure. Grotesque stories are told of Davis at this time. Captain McPhee, one of his sympathizing friends, used to relate that Davis, after being debarred from the Taylor home, and disdainfully treated in other ways, asked him to carry a challenge to the irate Taylor. McPhee declared he would act as second only in case Davis gave up all claims to the maiden. "I would not help him shoot his own father-in-law," was McPhee's quite understandable objection. Subsequent events brought Davis and Taylor closely together, both in the army and in politics, and soothed their mutual aversion. Probably the pathetic end of the romance had much to do with this new relationship. For the bride, taken to Davis's new plantation home in Mississippi, survived her marriage only three months. The fever-laden atmosphere of lower Louisiana, where she was paying a visit to one of Davis's sisters, took her in her twenty-third year. So vanished the one human being who was able to arouse the deepest emotions of this silent, undemonstrative man. Though Jefferson Davis married a second time, and married happily, he never recovered from the shock of his first and lasting love affair.

3
Scholastic Recluse

This tragedy brought to an end the earlier part of Davis's life and embarked him on a new path. In external circumstances, in aspiration and personal development, the Davis of this second period is a different character. From 1835 to 1844 the young man was what he had never been before, a definitely placed resident of a particular state. For his first twenty-seven years, as already described, he had led a wandering existence — as had his father and grandfather; practically every region of the South and a considerable part of the North and West had provided abiding places. Thus that loyalty to a particular region which is supposed to be the birthright of the traditional Southerner had not been his portion. Consider the ancestors of Robert E. Lee: for more than two hundred years they had been the sons, not only of Virginia, but, for the most part, of a particular county, Westmoreland; they had been born to long-established ideas, to ancestral loyalties, and to certain political and social standards. No influences of this kind had surrounded the days of Jefferson Davis. He was not a Georgian, a Kentuckian, a South Carolinian — probably not even a Mississippian. At approximately his thirtieth year Davis finally set up his tent in a particular state, but that was too late to acquire the sense of local patriotism which, in order to be powerful, must seize a man in his formative years.

And there was another reason why Davis was never really devoted to any one locality. The truth is that Mississippi had no special character of its own. It was itself, in population and social and political attitude, a composite of the South as a whole. At the time Davis selected it as his home, Mississippi had been in existence as a state only eighteen years; a generation before a good part of it had been Spanish territory. Its population, in 1835, was composed of recent immigrants from Virginia, South Carolina, Tennessee, Kentucky, and other

Southern states. Practically all of these regarded themselves as sons of older communities, not of the new section into which they had rushed in the pursuit of rapid fortune. Thus, Jefferson Davis was a new phenomenon in American progress; he was a Southerner, a citizen of the great region south of the Potomac and the Ohio, not primarily a denizen of any one commonwealth. In the growth of Southern nationalism his position may be compared to that of Alexander Hamilton in the development of the American Union; just as Hamilton, born in the West Indies, and thus destitute of local patriotism, felt no allegiance except to the nation as a whole, so Davis, unfamiliar with any long-established Southern community in his sensitive years, became rather the champion of that Southern nationhood which gained ascendency in the thirty years preceding the Civil War.

This Southern type differed materially from the familiar figure of colonial and Revolutionary times. Mississippi was a new country; its settlers were for the most part "new men" displaying many of the qualities of "new rich." Indeed they had many of those traits which many commentators have found odious in the industrialists of recent times. They were plutocrats, exploiters of natural resources, not so much agriculturists as the producers of the raw materials of manufacture. Their labors were tributary, not to the granaries of the nation, but to the textile mills of Great Britain and Europe. And the country they opened was as much virgin soil as were the forests, the oil wells, and the mineral fields into which the industrial adventurers of a later period found their precipitate way. The cotton barons of Georgia and the Mississippi delta exploited their land just as ruthlessly as did their successors in the West three decades afterward. The most important of these natural resources was a belt of black loamy soil, extending from South Carolina across central Georgia and Alabama, and bordering both banks of the Mississippi River from the Gulf to Tennessee. This area made the agricultural wealth of the new antebellum South; it made also its politics as well as the politics of the nation as a whole. It ultimately produced the Confederacy and the Civil War. It maintained, in this critical period, that ascendency, both political and economic, which Virginia had upheld in the colonial period and the fifty years following the Declaration of Independence.

It is an interesting circumstance that Virginian statesmanship, so potent in establishing the new nation, should have shown exhaustion almost contemporaneously with the exhaustion of its tobacco lands. By 1824, the year that marked the end of the Virginian Presidential "dynasty," the importance of the state as an agricultural region had also come to an end. Its social distinction still ruled supreme; but wealth, the export trade, and political ascendency were passing into other hands. Already Virginia's most adventurous sons, as well as those of the other long-established Southern states, — reënforced by a large contingent from North and West, — had discovered the fruitful opportunities for rapid riches in the southwestern cotton belt.

No soil so adapted to the cultivation of this indispensable staple had ever been placed at the disposition of man. The growth of the factory system, the invention of spinning machinery and the cotton gin, the development of a vast market for British and Continental cotton manufactures in all sections of the world, particularly the Far East, created a demand for the product of Southern plantations almost beyond their capacity to supply. Consequently hordes rushed into the new country, acquiring acres by the thousands for absurdly small sums, — frequently appropriating them without formalities of any kind, — transporting into the new fields droves of slaves, usually purchased in Virginia and neighboring states, sometimes building homes of miscellaneous architecture, frequently living in other regions, even in the North, and leaving management to overseers. The most wasteful method of agriculture prevailed. That preliminary to creating farms so common in other regions, especially New England, — removal of the forest, — was not the rule in this pioneer country. The trees were killed — "deadening" it was called — by ripping off the bark near the ground; the leaves fell, the smaller branches were torn away by the winds, and thus the needed sunlight gained access to the freshly planted seed. There were no attempts at conservation, either of trees or of soil. As soon as fertility had been exhausted in one area, the planter advanced to another, for land in that primitive era was cheap; so that the whole country was streaked by abandoned cabins and those gaunt, dead forests, fit symbols of the desecrating rapacity that impelled the advancing hosts. As late as 1857, Frederick Law Olmsted visited this country, and the account he wrote was a desolate one; it gave a shocking picture of that rapacious devastation of nature's resources for immediate profit which laid the groundwork for the agricultural poverty of the region so familiar as a fact to-day. The inevitable accompaniments of the slave system — the riches of the great planter, the poverty and ignorance of the unpropertied whites, the absence of schools, the lack of sanitation, the neglect of farming in its real sense — were visible on every hand. "The majority of negroes at the North," concluded Olmsted, "live more comfortably than the majority of whites at the South." [4]

To this sweeping generalization, of course, glaring exceptions must be noted. Many of these large planters became very rich; in fact there were more wealthy men in the Southwest from 1840 to 1860 than in the East and North. And wealth, as is always the case, inspired certain ambitions. These miscellaneous pioneers in a new country, many of them from the older South, began to gaze wistfully at the culture and social charm that had made Virginia and South Carolina eminent in the early days of the Republic. The old, romantic South of the Potomac and the James, — the South of statesmen, of Constitution framers, of philosophers and writers, of scholar-

[4] *The Cotton Kingdom* (London, 1861), Vol. II, p. 129.

ship and art, and of fine living, — was on the decline. The new-rich of the lower Mississippi and Alabama rivers now dreamed of establishing some system in their country to take the place of this vanishing Southern glory. They possessed the economic basis for a delectable society. The old Southern aristocracy had rested upon tobacco; could not a new Southern élite be built upon cotton? Naturally an extremely small part of the population would share this new splendor; but that was the case also in the old Virginia and Carolina; there was as wide a chasm between the occupants of the great Potomac houses and the "underprivileged" Virginia peasantry as there was likely to be in this projected new abode of social eminence.

And so, as money from the cotton crops poured in, selected oases of refinement — at least its external aspects — grew up on the lower Mississippi. Natchez was the most successful. To-day portfolios of "Georgian houses" always contain a few pictures of homesteads in this Mississippi region. Their occupants were for the most part Whigs, as Federalist in attitude as the old shipping magnates of Boston or the lords of the rice coast in South Carolina, despising Democrats, loathing Andrew Jackson and his ilk. Their sons were usually sent to Yale or Harvard; their daughters were educated by private tutors, frequently imported from New England; and, as was the case in the old Southern society so sedulously aped, cotton planting, combined with "law and statesmanship," was regarded as the only decent occupation for gentlemen. By 1860, much progress had been made in the establishment of this new order, not only in Natchez, but in other areas; the progress in "statesmanship" had been far greater than Virginia had ever secured, for, by the fifth decade of the nineteenth century, this Southern cotton belt had succeeded in obtaining control of all three branches of the Federal government — executive, legislative, and judicial — and was using this power to extend its own interest. It was the revolt of the North and West against this dominance that brought on the Civil War.

JEFFERSON DAVIS, SOUTHERN NATIONALIST 29

One of the earliest arrivals in this new district, as well as one of the most successful, was Joseph Emory Davis, that elder brother of the future Southern statesman. By 1835, his fortune was popularly assessed at one million dollars. If that popular estimate was correct, this Davis was not only the richest Mississippian, but one of the richest of Americans, for millionaires at that early day were rare in any section of the United States. Joseph Davis had reached the new land of opportunity early; in 1818, a year after Mississippi became a state, and before the rich quality of its soil was widely understood, he dropped his law practice in Natchez and, with the modest fortune it had brought him, purchased one of the most fertile pieces of land in a fertile region. About twenty miles south of Vicksburg the Mississippi indulges in one of those convolutions for which it is celebrated, making a detour which completely encloses a circular point of land, having a diameter of about ten miles. This river island was a wild and unkempt place at the time of the elder Davis's arrival, the earth covered with briers and bracken, the whole impeded by a growth of oak and magnolia. These obstructions once removed, in the usual barbarous fashion, the Davis plantation rapidly became one of the most profitable on the hemisphere. The house which Davis built hardly rivaled the more pretentious structures of the Natchez region but was much more spacious and substantial than the average Mississippi home. It had two stories, an upper and lower balcony, a wide entrance hall, drawing room and tearoom opening on the side, and the "office," "gun room," and storeroom that completed an old-fashioned Southern "mansion." Joseph Davis sold part of his domain to congenial friends and reserved five thousand acres for himself, which, cultivated by about a thousand slaves and managed with skill, rapidly made him rich. Joseph Davis represented the higher type of Mississippi planter; he was not an absentee landlord, but supervised the estate himself, treating his negroes with great kindness, even entrusting the ablest of them with important executive functions, and devoting much of his own time to reading and study, especially in his chosen field — politics and constitutional law. If the Mississippi delta was to realize its ambition of becoming a second Virginia, clearly Joseph Davis would be an effective instrument in the transformation.

This aspect of his chosen section much interested the man. To found a Southern family was his ambition, but to realize this aim his thoughts turned rather to his younger brother than to himself. Jefferson, twenty-four years younger, had enjoyed greater educational openings, was a man of more polish and finer bearing, and a graduate of West Point — in itself in that day a distinction fairly aristocratic. Moreover, his army career had been creditable, and he was generally regarded as a coming man. That Jefferson's engagement to Miss Taylor — despite the hostility of Zachary — greatly gratified Joseph may be assumed. Jefferson, selected by his brother as the founder of the new line, could have made no more auspicious beginning. Knox Taylor was directly descended from that Richard Lee, who, about 1640, became the ancestor of the most famous of all Southern families. An ideal bride, this, for the "new man" bent on lifting himself in the social scheme! Joseph Davis was as much opposed to surrendering this auspicious couple to the itinerant life of army posts as was father Zachary Taylor himself. He therefore sequestrated five hundred acres of his island kingdom, stocked it with an adequate supply of slaves, and, immediately after the honeymoon, established the newly married pair on a plantation of their own.

It is significant of the guardianship which the older brother maintained over the younger that he never gave him a free and clear title to the property; Jefferson operated it himself, and derived all the profit, but the ownership remained with Joseph. The latter had still more ambitious plans for his fraternal protégé. That public life — possibly a governorship, or a place in the lower House or the Senate — which had been the crown of the tobacco planter's life in old Virginia was the future that Joseph had decided on for "little Jeff." As he proudly regarded the handsome young man and listened to his discussion of public questions, the elder was confident that this programme would not miscarry. Then the malarial atmosphere of the Louisiana bayou, by killing the bride three months after marriage, apparently destroyed this dream.

And the young man's grief seemed for a considerable time to condemn him to a hermit's life. From 1835 to about 1843, that was essentially his existence. All social ambitions and all desire for political eminence vanished. Jefferson took up his abode at Hurricane, his brother's house, and gave most of his active hours to his farm. He did this so assiduously that he was soon earning a good income. But for seven or eight years he was a recluse. Sometimes a whole year passed without his leaving the island. His only close companions were his negroes — to several of whom he became warmly attached — and employees in the ginhouse; he never visited neighbors and had no desire to receive visits from them. Only with his brother, during those seven years of exile, did he grow more and more intimate.

Intellectually, the period proved the most fruitful in Jefferson Davis's life. All the time not given to the plantation was consumed in reading and study. The routine that Davis maintained from 1835 to 1843 does indeed recall the existence of the Virginian of olden time. The picture offered by the young planter among his books at Hurricane has many touches in common with that of Richard Henry Lee, as a young man, preparing himself for "statesmanship" in the library and garden of Stratford. Government, with Davis at this time, as with the Lees and Madison and Jefferson and Mason at an earlier day, became the unremitting subject of study. Again brother Joseph was the guardian angel. He had collected all the writings of the fathers — of Hamilton, Madison, and the rest — and all the histories and biographies and speeches of Southern and Northern giants, and these he and his young ward read, discussed, debated day after day and evening after evening. All the leading newspapers of Washington, Richmond, and Charleston were conned — and the discussions were exciting and engrossing, for the great slavery debate had started, the deeds of the abolitionists were enraging every Southern heart, and John Quincy Adams and his antislavery petitions seemed fairly to presage disunion. The *Congressional Globe* — nowadays called *Congressional Record* — came regularly to the Davis establishment, the two brothers reading it with the same eagerness that the modern world gives to novels and detective stories. And the object of greatest interest — and strange as it may seem, of adoration — was the Federal Constitution. Daniel Webster had no greater reverence for this great charter than Joseph and Jefferson Davis had at this time. The fact is that Jefferson Davis never outgrew his belief in this document as the greatest scheme of government ever framed by man; the first act of the Confederacy, as will appear, was the adoption of the Federal Constitution — with a few changes — as the basis of the new nation. Brother Joseph never ceased to portray the perfections of the labors of 1787. Was the Constitution not largely the work of Southern statesmen? Under it, so long as it was obeyed and not corrupted by the false reasoning of New England casuists, were not Southern liberties and Southern "rights" secure?

To grow one's crops and at the same time to browse among one's books, devoting attention chiefly to political and historic study, in preparation for public service — here was the old Southern tradition, and this Jefferson Davis, under the watchful eye of his brother, now proceeded to revive. That the senior was the supervising influence is plain enough. "Joseph," writes Mrs. Davis, "was well calculated to improve and enlarge the mind of his younger brother. Joseph Davis was a man of great versatility of mind, a student of governmental law, and took an intense interest in the movements of the great political parties of the day."[5] Thus Joseph was one of those obscure makers of history who work in the background, for he it was who, more than any other influence, trained the mentality of the great chieftain of disunion. In all crises of Jefferson Davis's career, indeed, this older brother is discovered as the propelling force. He gave the boy his education; he secured the appointment to West Point; he established him as a planter, and so started him to financial ease; he acted as mentor in his reading and in the formation of his political creed. And now the senior rendered another service — this time of a more personal kind. He redeemed the scholastic hermit from his solitary existence and selected for him a wife. Davis was only twenty-seven when his first marriage ended in tragedy; by 1845, at thirty-seven, he was still a young man; ten years he had spent as a lonely widower; that he should marry again was in the natural course of events.

For some time Joseph had had his eye upon a particularly desirable bride. Here again the old Virginian formula pointed the way. In the ancient South, a marriage was not, first of all, an impulsive romance; it was a social contract in which prudence as well as sentiment was considered. "Family and fortune" — such were the two imperative qualities to be kept in the foreground. Fortune was not so indispensable in the Davis case, for the clan was already part of the new plutocratic South; but "family" was essential to a young man who aspired to become the political spokesman of the most respectable Southern point of view. And so, scanning the field, this shrewd fraternal matchmaker hit upon the one matrimonial candidate in southern Mississippi who seemed most fitted to the high destiny appointed for the "little brother."

[5] *Memoir*, Vol. I, p. 171.

4

Varina Howell

When William B. Howell, son of a Revolutionary veteran who served for eight terms as Governor of New Jersey, floated down the Mississippi River in a flatboat, seeking, like many an ambitious Northerner, new pastures in America's richest cotton country, he finally came to a halt at the lofty bluff of Natchez, opened a law office, and rapidly attained a position of leading citizen. In those days the fact that a man was of Northern blood and a devotee of Alexander Hamilton constituted no bar to progress in a Southern community. Southerners always attached great significance to position; and the son of a governor, a man himself of education and distinction, could count on the most cordial welcome. Howell's Whig principles, his detestation of Andrew Jackson and Martin Van Buren, his unconcealed contempt for "hillbillies" and "fly-up-the-creeks" proved no handicap in that segment of Mississippi; its settlers had not come exclusively from neighboring states; New England family names — Dwight, Lovell, Lyman — were common; several of Mississippi's most famous men — Sergeant S. Prentiss, John A. Quitman — had come from the rocky New England soil. When Howell fell in love with Louisa Kempe, daughter of a Virginia "aristocrat," the marriage was generally hailed as a union of the richest strains of Northern and Southern blood.

The best man at this wedding was Joseph Emory Davis who, in the few years succeeding Howell's landing, had become one of his closest friends. That Joseph had a sentimental feeling for the bride was generally believed; however, this did not stand in the way of his own marriage soon afterward, or of an even closer friendship between the two families. Perhaps it explains the interest Joseph Davis displayed in the Howell children. The first, a boy, was named for him; the second, a girl christened Varina, born May 7, 1826, he regarded almost as a member of his own household. Varina was brought up to call the elder Davis "Uncle Joe" and no relative observed with more affection and admiration the girl's progress. From the first he regarded her as one of the most desirable of feminine humankind. Perhaps the station that Varina ultimately occupied — that of Lady of the Confederacy — explains the retrospective enthusiasm of the friends of her early days. Certainly admiration could go no further. Her biographer, Mrs. Rowland, sees in Varina Howell Davis a combination of Queen Elizabeth, Queen Victoria, and Andromache; Queen Elizabeth for her wit, shrewdness, tart epigram, haughtiness, and statesmanship; Victoria for her dignity, propriety, conservatism, and practice of the homely virtues; Andromache for the Trojan lady's unselfish absorption in fatherland, husband, and children. All these qualities, it is related, or at least their germ, Varina manifested as a girl. It is scarcely necessary to go to such extremes. Neither do the surviving daguerreotypes confirm the extravagant appraisals of the girl's beauty. She could be properly described as fine looking, even handsome, but these pictures hardly warrant the elder Davis's appreciation expressed to brother Jefferson. "By Jove, she is as beautiful as a Venus!" The slim body had a pleasing, graceful carriage; the dark hair, combed ruthlessly in the plaits popular at the time, its sombreness relieved now and then by twist curls at the sides, and the dark intelligent eyes, contrasting to her "creamy white" complexion, made her an arresting figure.

Another of Joseph's recommendations — also conveyed to Jefferson — was entirely justified. "As well as good looks, she has a mind that will fit her for any sphere that the man to whom she is married will feel proud to reach." Varina had had unusual educational opportunities to which she had congenially responded. These, like her father and her political principles, came from the North. The two years spent in a Philadelphia young ladies' school were not the most important of these Yankee influences. Among the many New Englanders who came to Natchez in this boom period was George Winchester of Salem, Massachusetts, a graduate of Harvard, a fine classical scholar, and a man to whom the English writers were second nature. Winchester rose to be one of the conspicuous lawyers of Mississippi, and a judge of its highest court. He never married, and, close friend and frequenter of the Howell home, he took the little girl under his wing. Her mental quickness, her eagerness for books, and her happy, quick retorts aroused both his admiration and affection. Judge Winchester was not technically Varina's tutor, for his business was the practice of the law, and he took no compensation from the Howell family. But for twelve years, from early childhood to her sixteenth year, he devoted himself to framing Varina's mind. A few evenings after Jefferson Davis's first meeting with his future wife, the girl entertained him and Joseph by reading one of the political speeches with which the American atmosphere was then resounding; the ease with which she pronounced certain Latin phrases and the readiness with which, in answer to their challenge, she translated them, astonished the brothers. This knowledge, unusual in a Southern girl of the day — in a Northern one for that matter — was the fruit of Judge Winchester's instruction. He taught Varina the Latin classics, introduced her to English literature, schooled her in the John Adams brand of Federalist principle. The influence of Judge Winchester never left her. Next to her husband, he was the idol of her life. Always in the crises that befell her — and they were many and terrible — Mrs. Davis's thoughts would revert to this companion of her childhood. What she was, intellectually and to a large extent in strength of character, she owed to him. To her he was "Greatheart," the name she invariably called him.

A rare experience this, and that a man of Winchester's quality should have thought Varina worthy of this patient care, from her fourth to her sixteenth year, and that she should have responded so appreciatively to his ministrations — no further testimony could be asked as to her own sensitiveness to the "things of the mind." Her home surroundings — the house was a large structure, poised on one of the loftiest bluffs near Natchez, with a magnificent view of the river, here a mile wide, the Mississippi steamboats, usually described in the literature of the day as "floating palaces," gracefully paddling by, the surrounding country a forest of magnolias, oak and gum trees, the evening sky tinged by the most brilliant of sunsets — harmonized completely with the stimulating mental world in which the child passed her days. In this region Chateaubriand had laid the scene of his *Atala;* and even his exuberant fancy hardly exaggerated its sylvan beauty.

This Natchez life, full of gayety, house parties, visits, and neighborly association, had little in common with the existence led by the Davis brothers in the malarial bottom lands of the Bend. Indeed, Varina had been brought up to regard the Vicksburg area as hardly in tune with her more elevated existence. First of all, this Davis section was Democratic, and Democrats were an obnoxious folk with whom "nice people," like the Whigs of Natchez, had nothing to do. In those days social barriers were drawn on party lines! Again, this lesser breed were Methodists and Baptists, at best Presbyterians, while the blue bloods of the Howell environment, like those of ancient Virginia, were Anglicans. But of course an exception could be made in the case of "Uncle Joe" Davis. All these years he remained on the friendliest relations with the Howell family; all this time he had solicitously watched the blossoming of the daughter of the house. The Howells were not surprised therefore at his repeated requests that Varina pay a visit to his home. In the winter of 1843 he was too insistent to be denied. The girl was then seventeen. A large house party had been arranged for Christmas 1843–1844 at "The Hurricane," and Miss Howell's parents acceded to Joseph's request that she be one of the guests. Not improbably the Howells fathomed "Uncle Joe's" romantic purpose in pressing this invitation. But the conspiracy, if it had been hatched, was a tacit one. "It is not verified by a single hint nor utterance preserved in any reminiscence either in verbal or written form, of any of the parties concerned, that there had been a premeditated plan on the part of anyone for a meeting of Varina Howell and Jefferson Davis. All of the circumstances, however, point to the fact that at least the shrewd elder brother Joseph was not without some design in bringing the lovely young Varina to 'The Hurricane' for the Christmas holidays." [6]

If such a romantic plot were afoot, at least one of the persons concerned was completely innocent. That was Varina herself. When she started north on the steamboat *Magnolia*, under the care of Judge Winchester, she did not know that such a person as Jefferson Davis existed. She presently showed signs of petulance that she had never been told of Joe's young brother. "Did you know he had one?" she asked her mother in her first letter from Hurricane. That letter is a remarkable document — it betrays in every line the instant impression Jefferson had made upon the girl. She had stopped for a short visit with Mrs. McCaleb, Joseph Davis's daughter; almost immediately a tall horseman appeared before Miss Howell and informed her that she was expected at Hurricane the next day; after delivering this message in his most courteous manner, the apparition vanished. Yet on the strength of this brief interview the famous letter was written. "I do not know whether this Mr. Jefferson Davis is young or old. He looks both at times; but I believe he is old, for from what I hear he is only two years younger than you are. [Jefferson was then thirty-five!] He impresses me as a remarkable kind of man, but of uncertain temper, and has a way of taking for granted that everybody agrees with him when he expresses an opinion, which offends me; yet he is most agreeable and

[6] *Varina Howell, Wife of Jefferson Davis*, by Eron Rowland, Vol. I, p. 46.

has a particularly sweet voice and a winning manner of asserting himself. The fact is, he is the kind of person I should expect to rescue me from a mad dog at any risk, but to insist upon a stoical indifference to the fright afterward. I do not think I shall ever like him as I do his brother Joe. Would you believe it, he is refined and cultivated and yet he is a democrat!" It is a puzzling, almost an incredible characterization. On its surface it was written on the very day of this first meeting;[7] and yet the young girl proceeds to psychologize her subject in all this detail. And the analysis shows insight, for it hits off several of the traits that marked Davis all his life. And if Joseph could have seen the passage in which she disclaims a liking for the man, and even pretends to prefer the sexagenarian brother, so wise a gentleman would have justly concluded that his scheme had already half succeeded.

The next few weeks provided all the essentials of an old-fashioned Southern courtship. They would have satisfied the most exacting requirements of a story by Thomas Nelson Page. December and January in that part of Mississippi are mild; and walks in the open, afternoons spent in the music room, evenings before a log fire, charades, dancing, singing — no one could ask a more typical setting. The interest which the young girl and middle-aged man felt in each other soon struck the whole company. Brother Joe could scarcely conceal his delight. In fact, there was not much subtlety in his behavior. Whenever the three came accidentally together, he usually found some excuse for slinking from the room, and his persistence in keeping intruders at a distance from the romantic pair caused a general smile. The truth is that Varina and Jefferson were soon very much in love and everybody was pleased. The fitness of the match was only too apparent. Varina's horror at her lover's political opinions was not feigned; he had made his beginning in politics, had already run unsuccessfully for the legislature and was soon to take

[7] "To-day Uncle Joe sent me his younger brother," it begins. *Ibid.*, Vol. I, p. 48.

the stump for Polk and Dallas; but his very presence disabused her of the conviction that only backwoodsmen and "dirt eaters" could be Jacksonians. In fact, her admiration for the man was unbounded. Her pride in the deference shown him by others was great, and when informed that on Jefferson's one brief trip to Washington, five years before, President Van Buren had invited the Mississippian to his breakfast table — this, she believed, was a fitting tribute to his gentility and handsome deportment. "Everybody bows down before the younger brother," she wrote. Jefferson's opinion of the girl, expressed to Joseph, was quiet and characteristic. "She is beautiful and she has a fine mind."

Before that Christmas party disbanded, the engagement had been virtually arranged. The wedding, however, did not take place until the next year, in February, 1845. It was a quiet one, with only the families present, probably because the groom was a widower. After a brief honeymoon the married life of Jefferson Davis and Varina Howell began at a newly constructed house on his plantation, famous in Southern history as "Brierfield."

5

State Rights

Davis had emerged from his self-imposed exile with a fairly complete stock of political ideas. In his unsuccessful campaign for the legislature in 1843, and in his stumping tour as a Presidential elector in 1844, he had given these a considerable publication. Naturally they embodied little that was original. In fact, they exhaled the flavor of the closet. They were the fruit of seven years of study and academic discussion; John Taylor of Caroline, Thomas Jefferson, Madison — the Madison, not so much of the Constitutional Convention and the Federalist as of the Report on the Virginia and Kentucky Resolutions — and Calhoun, in his later phase, were the political thinkers who formed the young philosopher's mind. The turning point in Jefferson Davis's progress, as in that of the country as a whole, was the Mexican War, still a year or two ahead. The era from 1835 to 1846 portrays Davis in what may be called his abstract mood; the after period, that in which practical issues produced a changed view of Southern destiny. It is true that Davis, to his dying day, insisted on opinions formulated during this political adolescence; as late as 1880, when his two-volumed apologia was published, he elaborated these ancient theses with tedious iteration; but his story, as Southern statesman and President, will disclose the little power an ancient creed wielded upon his practical life. Faithful to old Virginia, ambitious to restore the Virginian tradition to a frontier country, the old Virginia scholasticism was adopted as his professed doctrine. Thus his allegiance to "State rights" was of the most approved Virginia type. Only the state was "sovereign"; no sovereignty inhered in that entity known as the United States of America; the only powers it possessed were those delegated for specific purposes by its masters, the states; these powers had been conferred temporarily, during good behavior, so to speak; the "sovereign states" had, of their own free will, and as an expression of their "sovereignty," entered into this compact, and by virtue of the same right could withdraw at any time. That is, secession was justified, both by the spirit and the letter of the Constitution.

It necessarily flowed from this that that charter must be strictly construed. The Federal government could exercise only those powers entrusted to it by states. Above all, it could not appropriate money for local and state purposes; "internal improvements" were abominations to Davis as to his great preceptors, Thomas Jefferson and John C. Calhoun. The old familiar interpretation need not be rehearsed again in this place. But one or two examples may be cited showing the rigidity — one almost might say the priggishness — with which Jefferson Davis practiced his bookish faith. His first act as member of Congress — a new service that began in December, 1845 — was to introduce a resolution, which died in Committee, providing that all Federal troops be withdrawn from Federal forts, their places to be supplied by recruits furnished by the states, each state represented in proportion to its membership in Congress. At the end of the Mexican War, President Polk, as a reward for Davis's indisputably capable service, tendered him a brevet as brigadier general. Davis respectfully put aside the honor: it was an insult to the State-rights rubric. Strange refusal for a man who, as President of the Confederacy, was to be abused as the foe of local sovereignty and the "tyrant" of nationalism!

The Mexican War had both a propitious and a malevolent effect upon the career of Jefferson Davis. At Monterey and Buena Vista he displayed not only personal courage and dashing initiative but considerable ability as a tactician. Buena Vista in particular brought him reputation, both in his own country and in Europe, his famous V formation in meeting the attacking enemy being held by some as responsible for that decisive victory. A serious wound received in this engagement, making the use of crutches necessary for a considerable period, added the personal touch so indispensable in the creation of a popular hero. All this made Davis the most popular man in Mississippi and provided the groundwork for his political career. But not improbably it had a baneful influence on the fortunes of the future Confederate States. It not only strengthened the man's natural passion for military glory, but convinced him that his real talents lay in the martial field. General Grant said that Davis regarded himself as a military genius. Most experts to-day believe that President Davis's constant interference in army matters and his endless bickerings with his generals exercised an unhappy effect upon Confederate campaigns, especially in the last years of the war. Thus it is not impossible that the young man's exploits in Mexico and the widespread acclaim they received had an influence on history which no one at that time could foresee.

Davis, of course, was not a modern man; he lived through the period of Darwin, but all the science and philosophy of the age made no impress upon his rigid, straight-laced mind. His political beliefs, like his religion and morals and his conceptions of human society, were not the product of independent thought, but of the circumambient *mores*. His worship of slavery, for it was nothing less, led him into some queer divagations in biology and anthropology. In a faraway metaphysical sense this man was an abolitionist; that is, slavery did not represent ultimate perfection for the negro, in that distant golden age toward which mankind was slowly advancing. Thousands of years ahead, the black man would be free. This pious expectation in Davis took form in his weirdest paradox. The best way to abolish slavery, he insisted, was to extend it. Spread the institution all over the country, from the Mississippi River to the Pacific Ocean. Let the slave ships deposit their cargoes in California, in 1845, just as they had done in Virginia in 1620! Such new slave territory did not mean, he said, a single additional slave; it merely signified the wider distribution of the existing supply. The influence exercised on population by abundant food and economic demand was something overlooked by this amateur demographer. The Davis explanation of the origin of slavery and its justification was even more primitive. It was based on the most fundamental kind of religion. Father Noah, according to Genesis, had condemned all the dusky sons of Ham to "everlasting servitude." That was the reason, and all-sufficient justification, for the existence of 4,000,000 black bondmen in the United States of America. "It matters not," said Davis, "whether Almighty Power and Wisdom stamped diversity on the races of men at the period of the creation, or decreed it after the subsidence of the flood. It is enough for us that the Creator, speaking through the inspired lips of Noah, declared the destiny of the three races of men."

This fervid belief in slavery was genuine; it rested on even stronger grounds than "fundamental" religion or social convention; its solid basis was self-interest; it was making Davis rich as it was thousands of other men in his region. Not the same can be said for the other great item in his creed — State rights; his theories here seem a little artificial. Davis was probably not aware of this mechanical aspect himself, but, as will appear, he disregarded his own aggressively maintained doctrine when practical issues made that the course of advantage.

6

Leader of Secession

With the Mexican War new aspirations began to sway Southern ambition, especially in that miscellaneous Southwest of which Davis presently became the most vocal spokesman. This new American hinterland was hardly an appropriate place to set up the ancient Southern gods. It was as undisciplined and raw as those Western states that had sprung into existence at about the same time. Virginia and the Carolinas had a background of more than two centuries of symmetrical history; as colonies and states they were much older than the Federal government. Thus with some truth they could maintain that they and the eleven other original commonwealths had created this central government and therefore could not properly be regarded as its subordinate offspring. They had evolved distinct characters as political societies, had produced noteworthy families and statesmen of large stature; that is, they possessed, precisely as they claimed, distinct individualities. Virginia still bore the impress of the British "adventurers" who had settled it; probably the persistent quality of the Carolinas had its explanation, at least in part, in its large infusion of French Huguenot blood, a race marked by its reverence for institutions and its sense of historic continuity. When Virginia and South Carolina, therefore, set up their claims to independent existence apart from the recently established Central power, even when they called themselves "nations," the assertion was not entirely preposterous. But with new communities like Alabama and Mississippi, such pretensions seemed absurd. At the time of the Constitution Convention Mississippi was a wilderness. As a state, the Federal government could rightly insist that it was its own creation. In 1850, the period now under consideration, Mississippi had been in existence only about thirty years; its population, formed by accretions from all Southern sections as well as by thousands from New England and the North, had developed no distinguishing quality, none of the local genius which was stamped on the Virginian and the "Carolinian." An attempt to found its public life upon the concepts of an old established civilization was as absurd as the effort to establish on the lower Mississippi the social conditions that had flourished for two centuries and a half along the Potomac and the James.

The point is of great consequence in the present connection, for it was this parvenu South, rude in its culture, engaged in a mad scramble for wealth, which ruled the whole country in the twenty years preceding the Civil War, and which was chiefly responsible for that calamity. Of this new pugnacious force in the American imperium, Jefferson Davis came more and more to be the prophet. The annexation of Texas gave Davis and other statesmen of this new area their opportunity. The fight they waged was not so much one for State rights — whatever catchwords may have obscured the real issue — as one for Southern nationalism. The desire was not so much for separation from the Union as separation from the North. As sectional differences took on new intensity the conviction grew that two really distinct and discordant nations had been, by a monstrous error, incorporated into one;

that the Northern states, commercial, industrial, agricultural in a sense hardly known in the South, — that of raising food supplies both for the home market and export, — predominantly white in complexion, subsisting on free labor, extremely hostile to slavery and its extension, had little in common with the South, divided into huge plantations, worked by negro bondsmen, devoting all its energies to raising staple crops — cotton, tobacco, rice, and sugar. That there was a "Northern nation," intensely concentrated in sympathy and purpose, was evident; why not establish a Southern nation, just as widespread, just as unified? At first the lack of territory had made impossible such a dream. At one time there were hopes that the West could be drawn within the Southern orbit; but the growth of antislavery feeling in the West, the hostility of that region to the admission of new slave states, its teeming wheat and corn farms — crops more suited to cultivation by the independent white yeoman than by the African — presently showed that its future would lie with the North and East. Consequently any proposed Southern nation would be limited to the territory lying south of the Ohio and east of the Mississippi and that small segment of the Louisiana purchase allocated by the Missouri Compromise to slavery. As the map of the United States stood in 1845, the future clearly lay with the free North and West, and it is not strange that, up to this time, little had been heard of a great Southern empire.

The Mexican War changed the outlook. This ripped from the disorderly Republic of Mexico half of its domain, almost overnight. In addition to Texas, the vast country that subsequently was transformed into the states of California, New Mexico, Arizona, Nevada, Utah, and part of Colorado was added to the United States. In extent, this annexation was larger than the territorial expanse reaching from the Mississippi to the Atlantic Ocean, with which the United States in 1783 began its independent existence. Here was the opportunity for the expansion of the South into a country on almost equal terms with the North. From this acquisition may be dated the rise of Southern nationalism. The idea had many mutations; but the plan that now rapidly took shape in Davis's mind may be taken as the extreme of this new Southern "imperialism." He would have extended the Missouri Compromise line west to the Pacific coast — all territory north to be part of the old Union, all south to become Southern. This line would have struck the Pacific about 100 miles south of San Francisco; the rich country of Southern California, therefore, would have been included in the proposed Southern realm. But Davis and his confreres had far more ambitious plans. They expected to take in a large part of what was left of poor Mexico; at times their ambition included all of Central America as far as Panama. Yucatan Davis particularly coveted, and, as Secretary of War in Pierce's cabinet, he was the directing schemer in plans for the annexation of Cuba — out of which two or three states were to be carved. To flood this extensive country with slaves it would be necessary to reopen the African slave trade; and that Davis, at this time, favored such a revival is the opinion of his ablest biographer, William E. Dodd.[8]

It all looks rather insane to-day, but such was the new "imperialism," the new Southern nationalism, to which Davis began to give his thoughts. His political ambitions received a great impetus as a result of his service in the Mexican War. That made him Senator from Mississippi, member of the Franklin Pierce cabinet, and most commanding spokesman of the South; all Brother Joe's splendid wishes had been realized. The elder brother, it is true, had given Davis his opportunities, but it is also true that he rapidly developed talents and capacity for leadership that justified this patient instruction. "Little Jeff" was now a ready and persuasive orator, a forceful and arrogant debater; he was a man of impeccable

[8] *Jefferson Davis*, p. 177.

private life and the head of a charming family — his social eminence in Washington was enhanced by the dignity and grace of his accomplished partner. That there was nothing inspired in Davis's speech-making is true. Humor and a quick appreciation of human attributes had been denied him. Not one of Davis's hundreds of addresses has added a single gem to American literature. He appears in no anthologies. There are no Davis epigrams, no Davis witticisms, no Davis anecdotes; he had none of that genius for compressing the issues of an epoch into a single undying sentence that distinguished his great adversary. And this literary disqualification was evident not only in Davis, but in practically all contemporary leaders of the South. Take down such a volume as the recently revised *Bartlett's Quotations*. Here are enshrined quotations in plenty from Lincoln, Seward, Greeley, Stanton, Grant, Sherman, and other Northern chieftains, but practically nothing from Davis, Benjamin, Yancey, Robert E. Lee, Stonewall Jackson, or Jeb Stuart. If you go back to the older Southerners, however, — Washington, Jefferson, Madison, Marshall, Randolph of Roanoke, Andrew Jackson, John C. Calhoun, — the gift for phrasing is again apparent. Here once more we are confronted with the truth that the *nouveau riche* South, which made the war, was something very different from that of the olden time.

Though he lacked literary effectiveness, Davis did not lack adequate expression and certainly not programmes and ideas. The situation came to a crisis in 1850. Jefferson Davis now makes his first appearance as leader of Secession. That the nation came close to secession and civil war in 1850 is something most Americans have forgotten. It was the year of two simultaneous events, — the meeting of the Nashville Convention and the passage by Congress of the famous Compromise measures, — both the fruits of the Mexican War. These two proceedings represent the two forces then at work in the American drama, one making for disunion, the other attempting to bring into lasting compromise the forces, North and South, that yearned to perpetuate the prevailing order. The Nashville Convention was the achievement of the disaffected — the seceders. The hurly-burly that had distracted the nation since the acquisition of Mexican territory had persuaded them that there was only one way to obtain their "rights" — chief of which was the right to convert this new American empire into a stronghold of slavery — and that was by separation from the Union. Perhaps it would be more accurate to say that the threat of Secession was the way they hoped to accomplish this end. The Nashville Convention, called in January, 1850, to meet in June, was in reality such a threat. Jefferson Davis, its chief promoter, made no attempt to conceal this fact. Congress at the time had under consideration the future — the slavery future — of the Mexican cession. Decide this question as we demand — or we shall secede! That was the attitude of the Nashville Convention; it was really a club brandished over the head of a hesitating Congress. But it was not an enterprise with which the South as a whole showed much sympathy. The Nashville Convention was the creation of the new plutocratic South — of that lower tier of new Southwestern states which, as already observed, acquired great political influence at this time. Its promoters were Jefferson Davis, Albert Gallatin Brown of Mississippi, William Lowndes Yancey of Alabama, and Robert Barnwell Rhett of South Carolina. This latter name makes necessary a slight amendment to the statement above, for South Carolina must not be included in the new-risen Southwest. But Rhett's participation was on an entirely different basis from that of Davis and the rest. In his eye, Nashville was to be the vindication of the classic State rights for which he stood; he was not interested, as were the other leaders, in creating a new Southern Republic; his passion was for state sovereignty and state independence, even state nationality.

The fact is, however, that not even South Carolina, as a

whole, cared much for the Nashville Convention; Rhett's impassioned advocacy made him so unpopular in his own state that he was forced to resign his seat in the Federal Senate. This was 1850, remember, not 1860! What really gave the *coup de grâce* to Davis's Convention and made it odious not only in the North but also in the South, was Clay's compromise, which was generally accepted in both regions as permanently settling the great controversy. Even Mississippi, which had taken the lead, was sharply divided. In no place was the Secession Convention more unpopular than among the Mississippi Whigs, who represented the intelligence and culture of the state. One wonders if Davis found opposition at his own hearth; for it was Mrs. Davis's relatives and friends in Natchez who grew most emphatic against this scheme of disunion. Her husband's part in the proceeding so diminished his popularity in his own state that his political future seemed to have been destroyed. In 1851 the exigences of Mississippi politics compelled Davis to resign his Federal Senatorship and run as Democratic candidate for Governor. Only one short year before he had been the political darling of his people, the wounded, half-blinded hero of Buena Vista; but his opposition to the great Compromise, his sponsorship of Secession and the Nashville Convention had stained his escutcheon.

His opponent for Governor was Henry Stuart Foote, — of whom he was to know much more in the future, — one of those Virginians who, in the great southwestward migration, had wandered through Georgia and Alabama, finally anchoring in the Unionist Whig region of Natchez. Foote and Davis had been fellow Senators from Mississippi during the Compromise debates; their association had not been congenial, however; on one occasion they came to a fist fight in their boardinghouse; and on the floor their exchange of compliments was tart, Foote being an unrestrained advocate of Union and the Compromise — the bitterest denouncer of the futile Convention. To be defeated for the Governorship because of his programme of Secession was humiliation enough; to be vanquished by a man he so detested as Foote — for this was one of those personal antagonisms that litter Davis's life — was unbearable. Jefferson and Varina left Washington in sorrow, and resumed existence at the Brierfield plantation with their cotton, their slaves, and their books. So far as Davis could see, that political triumph of which he had dreamed was at an end. His fervor for disunion and Southern nationality had blasted it. It must have been a sad moment for Brother Joe, now sixty-seven years old. All that long time spent in preparation, all that startling success in the Mexican War, all those promising first steps in politics, including a seat in the United States Senate, had ended in sequestering Jefferson Davis, at the age of forty-three, at his modest cotton farm on Davis Bend, on the lower Mississippi. And he had been destroyed because of his championship of Secession!

7
Secretary of War

It was a gentleman from the far northern state of New Hampshire who rescued Davis from this new obscurity. Here we meet something novel in the Davis story — a friendship. For close intimate friends were almost unknown to Jefferson Davis. Even this friendship was not particularly warm, resting rather on a community of taste and convictions than on cordial personal affection. For Franklin Pierce was about as distant, rigid, and unemotional as Davis himself. Yet a certain sympathy did draw the men together. Davis, in his memoirs, never mentions the name of Franklin Pierce without praise; Pierce, even after Davis became the leader of a cause which he repudiated, still corresponded on terms of friendship; yet in their letters their salutations never advanced beyond the "Dear Sir" or "Dear Friend" stage. In those days

Clay was "Harry" to his senatorial intimates and Webster was "Dan'l," but Pierce and Davis never became "Frank" and "Jeff" to each other. Despite this, the men were sympathetic. This was evident on their first meeting, on the Mississippian's first visit to Washington in the winter of 1838. Pierce was then not a particularly conspicuous representative from New Hampshire. Davis met him at a Congressional "mess"; they saw much of each other; it was Pierce who took his new Southern friend to breakfast at the White House with President Van Buren. That a citizen of the New Hampshire granite hills and a denizen of the lower Mississippi river bottom should think alike on the great political issues of the time strikes the present generation as a paradox, yet this was not unusual. Pierce detested the Abolitionists, thought that the attitude of his fellow-Northerners was endangering the Union, accepted the Southern thesis on slavery, and wished, above all, to bring the controversy to an end. What Pierce believed was not of great public consequence in 1837, but sixteen years afterward it was a matter of national concern. For the strange sinuosities of politics has made this unassuming, far from brilliant or courageous Yankee President of the United States. Almost his first act was to reach over to Davis Bend on the Mississippi, rescue a more or less discredited statesman from what seemed likely to develop into permanent exile, and make him Secretary of War in his Cabinet. And Davis rose to be more than merely head of an important department. He quickly assumed the rôle of master of the Pierce Administration. He directed its destinies, both in domestic affairs and in foreign relations. This is another evidence of Davis's ability and force of character, for Pierce's Cabinet contained several able men, such as William L. Marcy of New York, Secretary of State, and Caleb Cushing of Massachusetts, Attorney General.

So begins Davis's second phase as a national statesman. And the man who took up life in Washington in 1853 to remain a national figure until his "adieu" in 1861 was something different from the more impetuous senator of the earlier period. In a sense he was chastened. The collapse of his Secession plans of 1850 had taught its lesson. Davis had learned prudence; an element of expediency now affected his programme. Not by the advocacy of disunion was political success to be achieved, even in Mississippi. Davis ceased — for a time — to be a Secessionist; even in 1861, contrary to opinion held by Horace Greeley and other Northern rhetoricians, Jefferson Davis was not a die-hard for separation — not a Toombs or a Yancey or a Robert Barnwell Rhett. The erection of a great Southern republic, stretching from the Atlantic to the Pacific, and incorporating a large part of Mexico, was an idea that ceased to trouble his dreams. Instead he became the orator of "Southern rights," — "extreme Southern rights," if you will, — but still to be achieved within the Union. His object of worship was now the Federal Constitution, and this he revered above all, because, he insisted, it guaranteed all the rights which the most aggressive Southern point of view demanded. The foremost was the constitutional right of the Southerner to go into any part of the national territory and take his slaves with him. All that new country lying west of the Mississippi to the Pacific Ocean, so long as it remained in the territorial state, was to be made accessible to slavery. The old Davis imperialism was not dead; he still aspired to add large slices of Mexico and Central America to the United States — all to be made sacred to slavery; and the most sensational diplomatic act of the Pierce Administration, an openly proclaimed determination to annex Cuba, was the outcome of his engineery.

A great, powerful new South, protected by all the safeguards which Davis perceived in the Constitution, resting upon slavery as its economic background, strengthened, if necessary, by reviving the slave trade, but a South within the Union — this was the end Davis worked for from this time forward. No man, indeed, was more fervent in affirming his love for the Union than Davis; its praises were constantly on his lips; but it was only by giving the South assurance of a great future on these lines, he declared, that the blessed work of the fathers could be preserved. And State rights of the old Virginia type? Again Davis gave the doctrine lip service; but a single advocacy shows how far he departed from it in practice. A test of allegiance to Jeffersonism was opposition to internal improvements. Federal money must not be used to construct huge public works! Both Monroe and Jackson had vetoed bills providing for the construction of Federal roads at the expense of the Federal Treasury. Davis had taken the same stand on many occasions. But, when the future of his beloved South was concerned, State rights went promptly into the discard. All through the fifties he was the irrepressible promoter of a Pacific Railroad, linking California with Memphis, Tennessee. This foe of "internal improvements" proposed that the national government spend $100,000,000 on this grand enterprise. It was through his exertions that $10,000,000 was appropriated for the "Gadsden Purchase" — a strip of Mexican soil adjoining New Mexico and Arizona, essential to the construction of this road. In acquiring this strip of land, Davis's foresight was justified; through it the roadbed of the present Southern Pacific extends. But this, as well as his whole plan, flew in the face of all his protestations on the limited powers of the central government.

Though Jefferson Davis in the decade from 1850 to 1860 ceased to be the protagonist of Secession, he was the champion of the idea that inevitably meant civil war. This was the extension of the negro system of the South into the new territory beyond the Mississippi. That was the one thing, and the only thing, that made inescapable a clash of arms. Except by a minority of Abolitionists, who were as unpopular in the North as in the South, there was no intention of disturbing slavery in the states where it existed in 1860. Beyond that it must not go. New Haitis or San Domingos were not to arise in the uncontaminated lands west of the Mississippi River. Such was Lincoln's attitude just before his inauguration. We promise not to interfere with slavery in those states where it is an established institution — the pledge appeared in his first inaugural; he was even in favor of a Constitutional amendment making this guarantee. But — slavery must not be extended into the new West; on that principle the new President took his stand, and for it he was prepared to wage a great civil war. It was the first step in that superb statesmanship for which posterity so honors his name. Imagine California, Oregon, Colorado, and all the rest of this vast territory to-day given up to slavery! Davis stood immovably for this very thing — the unlimited extension of the slavery system. That was the cause of the Civil War. Many modern historians have sought other explanations for the mighty conflict. Especially has there been manifest a desire to explain it on "economic" grounds. It was a great struggle, we are told, between the "agricultural" South and the "industrial" North. This theory ignores several pertinent facts, chief of which is that the states that remained in the Federal Union in 1861 were an infinitely greater agricultural country than those that comprised the Confederacy. In 1850 the hay crop alone of the free states had a higher value than all the cotton, tobacco, rice, and sugar produced in the South, and in the other essential agricultural crops — wheat, oats, Indian corn, potatoes, rye, barley, and the like — the future Confederacy was left far behind. The "agricultural" and "industrial argument" therefore does not suffice.

In a different sense the struggle may be described as an economic one. It was precipitated, not by the old traditional South but by the "new-rich" cotton millionaires who were exploiting the cotton lands of the Southwest — Alabama, Mississippi, Louisiana, Texas, Arkansas. These men might be esteemed industrialists; at least, their occupation was that of raising cotton, the raw material of the spinning factories of Great Britain and France. It was the determination of this new extreme-southern South — what, in modern days is usually described as the "deep South" — to extend ever and ever its domain into new western fields and obtain more rich soil for the cultivation of a great industrial crop, that brought North and South into conflict. Of this expansion of slavery Jefferson Davis, from 1850 to 1861, was the most successful exponent; not inappropriately, therefore, the new nation, the creature of this new region, found its head, not in Virginia, or in the Carolinas, the early home of Southern statesmen, but in Mississippi, a newcomer among states, and chose in Jefferson Davis, its foremost citizen, the man whose life and record as statesman completely echoed the Southern philosophy which had gained the upper hand.

II

THE GREAT GEORGIA TRIUMVIRATE

1

ALEXANDER H. STEPHENS

ONE of the men to whom Lincoln most tersely described his policy on slavery was Alexander H. Stephens, of Georgia. Lincoln and Stephens had served together in Congress during the Mexican War; both had opposed that aggression, and both had afterward fought in the same Whig Party for Taylor's election in 1848. Probably Stephens was one of the few public men of the South to whom Lincoln, in 1860, was not an ignorant abolitionist "baboon"; Stephens even then expressed admiration for the new President and respect for his conscientious motives in dealing with the crisis. A speech this independent Southerner made before the Georgia Legislature on November 14, 1860, profoundly affected the man who, about a week before, had been elected President of the United States. Stephens had addressed an impassioned plea to this pivotal Southern state, advising it not to secede! The episode led to an exchange of letters between the two former fellow Congressmen, in one of which Lincoln set forth, as clearly as it has ever been set forth, the main points in the argument that was tearing the nation apart. "I fully appreciate," Lincoln wrote to Stephens, December 22, 1860, "the present peril the country is in and the weight of responsibility on me. Do the people of the South really entertain fears that the Republican administration would, *directly* or *indirectly,* interfere with the slaves, or with them, about the slaves? If they do I wish to assure you, as once a friend, and still, I hope, not an enemy, that there is no cause for such fear. The South would be in no more danger in this respect than it was in the days of Washington. I suppose, however, this does not meet the case.

You think slavery is right and ought to be extended, while we think it is wrong and ought to be restricted. That, I suppose, is the rub. It certainly is the only substantial difference between us."[1]

The Southern opponent of Secession to whom Lincoln wrote in these terms, at a moment when events had practically reached the breaking point, was destined, seven weeks afterward, to become Vice President of the Confederate States. These two facts — the man's early hostility to forming a Southern Confederacy, and his prompt acceptance of second place in the new government — indicate the contradictory phases of what was perhaps the most brilliant and resilient mind in the whole movement. From all points of view, intellectual, physical, political, psychological, Stephens offers fascinating qualities lacking in the more correct and prosaic Davis. A study of his life and character is indispensable to any understanding of the rise of the Southern nation — even more of its fall. For both its establishment and its destruction he was one of the men chiefly responsible. No man formulated quite so vividly the ideas that led to the adoption, in February, 1861, of an independent Constitution, and no man, in the following four years, so persistently instilled into its veins the poisons that led to its collapse. The elements of this failure were inherent in the Confederacy at its birth and the scholar-statesman who became its Vice President was their most powerful exponent.

That the man should bear the name of Alexander Hamilton Stephens was itself symbolic, for in his earliest days of political thinking, and in all his activities up to the final parting, he was as belligerent an advocate of Union as the founder of the Federalist Party himself. Like Hamilton, Stephens was first of all an intellectual, a student of history and political institutions, a philosopher of government. Considering the

---

[1] Stephens published this letter in facsimile in *Constitutional View of the War Between the States*, Vol. II, p. 266.

physical equipment with which nature endowed him, Stephens could hardly have played any other rôle, for as both boy and man he was little more than brain. Of all leaders who have risen to eminence in the United States, none cut a more unfortunate personal figure. One day a Georgian follower, having heard that the famous Alexander H. Stephens was on board a train then halted at the station, pushed through the crowds and stalked into the car to gain a glimpse of his favorite statesman. "Good Lord!" he exclaimed when his hero was pointed out, then turned his back and departed from the presence. What this disgusted hero-worshiper gazed upon was a small, boyish figure, a little more than five feet high, weighing about ninety pounds, with a shrunken, consumptive chest, a sallow, mummified face, in which the bony structure stood forth like a death's head, capped by a vampirish wisp of brown hair, the unearthly aspect of the whole lightened by a pair of fierce, piercing dark eyes, deep sunken in their sockets. The body was so small, so frail, so childish that, long after Stephens had become one of the leading lawyers of Georgia, he was commonly mistaken for a boy. "Do you expect to go to college?" a stranger once asked Stephens, years after his graduation from the University of Georgia. "Sonny, get up and give your seat to the gentleman," was an admonition once addressed to him in the interest of a man younger than himself.

Stephens, at the age of twenty-two, wrote down, in his usual precise way, his physical statistics. "My weight is ninety-four pounds, my height sixty-seven inches, my waist twenty inches in circumference, and my whole appearance that of a youth of seventeen or eighteen. When I left college two years ago, my weight was seventy pounds." Several contemporaries have humanized these details with lifelike descriptions. "His form was the most slight and slender I had ever seen," says Richard Malcolm Johnston, Stephens's friend and biographer, "his chestnut hair was brushed away from a thin white brow and bloodless cheeks. The child looking at him felt sorry for another child." "The man looked as if he had two weeks' purchase on life," said the robustious Toombs. "An immense cloak, a high hat," so ran a newspaper description, "and peering somewhere out of the middle a thin, pale, sad face. How anything so small, sick and sorrowful could get here all the way from Georgia is a wonder. If he were laid out in his coffin, he needn't look any different: only then the fires would have gone out in the burning eyes. Set as they are in the wax-like face, they seem to burn and blaze."

Ill health represented the great tragedy of Stephens's life. He always had the appearance of one recovering from a long illness. From the first moment of consciousness, he himself declared, there had never been a day free from pain. His letters abound with references to the long disease that was his life. Neuralgia and what he described as "horrible headaches" had been daily inflictions. "Weak and sickly I was sent into the world with a constitution barely able to sustain the vital functions. Health I have never known and do not expect to know. But this I could bear; pain I can endure; I am used to it. Physical sufferings are not the worst ills I am heir to. I find no unison of tastes, feelings and sentiments in the world. . . . The torture of body is severe. I have my share of that; most of the maladies that flesh is heir to. But all these are slight when compared with the pangs of an offended and wounded spirit. The heart alone knoweth its own sorrow. I have borne it these many years. I have borne it all my life."

In Stephens we have a case, not only of physical suffering but of soul sickness. There has been a tendency to trace this melancholic state to his early life, its hardships, its sorrows, its struggles for social and educational betterment. Yet, though his early days were a time of poverty and physical toil, they did not differ particularly from those of many Americans who have risen to successful and contented lives. In ancestral inheritance the fates did not deal badly with Stephens. His grandfather was an English Jacobite who emigrated to America after the rebellion of 1745, settled first near the Juniata region of Pennsylvania, afterward in Wilkes County in Georgia, serving with considerable credit in the Revolution. His mother belonged to the Grier family of Pennsylvania, and was a relative of that Justice of the Supreme Court who figured conspicuously in the Dred Scott decision. Alexander's father was both country school teacher and small slaveless farmer. From him the sickly boy obtained his earliest schooling, supplemented afterward by fall and winter terms in a nearby "Old Field School." Despite a frail constitution, Alexander spent much of his childhood in arduous toil. At the age of six he was "corn dropper" on his father's acres; as such it was his task to follow the plow, letting fall the kernels in the spreading furrows. Later he became farm hand and sheep herder; as there were apparently no negroes on this little estate, most of the small and not especially dignified jobs they usually performed became his duty. Even then existence had its compensations. Always there was the father with Webster's spelling book, the Bible, and a few other volumes to stimulate the child's enthusiasm for reading. Glimpses suggesting the boy Lincoln survive. Alexander, like Abraham, even spent evenings conning his literary treasures by a pine-knot light! A great good fortune that came in his fourteenth year compensated for many days spent in "corn dropping" and guiding the plow. A rich patron appeared at the precise moment when he believed his education at an end. This gentleman had been observing Aleck for some time, and noting his eagerness for study and his piety he offered to send the boy to a neighboring academy where he could "learn Latin" and prepare for the State University at Athens. In this way Stephens grew up an educated man — and one educated far beyond the resources of the Georgia of that time, for education with him never ceased, and books took the place that mundane satisfactions provide for men physically better equipped for them. At the University Alexander's record was a brilliant one; his Greek remained a possession to the end, and history and political theory were absorbing themes. After graduation Stephens studied law, rapidly becoming one of Georgia's leading advocates, and this inevitably launched him on a career in the state legislature and the Federal Congress. But he was always a closet student, and the point is an important one in estimating his influence on the Confederacy, for he viewed every question from the doctrinal, not the practical standpoint. Stephens was that "scholar in politics" sometimes regarded as so desirable in a fumbling democracy; not improbably the cynical might regard him as a striking illustration of the evil which the pure theorist can achieve in everyday affairs.

The middle name, Hamilton, was not given Stephens at christening; he added it to Alexander as a tribute to a beloved professor whom he revered as chiefly responsible for his start in life. Like most promising young men, Stephens early received invitations to appear in his neighborhood as Fourth-of-July orator, just as Webster did in New Hampshire, and his exhortations proved to be quite as vehement in preaching State rights ·as had Webster's been in disseminating the soundest brand of Nationalism. Perhaps the man who exercised the greatest influence on Stephens's life, though an unconscious one, was his father. When Andrew Stephens, some time before Alexander's birth, used his first year's earnings as schoolmaster to purchase one hundred acres near Little River in Georgia, he performed an act that had a great effect on his son's development. The land was situated not far from Crawfordville, in that section of Wilkes County that afterwards was known as Taliaferro. Here Alexander was born; to this place as a successful lawyer he returned to make his home; here he lived the rest of a long life, and here he died, in 1883. Stephens added much to his domain as time went on, but he never had any other home and desired none. In fact, except for his service in Congress, and in Richmond as Vice

President of the Confederacy, he never spent much time anywhere else. His whole existence was passed in this same little environment. He was born in Wilkes County, went to an academy in the same place, attended the University at Athens in the same neighborhood, studied law and took up its practice at Crawfordville, three miles away, and confined his political and professional life to the surrounding region.

While Vice President, Stephens spent little time in Richmond; always he felt the pull of home. And this love for one spot of earth developed with him into a passion. Lovingly his recollection lingers over this piece of Georgia earth and the ugly frame house that made his lifelong abode. "That part of my life which is by far the most interesting," Stephens wrote in 1856, "was that which was spent on the 'old homestead' under the paternal roof, and in the family circle. That was the 'day-dawn period' with me. . . . The most liberal inducements were offered me to go to Columbus and become one of a firm. This I declined for no other reason but a fixed determination I had formed never to quit, if I could avoid it, those places nearest my heart, where I had played as well as toiled in my youth, about which I had so often dreamed in my orphan wanderings. This is what kept me in Crawfordville." The summer of 1865 Stephens spent as a prisoner at Fort Warren, Boston, every day expecting summons to a trial for treason; in his lonely cell the thought of this Georgia rooftree frequently moved him to tears. "No mortal," he wrote in his Diary at this time, "ever had stronger attachments for his home than I for mine. That old homestead and that quiet lot. Liberty Hall, in Crawfordville, sterile and desolate as they may seem to others, are bound to me by associations tender as heart strings and strong as hooks of steel. There I wish to live and die." "Let my last breath be in my native air! My native land, my country, the only one that is country to me is Georgia. The winds that sweep over her hills are my native air. There I wish to live and there to die!"

One will search the writings of Jefferson Davis in vain for any such apostrophe to Mississippi. Davis's enthusiasm, as already noted, was for the South as a whole — for the new Southern nation — whereas the allegiance of Stephens did not extend much beyond Georgia. And these different outlooks determined the two men's political ideas. As the war went on, Davis more and more became the Southern nationalist, while Stephens seemed to grow ever stronger in his loyalty to the state. At times, indeed, Stephens is the great pedant of that doctrine. His arguments are scholastic, fine-spun, frequently very tedious. His discourses on "centralization," "the Federal Compact," "state sovereignty," and the rest are more important than the similar discourses of Jefferson Davis, for with Stephens they represent a creed which he literally carried out in his public life — greatly to the discomfiture of the Confederacy. With him these things were not empty logic-chopping but realities intended to guide the life of a people. Such were the convictions Stephens advocated in the Federal sphere from 1843 to 1859. In all the disputations of that time, he was one of the most forceful participants. In the many crises from the Mexican War to John Brown's raid, this energetic and half-sepulchral figure, his dark eyes blazing with indignation, his bony arms waving with feverish emphasis, was a startling sight. There were even times when Stephens seemed to be a great orator. One impartial judge at least he deeply impressed. "I take up my pen," wrote Abraham Lincoln to William H. Herndon, February 2, 1848, "to tell you that Mr. Stephens, of Georgia, a little, slim, pale-faced consumptive man, with a voice like Logan's, has just concluded the very best speech of an hour's length I ever heard. My old withered dry eyes are full of tears yet."[2] This speech affected Lincoln because it radiated the quality that was conspicuous in Stephens, as well as in himself. That was consummate honesty. Nothing shocked Lincoln so much in that period as President Polk's

[2] Abraham Lincoln. *Complete Works*, Vol. II, p. 111.

justifying statement on invading Mexico — that he was repelling an attack from that country. This hypocrisy also aroused Stephens to the height of eloquence that Lincoln described. The common feeling on this basis was what brought Lincoln and Stephens into a sympathetic friendship.

2
THE MAN WITHIN

All this time Stephens was leading a strange inner life. He was a man of introspective, morbid psychology. To understand his character and the part he played in the Confederacy, this fact must be properly appraised. Few men ever wrote so many revelatory letters or indulged so remorselessly in self-analysis. Practically every day he wrote a long letter to the "light of my life," as Stephens calls his half brother Linton. Sometimes these epistles were so distressingly egocentric that Linton, in mercy for his brother's standing with posterity, destroyed them. Seldom has a correspondent so immersed himself in Stygian gloom. Introspective, self-torturing, hypersensitive, frequently reduced to tears, always shrinking from the vulgarities and obscenities of existence, furiously longing for that applause from humankind which he affects to despise, with it all profoundly religious and idealistic, high-minded and intensely ambitious — seldom has so bewildered and anguished a psyche been let loose in a matter-of-fact world.

"To live to-day and to be warm" — such is his idea of life — "to move and to think; tomorrow to be silent, cold and dead; devoid of mind and sense, fast mouldering into dust, fit food for worms." "Life is but a dreamy pilgrimage through an inhospitable clime." Man's part is "over mountains and in deep and dark valleys, through bogs and morasses, beset on all sides by brambles and thorns, by knats, mousquitoes, stinging insects, flies, and venomous reptiles." Cheerful communications of this sort Stephens was accustomed to address to Linton even during the Christmas season. The torments suffered from the disregard of his fellow men are duly set forth. "I have often had my whole soul instantly aroused with the fury of a lion by so slight a thing as a look! What have I not suffered from a look! What have I not suffered from the tone of a remark, from a sense of neglect, from a supposed injury, from an intended injury!" Despite all this, the man had a sense of humor. He describes how he was curing himself of his mental disease by homeopathic treatment — by reading the *Anatomy of Melancholy*. And he had all the joy of self-pity. The secret of his life was something that he called — rather ineptly, he admits — "revenge reversed." Perhaps by this Stephens anticipated the word "compensation" of which so much is heard these days. He repaid the "contumely of men" by rising superior to it — "by doing them good instead of harm." Thus the long black night of his existence on the whole proved to be a boon to his fellows. For it was Stephens's purpose, in his own words, "to master evil with good and to leave no foe standing in my rear. My greatest courage has been drawn from my greatest despair."

A modern age would have no difficulty in finding another "secret" for Stephens's maladjustment. For a nature of such keen sensibility, the absence of the domestic satisfactions must have amounted to little less than continual agony. This little caricature of physical man clearly regarded himself as a kind of Cyrano de Bergerac — a beautiful soul tragically encased in a most unprepossessing frame. This fact, in his morbid view, forever exiled him from a domestic hearth; love and wife and children were not for him. However, Stephens's life was not a solitary one; a proper insistence on his melancholy should not cause one to overlook a more genial side. Despite his sick body and sick mind, men and women flocked to him; the home at Liberty Hall was constantly filled with guests;

and his conversation, not so occupied with self-analysis as his letters, could frequently start roars of laughter. For the most part, however, his life was lonely. Having no wife or children, it almost seems as though he centred on another adoration. The man's character presents a series of contradictions, and nothing seems less in keeping with his Confederate career than his worship of the Constitution of the United States. "If idolatry could ever be excused," he said, in 1845, "it would be in allowing an American citizen a holy devotion to the Constitution of his country." [3] Four years of civil war did not diminish this piety. In July, 1865, when imprisoned in Fort Warren, Stephens wrote Secretary Seward: "I know that no man more true, more loyal, so ardently devoted to the Constitution of the United States and the principles of civil and religious liberty it embodies than I am ever breathed the vital air of heaven." [4] Lincoln's feeling for the Union, it has been said, had a mystical quality, and the same was true of the reverence which Stephens always felt for the charter on which that Union rested. Here was perhaps the source of the sympathy which drew the two men together.

But there was another statesman whom Stephens ranked above Lincoln. No American, he believed, compared for a moment with Daniel Webster; one of the most conspicuous ornaments of Liberty Hall was a bust of the New England statesman, the man who, in the "quality of moral greatness" Stephens put on a higher plane than either of his contemporaries, Clay and Calhoun. So greatly did he esteem Webster that, in 1852, Stephens deserted both the old parties and attempted to organize a new one to make Daniel President. In the election of 1852, Stephens cast his vote for Webster though at the time that statesman was in his grave. It was Webster, the orator of Union, the expounder of the Constitution, the leader whose patriotism embraced no one section but

[3] *Recollections*, p. 95.
[4] *Ibid.*, p. 372.

all parts of the United States — this was the man whom Stephens revered above all contemporary Americans.

Despite this, Stephens took issue with his favorite preceptor on his fundamental Constitutional tenet — that the document had created an integrated nation, not a loosely organized league of states. To this latter view Stephens adhered with all the syllogistic loquacity of a hair-splitting metaphysician. He admired the American Constitution above all earthly forms of government because, he never wearied of insisting, it had created precisely such an ideal society. His devotion to the document was like Jefferson's, who always protested his love of "the Constitution — properly understood." And that his own understanding was unimpeachable, Stephens never entertained the slightest doubt. The supreme achievement of this Constitution, as framed by the founders of 1787, was its concentration of "absolute, ultimate sovereignty" in the several states. Any theory that ran counter to this transcendent reservation was simply treason. The greatest critique of the Constitution he regarded as that which had been formulated by Jefferson in his Kentucky Resolutions of 1798, in which this fundamental thesis was displayed in irrefutable terms. Each state, under the Federal compact, was a sovereign, practically independent nation. Had then a state a right to secede — a constitutional right, that is, not a revolutionary one? To Stephens this right was as unassailable as truth itself. Had it, under this same instrument, the right to maintain slavery? Stephens simply pointed to those clauses which, if they did not authorize this system in so many words, certainly recognized and protected it. Was the right to take one's slaves into the territories — the argument that resulted in civil war — guaranteed by this same fountain of wisdom? Who could believe otherwise? Had not the Supreme Court of the United States, the final arbiter, decided the question in the affirmative? It was precisely because the Constitution did not organize a "Central Despotism," because it reserved sovereignty to the individual states, because it left the state's social and labor systems at its own discretion, because it permitted states to "resume their sovereignty" when circumstances, in their judgment, warranted such action, that Stephens regarded the Union it had formed as the greatest political achievement of man. Hence his love for that Union to maintain which had been, all his life, "my earnest desire, my highest aspiration."

3

THE TOOMBS–STEPHENS COALITION

That, at several crises, Stephens had fought, in his own Georgia, to preserve the Union, was no empty boast. And in this work he had formed one of a famous triumvirate of Georgia leaders — three men destined to play a conspicuous rôle in the Confederate States. His two co-workers in this noble enterprise had been Robert Toombs and Howell Cobb. Both these statesmen afterward became so identified with Secession that their earlier coöperation against Southern forces of disruption has been overlooked. Especially has fate dealt unjustly with Toombs. In the popular mind to-day Toombs is looked upon as the typical, swaggering Southern browbeater, constantly aflame with imprecations against the North, loud-mouthed, threatening, ferocious in his language, uncompromising and destructive in his acts. Most Americans have forgotten that for the larger part of his political life he was a Whig, a member of the party in the South for decades influenced by loyalty to the Union. Toombs was one of the ablest Southerners of his generation, its greatest parliamentarian and debater, and, in many ways, its most far-seeing and well-balanced statesman. Personally, it is true, he was a rather rough-hewn character. Not without significance is it that his favorite figure in literature — and his reading reached far — was Falstaff. In many ways he resembled immortal Jack. His huge bulky frame, with well-developed abdomen, his great round head, surmounted by a mane of unruly brown hair, his loud, roaring voice, given to ready jest and incessant epigram, his fondness for hard liquor — a habit that in his last years became a vice — all this made him fellow to the rollicking knight of Gadshill. Certain less agreeable Falstaffian traits Toombs did not possess; he was not a foolish braggart, least of all a coward; his family life was above reproach. But it was certainly a strange fortune that made Toombs the intimate friend of Stephens, who, if the former came to be regarded as the Falstaff of the Confederacy, may be considered its Hamlet. It is even stranger that a small area in Georgia — roughly a northeastern segment of the cotton belt, bordering on the Savannah River — should have produced all three men whom many consider the ablest leaders of the South — Stephens, Toombs, and Howell Cobb.

As young men and beginning lawyers, Stephens and Toombs were thrown into close association. Together they traveled the circuit, occupying the same rooms in hotels, eating their meals side by side, constantly helping each other in knotty legal problems. They entered Congress at almost the same time, and in Washington the bachelor Stephens found a most hospitable home with Toombs and his wife. When apart, the two men constantly corresponded, and usually they were sympathetic on public questions. That the anemic Stephens should have found his closest friend in the athletic Toombs, as open-minded in his religious convictions as Stephens was pious, as Rabelaisian in speech as the little companion was circumspect, as bibulous and Gargantuan in self-indulgence as the other was self-denying — this showed that Stephens had human qualities making him attractive to the more masculine type. And both were men of intellect — if Stephens was a bodiless brain, Toombs's mental power was almost as overwhelming as his physical presence; and both held similar ideas on the Union and the problems of the forties and fifties.

4
Robert Toombs, Unionist

Born in 1810, the son of a rich cotton planter and Revolutionary veteran; expelled — or practically expelled — from the State University for card playing, then educated at Union College, Schenectady, and the University of Virginia; at thirty among the most successful and prosperous lawyers of his native state, Toombs went through the several political gradations, until, in 1844, he found himself installed in Congress, as representative of the still powerful Whig party, and spokesman of the more moderate phases of the rising slavery dispute. Already he was a marked character, not only as a man of ability and political power, but as one of the most magnetic human beings in Washington. Throughout Georgia, despite his comparative youth, Toombs was a personal figure of almost legendary significance. There were few citizens of the Eastern circuit who did not know him well. Stories of his prowess on the hustings, quotations from the impromptu speeches at which he was so expert, anecdotes of his varying public moods, his fierceness in the face of injustice, his tenderness to the underdog, his hilarious laughter, his witty and fluent speech, filled every corner of the land. Like Lincoln, Toombs was the genial comrade in courthouse yards, taverns, stagecoaches, and other meeting places of the common man. He entertained the mob with stories, offhand speeches, and rapid give-and-take conversation. The young aristocrat was one of those companionable souls who will discuss all questions, even the most intimate ones, with chance acquaintances. Even though, with all his bonhomie, Toombs now and then became brusque towards dissentients, it was this personal quality that largely explained his rapid stride in public life.

This reputation naturally preceded him to Washington, and the whole capital was on tiptoe with expectancy. Nor did he prove a disappointment. The report that Toombs was to speak quickly filled the galleries. What made the man so interesting was his unexpectedness. He was a genius in debate because he almost never conned his speeches in advance, always depending on the circumstances of the moment for inspiration. His extemporaneous speeches rolled out with ease and swiftness, and his readiness in retort made him a terror to hecklers. On a second's notice his bulky frame would rise, his deep Southern voice never pausing for word or idea, his leonine head shaking in monitory earnestness, his stubby finger pointing opprobriously at the foe; and sometimes the great form would parade up and down the aisle. Meanwhile the speaker's argument, now menacing, now defiant, part persuasion, part mere assertion and epigram, would hold a dozen Congressmen at bay. On few orators has such extravagance of praise been bestowed by contemporaries. Some compared Toombs to Charles James Fox — rather to the disparagement of the Englishman; others saw in him a reincarnation of Mirabeau. What is plain is that, irrespective of oratory or exposition, Toombs was one of the greatest debaters that Washington has seen.

His achievement was the more remarkable in that, at this early period, the themes of Toombs's eloquence were not the sort that usually stir legislative chambers. On the subject that was the great inspiration of oratory at that time — "our sable population," as Toombs liked to refer to it — he was not the most conspicuous performer. It is strange that those who searched for European counterparts should have overlooked William E. Gladstone, for, like the already famous British statesman, Toombs was at his best in finance and fiscal policy. As with his British contemporary, the most abstruse financial problems yielded their secrets when Toombs proceeded to dissect them; and, in his hands, things like treasury balances and tariff schedules took on romantic quality. He was no dilettante, in this or other matters; few more thorough students of public documents ever graced the chamber. Toombs's

Democratic successors of to-day might profitably read his speech in 1844 expressing horror at the increase in appropriations; at that time the Federal Government was spending $30,000,000 a year! The designation "pork barrel" had not yet been invented, but the practice had been, and no fiercer critic of money spent for local purposes ever existed than Robert Toombs. "Bills for depleting the Treasury" is what he called these measures. "I will give you millions for proper legislation, but not one cent for jobs!" He turned a particularly fierce eye on New York state, believed to be especially skillful at extracting favors of this kind, and just as severely criticized the Southern states who similarly fed at the public crib. "I do not want a dollar of public money expended in the state of Georgia," he would say. Toombs, as a consistent Whig, favored a moderate protective tariff, but mercilessly exposed the statesmen, even those of his own South, who put forth exorbitant demands. In the Senate, he enjoyed holding up to ridicule that shining Democrat, Judah P. Benjamin, who violated all the principles of his party by advocating huge tariff favors for the sugar planters of Louisiana. One of Stephens's first expressions of disgust at Jefferson Davis as Confederate President was that he made Toombs his first Secretary of State. Had he selected him as Secretary of the Treasury, Stephens always opined, the story of the Confederate Government would have been a very different one.

But naturally the one absorbing topic of the day presently assumed first place in Toombs's Congressional work. He had the fatal gift of epigram, and aphorisms, some falsely and some truly attributed to him, have distorted his real character. Thus the statement — one he denied ever having made — that he would some day "call the roll of his slaves at the foot of Bunker Hill monument," has given a twisted idea of his attitude on the Southern question. Posterity has insisted on regarding him as one of the irreconcilable agents of the slave power. It is therefore something of a surprise to learn that

Toombs, like Lincoln and Stephens, opposed President Polk and his Mexican War. And the reasons for the Georgian's hostility? Such a war would lead to the acquisition of Mexican territory and that in turn would precipitate a disastrous argument on slavery. The really serious matter was that it would endanger the Union. For Toombs, though a thoroughgoing proslavery man, and never disposed to yield an inch on what he regarded as the fundamentals of that policy, was almost as much a worshiper of the Union and Constitution as Stephens himself. Once the Mexican War had ended, however, with all the dire effect on domestic tranquillity that Toombs had foretold, he accepted the result and became an unyielding champion of the "rights" of the South in the new territory. Still he was no extremist, no follower of Jefferson Davis, in a course that, if pursued as Davis was pursuing it, meant secession and civil war in 1850.

Davis opposed the admission of California with a no-slavery constitution, but Toombs favored such admission. Davis fought the organization of New Mexico as a territory without making it a slave country; Toombs was willing to leave that question to local determination. Davis opposed attempts to eliminate the slave trade from the District of Columbia; Toombs favored such prohibition. Davis promoted the Nashville Convention, an indirect move towards secession in 1850; Toombs combated that proposal. Davis opposed the Compromise measures of 1850; Toombs supported them with all his eloquence. No man more earnestly fought Calhoun's plan for organizing a sectional Southern party in 1849; no party that was not continental in sweep found favor in his eyes. "The temper of the North is good," he wrote, "and with kindness and patronage skillfully adjusted, I think we can work out of present troubles, preserve the Union and disappoint bad men and traitors." The all-important difference between Toombs and Stephens, on the one hand, and Davis, Yancey, and Rhett, on the other, appeared in those words

"Union and Constitution." The latter group, even in 1850, were the advocates of Southern independence and a Southern Confederacy, with African slavery, even the revival of the slave trade, as the foundation stone; the Toombs-Stephens coalition were believers in the existing national system and regarded those who were undermining it, in Toombs's own words, as "bad men and traitors."

5

HOWELL COBB

This aspiration was embodied in the name of the party which Toombs and Stephens, with Howell Cobb, organized in Georgia, to solidify the loyalty of that state to the Compromise of 1850. They called it the "Constitutional Union" party; its aim was thus to preserve the Constitution and with it the existing central government. The enlistment of Howell Cobb in this new cause gave it the desirable quality of nonpartisanship. Both Toombs and Stephens were Whigs, always the compromising element, but Cobb was a Democrat of ancient breed, and Democrats were contenders for the most advanced Southern claims. Moreover, Cobb was one of the bluest of Georgia blue bloods. At a time when prosperity in the South signified property in slaves, Cobb was the Rockefeller of the region. One thousand black sons of Africa cultivated his plantations. That a magnate of Cobb's standing should have joined contentious Whigs in 1850 in opposing disunionist movements had influential results, not only on those stirring events, but upon the subsequent Confederacy. His independence at this time made him deadly enemies in his native Georgia, as well as in all the cotton states; but for the hostility aroused by this championship Cobb would probably have been chosen President of the Confederate States, instead of Davis; in the opinion of many, he was immeasurably better fitted for that office.

Cobb was a massive creature, physically and mentally; a huge head, surmounted by billowy, abundant locks; great, wide, steady gray eyes, half searching, half pensive; a generous beak of a nose; an arching mouth, proclaiming thought and kindness, rather than geniality; a rippling double, even triple, chin, advancing through the spaces of a mighty wing collar; the broadest of shoulders, the bulkiest of bodies — here indeed was the type of the well-fed, confident, long-established Georgia aristocrat. Already honors appropriate to his birth and social standing, as well as to his political aptitudes, had come to Cobb. Elected to Congress, in 1842, at the age of twenty-eight, he won sufficient prominence to be chosen Speaker of the House in 1849, when only thirty-four; he was made Governor of Georgia in 1851, finally capping his career in the national field by becoming Secretary of the Treasury in Buchanan's Cabinet — having declined a previous invitation as Secretary of State. Such progress, at a time when the average of ability in American public life stood high, bespeaks character and attainments. Cobb possessed both. His fine parliamentary manners, his consummate courtesy, especially to Northern opponents, made him a popular figure in Washington; his speeches were never disfigured by sectional rancor, and his nationalistic point of view on questions arising from the Mexican War, while it may have angered extreme Southern partisans, evidenced a broad-minded statesmanship.

Howell Cobb's leadership in the early days of the Confederacy, as in the case of Stephens and Toombs, has misled historians in estimating his public work. Even Mr. Rhodes asserts that his "devotion to slavery and Southern interests was the distinguishing feature of his character." [5] This summary is fair in a sense, but it does not tell the whole story. In his early period Cobb upheld unorthodox Southern views; he did not believe, for example, in the right of secession. His writings against this sacred tenet came up to plague him in

[5] *History of the United States*, by James Ford Rhodes, Vol. I, p. 117.

Brown Bros.

ROBERT TOOMBS OF GEORGIA (1810–1885)

Brown Bros

ALEXANDER H. STEPHENS OF GEORGIA (1812–1883)

Robert M. T. Hunter of Virginia (1809–1887)

Howell Cobb (1815–1868)

after years. Especially did he ridicule the right of those new states, such as Mississippi and Louisiana, to withdraw at will from the Union. These communities were mere swamp and forest when the Constitution was framed; most of the territory of which they were formed had been purchased with Federal money; all that they were they owed to the Federal Government; how absurd to fancy that they could constitutionally depart from that guardianship! Cobb was another of the half dozen Southern Democrats who refused to join John C. Calhoun in his attempt to form a proslavery party in 1849. All over the South this young, daring Georgian was known as "the man who had opposed Calhoun." Cobb, in fact, was a Jacksonian Democrat, and, as such, an enemy of nullification and secession, and a Jacksonian devotee of the Union. In consequence, much to the astonishment of his fellow Southerners, and possibly to his own, he found himself in 1850 companion to Stephens and Toombs, fervent Whigs, in their effort to detach Georgia from the Secession movement then being engineered by Mississippi and South Carolina. Cobb had more to lose by this action than Stephens or Toombs, for he was a Democrat while they were Whigs; his behavior was courageous and public-spirited, a clear case of sacrificing his own interest to conviction.

This the future proved. Cobb's political progress — perhaps even the Presidency of the United States, for his qualifications for that office were heralded at the time — all lay with the extreme Democratic side; political annihilation seemed to await any Southern Democratic leader who joined the foe in giving comfort to slavery restrictionists. But Cobb never hesitated. His love for the Union was his all-persuasive emotion. He flouted Davis, Rhett, and Yancey and their Nashville movement; he supported Clay's Compromise and hailed its passage as a happy milestone in American history. When Georgia irreconcilables still proved recalcitrant, joining their Mississippi and South Carolina confreres in continued resistance, Cobb and Toombs and Stephens organized the "Constitutional Union" party, to uphold the banner of a united country. The plan succeeded beyond all expectations. Georgia had never witnessed such a campaign; the triumvirate were day and night on the stump; the canvass had the flavor of a religious revival, and the awakening of Union sentiment was profound. This puissant trio overwhelmingly defeated both the old parties; Cobb was elected Governor, Toombs Senator, and Stephens was again returned to Congress. This new burst of national feeling in Georgia was to a large extent responsible for a similar enthusiasm in other states, even in Mississippi and South Carolina. As recorded in a previous chapter, the corresponding rise of Unionism in these supposedly hidebound secession areas resulted in the retirement to private life of Jefferson Davis and Robert Barnwell Rhett. To that result Cobb, Stephens, and Toombs had eloquently contributed.

Eighteen-fifty and 1860! the change that ten years had made in the national outlook, particularly in the South, presents one of the greatest contrasts in American annals. The excitements that followed the settlement of 1850 explain this altered prospect. The rise of Stephen A. Douglas, the reopening of the slavery issue, the ascendency of Jefferson Davis in the Cabinet of Franklin Pierce, Kansas-Nebraska bills, fugitive slave laws, the repeal of the Missouri Compromise, the struggle of the North to make the new West free and of the South to make it slave, John Brown's raid, *Uncle Tom's Cabin*, Helper's *Impending Crisis*, the organization of the Republican Party, the Dred Scott decision, Lincoln-Douglas debates, the culminating blow of Lincoln's election to the Presidency — here were the forces that made the United States a different country in 1860 from that ten years before. The solution of slavery troubles to which the Georgia trinity had made such substantial contributions in 1850 was completely undone. Not only had these events, with the fierce discussions to which they gave rise, the sectional antagonisms they had aroused, produced a completely changed national prospect; they had as completely reversed the attitude of public men, particularly in the South. Especially had Toombs and Cobb receded from their earlier attitudes. Cobb, who in 1850 had held up to scorn the right of secession, acknowledged that right in 1861. Toombs, who had spent his splendid energy and matchless eloquence preaching Union in 1850, stood out as one of the most unmitigated disruptionists a decade later. In December, 1860, Cobb resigned from Buchanan's Cabinet, in disgust at that vacillating statesman's effort to play honest broker between the sections of a disintegrating country. A month afterward, Toombs had become the most vituperative Senator from the South. His harangue on leaving the Senate in January, 1861, is not yet forgotten. In this the "black Republicans" appeared as the "perfidious authors of this mischief." "The Union, Sir, is dissolved . . . You see the glittering bayonet, and you hear the tramp of armed men from yon capitol to the Rio Grande. It is a sight that gladdens the eye and cheers the hearts of other men ready to second them." Abraham Lincoln "is an enemy of the human race and deserves the execration of all mankind." Ignoring the valiant fight he had once made for the Constitution, Toombs now declared that it had been a mistake from the first. The South would have been better off had it never been adopted. Patrick Henry and Samuel Adams had been right in fighting it! The "glittering generalities" of the Declaration of Independence were held up to ridicule. Toombs defied the North to attempt to keep the South in the Union. "Come and do it! . . . Georgia is on the war path! We are as ready to fight now as we ever shall be. Treason? Bah!" The furious statesman stalked out of the chamber, walked up to the Treasury, demanded what was due him in Senatorial salary and mileage back to his home state. Cobb was not so intemperate in manner, but his sentiments were about the same.

The third member of the old Union companionship, however, Alexander H. Stephens, was, in January, 1861, still a Union man. He still held by the Constitution and still insisted that secession would be a mistake. To the last moment he strove to prevent Georgia from taking what he regarded as an unjustifiable step. In November of 1860 one of the most stirring scenes in the history of the South took place in the Georgia Legislature. South Carolina had not yet started the secession parade, yet there was a certainty that she would soon do so; the question in Georgia was, should this previously strong Union Commonwealth follow the example? At this time there was a powerful Union sentiment in the Georgia community; in fact, when the moment came for the vote, on January 19, 1861, in the special convention called to take action, there were 164 in favor of secession and 131 against — a majority indeed for taking the state out of the Union, but, at the same time, a most substantial minority opposed. The meeting of the Legislature that had authorized this convention took place in early November, 1860. At that time Union and Disunion sentiment was rather evenly divided. A high state of excitement prevailed and the two parties to the dispute were almost at one another's throats. In this dilemma the Legislature adopted an unusual procedure: it invited its most conspicuous public men to address it on the pending crisis. The most famous of these "elder statesmen" were Robert Toombs and Alexander H. Stephens. Their speeches were published far and wide, forming a landmark in a drama every day becoming more tense. Toombs spoke first, putting the case for secession in powerful, if intemperate, words. There were few evidences, in his scathing arraignment of the North, of the Compromise and Constitution advocate of ten years before. Secession, Southern Confederacy, and war, bloody war — this one-time Whig and curber of extremists was now ready for anything. His good friends of the North had now become "negro-stealers," breakers of their "oft-repeated oaths," tariff schemers who levied tribute on the South at the same time that they sought to destroy its property, inciters of John Brown raids, murderers who applied "the assassin's knife and the poisoned bowl to you and your family." "Do you not love these brethren? Oh, what a glorious Union, especially to insure 'domestic tranquillity'!" "Strike while it is yet time!" "Throw the bloody spear into this den of incendiaries!" "Withdraw yourselves from such a Confederacy; it is your right to do so; your duty to do so. Make another war of independence; fight its battles over again; reconquer liberty and independence."

To exclamations of this sort Stephens the next evening made an even more stirring answer. At that time the diminutive orator regarded his public career as ended. Less than a year before he had declined renomination to Congress and retired to private life. And now Stephens was facing the Georgia Legislature in his last attempt to save the Constitution and the Union. On the speaker's rostrum sat Toombs, who frequently interrupted his friend's discourse. A slight rift had taken place in this friendship, caused by the difference in opinion concerning the existing crisis — an estrangement that was quickly healed, when the larger conflict became a reality. Stephens's speech, which was extemporaneous, lasted for two hours. It was a refutation of Toombs's argument of the evening before. Its tenor was that the hour "to strike!" in Toombs's words, had not yet arrived. As always with Stephens in such contingencies, the chief emphasis was laid on the Constitution. He was as much its devotee in 1860 as he had been in 1850. "If our hopes are to be blasted, if the Republic is to go down," he said, "let us be found to the last moment standing on the deck — with the Constitution waving over our heads." "This government of our fathers, with all its defects, comes nearer the objects of all good government than any other on the face of the earth."

"England," interjected Toombs.

"Well, that is the next best, I grant!" Stephens rejoined. "But I think we have improved upon England. Statesmen tried their apprentice hands upon the government of England, and then ours was made. Ours sprang from that, avoiding many of its defects, and leaving out many of its errors, and from the whole our fathers constructed and built up this model Republic — the best which the history of the world gives any account of."

It was this worship of the Constitution which led Stephens to oppose secession. Why was South Carolina on the brink of departure, why were many Georgians advocating a Southern Confederacy? Because, Stephens said, Abraham Lincoln had been elected President! That was the only argument for thrusting the nation into an abyss. The South did not like the candidate the American people had chosen for the White House. He was the candidate of a sectional Northern party; not a single electoral vote had been cast for him south of the Potomac; in many states he had not received a solitary popular vote, for in these states no Republican ticket had been put into the field. All this, Stephens admitted, was true. The South feared Lincoln because his announced policy meant that the slavery system could not be extended into the new western country. Ultimately, Southerners insisted, it meant the abolition of slavery in the old slave states. Therefore, the only course to take, as Toombs had urged, was "to strike! strike, while there is yet time!" — withdraw from a Union that was hostile to their labor system, and set up a Confederacy that would insure its safety forever. But now Stephens propounded a few ideas on the other side. In the first place, no one denied that Lincoln's election had been strictly constitutional. He had been chosen head of the nation in definite compliance with the provisions of the basic instrument. To rebel against this orderly constitutional process would be little less than to desecrate the national charter. But, it was urged, Lincoln had been elected on a platform that pledged him to violate the Constitution. The Supreme Court had ruled that slavery could not be prohibited in the territories. Lincoln was determined on such a prohibition. His speeches for several years had denounced the Supreme Court for that very decision; he had openly declared his desire to obtain a tribunal that would reverse it. But, pleaded Stephens, you could not make war on a President for his words. Only for his acts. Should Lincoln, after his inauguration, attempt to disregard this judicial arbitrament and to restrain the South from its "right" in the territories, then he would be guilty of "overt acts" that would justify extreme measures.

However, the speaker insisted, there was not the slightest chance of this. At the election of 1860, the Democrats had indeed lost the Presidency, but a Senate and a House of Representatives had been elected that were safely Democratic. Lincoln could do nothing in the face of the Congressional majority against him. The Supreme Court was still Southern in its membership; the majority that had rendered the Dred Scott decision was still intact, and would remain so for years. The "black Republicans" had won an empty victory; the mere accident that their opponents had three candidates in the field had given them the Presidency; but in the real contest, that for the control of Congress, the Democrats had triumphed. In all the disasters of the preceding ten years the North had been guilty of only one transgression in the South. In only one respect, that is, had it run counter to the Constitution. That was in its refusal to surrender fugitive slaves, something Section 2 of Article IV required it to do. But that did not in itself justify secession; given a little time, and that error would be corrected.

What would Mr. Stephens do if Georgia, in spite of all his admonitions, decided to leave the Union? On that point the speaker's statement was just as precise as on the others. His gospel of State rights compelled him to recognize his state as "sovereign." His allegiance to that took precedence over his loyalty to the Federal "Compact." The decision of Georgia in this crisis would therefore become his own. He would go with his state. "Whatever the result may be I shall bow to the will of the people. Their cause is my cause, and their destiny is my destiny."

And so it proved. The Legislature took the advice of Toombs and not that of Stephens. It called its Convention, of which Stephens became an unwilling member. This Convention, Stephens still fighting the movement and voting against it, decided to join the Confederacy. And Stephens, as he had promised, accepted the verdict and became a citizen of the government of which he so strongly disapproved. But his attitude at this moment, and for the preceding twenty years, was to have important consequences for his country. The views that men acquire in their formative years invariably, if unconsciously, exercise their influence on mature life. The disintegration of the Confederacy is not to be understood if the pre-war convictions of a large segment of Southerners, of whom Stephens was the most eloquent spokesman, are not considered. Stephens, always a Constitutionist, always a Unionist, did not enter the new government willingly; he was forced into it by local circumstances. His heart was never in the movement, and, even when serving as Vice President, he looked back longingly to the Union he had forsaken. The reluctant cooperation of Georgia made the Confederacy possible. Had that state refused the approaches of its neighbors it might not have been formed; at least it would have presented a greatly weakened front. Georgia figured as the pivotal state not only in 1861, but in 1864–1865, and in this latter crisis its influence was directed to destroying the Confederacy it had played so indispensable a part in erecting four years before. And Stephens was the leader in this disruptive movement as he had been in the anti-Secession attitude of 1861.

III
THE COTTON BELT SETS UP A CONFEDERACY

1
THE MONTGOMERY CONVENTION

STEPHENS at first refused to go to Montgomery as a delegate from Georgia. His spirit revolted from a convention assembled to frame a government opposed to his beloved Union. He finally gave a kind of ultimatum, drawing up a set of resolutions; if the Georgia Convention would adopt these, Stephens declared, he would become a delegate. If not, then he washed his hands of the whole business! These resolutions provided that any Constitution adopted by the South should be based upon that of the United States of America. In all essentials it should be the same, with such minor alterations in detail as the new situation might require. Georgia accepted his terms, unanimously approving these resolutions. Stephens then consented to be one of Georgia's ten representatives, and, in due course, left for the Alabama capital.

Why did statesmen engaged in the lofty task of founding a new nation meet in so small, and comparatively unimportant a town as Montgomery? Why should they congregate at all in one of the new raw states of the Southwest? When the rebellious colonies, in 1776, decided on their bold move, they selected Philadelphia, one of the largest and most historic cities of America, as the scene of their declaration. The Confederate leaders, in 1861, liked to regard themselves as the spiritual inheritors of Washington and Franklin and their forthcoming gathering as directly descended from the Continental Congress. One fervid patriot proposed that the new government be called "The Republic of Washington"; another suggested as its name "The Southern United States of America"; and there were those who even maintained that the

Stars and Stripes be kept as the Confederate flag. They protested that all these things — even the name United States — really belonged to the South, and not to that northern section which had usurped them. Yet of the seven units that organized the Confederacy in its first incarnation, only two — Georgia and South Carolina — had been in existence in 1776. When the Montgomery Convention assembled, Virginia, North Carolina, and Tennessee had not joined the movement and showed little likelihood of doing so. The Confederacy, as first formed, was a slice of the cotton belt: its states were new communities that had only lately emerged from the primeval forest. Raphael Semmes, afterward famous as captain of the *Alabama*, described the new nation, in a letter to Howell Cobb, as "the Confederacy of the Cotton States"; that was precisely what it was. The pretty little town in which their delegates assembled was only about forty years old. Of the commonwealths involved, Georgia and South Carolina were the aristocrats and one would naturally suppose that these older members would have taken a preferred position. Charleston or Columbia, South Carolina, Savannah, Augusta, or Milledgeville, Georgia — here the Confederacy might naturally seek a dignified birthplace, instead of resorting to the new and, as it proved, inconvenient town on the Alabama River.

There was a theory, popular at the time, and upheld by such writers as Horace Greeley in the North and Edward A. Pollard in the South, that the whole movement, at the start, was a "conspiracy"; that it did not represent popular sentiment, but had been engineered by politicians in the interest of a minority of rich planters, determined, come what would, to protect their wealth and increase it. In other words, that the great Rebellion, like so many historic uprisings, was a plotting of vested interests. Upholders of this economic interpretation even fix the date and place when it all began It recalls a celebrated episode that, in fact or fable, served as a preliminary to the Great War of 1914. Survivors of that era

THE COTTON BELT SETS UP A CONFEDERACY 87

have not yet forgotten the "Potsdam Conference." On the eve of mobilization the Kaiser is supposed to have called a meeting of military and diplomatic chieftains at this ancient headquarters of the House of Hohenzollern. "Are you ready for war?" — such was the question that he addressed to the assembled "key men" of the Reich; receiving a unanimous affirmative, the ultimatums began to fly. The South also had its "Potsdam Conference"; this convocation was held on the evening of January 5, 1861, in one of the very committee rooms of the National Capitol. The participants were the Senators of six of the seven states that afterward formed the Southern Confederacy. The situation was canvassed in detail, the military status examined, and plans for an aggressive campaign determined. Telegrams were despatched to each of the state governments, recommending immediate secession; the centres of disaffection were instructed to seize all Federal property in the neighborhood — customhouses, forts, arsenals, lighthouses, mints. The seceded "sovereign states" were called upon to send delegates to a Convention to be held at Montgomery not later than February 15 for the formation of a new government. On this critical evening, so it was said, Jefferson Davis was definitely selected as the President of the contemplated Republic. From this Senatorial "conspiracy" flowed all the transactions that led up to the Southern convention. That the states in question did secede, that Federal arsenals, customhouses, and other valuable buildings were seized, that the Montgomery Convention was held, that a Southern Confederacy was organized, that Jefferson Davis was elected President — these events, following in rapid succession this Southern "Potsdam Conference," have given a semblance of truth to the narration. That its propounder should have been Edward Pollard,[1] editor of the Richmond *Examiner,* and ablest journalist of the Confederacy, made

[1] *The Life of Jefferson Davis, With a Secret History of the Southern Confederacy.* Chap. IV.

the whole thing plausible; it was no invention of Yankee enemies. Moreover, such a Senatorial meeting undoubtedly did take place. There was no secrecy about it at the time. The news was officially published in the press; in his *Rise and Fall*[2] Jefferson Davis tells the story briefly, though denying the version to which Mr. Pollard gave currency. This senatorial conference doubtless acted as one incentive to secession, but that it precipitated the war upon a reluctant Southern people can hardly be maintained.

Nor is it likely that Davis owed his selection as President to the initiative of his brother Senators. Their favorite, at the moment, seems to have been Robert M. T. Hunter of Virginia, — Virginia's early association in the movement was evidently expected, — a candidate who soon lost favor, on the charge that he was really a "reconstructionist" — the name used to describe Southerners who wished to patch up the quarrel. At this time Jefferson Davis, according to general belief, had no desire to become President. Neither did his state of Mississippi prefer him for that honor. Both had marked out for this leader a more Napoleonic, or, as they would have said, a more Washingtonian rôle. Mississippi had already created an armed force of its own and given Davis command with a commission as major general. It was the expectation in this region, as it was with Davis himself, that this command would prove the stepping stone to the generalship of all the Southern armies.

Nor was the idea in itself absurd. Davis was a West Point graduate, he had served ten years in the Federal army, he had proved an able officer in the Mexican War, he had made an excellent record as Secretary of War in the Cabinet of Franklin Pierce. As to his capability in the field, his tactics at the Battle of Buena Vista had won high praise from no less an authority than the Duke of Wellington. Moreover, Davis was first of all a military man; his type of mind was

[2] Vol. I, p. 200 *et seq.*

autocratic, imperious, self-confident, better fitted to give command in war operations than to cooperate with a group of civilians in managing a government. His book on the Civil War is a great disappointment, for a significant reason: it touches only incidentally on the matters we most desire to hear from him, the civil and diplomatic side, and deals at length with the military history on which knowledge is abundant from many sources. That illustrates Davis's type of mind. True, and this was probably what determined the choice, he was the "logical" candidate for President. He came from the deepest recesses of the Deep South, and represented more completely than any other man mentioned for the post the plutocratic cotton-growing section which was responsible for the war. For ten years he had been the foremost spokesman of the Southern pretensions which had finally ended in conflict. The dissolution of the Democratic party in Charleston, in April, 1860, — a dissolution leading directly to the election of Lincoln, — was more his work than the work of any other man. There was therefore a certain propriety in placing upon him the task of piloting the South through a crisis for which he was so largely responsible. Other considerations were important; above all, Davis possessed the dignity, the suavity, the correctness in personal and official behavior, the social position and manners, and the polished, if not inspired oratory desirable in the head of a Republic.

One detail about this meeting of so-called Southern "conspirators" in the Washington Capitol should not be overlooked. Here the first suggestion of Montgomery as the birthplace of the future "Confederacy of the Cotton States" was made; at least, a diligent investigation has disclosed no prior mention. The town was centrally situated — not an indispensable requirement, as was shown in the selection of Richmond, a few months afterward. But it was not a convenient place for such a meeting; the hotel accommodations were wretched, and buildings for temporarily housing the new government inadequate; above all, the place was infested with mosquitoes, which made the lives of the delegates miserable day and night. Health conditions were bad; Davis himself was ill a good part of the time.

There was a pretty little Greek temple of a Capitol building standing on a hill, and in this on February 4 the forty-four delegates of the seceded states were called to order. They composed both a Constituent Assembly and a Congress. They were both Constitution makers and a legislative body. In the exaltation of the moment the members saw themselves as the heirs not only of the Continental Congress of 1776 but of the Constitutional Convention of 1787. In certain outward aspects at least the Montgomery proceeding did resemble these earlier convocations. It consisted of a single chamber. It represented states, not individuals, and each state, irrespective of size, had a single vote — a vote determined by a poll of representatives from that unit. Like the Continental Congress and the Constitutional Convention, its sessions were secret, a fact that has furnished arguments to the proponents of the "conspiracy" charges, angered the newspapers at the time, and was particularly resented by the large contingent of ladies. Occasionally the galleries were opened to the populace, but the really important deliberations took place behind closed doors.

This exclusiveness is only one reason why so little material survives to reconstruct the sessions. Of the Montgomery Sanhedrin we know far less than of the great assemblies that adopted the Declaration of Independence and framed the Constitution. No detailed record was kept. A proposal that stenographers be employed to take down the debates was rejected. Only the most skeletonized journal was made by the secretary, and even this was carefully guarded from contemporary eyes, not being published until 1904, and then by the government of the United States. Mr. Edmund C. Burnett's recently published volumes of letters written by members of

THE COTTON BELT SETS UP A CONFEDERACY 91

the Continental Congress have given an intimate, day-by-day picture of the workings of that body. No one has yet essayed any such labors for the Montgomery Congress. Such letters of influential participants as have been printed — of Howell Cobb, Toombs, Rhett, Barnwell, even Davis himself — are scrappy and disappointing. Most unfortunate of all, there was no James Madison to make a painstaking abstract of debates for posterity. The only man who faintly — and very faintly — filled this place was Thomas R. R. Cobb, the brilliant younger brother of Howell Cobb, a delegate from Georgia and a member of the Committee that framed the permanent constitution. His letters to his wife and his hasty notes have been published, in part; but they are brief, not masterpieces of characterization, prejudiced by the writer's religious fanaticism and extreme slavery point of view, especially by chagrin over the failure of the Presidential ambitions he had nourished for the object of his idolatry — that older brother who, in the view of many Southerners, then and since, should have been chosen President of the Confederacy.

Still, anyone looking for the "atmosphere" and personality of this gathering is compelled to rely almost exclusively on the younger Cobb's day-by-day jottings. Phrases taken here and there do slightly reveal the prevailing emotions. Personal rivalries and antagonisms are inevitable whenever forty and more politicians come together, but these were pretty well kept under the surface at Montgomery. An overwhelming desire for harmony prevailed. Unanimity on all important decisions was held essential to success. The work of establishing one nation and of destroying another seemed to be something that ought to be undertaken solemnly: personal ambitions should be sacrificed to the public good, and above all, no outbreaks of hostility, no bickerings, no disintegrating quarrels should stain the new nation at its birth. Cobb's notes disclose this conviction; they also show that underlying the happy exterior plenty of human nature was at work. Let us take a few random extracts. "The universal feeling is to make Howell [that is, his brother, Howell Cobb] President of the Convention. As to the provisional President of the Confederacy, the strongest current is for Jeff Davis. Howell and Mr. Toombs are both spoken of and there seems to be a good deal of difficulty in settling down to any person." Even here that dislike of secession, so strong in Alexander Stephens, constantly raised its head. Alabama "is very much divided, some of the delegates being not only Reconstructionist, but absolutely Union men. The truth is there is a very bad state of things in this state. The minority are sullen and not disposed to yield to the fact of secession." "The Georgia delegation has already the most powerful influence on this convention and will undoubtedly control the concern." The Texas members "are a very conceited crowd with very little of statesmanship among them. The weakest delegation here is from Mississippi." "The atmosphere of this place is positively tainted with selfish, ambitious schemes for personal aggrandisement. I see it, hear it, feel it, and am disgusted with it." "The Convention was organized to-day. Howell [Cobb] was elected President of the Convention by acclamation. . . . The breakers ahead of us are beginning to appear." "We cleared the galleries this morning and went into secret session. The outsiders were very much outraged, especially the women. I am hopeful of more harmony today than I was last night. We are doing the most important work in 'secret session.' A member is expelled for divulging the matter in any manner. . . . Ben Hill[3] brought his wife with him and she is put out with the closed doors." "There is but little speculation as to the probable President. Jeff Davis is most prominent. Howell [Cobb] next. Toombs, Stephens, Yancey, and even 'Joe' Brown[4] are talked about." "Stephens is looming up for President since Howell's name has been almost withdrawn. I still

---
[3] A leading public man of Georgia.
[4] The famous Governor of Georgia, of whom more will be heard in succeeding pages.

think Davis has the best chance." "The crowd of Presidents in embryo is very large. I believe the government could be stocked with officers among them." But the rivalry was soon ended, for on February 9, four days after the Convention had assembled, it elected Jefferson Davis President and Alexander H. Stephens Vice President. "The latter," wrote Cobb, "is a bitter pill to us, but we have swallowed it with as good a grace as we could. The man who has fought against our rights and liberty is selected to wear the laurels of our victory."

The writer's disappointment comes out in his general comments on the Convention. "I am sick at heart with the daily manifestations of selfishness, intrigue, low cunning and meanness among those who at this critical moment should have an eye single to the protection of their people." "It looks now as if there was nothing but office seeking." Cobb had no great enthusiasm for Davis, and his dislike of Stephens had become intense. Stephens's attitude against Secession and his hardly concealed contempt for an independent South had estranged both the Cobbs. Thomas Cobb, one of the most fanatical of all Secessionists, could not but grieve that Stephens, holding the views that he did, had been given second place in the Confederacy, and his conviction that this meant trouble was only too amply justified.

He similarly showed insight in appraising Davis. The new President "is as obstinate as a mule. . . . Many are regretting already his election." "President Davis dines at our table every day. He is chatty and tries to be agreeable. He is not *great* in any sense of the word. The power of will has made him all that he is." This correspondent touches on qualities that were to make trouble in the next four years. "Mr. Davis acts for himself and receives no advice except from those who press their advice unasked." "Mr. Davis has not honored a man from Georgia, save Mr. Stephens, even with a consultation." "Stephens has the ear of Davis." This last fault was soon to be corrected for the war had not progressed far when Davis and Stephens were at daggers drawn.

Occasionally a few words give us an unforgettable picture. On February 17 the President arrived for his inauguration, "in a suit of homespun. . . . A crowd variously estimated at from 3,000 to 10,000 are collected at the west end of the Capitol and are now cheering vociferously as the President-elect descends from his carriage to enter the capitol. . . . Well, the ceremonies are over and the crowd dispersed. The inaugural pleased everybody and the manner in which Davis took the oath was most impressive. . . . Bouquets were showered upon him. At the head of the procession was Captain Semmes' Columbus guards in a beautiful uniform of sky-blue pants and bright red coats, carrying a banner with the Georgia coat of arms." Only one incident marred the occasion when Members of Congress took the oath of loyalty to the Constitution. "One man refused to kiss the Bible. He is Judge Withers of South Carolina. He is an avowed infidel." Other sentences reflect certain of the terrible misapprehensions with which the Confederate people launched their ship of state. "The almost universal belief here is that we shall not have war." "The firm conviction here is that Great Britain, France and Russia will acknowledge us at once in the family of nations."

Many who were to play important parts in the Confederacy appear in these notes. Stephens is never mentioned except to be assailed. "Mr. Stephens is most arrogant in his oracular announcements of what we should or should not do. . . . A poor, selfish demagogue, he is trying to ride on the wave of popular clamor, and create factions in opposition to everybody." Meanwhile the business of Cabinet making was under way. "Toombs is spoken of for the State Department, but says he would not have it. Yancey and Benjamin have been named for places, but I think no one has the slightest intimation of the views of the President." Of all Southern leaders

Benjamin was the most odious to the writer. "A grander rascal than this Jew Benjamin does not exist in the Confederacy and I am not particular in concealing my opinion of him."⁵ "I hear Mr. Davis had consulted no one save Mr. Stephens and Mr. Memminger. The latter will probably be Secretary of the Treasury. . . . He is very shrewd, a perfect copy of McCoy metamorphosed into a legislating lawyer." "It is understood that [Mr. Davis] offered the Treasury department to Toombs by telegraph and it is well known that Toombs will decline it. Yancey is to be Attorney General. Captain Bragg is to be Secretary of War. These are rumors." ⁶ "The State department was offered to Mr. Barnwell and declined by him, so says Keitt." ⁷ "Many are disappointed here. . . . I had the folly to believe that there was great patriotism in this movement. God help us! It looks now as if it was nothing but office seeking." "Mallory of Florida will be Secretary of the Navy. Yancey is one of the Commissioners to Europe." "The nomination of Mallory as Secretary of the Navy was confirmed to-day after a struggle. His soundness on the Secession question was questioned." ⁸

The young man who wrote these notes — Cobb was thirty-eight at the time — did not believe that the gathering meant war. He was killed, twenty-two months afterward, in the battle of Fredericksburg.

2

DAVIS ELECTED PRESIDENT ACCIDENTALLY

Just how did it come about that Jefferson Davis was elected President of the Confederate States of America? On this

⁵ This entry was made several months later, when Judah P. Benjamin was Secretary of War.
⁶ Rather wild ones, as it turned out.
⁷ Of South Carolina. Keitt had been one of the fire-eating South Carolina Congressmen before Secession
⁸ These extracts are from a collection of Cobb's letters in *The Southern Historical Society's Papers*, Vol. XXVIII, and *Proceedings of the Southern History Association*, Vol. XI.

question his biographers have ruminated without finding any satisfactory answer. Of course the upholders of the "conspiracy" theory, of the furtive meeting in the Washington Capitol on January 5, have no difficulty in solving the problem. According to this explanation his selection was automatic. Davis had been decided on then and there and the Convention really had no choice. Certain impediments to accepting this simple elucidation have been noted above. Far from being the mechanical result of a precisely arranged programme, there are facts that make the election of Davis a pure accident. His elevation was, it almost seems, the outcome of a misapprehension. Stephens maintained to his dying day that such was the case. Had the Montgomery Convention really exercised a free choice, he insisted, it would have unanimously elevated Robert Toombs. That he was a far more attractive man than Davis, a far more brilliant orator, far more human, and probably abler as a statesman, most commentators agree. Now and then, it is true, Toombs was lacking in seemly behavior. Sometimes his tobacco juice oozed from the corners of his mouth upon a white shirt front; and, according to one legend, his bibulous habits at the Montgomery Convention got the better of him; in plain words, like Andrew Johnson in a fateful moment, Toombs was palpably drunk. It was this slip, according to the story, — not satisfactorily authenticated, — which kept Toombs from the Presidential chair. The mere fact that Toombs came from Georgia stood much in his favor. "As Georgia goes, so goes the Confederacy," soon became a byword. An indication of its preëminence is that, of the four men conspicuously suggested for President, three were Georgians. Two of these, however, presented difficulties. Howell Cobb, as already related, had deserted his Democratic party in 1850 and joined forces with the antislavery Whigs in upholding the Compromise measures of that year. The memory of Democrats was retentive and Cobb's unpopularity, particularly in the cotton states, offered a serious bar to his candidacy. Due obeisance was paid to his eminence as Secretary of the Treasury in Buchanan's Cabinet by making him the presiding officer of the Montgomery Convention, but the forcing of his name for chief executive would have ruined that harmony which was deemed so desirable at this momentous hour. The sad feature is that Cobb and his friends and family so heartily yearned for the honor.

So, it is quite apparent, did the second available candidate, Alexander H. Stephens. The reason he was not seriously considered appears in the note of Thomas R. R. Cobb, quoted above. He was regarded as an eccentric and chameleonlike man, holding one view to-day, another to-morrow. His speech opposing Secession in the Georgia Legislature had aroused the enthusiasm of Abraham Lincoln, but had weakened his standing in the lower South. Clearly here was the most insidious of those "Reconstructionists" against whom all earnest proponents of Southern independence were continually on the defense; make Stephens President and he would at once — so it was urged and the fear was doubtless real — begin negotiations to reinstate a repentant South in the Union! Had the Montgomery delegates been in possession of Stephens's letters written at the time, their distrust would have turned to violence. These letters show that this Georgian had no faith in the proposed Confederacy or in its leaders. His melancholic disposition became black when viewing the prospect before him. Only a month before going to Montgomery, Stephens had declared to his brother Linton that the South had no real grievance against the North. The complaint "arises more from a spirit of peevishness or restless fretfulness than from calm and deliberate judgment. . . . With but few exceptions the South has controlled the government in its every important action from the beginning. It has aided in making and sustaining the administration for sixty years out of the seventy-two of the government's existence. Does this look like we were or are an abject minority at the mercy of a despotic northern majority, rapacious to rob and plunder us?"[9]

His letters ridicule and depreciate the leaders of the movement. "My apprehension and distrust of the future arise from the want of high integrity, loyalty to principle and pure, disinterested patriotism in the men at the head of the movement, who necessarily control it, at least for the present. . . . Whatever feelings of despondency I have in looking to the future come from my knowledge of the men in whose hands we are likely to fall. They are selfish, ambitious and unscrupulous. . . . My word for it, this country is in a great deal worse condition than the people are aware of. What is to become of us I do not know."[10] Perhaps the Convention acted wisely in frowning upon Stephens's very mild Presidential "boom."

None of these arguments, however, held against Toombs. Except for a miserable blunder, so Stephens afterward explained and so Toombs's biographers believe,[11] he would have been chosen. This mistake hinged upon the general distrust felt towards Howell Cobb. There was almost a morbid insistence that the President should be elected on the first ballot and that this election should be unanimous. Again the Washington precedent should be observed! Every member was prepared to sacrifice local ambitions in order to produce this result. On the evening preceding the balloting all delegations except the one from Georgia met to pick their candidate. The next morning at ten o'clock the men of Georgia gathered for the same purpose. A large majority in this meeting expressed their desire for Toombs. "Will you have it?" Stephens asked. There was nothing which Toombs yearned for more. If it came to him cordially, he answered, he would accept. But now spoke up Thomas R. R. Cobb whose notes, breathing fierce animosity against Stephens and strong desire for the selec-

[9] *Life of Alexander H. Stephens*, by Johnston and Browne, p. 376.
[10] *The same*, p. 384.
[11] See *Life of Robert Toombs*, by Ulrich B. Phillips, p. 224.

tion of his brother, have been quoted above. All the other delegations except Mississippi, he declared, had united at their meetings the previous evening on Jefferson Davis. Should Georgia take the responsibility of advancing their "favorite son" and thus break the hoped-for unanimity? All present were agreed that this would be a tragedy, and one of their number was sent to make inquiry as to the truth of Thomas Cobb's statement. This messenger quickly returned. Yes, it was indeed true; all the states, except Mississippi, had gone for Davis; his own state held back, not because of hostility to the man, but because it wished him — as he did himself — to become Commander in Chief of the Confederate Army. There seemed nothing left for Georgia to do therefore except fall in line and make the selection unanimous. As consolation, another of Georgia's sons, Alexander H. Stephens himself, was made Vice President while the disappointed Toombs received the highest appointment as the gift of the new executive, that of Secretary of State.

Too late did the Georgia men learn why their compatriots of Alabama, Florida, South Carolina, and Louisiana had rushed so precipitately to Davis. Not one of them, it presently appeared, had actually wanted this candidate for President; their choice of all of them was Toombs. But all had been informed that Georgia intended to present Howell Cobb. Clearly this attitude placed Toombs in an unfortunate position. His own state evidently did not desire him for President of the Confederacy; it had centred upon the obnoxious Howell Cobb. Under these circumstances, the enthusiasm that had previously been marked for Toombs throughout the South rapidly dissolved. The supposed injection of Howell Cobb stirred up the old antagonisms. If his name were to be seriously advanced, that harmony to which the delegates had pledged themselves would disappear. The Convention would soon be engaged in a battle over the most important matter on the programme. For under no circumstances would the other states accept the "apostate" of 1850. Nothing was therefore left to do but to concentrate on Jefferson Davis. In this way did the half-invalid and reluctant statesman of Mississippi become President of the Confederate States of America. The election, as had been planned, was unanimous. Six states voted as states, and all six votes went to Davis. The disappointed militarist at once resigned his commission as major general of the army of the "Republic of Mississippi" and departed for Montgomery.

3

THE CONSTITUTION FOR SECESSION

In the second great task of the Convention, Stephens for the most part had his way. In the brief space of a month, the delegates adopted both a provisional and a permanent charter of government. The form decided on was the Constitution of the United States, with such alterations as were deemed necessary to bring it into harmony with the new Southern situation, or, as Davis phrased it, to express "the well known intent" of the fathers of 1787. For example the first seven words of the Federal preamble had led to hot contention for three quarters of a century: "We, the people of the United States." Centralists had declared that this clause itself settled the greatest of all Constitutional arguments. Did it not describe the American government as a national Union, the work of the American people as a homogeneous mass? State-rights philosophers had met the admittedly difficult point with a variety of ingenious contentions, and this dispute the Confederate Constitution decided to clear up definitely. Its very first sentence, therefore, sounded the quintessence of Calhounism. "We, the people of the Confederate States, each state acting in its sovereign and independent character." This explanatory clause, according to the State-rights school, the fathers of 1787 had intended to add to the original proclamation, but for some strange reason had neglected to do so;

Montgomery now corrected this fatal omission of Philadelphia. There could be no argument as to meaning after that!

Another hiatus in the Federal Constitution had long been a grievance to the more religious part of the American population; this was its failure to mention the Deity. And so the Confederate preamble invoked "the favor of Almighty God" though the attempt of Thomas Cobb to secure the insertion of a clause forbidding the transportation of mails on Sunday was disapproved. An even more significant change than any of these was the use of the word "slave." This word does not appear in the Federal Constitution, though the existence of this type of property is clearly recognized several times. Most of the fathers of 1787, especially those from the South, detested slavery, and could not bring themselves to use the hated syllable in their charter. In this document black bondmen appear as "persons," "other persons," or "persons held to service." But much history had been made from 1787 to 1861; how much, the Confederate Constitution disclosed. An institution that was abhorred by the Virginians of the earlier time had become respectable in this later age. The constant hammering of the Abolitionists, the Garrisonian cry that slavery was a "sin," that a nation encouraging it was eternally damned, had seared the Southern mind and produced an attitude of defiance and assertion. Southerners for a generation had winced at the shamefacedness of the Constitution in refusing to mention specifically "slaves"; they regarded this reluctance as an insult to their section. Consequently, in their revised document the obscured African of 1787 leaps into the sunlight. He ceases to be a "person," and emerges challengingly a "slave." Certain members made a precise point of this change; they looked upon it as a matter of honor; the South must not be ashamed of something which was really much to its credit. At the same time the Confederate Constitution peremptorily prohibited the slave trade. The only state that protested to the end against this outlawing was South Carolina, and for some strange reason, that inscrutable person, Alexander H. Stephens, voted with South Carolina on this question.

But one studied omission from this paper comes almost as a shock. Several attempts were made to include in the Constitution a declaration asserting the right of Secession. The Convention stonily refused to make such a declaration. The principle on which the constitutionality of their entire movement depended the delegates at Alabama utterly declined to proclaim. South Carolina's effort to have the right of nullification acknowledged similarly did not succeed. But the Constitution did include a clause settling a controversy that had raged between the sections for decades. Congress was imperatively forbidden to pass a protective tariff. Another clause that reads strangely to-day is one forbidding the appropriation of money for public improvements! Here orthodox Jeffersonism scored another victory.

Toombs had visited Europe in 1855; in London he liked to drop in on the House of Commons and listen to the debates. This experience, as well as his wide reading, had given him a great respect for the British parliamentary system. One must remember his interruption of Stephens's November speech when, in response to the statement that the United States government was the best in the world, he ejaculated the word "England!" Stephens also thought that, in certain details, parliamentary government was better than our own. They were undoubtedly the two most statesmanlike of the minds that framed the Confederate Constitution, and their admiration for the English House of Commons appears in several details. But the most radical change they sought to incorporate, giving the President power to select his Cabinet from the membership of Congress precisely as the British Premier does from Parliament, did not meet approval. However, they did obtain a clause making it possible for Cabinet members to sit in the House of Representatives and to participate in debates affecting their departments. More important still, the Constitution contained a section that provided for what was essentially the British budget system. There can be no real budget, of course, so long as individual lawmakers can introduce appropriation bills of their own, or increase the estimates. Making the budget is an executive function, not a legislative one. The departments should inform Congress the amounts they need for the conduct of the nation's business; it is the prerogative of Congress to vote these requests or refuse to do so. This rational procedure is completely destroyed when individual members, helter-skelter, can bring in money bills. The Confederate Constitution most wisely prohibited this practice. "Congress shall appropriate no money from the Treasury, unless it be asked and estimated for by the President or some one of the heads of departments, except for the purpose of paying its own expenses and contingencies." How the legislative process at Washington would be simplified if such a rule prevailed to-day!

Another innovation introduced by the Confederate Constitution is one which reformers have advocated for years, so far unsuccessfully. That is a clause permitting the President to veto single items in appropriation bills. Thus was cured one of the greatest abuses of Congress, that of putting in general appropriation bills all kinds of undesirable expenditures — items that the President must accept if the government is to continue, for he cannot disapprove them except by vetoing the measure as a whole.

This review of the Convention and its constitution reveals again the overwhelming dominance wielded by the most populous and enlightened of the seven states that organized the Confederacy. One of Georgia's ablest sons, Toombs, would have been President except for an absurd misunderstanding. The Georgia delegation towered over all the other states in the eminence of its representatives. No other unit could display a group so statesmanlike and so gifted for leadership as Stephens, Toombs, Benjamin Hill, and the Cobb brothers. These men furnished the ideas for the Constitution and exercised the chief influence in framing it. They added to the old Federal Constitution certain innovations — such as that providing for a genuine budget system and that giving the President power to pick out obnoxious items in appropriation bills and veto them — that enhanced its value as a system of government. Whether the provision making the Presidential term six years, with no re-election, marked an improvement may be fairly argued, but it at least removed forever that nightmare of a "third term" which has so frequently demoralized national politics.

4

THE FIRST CABINET

The first Cabinet of Jefferson Davis was selected on what would be called to-day a "pork-barrel" basis. Besides Mississippi, there were six states in the government, in its first phase; each was duly "recognized" by the appointment of one of its prominent citizens to the President's Council. Toombs, of Georgia, became Secretary of State; Charles G. Memminger, of South Carolina, Secretary of the Treasury; Leroy P. Walker, of Alabama, Secretary of War; Stephen R. Mallory, of Florida, Secretary of the Navy; Judah P. Benjamin, of Louisiana, Attorney General, and John H. Reagan, of Texas, Postmaster General. This Cabinet had its offices in a commercial building in Montgomery, while the President transacted business in the Exchange Hotel. Its existence in Montgomery lasted for about three months. In that time only one of its sessions looms large in history and that one looms large indeed. Lincoln's inauguration on March 4, and his address, which clearly foreshadowed the use of force to put down the "rebellion," suddenly awoke the officials of Montgomery to a realization that war, after all, might be the sequel to their separation. Lincoln's dilatory action on the affair of Fort Sumter also disquieted and puzzled them. The basis of Lincoln's conduct is now no secret. He was determined to restore the Union, using, if necessary, all the men and resources of the North for that purpose. But an embarrassing fact was that the North at the beginning was not united for offensive purposes; and the President completely understood the foolhardiness of entering on such a stupendous conflict without a unanimous nation at his back. Only one thing would produce this unanimity: an act of aggression by the South, an armed attack on the Union. Above all other wars, the side that struck the first blow in this one would reap a great disadvantage. Lincoln's romantic, imaginative nature accurately appraised the instantaneous effect that would be produced in the North by such an overt act as firing on the American flag. This was one of the imponderables that Davis, less sensitive, did not gauge. Such an affront, Lincoln knew, would unite the North in an instant and bring all the people to a furious understanding of what these strange performances at Montgomery implied. Up to April, the Montgomery deliberations had half angered the North, half amused it. Secession struck most observers on the national side of the Potomac as a mixture of menace and burlesque. Its real purport — a most formidable attempt to split the nation in two, to set up an independent and necessarily hostile Republic on the Southern border — had entered the consciousness of only the most discerning. Politics still raged supreme; Democrats were still too inclined to look sympathetically upon the grievances of their Southern brethren; in the Northern states Secessionists were uncomfortably numerous. In consequence that unanimity of feeling essential to crushing the uprising did not exist, and Lincoln's first task as a statesman was to establish such oneness of feeling. An aggressive act on the part of the South would tremendously help him in this work. His behavior during the critical month from March 4 to

April 12 shows that in his own quiet, subtle way, he was goading the South into committing this mistake.

One man in the Confederate Cabinet — and only one — completely understood Lincoln's maneuvers. That was Robert Toombs. All the influence he possessed was exerted to prevent Davis from playing into Lincoln's hands. The fatal Confederate Cabinet meeting was held on April 9. Lincoln, evidently thinking the moment had arrived, notified South Carolina that he intended to replenish the supplies of the garrison at Fort Sumter. Davis had called his Cabinet to consider action on the crisis. Every member, except one, urged him to resort to drastic means of reprisal. Toombs entered the Cabinet meeting after the discussion had begun. He immediately opposed Davis and his colleagues. "The firing on that fort," he warned, "will inaugurate a civil war greater than any the world has ever seen; and I do not feel competent to advise you." Then, at the incredulous smiles of his associates, he became more serious. His hands behind his back, the Secretary of State stalked up and down the room. Suddenly he stopped before Davis. He was an impressive sight with his burly figure, his large round head, with its tangled forest of disordered hair, his flushed ample cheeks, his dazzling blue eyes. "Mr. President," he said, "if this is true it is suicide, it is murder, and will lose us every friend at the North. You will wantonly strike a hornets' nest which extends from mountains to ocean; and legions, now quiet, will swarm out to sting us to death." Then, after a pause: "It is unnecessary, it puts us in the wrong. It is fatal."[12]

But Toombs found no supporters — above all, not the President. A telegram was written and handed to a boy, who rushed to the telegraph office across the street. It was a message to Beauregard, virtually ordering the bombardment of Fort Sumter. The Civil War had begun — and was begun, as Lincoln intended it should be, by the South.

[12] *Robert Toombs, Statesman, Speaker, Soldier, Sage*, by Pleasant A. Stovall, p. 226.

IV

DIPLOMACY ON THE MEXICAN FRONT

1

Recognition by Europe

Upon Robert Toombs, Secretary of State, was laid perhaps the most delicate task facing the new government. It was his duty to cultivate the friendship of Europe and to win recognition from its greatest powers. Success might well have meant immediate triumph, for it would have involved the Federal Union in war with Great Britain and France. Was it conceivable that the North could wage a great conflict on its own borders, and, at the same time, fight the most powerful naval and military nations of Europe? Recognition would end the blockade, perhaps the North's most destructive measure against the South, open the markets of the world to cotton, and thus give the Confederacy a financial strength which in itself would have made the cause secure. Toombs may have felt a justifiable grievance in failing to gain the Presidency of the new republic, but he could not complain about the importance of the office assigned him.

The first Davis appointments in this field proclaimed the complexity of the interests at stake. To a commission of three men — William L. Yancey of Alabama, Pierre A. Rost of Louisiana, and A. Dudley Mann of Georgia — was assigned the task of winning recognition from Great Britain and France. At the same time a not widely known Kentuckian, John T. Pickett, was despatched on a similar mission to Mexico. England, France, and Mexico — such were the Governments whose friendship was deemed most essential to Confederate success. That England and France should be sedulously courted arouses no surprise, but why should recognition by Mexico be so highly esteemed? Yet Toombs was not the only statesman who conciliated the disorderly republic to the south. Lincoln and Seward similarly sought its friendly aid. "The President," wrote William H. Seward, Federal Secretary of State, in his instructions to Thomas Corwin, the new Minister to Mexico, regarded the Mexican mission [1] "at this juncture as perhaps the most interesting and important within the whole circle of our diplomatic relations." Even before the firing on Fort Sumter influential Southerners began stressing the importance of Mexico to the Confederate cause. One of these was William M. Burwell, of the well-known Virginia family — a Virginia conservative who took an exclusively aristocratic view of the crisis. "Lincoln and Seward," Mr. Burwell wrote Toombs as early as March 14, "properly perceive that their main battle with the South is to be fought in Mexico. . . . You are ready for that battle and I trust in God you will whip it. There lies, I think, the future of your country." [2] Another pressing correspondent was John Forsyth, of Alabama, from 1856 to 1858 American Minister to Mexico and negotiator of an unratified treaty which represented the widest expansionist desires of the Buchanan Administration. In March of 1861 Mr. Forsyth was sojourning in Washington, D. C., as a member of the Confederate Commission to the United States. Not meeting with a hospitable reception from Lincoln, Forsyth consoled himself by writing letters, one addressed to the new President at Montgomery. In this Mr. Forsyth urged that his chief despatch immediately a secret agent to Mexico.

Why was this emphasis laid on Mexico as the focal point of Confederate diplomacy? For the preceding forty years the Aztec republic had been the most tempestuous nation in two hemispheres. Since the expulsion of the Spaniards, in 1821, Mexico had had seventy-five presidents — nearly two a year. No country enjoyed less respect or influence in the foreign

---
[1] *U. S. Instructions*, Vol. XVII, No. 2, Apr. 6, 1861. National Archives.
[2] *Pickett Papers*, Library of Congress.

offices of the world. None would seem less likely to be flattered by a proud young people, like the Confederacy, seeking international standing. Yet this very turbulence in itself made Mexico an important pawn in the diplomatic game which now began. For it was through Mexico that recognition by Great Britain and France might be obtained. The most successful diplomatic attack was not to be a frontal one on London and Paris, but a flank one on Vera Cruz and Mexico City.

To understand this, we must erase all realization of the present world, forget the situation which the United States now holds in world affairs, and reconstruct the conditions of 1861. At that time European nations were casting covetous eyes upon Central and South America; Mexico, the richest jewel of all, was the particular object of desire. The one thing that this republic had seemingly demonstrated, in its less than half century of existence, was an inability to govern itself. It was not that it governed badly; the difficulty was that it did not govern at all; the nation for nearly fifty years had lain at the mercy of roving bands, each of which, in a period of temporary power, robbed and murdered at will. In no place were life and property safe. Foreigners had suffered even more than the simple, poverty-stricken peon. Neither private nor public debts had been secure. To the old-fashioned statesmen of those days only one solution of the Mexican problem seemed conceivable. Since Mexicans showed no signs of governing their country it was obviously the duty of the "powers" — especially of those whose citizens had been robbed and killed, whose property interests had been constantly jeopardized, and whose debts had for decades been in arrears — to step in and take control. That was the mid-nineteenth-century view of the proper way to handle disorderly peoples. Doubtless the vast riches of Mexico considerably whetted this European concept of duty; happy the nation that could add this unexampled empire to its possessions!

Another nation had not only cherished a similar ambition, but, to the extent of "robbing" Mexico of one half of her area, had carried it into effect. The ten years preceding the Civil War had clearly demonstrated that "the new colossus of the North" was quite prepared to complete the work of evisceration. Mr. Forsyth, who addressed President Davis on the Mexican problem in March, 1861, had been one of the greediest of land grabbers; another was Judah P. Benjamin, now Attorney General in the Davis Cabinet, previously the spokesman of President James Buchanan in Mexican affairs, and eager pursuer of concessions which would have given him control of a railroad across the isthmus of Tehuantepec. Thus the most formidable rival to British, French, and Spanish ambitions in Mexico was that nation's closest neighbor. Its Monroe Doctrine prohibited any European country from acquiring an additional foot of land in the Western Hemisphere. Its own history showed that what it denied to Europe, it reserved the right to appropriate itself.

At that time Great Britain had not yet reached the point of satiation in engulfing foreign territory. A people that had not ceased to grieve over "the loss of the American colonies" would have gladly found consolation in a land perhaps even naturally richer than the great Republic. Spain, feeble and poverty-stricken, still lived in her ancient pride, and still dreamed of regaining the lost Mexican Empire. But the most aggressive of all contenders was France. Louis Napoleon, nephew of the great Napoleon, had ruled France for nearly ten years. Splendid as the Second Empire appeared in its external trappings, its future was by no means secure. Founded chiefly on the prestige of a great name, itself the product of a barrack usurpation, it could maintain its power only by adventure and expansion. Napoleon III, no mighty statesman, had reached his lofty height by assurances that, under him, France would regain the power that had been achieved under his great namesake. Only triumphs in the dangerous foreign field could solidify the dynasty. *Gloire* thus became the watchword of his reign and restless ambition the one rule of its existence.

Had Napoleon himself lacked the zeal necessary to this purpose, a fiery and tireless influence constantly stood at his side, urging the more sluggish temperament to action. Napoleon III had married the beautiful and ambitious Eugénie de Montijo, a Spanish lady of noble but not royal birth. She had all the zest of a Spaniard for Empire and for Church. A France that should regain the mastery of Europe did not satisfy her imperial designs: she aspired to establish once more that power in the Western world which had been lost to Great Britain and the United States. France had once ruled Canada, and had ceded it to Britain; she had dominated the large domain of Louisiana, and had sold it to the new American Union. What more fitting enterprise for the new Napoleonic empire than the restoration of French prestige in the Western world? Eugénie was thinking of more than political success. She was a fervid Catholic and upholder of the temporal power of the church, then assailed in many lands. The greatest sin of the Mexicans, in her eyes, was the warfare on the Papacy. That had been the question at stake in the latest of Mexico's civil wars, that between Zuloaga, fighting with the clericals, and Benito Juárez, the church's bitterest foe — a contest that had ended in January, 1861, a month before the outbreak of the American civil war, in the complete success of Juárez. The result had been the secularization of religion and the seizure of church property. Eugénie's soul burned with a passion to right what she regarded as a monstrous wrong. French domination in Mexico was the one way to do it.

Only one enemy stood in the path of this magnificent enterprise. The preposterous Yankee Republic, with its even more preposterous Monroe Doctrine, alone disturbed the imperialistic dream. All European statesmen, including Napoleon

III, understood that any attempt to establish a foreign power in Mexico, or in any part of North or South America, would be accepted by Washington as a declaration of war. Until 1861, therefore, Napoleon had remained quiescent. For the preceding few years Mexico had offered a serious problem to three European powers, England, France and Spain, but in all these activities the secret purposes of the French emperor had been kept in abeyance. Mexican carelessness in paying her debts now brought these three nations together for joint action. In those days the use of ships of war as debt-collection agencies was accepted as one of their natural functions, and the news that England, France, and Spain had decided to send a persuasive flotilla on such a mission to Vera Cruz caused no anxiety in Washington. The three powers explained that mere seizure of a port, with its customhouses, for the satisfaction of long-standing claims, was the only end in view; above all, that no occupation of Mexican territory entered into the plans. So long as the expedition limited itself to such a demonstration, the United States raised no objection. The Monroe Doctrine was not involved.

But at least one of the intervening powers was meditating schemes far more imperialistic than a dunning expedition. Already, in the spring of 1861, Napoleon and Eugénie had formed the plan of invading Mexico, seizing the government, and creating a throne for some European royalty, preferably the Archduke Maximilian of Hapsburg, brother of the Emperor Francis Joseph. Maximilian himself, at that time twenty-nine years old, second in succession to the empire of Austro-Hungary, a man of cultivated mind and gentle disposition, was largely under the influence of his wife, the impetuous, ambitious Charlotte, just as Napoleon, in this enterprise, was dominated by the Empress Eugénie. Thus it would be no exaggeration to say that the proposed Hapsburg Empire in Mexico was largely the work of these two restless, imperious women. Except for one turn of history, however, it would have remained a fantastic dream. The happening that changed it from a wild, feminist imagining into a reality was the new political prospect opening in the Western Hemisphere.

The break-up of the American Union had apparently removed the single impediment to European ambitions on the new continent. To most European statesmen, in 1861, the organization of the Confederacy signified the end of the United States — at least its end as a great power. The Battle of Bull Run confirmed this belief. William H. Russell, the *Times* correspondent already quoted, returned to England in the spring of 1862, convinced that the Union could never be restored. Most European countries held the same view. It was not only the apparently hopeless military task confronting the United States that induced this unanimity. Nations, like individuals, are likely to believe what they wish to believe. The sudden rise of the United States, its growth in wealth and population, its truculent attitude towards European powers — an attitude natural enough to exuberant youth — had alienated most of Europe. The expanding American merchant marine was especially disturbing to Great Britain. But above everything else the thing that offended the Old World was the Monroe Doctrine, the declaration that no longer could Europe carve up the American continent, and the threat of war constantly held out to any nation that should make the attempt. To European statecraft, therefore, the impending break-up of the United States was a most welcome event. Especially was it hailed almost as a deliverance by Napoleon III, by Leopold I of Belgium, by Maximilian of Austria, by the Empress Eugénie and the Archduchess Charlotte. Heaven had delivered Mexico into their hands! No American fleet could now oppose their approach to Vera Cruz; the Yankee navy was too much occupied blockading three thousand miles of Confederate coast line. No American army would now venture to cross the Rio Grande and expel foreign troops; that border was the possession of a hostile

Confederacy. Not only was this obstacle removed for the time being, but seemingly forever. A powerful southern people, strong in arms, rich in products, commercially and economically a complement to Europe, would stand indefinitely as a buffer between what was left of the arrogant United States and the contemplated Mexican Empire. European diplomacy in the future should maintain the friendliest relations with the Confederate States, for, so long as this new virile power upheld its independence, the Monroe Doctrine could be treated as a dead letter. Again, almost in a twinkling, both North and South America had become a field of conquest, helpless before European exploitation. In a world-wide sense the chief importance of secession was that it had transformed the Western Hemisphere into a gigantic Poland, ripe for partition by the powers of Europe.

Not only did European plotters perceive this opportunity, but Confederate diplomacy as well. An unfortunate phase of war is that the foe usually looks for advantages where they may be found, and the immediate necessities of the case frequently result in strange, even disastrous combinations. In 1861 the enemies of the Federal Government, wherever found, were regarded, from that very fact, as the destined friends of the Confederate States. Thus events had apparently made the South an ally of France, even at the cost of advancing the predatory schemes of Napoleon. Davis had something definite to offer France, and Napoleon in return could do much for the South. Was it mistaken policy to promote the Maximilian usurpation in Mexico, in exchange for French recognition of the Government of Jefferson Davis? Confederate statesmen accepted this as good international politics.

Recognition by France, they fondly believed in these early days, would have, as a necessary accompaniment, recognition by Great Britain. That France and Great Britain were acting as a unit in the American crisis was no secret for, as soon as hostilities began, the French and British Governments officially made an announcement to this effect. Both at the same time recognized the belligerency of the Confederate states and simultaneously issued proclamations of neutrality. Both publicly declared that, on the more vital question — the acknowledgment of Southern independence and the negotiation of treaties of friendship and trade — they would act as a single nation. One morning Mr. Seward was astonished by the appearance of Lord Lyons and M. Mercier, British and French Ministers in Washington, on a joint visit to the State Department, demanding that they be received together. Mr. Seward deftly but firmly declined to grant this startling request, but the proposal disclosed the extent to which the two Governments were carrying out an allied policy in the treatment of all American questions. It was therefore natural to suppose that French recognition of the Confederacy would simultaneously bring similar action by Great Britain. Mr. Toombs therefore regarded it as good diplomacy to take all means of enticing Napoleonic France into such an accommodating gesture. To promote Napoleonic schemes in Mexico was the quickest way of reaching this goal. To offer the same opposition that was stolidly presented by Washington would utterly destroy any chance of French and European support.

Thus the quickest way to a possible diplomatic triumph in Europe lay through Mexico. From the standpoint of American continental history, such a policy involved great sacrifices. It might indeed be regarded as a betrayal of the whole North American tradition. It implied a complete reversal of the American system It meant the introduction of European principles and of European dynasties into a hemisphere that had forever cast them out. Should France establish an imperial regime in Mexico, other European states had plans ready for advancement in other American quarters. The work of Washington, who insisted that America was something quite distinct from Europe and should be kept free from European ideas, would go into the discard. The policy of another Southern President, Monroe, vetoing for all time any extension of European influence in the New World, would be jettisoned. These concessions, however, the South was prepared to make. As a result, the struggle of the Lincoln Government involved far more than is ordinarily understood. What the North was supposed to be fighting for was the preservation of the Union. But the problem was vaster than that. The North was really fighting for the preservation of the Western Hemisphere, of both North and South America — at least their preservation from seizure by the autocratic dynasties of the transatlantic world.

The triumph of Juárez over Zuloaga, in January, 1861, did not settle Mexico's internal conflict. Again two parties rose, struggling for control in the time-honored Mexican fashion. And the issues remained the same. The Constitutionalists, still led by Juárez, had been recognized by the United States as the established government. The Juárez regime was usually pictured as the liberal, anticlerical popular majority. By April, 1861, Juárez dominated the capital and most of central and southern Mexico. The opposition party was the Conservative, composed of the "respectable classes" — property owners and good churchmen, devoted to the restoration of the hierarchy and its ravished lands. This combination, it was asserted, favored the establishment of an empire, under a European prince, believing that only in this way could peace and order be brought to a distracted people. With this latter element the fortunes of the Confederacy clearly lay. On this point the letter of Mr. Burwell, addressed to Robert Toombs, is illuminating. In this writer's view the success of the North would endanger, not only the Southern labor system, but religion. "To-day their special animosity is against slavery; tomorrow it will be against peonage. Here they are restrained from imposing Congregationalism and Presbyterianism upon dissenters by the terms of the Federal Constitution; in Mexico they would attack Catholics with an appetite sharpened by compulsory abstinence. If you deem important to be placed in confidential relations with the leading Catholic authorities in this country and in Mexico, with a view to impressing on the Mexican mind the superior safety of an alliance with the Confederacy I can bring into communication with you an intimate friend and *devotee* of Archbishop Hughes [Archbishop of New York]. He is also a man long and intimately acquainted with Mexico, socially, commercially, ecclesiastically and politically, and he will, I am conyinced, afford you any assistance in that respect which you may desire."[3] This letter clearly contemplated an alliance with the Catholic Conservatives and Maximilianists. The Confederate ambassador selected for Mexico believed in his heart in the wisdom of the policy outlined. John T. Pickett, the man sent to bring the distracted republic into coöperation with the Confederacy, never wavered in this conviction. Before departing he wrote John Forsyth (March 13, 1861) that "only foreign intervention can bring peace and tranquility to Mexico."[4] After spending eight months in that country, his expressions on the subject were even stronger. He then informed Secretary Toombs that "President Zuloaga, the clergy and the old army chiefs would gladly throw themselves into the arms of the Confederate States. We may thus have forced upon us the policy of *divide et impera*."[5]

2

COLONEL JOHN PICKETT

The two men selected to represent their two Governments in this critical capital had only one point in common — both were native Kentuckians, Pickett a member of the family

[3] Letter of William M. Burwell to Robert Toombs, the Confederate Secretary of State, Liberty, Virginia, 14 March 1861. *Pickett Papers*, Library of Congress.
[4] *Pickett Papers*, Library of Congress.
[5] *Pickett Papers*, Despatch No. 10.

that produced the fateful general of Gettysburg, Thomas Corwin the descendant of a similarly worthy New England line. In temperament, in character, in tastes, in political ideas, in career, it would be hard to imagine two men more unlike. Pickett was one of those adventurers about whom legends gather. He was a Southerner of traditional type. Proud, fiery, generous, quarrelsome, sensitive on points of honor, brave in a reckless, devil-may-care fashion, his whole existence had been a succession of excitements. Born in 1823, educated at West Point, Pickett gave up a comparatively quiet existence in the American army for more pleasing diversions in foreign lands. Co-conspirator with Kossuth, general — at least by appointment — in that patriot's Hungarian army, fomenter of revolution in San Domingo, colonel on the filibustering expedition of Narciso Lopez in Cuba, Pickett finally settled down as United States consul at Vera Cruz, where he became the intimate of *insurrectos*, the boon companion of banditti, and the right-hand man of American ministers and their co-plotter in schemes not necessarily friendly to Mexico.

John Forsyth of Alabama, American minister in the trying period preceding the Civil War; Judah P. Benjamin of Louisiana, future Secretary of State in the Confederacy, and steadfast seeker of Mexican concessions; John Slidell, another Louisianan who spent nearly a year — 1859–1860 — as unreceived Minister of the United States to its suspicious southern neighbor — such were Pickett's closest confidants. Forsyth owed much to Pickett's tutorship. No better instructor in the complexities of Mexican politics could have fallen in Forsyth's way. In his Mexican sojourn, from 1856 to 1859, Pickett had been his constant companion and adviser, a relationship that continued when Pickett, a ferocious Confederate, returned to the United States on the eve of Secession. When Forsyth went to Washington, in February, 1861, as a member of the Confederate commission to the United States Government, he took Pickett along as secretary. On the failure of this attempt at accommodation, Pickett returned to the centre of operations, Montgomery. Everywhere Pickett and Forsyth were found in company. William H. Russell, correspondent of the London *Times*, met the two men both in Washington and in the Confederate capital. The Englishman evidently liked Pickett, spent many convivial evenings with him discussing various aspects of the Confederacy, and learned much of Central American politics. "Mr. Colonel Pickett," wrote Russell, "is a tall, good-looking man, of pleasant manners and well educated. But this gentleman was a professed buccaneer, a friend of Walker, the grey-eyed man of destiny — his comrade in his most dangerous razzie. He was a newspaper writer, a soldier, a filibusterer, and he now threw himself into the cause of the South with vehemence; it was not difficult to imagine he saw in that cause the realization of the dreams of empire in the south of the Gulf, and of conquest in the islands of the sea, which have such a fascinating influence over the imagination of a large portion of the American people." [6]

With such admirers at court as John Forsyth and Judah P. Benjamin, and with his long experience in Mexican affairs, acquaintance with Mexico's public men, and skill in the Spanish language, Pickett's appointment to the Aztec capital followed in the natural order of things. Above all, his ambitions in Mexico and Central America accorded with those of the men directing Confederate affairs. Davis himself was no more an "imperialist" in this quarter of the hemisphere than Pickett. The genial "Colonel John" — in Mexico this name quickly became Don Juan — pinned his faith on the conservative and clerical party; he loathed the Juárez regime, and believed that the South should seek alliance with the counter-revolution then attempting to destroy it. His rival, the new American minister to Mexico, Thomas Corwin, sympathized just as

---

[6] *My Diary, North and South*, Vol. I, p. 95. Pickett's title of "Colonel" came from his service in the Lopez expedition.

strongly with the Liberal or Constitutional party. None of Lincoln's diplomatic appointments so angered the South as this one. If the new President at Washington had searched the country to discover the one man most hateful to the hot spirit of "Colonel John" he could have made no better selection. That Corwin, like himself, was a native Kentuckian only added to his fury. But the very things that made Tom Corwin odious to Southerners assured him the warmest reception in Mexico. Mr. Burwell, the already quoted Virginian who intended to approach the Mexican problem by way of the Catholic Church, expresses this anger in a letter to Toombs, March 14, 1861. As his first diplomatic appointment, Mr. Burwell says, Lincoln sends to Juárez the man who "welcomed Americans with bloody hands to hospitable graves in Mexico." Evidently Mr. Lincoln thought that the main battle was to be fought south of the Rio Grande, since he had sent there "a man who sided with Mexico in a war with his own country for the free-soil cause."[7] The episode in question concerned the most important fact in Corwin's career — his hatred of slavery, and the part he had played in obstructing its extension. A Kentuckian turned Abolitionist — such was the spectacle that made the Corwin name detested throughout Dixie. For Corwin was no mild or philosophic dissentient; he carried his opposition into every phase of life. His career had been a conspicuous one. Congressman in 1830, Governor of Ohio in 1840, United States Senator in 1845, Secretary of the Treasury in the Cabinet of President Fillmore — such were the rewards that had crowned Corwin, largely as the result of his fight against the Southern tenet. And his opposition had been effective, for he was one of the most brilliant stump speakers of a period prolific in that art. Though soaring earnestness was his main quality, Corwin's speech at times became biting, dangerously witty, compact of those unforgettable phrases which pass into contemporary speech. Mr. Burwell recalls above one

[7] *Pickett Papers*, Library of Congress.

THOMAS CORWIN (1794–1865)

Brown Bros

BENITO JUÁREZ (1806–1872)

Brown Photos

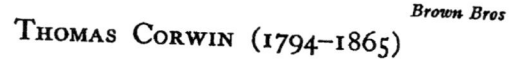

William Lowndes Yancey of Alabama
(1814–1863)

John T. Pickett of Kentucky

of these epigrams, uttered in a Senate debate on the Mexican War. It had dogged the Kentuckian for the rest of his days. Corwin formed a member of the Congressional coterie opposed to this aggression. In this he had distinguished associates. While Corwin berated President Polk in the Senate, Abraham Lincoln and Alexander H. Stephens were assailing him in the House, but the eloquence of the Representatives reached no such vituperative stage as that of the gentleman in the upper chamber. "If I were a Mexican I would tell you: Have you not room in your own country to bury your dead men? If you come into Mexico we will greet you with bloody hands and welcome you to hospitable graves." In the South this oration transformed Corwin into the inevitable "traitor," but in the North the orator became something of a hero; Horace Greeley, in the *Tribune,* promptly nominated him for President. Corwin did not attain that office, but, from 1850 to 1860, he was one of the most forceful characters in America, more and more impassioned on the antislavery side.

That speech had metamorphosed him into one of the heroes of Mexico. The ministers who had been accredited from Washington in the fifties — Gadsden, Forsyth, McLane — had all been Southerners. They had spent most of their time attempting to slice off large segments of Mexican soil to swell the territory of an already fat Northern neighbor. But Corwin was a diplomat whose career disclosed his opposition to this kind of treatment. Here was a *Yankecito* after Mexico's own heart! Corwin had still other advantages. He was by nature a diplomat. Impressive personally, — a man of big frame, muscular, active, with an open, genial countenance, frequently given to laughter, — he presented a different type from the grim, forbidding, self-satisfied American temperament which too frequently marked the opponents of slavery. He had taken over the opinions of New England, but he had remained, in disposition, completely Kentuckian. Nor did his exhortation to "hospitable graves" represent his usual platform manner.

Corwin really believed that his reputation for wit had destroyed his political career — at least, that it had prevented his progress to even higher posts than he reached. "Tom" Corwin's humor and charm had made him the most popular man in Ohio, but had injured his standing as a serious statesman. His advice to young men about to embark in public life was always the same: Never be funny! Always assume an air of the most profound gravity! "The world," he said, "has a contempt for the man who entertains it." That may be true of statesmanship, but it is not so true of diplomacy, where the ability to amuse people, to fraternize, to be always good-natured and unruffled is a priceless asset. Especially was this the case with people so childlike as the Mexicans. The politicians then uppermost in Mexico naturally felt suspicious of Pickett, familiar to them for years as a filibusterer in Central American countries and an agent of annexation, and at once attached themselves to Corwin, their friend in difficult times and the representative of that part of the United States less conspicuous in efforts to dismember their country.

In June of 1861 these two diplomats stood facing each other, in a sense literally, for Pickett had taken up headquarters in the Hotel Iturbide, directly opposite the modest United States legation. "Your mission is a difficult one," a Mexican friend of Pickett, Señor Mata, wrote him on his arrival at Vera Cruz. That remark did not lack a sardonic quality. The Mexican himself was not destitute of humor, and the appearance of a representative of Jefferson Davis in the guise of conciliation was rated at its true worth. Davis had for years been the articulate spokesman of the American advance in Latin America. It was his desire to transform all Central America, as well as Cuba and the Caribbees, into American soil, all to the greater glory of slavery. It now became Pickett's mission to persuade the suspicious Latins that Davis, not Abraham Lincoln, was their friend, and that his chief ambition was to prevent their being swallowed up by an avaricious

North. His general purpose was to convert them into allies in the great American conflict and to forestall assistance to the foe. In case of foreign intervention, the Confederacy — so ran Toombs's instructions to Pickett — could offer more protection to their Southern neighbor than the Federal Government. This latter was the all-important point, but there were other tangible ways in which Mexico could help. After all, only one boundary of the Confederacy was free from the Federal blockade; this was the Rio Grande River, the Mexican-Confederate frontier. Munitions and other supplies transported to Mexico from Europe could be smuggled across this line into the Southern states; Confederate products, above all, cotton, could be shipped in the opposite direction to a transatlantic market. Across the same frontier, Confederate forces could easily invade Mexico, in case of misbehavior: it therefore offered a vantage point from which the new nation could constantly threaten her neighbor. "Mexico being co-terminous with the Confederate states," read Toombs's ominous letter, "renders the existence of a friendly alliance with the latter of the highest importance to the former." Then Vera Cruz was an important port; its docks were constantly full of foreign ships. Could not these, or some of them, be enlisted in the Confederate service as privateers? Pickett carried to Mexico twenty blank commissions of this kind, signed by Jefferson Davis, though he does not seem to have met such success in persuading sea captains to accept them.

Obviously the first duty laid upon the American minister was to prevent Mexico from entering into any treaty or alliance with the enemy, and not to permit its territory to be used in any way that would advance the interests of the South. On the other hand he was expected to make Mexico, in so far as possible, an agency of the American government. Both these objects Corwin accomplished. Pickett resided in Mexico seven months, from June until December. In that time he obtained only one interview with the Minister of Foreign Affairs, and though he addressed many communications to that official, received only one or two replies. President Juárez never received the Confederate and practically all the other functionaries gave him a wide berth. Pickett first addressed the government in a well-written, if bombastic, letter, given up largely to drawing comparisons between Mexico and his newly risen nation. They were both agricultural countries, Pickett explained, interested only in exchanging their natural products for articles of use from abroad. Their labor systems, while not identical, did not materially differ: African slavery and peonage after all were essentially the same thing! Pickett detected a close resemblance between the many uprisings in Mexico and the present upheaval in his own country. "What have your revolutions been," he asked, "but constant struggles of state sovereignty against controlled usurpation of power? We have but imitated the example of our southern neighbors." In both nations the motive for action had been "that noble spontaneous sentiment which yearns for political freedom." Beware of that northern nation! "What will become of Spanish America when Yankee meddlesomeness and Puritan bigotry run riot throughout the hemisphere?" Trust the South! "By whom were belligerent rights first conceded to Mexico? By a Virginia President.[8] By whom was her absolute independence first acknowledged and vindicated? By a Tennessee President, a Kentucky Senator and a South Carolina Envoy.[9] Who defeated the McLane treaties?" "Yankee senators."

Five days elapsed before the agent of the Confederacy received a reply. Then Zamacona "kissed the hands of Señor Don Juan Pickett," and appointed the next afternoon for a meeting. The wary Mexican did not desire an interview at the Foreign Office, but requested Pickett to call at his home. His greeting had all the suavity to be expected from a Mexican but his remarks were mainly limited to congratulating Pickett

[8] James Monroe.
[9] Andrew Jackson, Henry Clay, and Joel R. Poinsett.

on not asking for recognition or for a treaty of alliance; that caution was wise and very acceptable to Mexico! "We parted with mutual assurances of friendship and esteem," Pickett reported to Toombs. So far as practical results were concerned, that ended the first attempt of the Confederacy to establish diplomatic relations with Mexico.[10] Pickett had been granted the courtesy of a personal — not an official — reception, the usual procedure in situations of the kind, but had not obtained anything that suggested even remotely the coöperation of the Mexican Republic.

3

Señor Corwin

Meanwhile, Thomas Corwin was meeting with considerably more favor. A regularly accredited diplomat, his position was more secure than that of Colonel John. Besides, for other reasons, Juárez wished to make his residence successful. His Government possessed, in considerable abundance, the one commodity of which Mexico then stood in urgent need. Fair words and promises Juárez might obtain from the Confederacy, but hard cash could be secured only from *El Norte*. Probably this pure-blooded Aztec had no greater love for the section lying north of the Potomac than for the South. Both Unionists and Confederates were Gringos and therefore obnoxious to patriotic Mexicans. "These jealous, exclusive people heartily wish there were a Chinese wall or Gulf of Fire," wrote Pickett, "surrounding their country and separating them from the eternal enemies of their race. . . . They shed each other's blood in torrents, but the fear of losing any portion of their unpeopled waste is the nightmare which haunts their imagination constantly."[11] True as it is that Southern statesmen had led in the dismemberment of Central America, the North had not been entirely a disinterested

---

[10] Pickett correspondence, Library of Congress, No. 3, 4, 5.
[11] *Pickett Papers.*

spectator; not only the extension of slavery, but "manifest destiny," a term already in use, had been an inciting motive. Even Señor Corwin himself, as his correspondence discloses, looked upon Lower California as legitimate prey. In June, 1861, however, this was not the matter that weighed heaviest on the Mexican state. No *Presidente* ever occupied so hazardous a seat as that on which Juárez was sitting when Corwin presented his credentials. He dominated the central section of his country with the City of Mexico as capital, and exercised an uncertain sovereignty over the South and East. He ruled this empire as the prize of a successful struggle against the Conservative party, composed of large landholders, aristocrats, and the Catholic Church; but these forces were still extremely vigilant, and were undermining Juárez in a hundred places.

Mexico as a nation stood on the precipice of extinction. The patience of European powers had been exhausted. In July, two months after the American and Confederate envoys reached the country, Mexico announced the suspension of interest payments on the national debt. Poor Juárez could hardly do otherwise; local chieftains were absorbing the Federal customs revenues; there was not a dollar in the treasury and even government troops and civil employes had received no pay for a considerable time. But this moratorium on debt service gave the European powers the excuse they had been seeking for several years. France and Great Britain suspended diplomatic relations; soon afterward, they drew up a Convention — in which Spain also joined — for the seizure of Mexican ports. William H. Seward distrusted all three nations. With Corwin he now worked out a scheme for checkmating the European advance. Why, asked Corwin, should the Federal Government not lend Mexico from $5,000,000 to $10,000,000 for the liquidation of the foreign claims and the reëstablishment of domestic order? This would deprive European powers of all decent excuse for intervention. Seward was more canny: it would hardly do to place so large a sum as this in the hands of the needy *Juáristas!* They might not use it to pay their debts, but might spend it in foolish enterprises of their own. A better plan would be for the United States to assume payments of the interest on the Mexican foreign debt. That would, or should, satisfy European creditors and give them no respectable excuse for bombarding the ports of Mexico and, what was more than likely, invading and seizing the choicest parts of its territory.

Corwin and Juárez at once began negotiating a treaty on this basis. The American government was to advance for six years the money to pay interest, at three per cent, on Mexico's European debt amounting to $62,000,000. What guarantee of repayment was the friendly northern Republic to obtain? Obviously there should be some security for the reimbursement of these considerable sums. Corwin pointed to the rich mineral lands in the states, Sonora, Sinaloa, Lower California, and Chihuahua; there were also great public dominions, so far uncultivated, in the same region. Above all, there were the rich estates of the Church which the Constitutionalists had expropriated — could not Mexico mortgage these assets to obliging Uncle Sam? Not improbably both Corwin and Seward, in stipulating these conditions to the bond, had an eye to the future. "It would probably end in the cession of the sovereignty to us," remarked Corwin. Seward injected into the treaty a definite clause that all these lands and mineral rights should become absolute in the United States in case Mexico defaulted after six years. Despite these concealed advantages, Corwin viewed the whole matter from a lofty plane. "The United States," he wrote Seward, "are the only safe guardians of the independence and true civilization of this continent." [12]

This treaty, which would have had such vast historic consequences, never went into effect; if it had done so, the American Union at the present moment would contain the states

[12] *United States Instructions,* Vol. 28, No. 3.

of Sonora, Chihuahua, Lower California, and Sinaloa — commonwealths which, in their essential characteristics, would not differ much from the present Arizona and New Mexico. The United States Senate ended the splendid plan by withholding its approval. An overburdened Federal treasury was one reason for its unfriendly attitude; another was the refusal of France and England, on being questioned, to accept this guarantee of interest as a pacification of their claims; they stood out for the principal. But strange are the revenges of diplomacy. This rejected treaty exercised almost as much influence on Mexican relations at a critical moment as it would have, had it received the benediction of the Senate. The main purpose in the negotiations was to keep Mexico friendly to the North and hostile to the Confederacy. The abortive treaty accomplished both ends. For the year that the treaty was under consideration Juárez, in his foreign policy, remained a submissive friend of Corwin and Seward. By the time it had failed in the Senate, Juárez was himself in flight and in no position to do the Federal Government good or ill. For the twelve months that Juárez held sway in Mexico, Thomas Corwin, by constantly dangling before Mexican eyes the prospect of ready money, had the whole situation in his hands. He had been instructed to frustrate any drawing together of Mexico and the Confederate Government. Above all, Seward insisted, it was his task to hold the European nations at bay, to prevent the invasion of Mexico, to make impossible any coöperation between France and the Confederacy in Mexico — coöperation that might have gone far towards the general recognition of the Southern States. This struggle was fought out in other places than Mexico; in fact, it was then taking place in foreign capitals. American diplomacy in this great enterprise, as will appear, was ultimately successful. But to this great triumph Corwin made his contribution. Sir Charles Wyke, British Minister, kept assuring Corwin of the sincerity of British purposes, and Lord Lyons, the British Minister at Washington, protested to Seward that Britain had joined France in the intervention merely to secure payment of their claims, and had no ulterior ends to serve, above all no desire to acquire territory. Both Corwin and Seward received these statements suspiciously, but when, in April, 1862, the British sailed away from Vera Cruz, declining to have any part in the French invasion, it was evident that Great Britain's disavowal had been made in good faith. The dream of Empire in Mexico thus became the exclusive possession of Napoleon. That was a mad adventure for which more experienced and more hard-headed British statesmanship had no stomach.

4

FARCE IN MEXICO CITY

Not for several months did Pickett learn how farcical his sojourn in Mexico City had been, and how utterly the Mexican officials had become wax in the hands of Thomas Corwin. Just before his departure, a letter came from the Confederate State Department informing its representative in Mexico that only one of his many and voluminous despatches had been received. For half a year his superiors had been left in the dark about transactions in this important capital. Such a discovery would have startled a more even-tempered emissary than this Kentucky filibusterer. What, he anxiously asked himself, had become of these confidential documents? At Tampico, where Pickett sojourned a few days on his way home, all curiosity was satisfied. Here was stationed Don Santiago Tapia, commander in chief of the state of Taumalipas, through whose hands passed mail destined from Mexico to the Confederate States.

"What became of such mail?" asked Pickett. It had all been intercepted, Don Santiago innocently replied, on the request of the American minister in Mexico. Señor Tomas Corbin was very *exigento* (exacting) in matters of that kind. Again we behold the power of the purse! Here appears another of Corwin's demands upon Juárez, which, in view of that anticipated loan, could not be denied. All of Pickett's secret communications, intended exclusively for the eye of Robert Toombs, had been sent to Juárez; that statesman, after reading the letters, transmitted them to the United States Minister, who in due course passed on the packets to Washington. "We should not be surprised," groaned Pickett, "that an impotent and cowardly nation, such as Mexico, should have practiced such neutrality."

Certainly the unfortunate man had every reason to be appalled when he remembered the contents of his letters. If Don Juan needed any further explanation of the indifference and even contemptuous hostility with which he had been treated, he had it now. Indeed, Pickett probably congratulated himself on getting out of the country alive. Mexicans are a hot and sensitive people, disposed to give vigorous and bloody expression to their emotions, and that Pickett should have been left undisturbed, while penning these sketches of the Mexican environment, is something of a mystery. But perhaps the sense of humor which Mexicans undoubtedly possess eased their anger. The turgid sentiments uttered by Pickett in his messages to the Foreign Office, placed by the side of his real opinions in his despatches to Robert Toombs, would appeal to any man's comic instinct. The contradictions must have delighted Thomas Corwin — the Senator whose public career, in his own judgment, had been ruined by a too lively appreciation of the ridiculous. Even at this late day the process of looking on this picture, and then on that, is not without entertainment.

For Pickett's official proffer of friendship had been most complimentary, even wheedling. He had discovered, as already related, a close affinity between the purposes inspiring his own country and those that had guided Mexico for several decades. In striking a blow for liberty, "we have but imitated the example of our southern neighbors." Mexicans were "a people whom I have learned to appreciate and esteem." Compare these salutations with the judgments he was confiding to the private ears of Robert Toombs. "Mexicans are a race of degenerate monkeys." "This country is in the hands of robbers, assassins, blackguards and lepers." "The government is the biggest robber of all." "Mexico City is the most disorderly city on the continent — perhaps on the globe." The nation was in a state of "moral, political and financial anarchy"; eminent Mexicans were daily "put to death in cold blood." One popular phrase affords this commentator endless amusement. *Cosa de Mexico* — the fashion of the country. Are the judges on the bench frequently well-known criminals? *Cosa de Mexico!* Can justice be purchased at a regulated tariff? *Cosa de Mexico!* The Chief of Police of Mexico City, Pickett reports, is "one Porfirio Diaz — a notorious highwayman." [13] *Cosa de Mexico!* The Deputy Chief was the graduate of a chain gang. "The highway is literally the highroad to riches, preferment and honor in this country." All such phenomena are *Cosas de Mexico!*

Pickett was evidently doing even more indiscreet things than inscribing these thoughts on paper; he rather proudly repeats to Toombs the witticisms with which he frequently entertained jollifying friends. He was many times asked if the Confederacy was looking for recognition by the Mexican Government. Not at all, replied Pickett. "To the contrary my business is to recognize Mexico — provided that I can find a government that will stand still long enough." Informed that many Mexicans were receiving commissions in Federal forces, Pickett expressed regret that the whole Northern army could not be officered by Mexicans. "I added also that they ought to be very careful not to be taken prisoners by the South, as they would, in that event, probably find themselves, for the first time in their lives, usefully employed in agricultural pursuits,

---

[13] Afterward the famous statesman. President of Mexico from 1877 to 1880 and from 1884 to 1911.

— that is, hoeing corn and picking cotton." Pickett publicly repudiated suggestions, constantly made, that the South lusted for Mexican territory. "We would not take it as a gift — with its population." Reform is impossible in Mexico because of "the gross ignorance and superstition of the people — if Mexico may be said to have a people."

The utter venality apparent on every hand came in for castigation. Had the Government obtained the memorandum appended to the private instructions from Mr. Toombs — as is not impossible that they did — it would have appeared that Pickett intended to make corruption the foundation of his policy. For this paper was written by Pickett himself. "A million or so of money judiciously applied would purchase our recognition by the government. The Mexicans are not overscrupulous and it is not our mission to reform their morals at this precise period." Sprinkled all over Pickett's despatches are references to this, the all-prevailing sin of Mexican politics. "Every Mexican has his price. He has an acute sense of touch as regards a certain yellow metal." The diplomat repeatedly complains of "the high price one has to pay for justice in this country."

But these were merely general insults; more disastrous was the revelation afforded by Pickett's letters of Confederate policy. He was constantly proposing to Davis and Toombs that they join hands with the foreign powers then making war on the government to which he was accredited. Should Mexico make a treaty with the United States "it will be to our advantage at once to take up the Conservative party and aid in restoring its leaders to power. . . . The Church is by no means dead there. . . . Southward is our destiny." At this very time Pickett was assuring Mexican officialdom that the Confederacy had no desire to expand in their direction. One proposal in his diplomacy anticipates an offer made by Germany fifty years subsequently to Mexico. Americans have not yet forgotten Herr Zimmerman's offer to Venustiano Carranza, in 1917, on the verge of American participation in the World War. If Mexico would join Germany, the German Foreign Secretary proposed on this occasion, that nation, in the event of expected victory, would take back Texas, Arizona, and New Mexico, of which the United States had robbed her seventy years before. It is curious to discover this same idea in Confederate diplomacy of 1861. Let Mexico join forces with the Confederate States, and this same territory, when the war ended favorably, would be re-ceded to her. Whether Zimmerman would ever have redeemed his pledge we do not know; how seriously Pickett, in 1861, regarded his offer his intercepted correspondence reveals. "There is no prospect of improvement, so long as Mexico is governed — or attempted to be governed — by Mexicans." The Confederacy should join the states then intervening in Mexico — France, Great Britain, and Spain — and with them carve up the country. "An alliance now is afforded," writes Pickett to Toombs, "the first, last and only opportunity of effectively excluding the United States from the possession of any of these magnificent territories upon our southern border, or laved by the Gulf of Mexico. Indeed, we might be able, in conjunction with those powers, and that of Spain, to render this Gulf forever a *mare clausum* to the United States, which would also be conclusive as to one aspect of the Mississippi River navigation question." "Our people must have an outlet to the Pacific. Ten thousand men in Monterey could control the entire northern part of this Republic." "Our revolution has emasculated the Monroe doctrine. . . . I am now prepared to advocate any alliance which may check the expansion of the North." "We have a very bad neighbor across a narrow shallow stream and we must invoke the God Terminus and make new limits. There is no fear that the Rio Grande would prove our Rubicon." How about his protestations to the Mexican Government that the Confederacy did not aspire to annex any Mexican state, and, indeed, was prepared to return great areas taken in the Mexican War?

"It must not be supposed from the expression of the foregoing in diplomatic language that I am not fully impressed with the fact that 'manifest destiny' may falsify the disclaimer. No one is more impressed than the writer with the great truth that Southward the star of empire takes its way." Capture Monterey at once! "It would secure us the permanent possession of that beautiful country." Take up a military position on the Rio Grande! All pending problems with Mexico would be solved, and the future empire of the Confederacy made certain by the simple process of sending "30,000 Confederate diplomats" across the boundary line.

The "sly Corwin," as Pickett termed him, presently committed an even meaner act than intercepting this correspondence. Pickett himself fell a victim to one of those *Cosas de Mexico* with which he so liked to enliven his despatches. This humiliation — so he always insisted — was the handiwork of the American diplomat in Mexico and "other wretches." Yet the blame, at least in part, attached to himself. It was the outcome of that intemperate, swashbuckling manner in which he took such pride. The whole story can be read in his lengthy, angry description. For Pickett, not only in his garrulous literary exercises but at the festive board in Mexican cafés, was frequently surrounded by admirers to whom his inmost thoughts were an open book. Any military success of the boys in gray elicited a bibulous celebration. Bull Run naturally called forth the liveliest outburst. Toasts were drunk to Beauregard — at that moment believed to have captured Washington. These *fiestas* naturally irritated the many Union sympathizers in Mexico and harsh words were bandied between the two groups. Yankees did not hesitate to hurl imprecations at Confederate leaders — insults that quickly reached Pickett's sensitive ears. Jeff Davis was openly referred to as a "traitor," "a thief," and "a rebel." Ill-feeling waxed especially hot the day news arrived that Mason and Slidell, new Confederate envoys to England and France, had safely arrived in Havana. The Confederates in Mexico City held a special celebration in honor of this achievement, all unconscious of the fate that quickly overcame those gentlemen. An American resident in Mexico, whom Pickett describes as "an unlucky pill-vendor by the name of Bennett," began to cast doubt on that information. "Pickett is spreading lies, as usual," this obnoxious Yankee reported. Clearly the time had come for action. Details of the subsequent combat are a little obscure; just which man came out on top cannot be determined from Pickett's narration, the only one at hand. The diplomat broke into Bennett's headquarters and slapped his face "with the back of my hand." Among Southern gentlemen such an affront could have only one sequel. Bennett was not a Southerner; being a peddler of patent medicines it is not quite certain that he was a gentleman; but, relates Pickett, "he is a larger and more powerful man than I." If so, Bennett must have been huge indeed, for Pickett was more than six feet tall. But he "refused the proffered gauntlett," and caused the fight "to degenerate into a mere bout of strikes and fisticuffs." The gigantic Yankee seized a club and made a frontal attack upon the intruder. "It became necessary to inflict upon him some chastisement," the latter records, "which I accomplished with no other weapons than my hands and feet." "Despatching that business I withdrew immediately" — the reader gets the impression it was rather precipitately; it is plain that the honors of the occasion were not all one-sided.

At any rate, the Yankee, who seems to have been fundamentally a good-natured creature, was entirely satisfied with his showing and had no responsibility for subsequent proceedings. In a crestfallen explanation to his State Department the Confederate emissary insisted that there was more in his belligerency than lay upon the surface. "Chastisement" of the abusive Northerner was only a by-product of a deep diplomatic plan. Pickett intended to create an "incident" that would result in his expulsion from Mexico as a "pernicious intriguer." Such a culmination would have had something of an heroic aspect. After all, was he not an ambassador and has not the person of an ambassador been sacred from time immemorial? An affront like this would demand summary action. Those "thirty thousand diplomatic agents of the Confederacy" would quickly cross the Rio Grande and add all the northern provinces of Mexico to the Confederate empire.

The next evening, just as he was disrobing for bed there came a knock on Pickett's door and four heavily armed villainous-looking "scoundrels" came into the room. The critical moment had arrived; evidently the ruse had succeeded. But a terrible humiliation lay in store for Don Juan. Instead of being served with an order commanding his departure from Mexico, Pickett found himself under arrest on a charge of "assault and battery." The Government was treating him, not as a diplomat who had incurred its displeasure, but as an ordinary street brawler. Conducted to the assistant chief of police, he loudly insisted on his "diplomatic immunity." "I presume even a diplomatic agent has no right to go into a man's house and pound him," said this functionary. The rest of the story is long and tedious. The Confederate agent, protesting at every step the inviolability of envoys, was conveyed to the *Disputacion* — city jail — placed in an unlighted cell, already occupied by three derelicts of the Mexican gutters, and forced to spend twenty-four hours in this durance without food or bed clothes or fire. Release was offered on the most humiliating terms. Only an apology to the "pill-vendor" and an indemnity could set him free. "I would rather suffer death in its most hideous form," responded the envoy, "than to submit to such terms." He therefore remained a prisoner for thirty days, finally obtaining release by bribing the court — in his own words, "by purchasing several hundred dollars' worth of justice."

The experience taught the unlucky gentleman one truth — that the Confederacy had no friends in Mexico and that further negotiations were a waste of time. He therefore left as soon as he could find a passage north. And like all governments, the Confederacy had no use for unsuccessful diplomats. All Pickett's attempts to exculpate himself made him only more odious in the eyes of Jefferson Davis. "Mexico is the grave of diplomatists," he wrote that statesman. Pickett returned to New Orleans, went into the Confederate army, and served with credit. This was his natural forte; as a diplomat, fate was always against him. How impishly misfortunes followed in his train Pickett did not learn until long after his return. The capture of his despatches he regarded as the evil stroke that had ended his usefulness. "This was a very unfortunate incident for me," he wrote President Davis, "or may I be permitted, so to speak, for my policy towards Mexico." Except for this, Pickett evidently believed, his darling scheme of an alliance with Napoleonic France would have succeeded. Naturally, on his disembarking at New Orleans, attempts were made to repair the loss. Pickett spent several days and nights patiently making duplicates of the purloined communications. The task must have been a burdensome one, for the missing documents filled a fair-sized copybook. Taking all precaution against another miscarriage, Pickett carried the precious packet in person to Dr. Riddle, Postmaster of New Orleans. He explained to that functionary the nature of the contents, enjoining the utmost care and secrecy in forwarding the documents to Richmond. Dr. Riddle, greatly impressed, promised that he would give his personal attention to ensure safe transmission. This promise was carried out only too faithfully. For this Dr. Riddle was a spy in the employ of the Federal Government. Instead of sending the documents to the State Department in Richmond, he forwarded them to Mr. Seward in Washington. Naturally enough, Pickett's further commentaries on the Mexican mission lacked his customary exuberance. "Punching of heads by diplomatic agents," he wrote Davis, who never answered his letters, "is not exactly the style of thing for the latitude of Mexico. I did all of that sort of business which was necessary. *Hos ego versiculos feci; alteri ferent honores.*" [14]

An appropriate memorial to Pickett survives to-day in Washington, in the manuscript division of the Library of Congress. This first of Davis envoys not only played his part in Confederate diplomacy; it is owing to him that we possess the materials with which its history can be written. In some way never satisfactorily explained the whole diplomatic correspondence of the Confederacy passed into Pickett's control. That train which left burning Richmond on the direful evening of April 2, 1865, carrying away the archives and treasure of the fleeing government, did not contain these valuable papers. Instead they were secretly placed in five trunks and hidden in a barn in Virginia. After many adventures they finally turned up in Canada, under the custody of Don Juan Pickett. Just what right he had to the documents, and just why he became the dictator of their fate has never been disclosed. The papers of the Confederate State Department naturally had great historic value. Inevitably the Federal Government desired to add these records of the "rebellion" to its archives. After protracted negotiation Pickett turned his treasure over to the Federal Government for a cash consideration of about $75,000. The transaction has left a stain upon his memory, but it has proved a priceless boon to students of Confederate diplomacy. The collection was brought to Washington, and, after leading a somewhat precarious existence in government buildings, at last found a definite resting place in the Congressional Library. It has formed the basis for the account of Pickett's mission given in the preceding pages, and will serve a similar purpose in other chapters dealing with the efforts of the Richmond State Department in foreign fields.

[14] I made these little verses; let others carry off the honors.

V

A DIPLOMATIC DEBUT IN ENGLAND AND FRANCE

1

THE QUEST FOR RECOGNITION

MEANWHILE the European continent was serving as a field for Mr. Toombs's diplomacy. Between Confederate efforts to "restore the Empire of the Montezumas" and its approaches to European thrones there existed a close connection. Probably, in the minds of Confederate statesmen, Great Britain and France presented the simpler problem of the two. The cooperation of these European powers, indeed, was regarded as a certainty from the first. The South would never have undertaken its hazardous enterprise had alliances with the leading Governments of Europe not been assumed as an essential part of the programme. Its attitude towards Great Britain and France was almost complacent. In seeking their friendship and trade, the Confederacy at times took the position of almost doing them a favor. The largest industries of both England and France had developed with Southern cotton as a basis. Both nations had many times tried to break this subserviency and find their raw materials in other lands, only to return to the cotton fields of the American Southwest as the inescapable reliance. What if England and France did hate slavery? The fact remained that the spinners of Lancashire and northern France were as much a part of the American slave system as the Southern states themselves. In 1861 Jefferson Davis believed that he held the economic salvation of these countries in the hollow of his hand; stop the supply of cotton and poverty and starvation would stalk their cities and countryside. Would France and England recognize the Confederacy? The real question was: would France and England survive as manufacturing nations? In view of this fundamental fact there seemed to be no doubt concerning the outcome. So firmly was this belief settled in the Confederate mind that Toombs seemed to think that the appointment of a Commission to Europe and a polite call by these diplomats on foreign Governments would quickly result in recognition. Of the trio selected for this mission, William Lowndes Yancey, of Alabama, was the only man who possessed the essential reputation and distinction. Pierre A. Rost was a Louisiana lawyer and judge, not nationally known; his chief recommendations were his French origin, and a supposed familiarity with the Gallic tongue. Both these considerations rather injured than strengthened his position in France. His broken French made him an object of ridicule on the boulevards; moreover, the selection of a man of French antecedents, who had left France as a small child, rather offended than pleased French officials. An American with ancient American background and of laudable American career would have flattered this susceptible people, but a *nouveau riche,* even though one born in France, who took up his abode on the Rue Montaigne, and paraded up and down the Bois, airily announcing to all acquaintances, when asked for Southern news, "*tout va bien,*" soon became something of a joke. That phrase in particular passed into a byword, and was quoted with characteristic French malice when news reached Paris that Mr. Rost's Louisiana plantation was in possession of Federal troops. "Did President Davis," the Marquis de Lapressange asked Paul du Bellet, another Louisianan then sojourning in Paris, "have a special reason for confiding such a mission to a person of French birth? Has the South no sons capable of representing your country?"[1]

[1] *The Diplomacy of the Confederate Cabinet,* by Paul du Bellet. Manuscript in Library of Congress.

Neither did Mr. A. Dudley Mann prove more acceptable. British representatives in the United States sent most unfavorable accounts of Mann to the Foreign Office. According to information forwarded by Robert Bunch, British Consul at Charleston, Mr. Mann was the son of "a bankrupt grocer"; moreover, his personal character was "not good." [2] This statement does the envoy injustice. Mr. Mann belonged to an excellent Virginia family, was well-educated and well-mannered, and had had some political and diplomatic experience in the service of the United States. But, as his career in Europe evinced, he lacked good sense and judgment, was too unobservant to see what was going on under his eyes, was turgid in conversation and in correspondence — a kind of diplomatic Polonius, who hardly touched a situation without doing his Government harm.

The third member, the leader of the delegation, was a man of different calibre. William Loundes Yancey was one of the best-known Americans of his day. Davis chose him for this mission, not because he liked the Alabamian, but because Yancey was too influential a character in Southern public life to be ignored. Possibly there was also some truth in the malicious explanation prevalent at the time. The real reason for sending Yancey abroad — so the whispers ran — was to get him out of the country. His name had already appeared as a candidate for the Presidency. In a few months the Confederacy was to chose its permanent chief; and Yancey's unguarded eloquence and chronic dissatisfaction with the existing regime made him a perpetual nuisance to those in power. He had no desire to go to Europe as Confederate envoy. Only the persistent urging of Davis finally elicited a reluctant consent. Davis's personal hostility to Yancey is evident. In his *Rise and Fall of the Confederate Government* the President never once mentions Yancey by name, though Rost and Mann receive a complimentary word. For twenty years this Alabamian had been a

[2] E. D. Adams, *Great Britain and the American Civil War*, Vol. I, 63.

leader of the proslavery cause. He won state leadership swiftly by his eloquence as an orator. He was not a public man in the national arena, his service having been limited to a single term in Congress. Significantly this had been marked by a speech so extreme in its slavery views, so violent in its criticisms of opponent views that it led to a duel — bloodless though several shots were exchanged — with Thomas L. Clingman of North Carolina. For fifteen subsequent years Yancey's occupation had been that of "firing the Southern heart." In the slavery campaign he figured as the antitype of William Lloyd Garrison and Wendell Phillips; Yancey was just as rash and irreconcilable in eulogizing slavery as were the New England brethren in denouncing it. Like them he proposed, in the interest of his cause, to destroy the Union and tear up the Constitution. Thus the fame of Yancey which reached every American household and even penetrated the villages of Great Britain was that of the extremest of Southerners, an advocate of Secession, of a Southern Confederacy, even of reopening the African slave trade. Enough black men should be imported from Africa, insisted Yancey, to provide every Southerner, rich and poor, city dweller or hillbilly, with at least one slave. Since both England and France detested slavery, — "France," one writer of the period said, "trembled" with rage at the very word, — to send the foremost stump speaker of the institution as ambassador to these nations looks, at least in retrospect, rather short-sighted. The mere appointment of Yancey emphasizes again the Toombs and Davis confidence in recognition by foreign powers. They apparently believed that Europe was so dependent on the Confederacy that Southern envoys, however obnoxious their opinions might be to European sentiment, would receive a cordial reception.

"To-night it was Yancey who occupied our tongues," Mrs. Chestnut writes in her *Diary from Dixie* for September 2, 1861. "Send a man to England who has killed his father-in-law[3] in a street brawl! That was not knowing England or Englishmen, surely. Who wants eloquence? We want somebody who can hold his tongue. People avoid great talkers, men who orate, men given to monologue, as they would avoid fire, famine or pestilence. Yancey will have no mobs to harangue. No stump speeches will be possible, superb as are his of their kind, but little quiet conversation is best with slow, solid commonsense people who begin to suspect as soon as any flourish of trumpets meets their ear."

That was admirable, as a general statement of the case; yet one fact made a gift for monologue useful in the present instance. In response to a request for an interview, Lord John Russell, then Secretary of State for Foreign Affairs, informed the Confederate Commissioners that it would give him pleasure to hear what they had to tell him, "though, under present circumstances, I shall have little to say." The conversation, under the rules laid down by his lordship, necessarily became a one-sided one. Yancey, in accordance with Toombs's instructions, enlarged on the righteousness of the Confederate cause, gave an exposition of State rights, and declaimed on the justice of secession. Inevitably his discourse involved the vital importance of King Cotton. Unlike Pickett in Mexico, who had placed the question of recognition in abeyance, Yancey and his associate Mr. Mann — Judge Rost was in Paris — requested in so many words that the Queen acknowledge the Confederacy as a free and independent state and enter into a treaty of amity and trade. His lordship listened to the plea with all the polite attention and frigid reserve of which the English statesman of that era was so consummate a master. To not the slightest extent did he commit his Government. He thanked the Commissioners, said that the whole subject would be placed before the Cabinet at an early day, and bowed them out. Three days afterward, Yancey and his confreres had

[3] Mrs. Chestnut was in error. It was Mrs. Yancey's uncle, Dr. Robinson M. Earle, who was the victim of her husband's homicide.

another, briefer meeting with the Foreign Secretary. That ended their personal intercourse. They remained in London, with occasional trips to Paris, for ten months, but the treatment received was certainly not that usually extended to accredited diplomats. This affected a haughty Southerner like Yancey, one of the greatest planters of his day, almost as sadly as did the total failure of his mission. One important act took place during Yancey's sojourn in London: the Queen's proclamation of neutrality, giving the South the rights of belligerents. But the Commission was not consulted on this, and knew nothing of it until the news appeared in the press. It would have been decided on, had the three eminent gentlemen never left the Southern states. British statesmen, always the most accomplished of snubbers, never exercised their art more expertly than in their disregard of this embassy. "It is perhaps proper to state," the agents wrote Toombs, after four months of weary exile, "that the Commission has not received the least notice or attention, official or social, from any member of the government since its arrival in England. This is mentioned in no spirit of complaint, but as a fact which the President may or may not deem of any consideration in weighing the conduct of this government towards the Confederate States." [4]

What is the explanation for this apparently studied disregard? It forms one of the most astonishing chapters in the history of American diplomacy. William H. Seward, Secretary of State in the Lincoln Cabinet, presents a fascinating character, combining, as he does, so many contradictory traits. At times he was magnificently blunt and blustering, again he was fairly Jesuitical in subtlety. At one moment he showed a purring side, at another he could become fairly savage. One day he was proposing plans that seemed to involve the wreckage of his country, the next he moved with a silent caution

[4] Yancey, Rost, and Mann to Toombs, August 7, 1861. *Official Records, Union and Confederate Navies*, Series II, Vol. 3, p. 237

which suggested the unscrupulous Italian with whom he has inevitably been compared. Seward had been the chief contender with Lincoln for the Republican nomination in 1860, and, after the November election, was looked upon as the inevitable man for the premier post in the new administration. Even before Lincoln's inauguration, while Seward was still Senator from New York, he had evidently fixed upon the one possible way of forestalling unfriendly action by Great Britain and France. At that time neither of these nations desired war with the United States, even a United States weakened by domestic convulsion. The general political situation in Europe made such an adventure unwelcome to either power. The one way of preventing recognition, in Seward's opinion, was to play upon this apprehension. British aversion to war — here was Seward's one diplomatic card. That it required courage, even audacity, to play it, was evident, but in this threat of war lay America's best chance to defeat Southern plans for European help. Presently Lord Lyons, British Minister in Washington, was sending disturbing reports about this disagreeable Yankee, destined soon to head the American State Department. The man seemed determined to pick a quarrel with England. At dinner tables in Washington he was talking without the slightest restraint. On such occasions Seward openly proclaimed his favorite plan for solving the problems of Secession and reuniting North and South. This was nothing less than embarking on a war with Great Britain or France, or even with both. Once engaged in such a contest, Yankee and Rebel would lay aside their family row, and join forces in fighting the foreign foe. It comes as something of a surprise to discover, from the diplomatic correspondence of the time, that this kind of talk produced uneasiness in high British circles. Lord Lyons was particularly disturbed. Mr. Seward, as Secretary of State, he wrote Russell, "would be a dangerous foreign minister." That the Foreign Secretary held similar views his despatches indicate. "If it can possibly be helped," he wrote Lyons, "Mr. Seward must not be allowed to get us into a quarrel. I shall see the southerners when they come, but unofficially and keep them at a proper distance."

Most commentators look upon Seward's blustering tactics as verging close upon madness. Engage in a war with Britain at a time when the Union was battling for life with the Confederacy? Perhaps, however, the man was not insane, after all. At least it is evident that had Seward's purpose been to create a certain impression in the British mind, it actually did produce that effect. As the story of American relations with Great Britain unfolds, the one fact that stands out above all others is the desire of Britain to avoid war with the United States, even in its crippled condition. In certain diplomatic crises the proper procedure is suavity, insinuation, persuasion; in others, directness and defiance are the only measures to success. Seward evidently believed that the European crisis of 1861 demanded diplomacy of the latter type. Therefore he continuously and in public preached European war as the one way out of the domestic impasse. When he entered the Cabinet, the ideas so unguardedly set forth in conversation became his official attitude. His famous "Thoughts" to Lincoln — a memorandum on perils, domestic and foreign, submitted to the President in April, 1861 — again advocated foreign war as the one way to national safety and reconciliation. At almost the same time he conveyed the same warning officially to both the British and French Governments. Both Lord Lyons and Mercier were notified, face to face, that recognition of the Confederacy would mean war with the United States. Seward instructed Charles Francis Adams, American Minister to the Court of St. James's, to serve this notice on the Foreign Secretary. "If any European power provokes war," Seward informed him, "we shall not shrink from it." The instructions sent to William L. Dayton, the new Minister to France, were the same. "Foreign intervention," Dayton was ordered to say to the French Government, "would oblige us to treat those who should yield it as allies of the insurrectionary party and to carry on the war against them as enemies. . . . The President and the people of the United States deem the Union, which would then be at stake, worth all the cost and all the sacrifices of a contest with the world at arms, if such a contest should prove inevitable." In conversation with Mercier, the French Minister in Washington, Seward abandoned all restraint. The United States, the French diplomat was bluntly told, would go to war with any nation that attempted to interfere in the prevailing quarrel. "We may be defeated," Seward added, "but France will at least know that there has been a war."

It would be interesting to speculate on the course of history had these American threats failed of their purpose, had England and France, despite them, recognized the Confederacy as an independent nation. The likelihood is that had these Governments taken this step, the American civil contest would have been transformed into a world war. This fact Seward completely understood and he understood also the unwillingness of England to start such a conflagration. If his attitude was therefore audacious it was an audacity of a splendid kind, and it had the supreme justification of success. When news reached Washington that Lord John Russell had received the Yancey Commission "unofficially," Seward acted in a way that persuaded the English statesman that America had decided on its course of action. The message sent to Mr. Adams for transmission to the British Government was one of the most formidable that ever issued from the American State Department. It was so menacing, indeed, that President Lincoln spent much time revising it — blue-penciling certain passages, obliterating others, and adding phrases of his own that gave the document a more friendly character. And Lincoln overruled Seward in an even more important respect. The Secretary had instructed Mr. Adams to read this despatch to the Foreign Minister and present him with a copy. But Lincoln refused to permit this. As finally sent, the paper was for Adams's eyes alone, and was intended to form the basis of representations to the British Government. Seward's disappointment with this Presidential veto had a characteristic sequel. If he could not get the paper before Lord Russell directly he was apparently determined to do so in subterranean fashion. One evening, about two weeks after the censored despatch had started on its way to London, the Secretary of State summoned to his house Mr. William H. Russell, correspondent of the London *Times*. "The Secretary lit his cigar," the journalist relates, "gave one to me, and proceeded to read slowly and with marked emphasis a very long, strong and able despatch, which he told me was to be read by Mr. Adams, the American minister in London, to Lord John Russell. It struck me that the tone of the paper was hostile, that there was an undercurrent of menace through it, and that it contained insinuations that Great Britain would interfere to split up the Republic, if she could, and was pleased at the prospect of the dangers that threatened it. . . . I ventured to express an opinion that it would not be acceptable to the government and people of Great Britain."[5] As W. H. Russell was on the most confidential relations with Lord Lyons, news of this seance undoubtedly reached the destination Seward intended, and it also gave this influential writer an insight into the state of mind of Washington at that critical moment.

Even in its amended form this communication came very close to being an ultimatum. It practically instructed Adams to desist from personal relations with Great Britain if that nation persisted in having further dealings with Yancey. "Intercourse of any kind with the so-called commissioners is liable to be construed as a recognition of the authority which appointed them. . . . You will in any event desist from all intercourse whatever, official as well as unofficial, with the British government so long as it shall continue intercourse of

[5] *My Diary· North and South*, Vol. I, pp. 102–103.

either kind with the domestic enemies of this country. When intercourse shall have been arrested for this cause, you will communicate with this department and receive further instructions."

When Adams called at the Foreign Office, in early June, to fulfill what he called "the most delicate portion of my task," Lord Russell was prepared to receive him. His Minister in Washington had kept him well informed on the excitement caused in America by the presence of the Confederate Commissioners in London and by the British recognition of Southern belligerency. Lord Lyons knew all about Seward's threatening despatch and Lincoln's modifications, and his recent letters from Washington had contained much about the behavior of this forthright Secretary of State. Lord Russell believed that the time had come to pacify the high-tempered Yankees. He had been favorably impressed by Mr. Adams as Minister, and he was particularly gratified at the very tactful manner in which the views of the American State Department were now set forth. Adams did not omit a single detail of his instructions, but he did it in the most courteous way. "It was not to be disguised," so Adams paraphrased his remarks in his official report, "that the fact of the continued stay of the pseudo-commissioners in this city, and still more the knowledge that they had been admitted to more or less [sic] interviews with his lordship, was calculated to excite uneasiness. Indeed it had already given great dissatisfaction to my Government. I added, as moderately as I could, that in all frankness any further protraction of this relation could scarcely fail to be viewed by us as hostile in spirit, and to require some corresponding action accordingly."

Here was extremely plain talking, politely as it might be phrased, but Lord Russell was in the most amiable frame of mind. There was nothing unprecedented in receiving unofficially such envoys, he said. He had recently given interviews to Polish, Hungarian, and Italian revolutionists — all engaged in operations against Governments with which Great Britain was at peace. Such interviews represented merely one method of obtaining desirable information; not remotely were they intended as recognition of insurrectionary movements. Now Russell came to the crux of the matter. He had seen the Southern gentlemen once some time ago and "once more some time since."

"But," he concluded, "I have no intention of seeing them any more."

This was not a positive pledge, but it came pretty close to being one. Mr. Adams retired content with the agreeable outcome of what had promised to be a difficult meeting.

2

Lord Russell's Compliments

The final scene in this diplomatic drama was enacted in the latter part of August. The setting, however, was not a distinguished one. There was no face-to-face association of Confederate Ministers with the chief dignitary of the British Foreign Department; in this Lord John Russell faithfully kept his word. Naturally the battle of Bull Run strengthened the position of the Confederacy in London, and correspondingly raised the hopes of Yancey that a new prospect had been opened for recognition. Clearly, so he reasoned, the one doubt that had made the British Government hesitate had now been removed. After that picture of the Federal troops, so luridly drawn by W. H. Russell in the London *Times*, — troops scampering from the Southern lines, and pouring into Washington a half-crazed, muddy, disheveled mob, — could there be any longer doubt of the ability of the Confederacy to maintain its independence? Now was there any question that the South was invincible? Was this not all the evidence the world, including the British Foreign Office, needed to prove that a new nation had been established? At once Yancey and Mann and Rost presented a demand on the Foreign Office for the recognition of the Southern States. A note was despatched to Russell, asking for an interview. In reply the Southern legates received the following: "Earl Russell presents his compliments to Mr. W. L. Yancey, Mr. A. Dudley Mann, and would be obliged to them if they would put in writing any communications they wish to make to him."

One did not have to be a proud and high-tempered Southern gentleman to feel, to the full, the almost studied insult of this rejoinder. It was not a note from Her Majesty's principal Secretary of State for Foreign Affairs, but from "Earl Russell," a private citizen. It was not dated from the headquarters of the British Foreign Department, but from "Pembroke Lodge," the writer's residence in the country. Despite this, Yancey and his fellows swallowed their pride and wrote a lengthy letter, describing Southern triumphs and basing upon them a claim for the recognition of independence. In reply little more than an acknowledgment was received. Yet the bewildered Southerners still kept at their ungrateful task, even addressing further letters to the Foreign Secretary. In early December, however, the farce came to an end.

"Lord Russell," read that diplomat's final note to the Commissioners, "presents his compliments to Mr. Yancey, Mr. Rost and Mr. Mann. He has had the honor to receive their letters of the 27th and 30th of November, but in the present state of affairs he must decline to enter into any official communication with them."

Here was a different attitude from the one that the Cotton Belt had anticipated when it formed its Confederacy, depending, as a matter of course, upon recognition from Great Britain and France. The famous theory of "King Cotton" had proved to be a delusion at the first test. Great Britain did not have the most distant intention of risking an unnecessary war with the United States in order to assure itself regular supplies of an almost indispensable material of manufacture. Similarly

Mr. Seward's diplomacy had succeeded at this, its first trial. He had almost peremptorily demanded that the British Foreign Office shut its doors on any envoys speaking in behalf of the Confederate States. In reply Lord Russell had promised Mr. Adams not to see the Southern Commission "any more" and, in this final brusque note to Yancey and his companions, had declined to receive even written communications in the future. This experience ended Yancey's brilliant but futile career. He served for a brief period, after returning from England, as a Confederate Senator from Alabama, but he was already afflicted with a mortal and painful disease. He died in July, 1863, at the age of forty-eight. Pierre Rost lingered for a time in the congenial atmosphere of Paris, but not as a Confederate envoy. A. Dudley Mann spent the next three years in several diplomatic ventures, all as unsuccessful as this first attempt in London. With the collapse of these first Mexican and European missions the diplomacy of Robert Toombs came to a close. His work as Secretary of State can hardly be regarded as a success; the fact is that he had little interest in that department, and gladly retired, long before the Yancey embassy came home, and entered the Confederate army as Brigadier General.

VI

"THE BRAINS OF THE CONFEDERACY"

1

JUDAH P. BENJAMIN

ONE member of the Davis Cabinet viewed with little pleasure these awkward essays in the foreign field. This was the adviser nearest to the Presidential ear, the gentleman known, then and since, as the "brains of the Confederacy." Judah P. Benjamin's official status in 1861 did not warrant so pretentious a title. His position, that of Attorney General, was the emptiest one in the Government. The Confederacy never developed a judicial system. The vast mechanism of law enforcement created by the Federal organization played no part in the Davis scheme of things. The Confederate Constitution provided for a Department of the Judiciary but, in the more pressing need of forming an army, a navy, a treasury, and other indispensable forces of warfare, the establishment of civil courts was postponed. The already existing state and local tribunals fulfilled the ordinary demands of law and justice. Thus the ambitious lawyer who enjoyed the distinction of Attorney General found himself with little occupation. Now and then he gave advice on constitutional points, made studies of such questions as privateering and the status of belligerents; for the larger part of the time, however, the man generally regarded as the ablest in the Davis Cabinet was obliged to find other employment.

His little office was bare of furniture, and entertained few visitors; even that throng of placemen who pestered his colleagues, most of whom, unlike Benjamin himself, were the dispensers of jobs, passed it by. Russell of the London *Times,* most persistent ferret of notabilities, did indeed discover the "most brilliant of the Southern orators," while making his famous tour of the Southern Cabinet, in May, 1861. The picture he drew for the British public did not gratify its subject. "Mr. Benjamin is a short, stout man, with a full face, olive-colored, and most decidedly Jewish features, with the brightest large black eyes, one of which is somewhat diverse from the other, and a brisk, lively, agreeable manner, combined with much vivacity of speech and quickness of utterance. He is one of the first lawyers or advocates in the United States, and had a large practice in Washington, where his annual receipts from his profession were not less than £8,000 to £10,000 a year. But his love of the card table rendered him a prey to older and cooler hands, who waited till the sponge was full at the end of the session and then squeezed it to the last drop. Mr. Benjamin is the most open, frank and cordial of the Confederates whom I have yet met." [1]

It is not surprising that Russell felt an interest in the bright-eyed, energetic little man then impatiently filling a purely honorary post. Most Englishmen found him the most beguiling character in the Southern group. There was one reason, above all, for this curiosity. At that moment another member of the Jewish race was rising to power in Great Britain. Benjamin Disraeli was rapidly advancing to the primacy of the British Cabinet — the same height which his Secession compatriot reached in the Confederacy at an earlier day. "Have you read Benjamin's speech?" asked Sir George Cornwall Lewis of Lord Sherbrooke, referring to the Louisianan's farewell address to the Senate in February, 1861, recently printed in the London papers. "Yes," was the reply, "it is even better than our own Benjamin could have done." Inevitably these two Jewish leaders in Anglo-Saxon lands have been compared. And they had more in common than their admirers are inclined to admit. First and all-important they were both Sephardic Jews. Vast differences exist among the several divisions of Israel, but the descendants of the people who wielded such great in-

[1] *My Diary North and South*, Vol. I, p. 254.

fluence in the Iberian peninsula before their expulsion in 1492 have always been accepted as the aristocracy of the race. At this dispersion the ancestors of Disraeli fled to northern Italy, whence they found their way, in the course of three centuries, to England. At the same tragic moment the progenitors of Judah P. Benjamin fled to Holland, making an easier transit to London three hundred years afterward. The immediate parents of these two statesmen arrived in the British capital at almost the same time, in the latter part of the eighteenth century. Thus both the American and the British Benjamins were born British subjects. Disraeli's father, author of the *Curiosities of Literature*, was a more distinguished person than Judah's, the keeper of a dried-fish shop in Cheapside, and one of those rarest of mortal men, a Jew who was an unsuccessful merchant; but the atmosphere of their early lives, particularly on the social side, had much in common.

Spanish and Portuguese Jews, then and since, have occupied a place apart. They are physically and mentally as different from the German and the Eastern Jews who have immigrated in such vast numbers to America as they are from their "Aryan" brethren. Sharp-featured, thin-lipped, long-skulled, black-haired, with high foreheads, frequently with slender, lofty stature, they have stood out, above all, for intellectual attainments, for artistic talents, for careers in the professions and in scholarship. Few in numbers, usually having maintained a long residence in their homes of exile, — the Sephardic Jews of New York have been part of that city's life since the days of Peter Stuyvesant, — they walk with a haughty reserve amid their coreligionists. The time was when intermarriage between a Spanish Jew and one from Germany or Russia was as rare and as much frowned upon as one between Protestant and Catholic. Both Disraeli and Benjamin were intensely proud of this origin. Significantly the same well-worn anecdote is told of both. Once declaimed against in the United States Senate as "that Jew from Louisiana," Benjamin, it is said, replied: "It is true that I am a Jew, and when my ancestors were receiving their ten commandments from the immediate hand of Deity, amidst the thunderings and lightnings of Mount Sinai, the ancestors of the distinguished gentleman who is opposed to me were herding swine in the forests of Scandinavia." Precisely the identical retort is attributed to Disraeli, on a similar provocative occasion in the House of Commons. As an anecdote, it is probably true of neither, but as a story picturing racial haughtiness and contempt for a hostile Gentile world, it is absolutely true of both.

Yet, Disraeli and Benjamin, despite their pride of origin, departed from their ancestral inheritance. Neither was what the orthodox call an "observant Jew." Disraeli joined the Church of England; Benjamin, so far as can be learned, died a Roman Catholic and is buried in consecrated ground. Both men married outside their faith — Disraeli one of the most English of Englishwomen, Benjamin one of the most French of French. Both had a favorite sister — Disraeli his beloved Sarah, Benjamin his "darling Penny." Both men rose to high political station as orators; both became leaders of conservatism, defenders of established things; both were protectionists. Disraeli battled for the rights of landlords no less valiantly than did Benjamin for the sugar planters of his chosen state. In the outlook of both statesmen the sense of grandeur, of Oriental splendor, of imperialism exercised its spell. Benjamin strove to extend American prestige over Mexico, Central America, and the Caribbean, just as Disraeli struggled for British empire in the East. Disraeli's great coup in preserving the Suez Canal for England even finds a parallel in the persistence with which Benjamin strove to link Atlantic and Pacific Oceans by a railroad across the Isthmus of Tehuantepec. "When we cross this isthmus," cried Benjamin, in one of his rare outbursts of exuberance, "what have we before us? The eastern world!" It might have been Disraeli who was speaking.

The careers of both abound in those picturesque contrasts

that make up the glamour of biography. The derided dandy who became ruler of the British Empire found a fellow adventurer in the friendless youngster, who, reaching New Orleans with four dollars in his pocket, rose to be one of the most successful lawyers of his day, Senator of the United States, the occupant of three Cabinet posts in the Confederacy, and finally, in old age, dressed in judicial white wig, black silk breeches, black silk stockings, and silver buckled shoes, ended his career as Queen's counsel and leader of the London bar. In one respect, however, the two men were unlike, and it is a difference that has harmed Benjamin's fame. Disraeli was talkative, showy, given to extravagances of speech and behavior, much inclined to set down his thoughts in letters to a multitude of friends, men and women. When he died a huge accumulation of such memorials provided abundant harvest for his biographers. Benjamin was close-mouthed, retiring, instinctively shrinking from confidences, never displaying his inmost thoughts to outsiders. He never talked of himself or his past, kept silence on his early life and struggles, seemed, indeed, to have almost a pathologic reluctance to self-exploitation. This constant living in an inner sanctuary made the world suspicious, critical, even at times denunciatory. Few men in American public life have been the victims of more unpleasant adjectives.

Only the uncomplimentary terms used to describe the person of detachment have been lavished on Benjamin. "Furtive," "sphinx-like," "enigmatic," "secretive," "wily," "sly" — such are the words leveled at a man whose only sin was perhaps a fastidious disinclination to share his personal life with his fellows. James G. Blaine called him the "Mephistopheles of the Rebellion, the brilliant, sinister, secretary of state." Benjamin insisted on keeping an intrusive world at a distance, not only in his lifetime, but forever. He took all possible pains that posterity should know no more about him than his contemporaries. His habit of destroying papers grew to be a mania. No adequate biography of Benjamin will probably ever be produced. All his days he struggled against such a possibility. As soon as he read a letter, it vanished into the flames. In old age Benjamin sought out his own correspondence in all possible quarters and destroyed it. His last days were devoted to this task of incineration. To an Englishman who wished material for writing his life and asked for help, Benjamin replied, "I have never kept a diary or retained a copy of a letter written by me. No letter addressed to me by others will be found among my papers when I die." At death, says Mr. Pierce Butler, his only biographer, "he did not leave behind him half a dozen pieces of paper." Neither Benjamin's wife nor his daughter possessed any memoranda that gave the slightest data on his career. His New Orleans relatives, it is true, have preserved a dozen or so letters written to Benjamin's sisters, and these are so delightful and revealing, so full of affection and warm human instinct that they go a long way toward disproving the "sinister" nature imputed to the writer. The man who could write so genuinely to "Sis, Hatty and Leah," display such tender solicitude for nieces and nephews, was not the acrid, unprincipled despiser of humankind that, in an era vibrant with hate, he was pictured. One wonders if this aversion to the literary prowlings of another time did not have a palpable explanation. Was there some passage in Benjamin's life which made a sensitive nature shrink from intimacy and personal confidence?

Probably the nature of the man himself explains this tendency always to keep his ideas and his motives secluded from the outer world. It is true, on the other hand, that one unhappy incident of his early life must be taken into consideration in any attempt to understand his career. This took place when Benjamin was little more than a boy, in his sixteenth year. It is significant of his precocity that he should have entered Yale at fourteen. Of the circumstances attending his earliest days little is known. Born in Saint Thomas, in 1811, taken to Charleston with his family as an infant, he grew up in a home which, while impoverished by the father's lack of business success, was not completely destitute of refinement. Of the family of seven — three boys and four girls — Judah Benjamin was the most promising. Though authentic details of his childhood cannot be obtained, such reminiscences as survive emphasize the traits that became familiar in after life. The boy was bright, handsome, ambitious, invariably leading his class in school. At Fayetteville Academy, according to all accounts, he made a brilliant record; the next chapter rather abruptly discovers him a freshman in Yale College. This New England institution had long been a favorite with South Carolina, despite the high order of Federalism inculcated and the strong antislavery sentiments of its teaching staff. Young as he was, Benjamin plunged into the lively debates that then comprised the main extra-curricular activity, upholding, against the prevailing views of his associates, the most destructive opinions of his own section. On the personal side he was liked and admired, and in scholarship his rank was an excellent one.

Benjamin's name appears in the catalogues of 1825, 1826, and 1827 — then silently and mysteriously vanishes from the college records. Soon after the beginning of junior year, just before Christmas, Benjamin departed from New Haven for reasons that have never been adequately explained. The reason which he himself afterward gave — that his father's pinched circumstances made it impossible to remain longer — is demonstrably untrue. The cause assigned by certain apologists — that he had become involved in a student plot against the course of study prescribed by the college authorities — is unsatisfactory. In the early part of 1861, when Benjamin, a Senator from Louisiana, was a leader of Secession and one of the Davis group that met in the Capitol at Washington to speed the Southern movement, especially to incite Southern states to seize all Federal property in their regions, a fellow alumnus of Benjamin's came forth with a more serious accusation. In every sentence of this publication the bitterness of the time stands revealed; it echoes, more eloquently than a thousand volumes, the emotions which the Southern separation, and its causes, aroused in the most respectable Northern breasts. For the journal in which this indictment first appeared was the New York *Independent,* one of the most widely read religious papers of the day, an organ of the Abolitionists, especially of Henry Ward Beecher. The article, entitled "The Early History of a Traitor," was signed in large type by D. Francis Bacon, Yale, 1831, a distinguished physician and a member of one of the most famous of Yale families. It was as follows: —

"The class of 1829 in Yale College (two years in advance of mine) was the finest body of young men that I ever saw in college. There was one of the class whose name cannot be found on the list of graduates, or in any annual catalogue after 1827. He was and still is a handsome little fellow, looking very small in his class, who, with few exceptions, were of full manly growth. This youth haled from a great state of 'the chivalrous sunny south,' bright-eyed, dark-complexioned, and 'ardent as a southern sun could make him.' In the early part of 1828 there was a mysterious trouble in that class. Watches, breast pins, seals, pencil-cases, pen-knives, jack-knives, two-bladed knives, four-bladed knives, etc. etc. etc. and lastly, sundry sums of money 'lying around loose' in students' rooms, disappeared unaccountably. The losers looked gloomily at each other and suspiciously at others. Something must be done. They finally constituted themselves a volunteer 'detective force,' set their trap — baited with thirty-five dollars in good bank notes — and soon caught the thief. He confessed. On opening his trunk in his presence, they found it nearly full of missing valuables — jewelry, pocket cutlery and horlogery enough to stock a Chatham Street store. He begged pitifully not to be exposed; they looked piteously on his handsome young face, and relented at the thought of blasting his opening young life. He had been a universal favorite, a pet of his class; so they agreed not to inform either the city magistrates or the faculty of the University, but ordered him to 'clear out' at once and forever. He went instantly to good President Day, obtained a certificate of honorable dismissal and vanished. That little thief is now a senator in Congress, advocating and justifying and threatening the robbery of forts, and the stealing of the military hardware and cutlery generally of the Federal government, without any more color or shadow of pretext than he had for his like operations on his fellow students just thirty-three years ago. A third of a century has not made and can never make, any change in such an originally born rascal. Had these early filchings been a mere boyish escapade, a momentary yielding to temptation while in great want, they would not deserve mention now; but they were systematised theft — long continued, accumulated, and hoarded pilferings from trusted bosom friends. Had the fellow not at length reproduced his private morality in public life, I would have allowed the secret of these early crimes to remain in the hearts of the few who then knew and now remember it." [2]

The name of Benjamin did not appear, but the identification was complete. Only one Senator in 1861 had been a member of the class of 1829 at Yale. The article went the rounds of the Northern press, which accepted it as completely explaining the moral nature of one of the most formidable enemies of the Union. The boldness of the accuser in signing his name, the high standing of the journal in which the story was published, seemed to be a direct challenge to a suit for libel. Under ordinary circumstances, a failure to defend one's reputation in this manner would be accepted as a confession of guilt. At the time this article appeared, however, such a procedure had become impossible. Four days after this so-called disclosure, the Confederate States came into existence in Montgomery; two months subsequently North and South were locked in war. Obviously it would not have been practi-

[2] *The Independent*, New York, January 31, 1861.

cable for any Southerner, under such conditions, to have maintained an action in a Northern court. Benjamin, therefore, cannot be criticized for not instituting legal proceedings. But his absolute silence under such charges is not so easily explained. Benjamin never gave the slightest public notice to this onslaught. His only comment appears in a letter to his close friend, Thomas F. Bayard of Delaware — one of the few of his letters that have been preserved. The question of a libel suit, he relates, had been laid before Charles O'Connor, the distinguished New York lawyer, who had counseled against it. "I have determined," says Benjamin, "to yield to the advice of my friends, and let a lifelong career of integrity and honor make silent and contemptuous answer to such an attack." "I am decided in one conviction,"[3] he wrote Bayard, in the same letter, "that it is not advisable to have any publication in any manner or form on the subject, whether from myself or friends." Mr. Bayard had written Benjamin soon after the article began its rounds of the Northern press advising him to make a public denial and offering to act as a medium of communication to the world. Benjamin's reply was a courteous refusal to take this means of vindication.

All through life Benjamin evinced this lofty disregard of popular opinion; his disinclination to refute this imputation on his character as a young man may have been a splendid manifestation of the same haughty reserve. Yet this silence inevitably prejudices his case. This is particularly so because the explanation he privately gave Mr. Bayard of his departure from Yale, in this same letter, the records disprove. "I left Yale College in the fall of 1827," he wrote, "in consequence of my father's reverses rendering him unable to maintain me there any longer."[4] A letter written by Benjamin himself, January 14, 1828, now in the archives of Yale University, contradicts this statement. Financial difficulties did not prevent

[3] *Judah P. Benjamin*, by Pierce Butler, p. 30.
[4] *The same*, p. 29.

the young man from finishing his course and obtaining a degree; Benjamin's own statement indicates that he was dismissed for reasons which the authorities regarded as discreditable. This letter was first published in *Memorials of Eminent Yale Men,* by Anson Phelps Stokes, in 1914.[5] It was a plea from Benjamin, addressed to Jeremiah Day, then President of Yale College, begging for reinstatement. "Highly respected sir," it begins. "It is with shame and diffidence that I now address you to solicit your forgiveness and interference with the faculty in my behalf. And I beseech you, sir, not to attribute my improper conduct to any design or intentional violation of the laws of the college nor to suppose that I would be guilty of any premeditated disrespect to yourself or any member of the Faculty. And I think, sir, you will not consider it improper for me to express my hopes, that my previous conduct in college was such as will not render it too presumptuous in me to hope that it will make a favorable impression upon yourself and the faculty. . . . Allow me, sir, here also to express my gratitude to the faculty for their kind indulgence to my father in regard to pecuniary affairs: and also to yourself and every individual member of the faculty for their attention and paternal care of me, during the time I had the honor to be a member of the Institution."

Benjamin's petition fell on unresponsive ears. "There is no evidence," comments Dr. Stokes, "that President Day even presented the letter to the faculty." Yet in certain respects this communication only serves to mystify the problem. The reason for his dismissal which Benjamin here intimates — some infraction of college discipline — is certainly not the one that Dr. Bacon's article definitely asserts. If the young Benjamin's statement of the case is trustworthy, it would also seem that he left as a consequence of faculty action, not, as the Bacon charge declares, on the unofficial and secret demand of his fellow students. Of course, it is not impossible that both his classmates

[5] Vol. II, pp. 262–263. Dr. Stokes was Secretary of Yale University from 1899 to 1921.

and the college authorities speeded the young man's departure. There are other contradictions in the several incomplete narratives of this expulsion — for it virtually amounted to that — but it is hardly worth while to enter into these minute details at this time. The real history of the incident has never been determined and probably never will be. The records of Yale, with the exception of the letter quoted above, provide no information. All that we can say with any definiteness, at this late day, is that Benjamin left Yale, not of his own volition, and not because of financial stringency; that his offense was so serious that the authorities declined to consider his request for a rehearing; that he himself misstated the reason for the separation; that the charge was made, in a responsible journal and by a college mate of standing, that he had been caught stealing from his fellow students; that Benjamin made no public denial of this charge; that all his life he showed a constant apprehension of a biography and destroyed all papers and documents that would facilitate inquiries into his past. Perhaps an oversuspicious mind might detect some significance in the fact that, on leaving Yale, he did not settle in Charleston, the town in which he had spent his early years and which offered abundant opportunities for the profession which he had decided to adopt, but departed for the then distant city of New Orleans, and began life anew. Under the most favorable interpretation, Benjamin's start in life had been an unfortunate one, and it is understandable that, in making his serious attempt at fame and fortune, he should have broken away from his early environment.

2

Creole Marriage

This creole community was precisely the place in which a person of Benjamin's talents and tastes would find congenial surroundings. Like the young man himself, its atmosphere was exotic. In 1828, when Benjamin started his career there in a commercial office, it was a French city. The Gallic influence pervaded all phases of social and civic life. French was the language, not only of ordinary intercourse, but of business and the courts. Its legal system had been founded upon ancient French practice. Originally settled by French immigrants in the time of Louis XV, the customs, language, and legal principles that had then prevailed still ruled this minute France beyond the seas. Benjamin soon identified himself with the place in all its phases. Presently entering the office of a New Orleans notary, he quickly qualified for admittance to the bar, and, in a few years, acquired a lucrative practice. He had enormous industry, genuine legal talent, a fascinating lucidity in the presentation of his subject, a clear-cut, mild-mannered, sincere eloquence, and, above all, an engaging person. He rapidly became the most sought-for commercial lawyer of New Orleans; but law did not confine his energies — he was one of the first to experiment in the new agriculture that proved even more adapted than cotton to the soil of the swampy delta. In the early thirties natives looked skeptically upon those hardy adventurers, like Benjamin, who believed that the future of lower Louisiana lay in sugar growing. With the profits of his law business the ambitious young man purchased a plantation, Bellechasse, in the parish of Plaquemines, a few miles below New Orleans. Here in a fine old Creole mansion, with gardens and stately groves of oaks, life for Benjamin assumed new dignity. His father, a struggling Jewish shopkeeper on a petty scale, had never attained that kind of property which spelled social success in the old South. But at Bellechasse the son became the proud possessor of slaves. With their labor he embarked on what was then almost an untried field, the growing of sugar cane. He succeeded from the start. So farsighted was Benjamin in the equipment of his estate that most of the machinery and buildings he installed in the 1840's were being used as late as 1895.

On the personal side Benjamin's life presents alternating lights and shadows. Nothing could be more charming than the story of his courtship and marriage. Arriving in New Orleans in 1828, with no friends and practically no money, the first handicap to success proved to be his unfamiliarity with the language. The sixteen-year-old boy found a romantic solution to this problem. Not only did Benjamin require French, but the natives of the town, in view of the influx of Americans, felt the need of English. So the beginning lawyer let it be known that he would hire out as a tutor in English to any family that would agree to teach him French. One wise Frenchman, seeking such a mentor for his daughter, rejected the young man on sight. "He's so fascinating," he said, "that my girl would fall in love with him and run away before the month was out." One of the most substantial of the Creole society, Auguste St. Martin, decided to take the risk. This gentleman had been born in France, having reached New Orleans by way of Santo Domingo, in which island he had had many experiences with bloody negro uprisings. The name of the daughter whom he wished instructed in conversational English — Natalie St. Martin — was, Benjamin insisted, a poem in itself. Moreover, she was a girl of beauty, intelligence, and charm. The young man spent many entrancing hours in her society, conveying to her the English he had acquired in Charleston and at Yale, while she in turn taught him the accents recently transported from France. The experience proved that the father who had balked at so engaging an instructor was right. A few months after being admitted to practice, in 1832, Benjamin married his pupil. Old Auguste St. Martin did not disfavor the handsome young Jew as a son-in-law. All signs indicate that he admired and liked Benjamin intensely, as did his son Jules. The sad fact is that the one member of the St. Martin family who grew dissatisfied with the marriage was the young lady who had so impetuously rushed into it. As mutual pedagogues in French and English the couple were a success; as man and wife they were failures.

This marriage presents another of those mysteries with which the life of Benjamin is so full. The obvious explanation of their unfitness for each other is the religious one. Natalie St. Martin was one of the most devout of Catholics; indeed, her chief personal interest in her husband seems to have been anxiety concerning his soul; she never abandoned hope of incorporating him in her faith; it was she who brought a priest to his deathbed and had extreme rites administered to the probably unconscious man; she saw that he was buried from a Catholic church and interred in a Catholic cemetery. But it is not likely that Benjamin's philosophic resistance to her lifelong efforts caused the difficulty. Differences in temperament probably explain this strange separation. Of Natalie, as of Judah Benjamin himself, there are virtually no literary remains. Only one sentence of hers survives, yet, in its unfoldment of her nature, it is worth volumes. In a moment of financial reverse, Benjamin, who scrupulously provided for his absent wife's support, had evidently written, suggesting a curbing of expense. "Don't talk to me about economy," she replied. "It is so fatiguing." That the lady possessed wit is apparent; in this epigram appear likewise the liking for languorous ease, the impatience with sordid details, the selfish disinclination to share burdens, that characterized the Louisiana Creole. And in this sentence we probably have the key to the failure of this ill-advised marriage. Natalie loved gayety, lively society, perpetual association with a multitude of friends. Bright-minded though she was, her husband's intellectual life did not afford the distraction her spirit craved. Benjamin, in his brief married career, maintained two homes, one in the city of New Orleans and one in the sugar country. Natalie was unhappy in both. The legal and political friends who gathered in the home on Bourbon Street, the constant discussion of State rights and slavery expansion bored this irrepressible French girl. Bellechasse, with its negroes, its tall fields of cane, its sugar refineries, she found *triste*. One day, in the early forties, Natalie, with her little daughter, Ninette, the one surviving child of the marriage, crossed the ocean and took up her abode in Paris, the city to which she really belonged. Louisiana saw her no more. She lived to be an old lady, dying in 1891, but never returned to her American home. The daughter, five when she left the bayou country, grew up a complete French woman, marrying an officer in the French army, and living until 1898.

But now begins the strangest part of this amazing marriage. Mrs. Benjamin played no rôle in her husband's public life, yet there was no quarrel between them, and really no separation. Benjamin maintained his wife and daughter in luxury for fifty years. In the last period of his career, when he became a leader of the English bar, he built Natalie and Ninette a beautiful home costing $80,000 on the Avenue d'Jena, almost impoverished himself by providing his daughter a handsome *dot* on her marriage, and then weary, ill with a mortal disease, spent his final year as a member of their household. Except for the four years of the Civil War, he made an annual summer pilgrimage to Paris, to visit his family and take care for their comfort. After becoming a resident of London, these visits became more frequent. Yet, though only the Channel separated man and wife, no effort was made to establish a common domicile. Existence did not lack even its tender moments. Once, when Mrs. Benjamin was on the verge of a serious operation, Judah crossed to Paris, took his post at her bedside, and held her hand all through the ordeal. On these surface facts, the marriage looks like one of unremitting devotion on his part, and callous, selfish indifference on the part of the wife; yet it is doubtful whether Benjamin greatly grieved over the situation, or had any deep-seated love for the woman who treated him as a convenience and avoided matrimonial duty. His domestic affections were seated elsewhere. The man was a genuine Jew in his devotion to kin. His mother and sisters monopolized the warmer side of his being. As soon as Natalie left the Louisiana home, Benjamin sent for his oldest sister Rebecca, whom he called "Penny," and installed her as mistress. Tradition describes her as a woman of fine mentality; for years she performed well the part of hostess to the brother in whom her pride was unbounded. Unlike Natalie, Mrs. Levy did not find the Bellechasse plantation, or the city home in New Orleans, dull and forbidding: she extended unceasing hospitality to all his friends; and her children seem to have become part of Benjamin's existence more than that distant Parisienne who always addressed him as *"mon père."* "Now I must bid you good bye, my darling," reads one of his wartime letters to Rebecca, "with a thousand kisses for you and the dear little ones, and a thousand affectionate remembrances to Kitt, from one who loves you dearly, and need not sign his name." Even in those early days in London, after 1865, when Benjamin, studying for admission to the English bar, dined furtively in cheap restaurants on bread and cheese, and walked the London streets to economize on cab fare, he still managed to smuggle small sums across the Atlantic for the maintenance of his relatives, utterly ruined by the war.

3

"Smiling As Usual"

Probably any Southern statesman called upon to form a cabinet for the Confederacy would have assigned a place to Judah P. Benjamin. Louisiana, like the other "sovereign" members of the new Government, was entitled to "recognition." Its two foremost men, in 1861, were John Slidell and his fellow Senator from New Orleans. In intellectual power, legal knowledge, capacity for work, skill in manipulating men, and subtlety in gauging human motives, Slidell hardly approached his brainy colleague. Probably Benjamin's views on the

Southern question more completely represented those prevailing in Montgomery, in February, 1861, than those of any other member of the Davis Cabinet. From the earliest days Benjamin had championed the most extreme of Southern pretensions. Most Southerners who emphasized the property aspect of the negro rested their thesis upon the right of the state to fix his status by statute. Not so Benjamin. He insisted that slavery existed under the common law of the English people, and traced prevailing conditions back to English soil. The same English common law that vested ownership of the retainers in the lord in the days of King John guarded the rights of American slaveholders in 1856. In the formation of the Davis Cabinet this ultra attitude was a recommendation. Suspicion of "reconstructionists" — of Southern leaders who still secretly yearned for reunion with the Federal Government — was active in Montgomery. More than one member of the new Cabinet, even Davis himself, so the whisperings ran, still cherished a furtive fondness for the old flag. But no such doubt stained the reputation of Benjamin. If any evidence were needed his speech in the Senate on December 31, 1860, just on the eve of Secession, provided it. The defiance of his final sentences still rang through the Southern States. "The fortunes of war may be adverse to our arms," he concluded. "You may carry desolation into our peaceful land, and with torch and fire you may set our cities in flames . . . you may do all this — and more too, if more there be — but you can never subjugate us; you can never convert the free sons of the soil into vassals, paying tribute to your power; and you never, never can degrade them to the level of an inferior and servile race. Never! Never!"

When Benjamin hurled this defiance, he had reached the apex of his personal and political power. The pro-Confederate audience in the Senate, wildly applauding his sentiments, had before their eyes the most romantic, because most extraneous, figure in American public life. All through the two hours he was speaking, Benjamin maintained the characteristic pose that had been familiar to the upper chamber for nearly ten years. A short, stout figure — some called it squat or "pudgy" — immaculately dressed in black, unadorned except by a heavy watch chain with which his hands kept fingering; a round head, black hair, black silky beard; an oval, slightly puffy face which, if not handsome, was certainly fascinating and lightened by intelligence; a melodious voice seldom betraying stress or excitement; eyes full of fire and penetration — such was the unimpassioned statesman, who, standing imperturbably between two desks, the voice seldom raised above a conversational temper, poured forth a biting discourse that, for its very gentleness and logic, enraged the North far more than the savage onslaughts of a Toombs or the tearful pleadings of a Davis. And this had been Benjamin's quality throughout his whole public life. Though the South rates him as one of its finest orators, there was nothing Websterian about his manner. The roaring accents of a Yancey he despised. Everything was quiet, stealthy in its attack, exasperatingly calm. Slidell once expressed his annoyance at Benjamin's "debonair" behavior. The same thing annoyed his Northern brethren on this occasion. Gentleness, courtesy, ingenuousness, even innocence — these were the qualities that Benjamin embodied, not only in this critical hour, but always. He never showed anger, excitement, or distraction, or, in fact, emotion of any kind. He was incarnated intellect and logic — all set forth in ingratiating accents. Though one of the most industrious men who served the Confederacy, he was never in a hurry. For even casual and bothersome callers on his busiest days, this unruffled soul always had plenty of time. Benjamin's most emphasized physical traits expressed this equanimity of spirit. His voice and his smile — those are the two things on which all commentators lay chief stress. "The birdlike, gentle persuasive tones of that oratorical siren," says one; "the sweet and beautifully modulated voice," records another; "high-pitched but articulate and resonant," to quote a third. The man's "perennial smile" similarly affected all beholders. Whether addressing judge or jury, speaking on the hustings or in the Senate, sitting quietly at his desk or walking along the street, this smile never departed; people even wondered whether Benjamin slept smiling. "There goes Mr. Benjamin, smiling as usual," was a common remark in Richmond, as the little Secretary of State passed on the way to his morning toil. Jones, the "rebel war diarist," insisted that this expression was not a smile at all, but a kind of permanent arrangement of muscles that gave it the semblance of one; Thomas F. Bayard, one of Benjamin's closest friends, insisted on calling it a "simper." But most found it inviting to friendly intercourse.

Significantly women found his society entrancing. His wife may have thought him wearisome at times, but the ladies of the Confederacy did not. Mrs. Chestnut, that tart memorialist of Southern statesmen, does not fix her barb in Benjamin. "Everything Mr. Benjamin said we listened to, bore in mind and gave heed to it diligently. He is a Delphic oracle of the innermost shrine, and is supposed to enjoy the honor of Mr. Davis' unreserved confidence." [6] Mrs. Burton Harrison, who, as Constance Cary, was one of the belles of Richmond, delighted in "the silver-tongued secretary of state," as she calls him. Nothing could surpass "his charming stories, his dramatic recitations of scraps of verse, and clever comments on men, women and books." [7] With Mrs. Davis, Benjamin was a favorite. No man was more welcome to her tea table. "Do come to dinner or tea this afternoon," she would write, "we succeeded in running the blockade this week," — meaning that she now could serve him real tea or coffee.[8] Men sometimes treated him more harshly. Henry S. Foote — who, with all his genius, was considerable of a blatherskite — denounced him in the Confederate Senate as "Judas Iscariot Benjamin"; the wittier

[6] *A Diary from Dixie*, p. 278.
[7] *Recollections, Grave and Gay*, pp. 129, 160.
[8] Pierce Butler *Judah P. Benjamin*, p. 335.

Ben Wade, of Ohio, called him "an Israelite with Egyptian principles." This was evidently intended as a thrust at a man who, despite the historic experiences of his own race in captivity, could be an apologist and practitioner of slavery.

Benjamin was educated beyond most of his time; he was well read in general literature — sometimes interrupting a legal discourse in Congress to eulogize Tennyson; he not only spoke fluently French and Spanish but was deeply versed in French and Spanish law. He once left Washington on what was regarded as a mysterious errand; its real purpose was to make an argument, in Spanish, before the Supreme Court in Ecuador. President Pierce esteemed his judicial qualities highly enough to offer him a place on the United States Supreme Court; President Buchanan sufficiently regarded his diplomatic talents as to offer him the Ministership to Spain. Benjamin's passion for the law, as well as his fondness for the work of Senator, made him decline approaches of the sort. In law, indeed, he was a man of great learning. His *Digest* of Louisiana Supreme Court decisions, prepared in association with Thomas Slidell, is still indispensable; while *Benjamin on "Sales"* became a classic in England and America on the day of its appearance, and largely explained his sudden rise at the English bar. Perhaps the quality that most surprises in this bland, placid jurist and statesman was his unremitting industry. It comes almost as a shock in a man so devoted to the elegancies of life. He always had leisure for a card game, he loved the table, being a good deal of a gourmet, but hard work he seemed to prefer above everything. "I like to bask in the sun, like a lizard," Benjamin would say, but his associates told a different story. "His power of work was amazing to me," said General Gorgas, Chief of Ordnance, "and he appeared as fresh at twelve o'clock at night, after a hard day's work, as he had been at nine o'clock in the morning."

Whether or not Benjamin merits his fame as "brains of the Confederacy" he certainly was the most subtle intellect in the

Cabinet. He enjoys another distinction: he was the closest of all Southern leaders to the President, the only one of his official family, indeed, to whom that reticent statesman seemed personally drawn. Davis, it is true, says little about him in his *Rise and Fall*. The most interesting statesman of the Confederacy elicits only the formal notice impartially bestowed on his colleagues. "Mr. Benjamin, of Louisiana, had a very high reputation as a lawyer, and my acquaintance with him in the Senate had impressed me with the lucidity of his intellect, his systematic habits and capacity for labor. He was therefore invited to the post of Attorney General." [9] The ten large volumes of Davis papers add little to this perfunctory tribute. The fact is that, before their association in the Confederacy, the relations between Davis and Benjamin had not been intimate, at times not even sympathetic. Once, in the Senate, Davis, affected by one of his spells of irritation, spoke insultingly to the Louisianan; at least, Benjamin so regarded his remark. The Senator from Mississippi described a paragraph of the Senator from Louisiana as "an attempt to misrepresent a very plain remark." That was a parliamentary way of calling his colleague a liar. Benjamin was not a proud "Baron" from Virginia, but he accepted this challenge in the spirit of Randolph of Roanoke. He scribbled a few words at his desk, handed the paper to a friend, with a request for its immediate delivery to Davis. The Mississippian's response forms one of the finest episodes in his career. "I will make this all right at once," he said to Benjamin's second. "I have been wholly wrong." Not only did he reënter the Senate and apologize in full view of that body to Benjamin, but confessed to the infirmities of temper that had caused him to make his unjustified criticism. "I cannot gainsay," he said, "that my manner implied more than my heart meant." He expressed regret that his behavior was "sometimes unfortunate, and is sometimes, as my best friends have told me, of a character which would nat-

[9] *Rise and Fall of the Confederate Government*, Vol I, p. 242.

urally impress that I intended to be dogmatic and dictatorial. . . . When I am matched by one as skillful, as acute by nature, and as trained by his profession, as the Senator from Louisiana, it is but natural that I should appear to have been the hasty man in the debate, whilst he must have the advantage resulting in that skill which his training gives." [10]

And so the incident that at first threatened bloodshed ended in a love feast. Benjamin accepted the disclaimer with all due suavity; he would be glad to forget all the honorable gentleman's remarks in the debate, he said, "except the pleasant passage of this morning." That Benjamin's quick resentment increased the Mississippian's respect for the "little man from Louisiana," as he called him, was natural; Davis admired courage, and a refusal to sit quiet under insult, even though he was himself the transgressor. Another conflict between the two men took place afterward, this time on a question of policy. Davis's heart, as already noted, was set on a transpacific railroad, from Memphis to San Francisco. Benjamin's darling scheme was to connect California with the South by means of a railroad, or canal, across the Isthmus of Tehuantepec; its terminus would be New Orleans. Davis proposed to have the Federal Government finance his enterprise to the extent of $100,000,000, while Benjamin's railroad was to be built by private capitalists. In the debate Benjamin pointed out the inconsistency of a State's-right Democrat proposing to dip into the Federal treasury for a grandiose "public improvement" on this scale, and did so with fine sarcasm and irrefutable logic. This difference, however, did not result in ill-feeling. But before 1861 there had been no intimacy between the two men. "Mr. Benjamin and Mr. Davis had had," says Mrs. Davis, "little social intercourse; an occasional invitation to dinner was accepted and exchanged, but that was all."

Benjamin had not long been a member of the Davis Cabinet, however, before the President and his secretary were drawn

[10] *Congressional Globe*, June 9, 1858, p. 2823.

closer together. Nor is this strange. What the President needed in his loneliness was some person of superior mind and judgment, of equable, sympathetic temper, to whom he could turn for assistance and advice; above all, one who knew his failings of temper and physical state, who, though he might at times differ with him, would never do so in a way to rasp his nerves, and who would not sulk if his recommendations were ignored. A man who was always affable and smiling, who never became discouraged when difficulties grew thickest, who always saw the bright side of things, and yet at the same time was not a vacuous optimist, but had his eyes on realities, and usually had in readiness some definite practical suggestion — this was the companion that Davis needed. Benjamin was also expert in handling another problem that irked the soul of the President. No man could more urbanely dispose of the army of office-seekers and commission hunters who abounded as numerously in the Confederate capital as in Washington. Thus early Davis began to turn to this associate in all critical moments. Benjamin was "personally devoted to Mr. Davis," records H. A. Washington, the Assistant Secretary of State, "and probably had more influence with him than any other man." Mrs. Davis says the same thing, in a vivid passage, which shows that not only Benjamin's intellect but his placidity of disposition made him a never-failing solace to her husband. Not only his political advice but his soothing nature came as balm to the dyspeptic and neurotic head of the Confederacy. "It was a curious spectacle," she writes, "the steady approximation to a thorough friendliness of the President and his war minister. It was a very gradual rapprochement, but all the more solid for that reason. . . . Mr. Benjamin was always ready for work; sometimes, with half an hour's recess, he remained with the executive from ten in the morning until nine at night and together they traversed all the difficulties which encompassed our beleaguered land. . . . Both the President and the Secretary of State worked like galley slaves, early and late. Mr. Davis came home fasting, a mere mass of throbbing nerves, perfectly exhausted; but Mr. Benjamin was always fresh and buoyant. There was one striking peculiarity about his temperament. No matter what disaster befell our arms, after he had done all in his power to prevent or rectify it, he was never depressed." [11]

Others, of course, attributed this influence to Benjamin's "sinister" side. Blaine's "Mephistopheles" conception of the Secretary reigned in certain quarters in Richmond. The diarist J. B. Jones, Chief Clerk in the War Department, is particularly insidious on this point. "Mr. Benjamin is a frequent visitor to the department and is very sociable; some intimations have been thrown out that he aspires to become, some day, Secretary of War. Mr. Benjamin unquestionably will have great influence with the President, for he has studied his character most carefully. He will be familiar not only with his 'likes,' but with his 'dislikes.' " The extent to which Benjamin was making his own the most persistent of the Presidential animosities the diarist gleefully records. Already the Davis-Beauregard feud had embarked on its unhappy course. Benjamin loyally championed Davis in this dispute, as he championed him in a similar controversy with Joseph E. Johnston. Beauregard's prominence as a candidate for the Presidency did not improve relations between that general and his chief. "There is a whisper," Jones records on August 11, "that something like a rupture has occurred between the President and Gen. Beauregard; and I am amazed to learn that Mr. Benjamin is inimical to Gen. B." And later: "Mr. Benjamin's quarrel with Beauregard is openly avowed. Mr. Benjamin spoke to me about it to-day and convinced me at the time that Gen. B. was really in the wrong." In the wrong, that is, as to his responsibility for the failure to pursue the Federal armies and capture Washington! Whether or not the influence which Benjamin acquired with Davis can be explained by such sycophancy as this

[11] Quoted by Pierce Butler in his *Judah P. Benjamin*, p. 32.

biased writer intimates, there seems to be little doubt that soon after entering the official family Benjamin became the Presidential favorite. The executive who was distant with most of his constitutional advisers immediately felt an affinity for his erstwhile "little man from Louisiana."

The first Cabinet was, in fact, an ineffective lot. Toombs's mishandling of foreign affairs has already been described. The War Secretary, Leroy P. Walker, was a failure from the start. Mr. Walker was a typical Southern gentleman — on that word "gentleman" he was inclined to lay more emphasis than was customary even in the South. He had been advanced to this commanding duty, as had all his colleagues, not on the ground of fitness, but because he was regionally acceptable. He represented Alabama in the Cabinet, just as Memminger represented South Carolina and Mallory Florida. He had one desirable attribute: he was full of fire for the cause. The Confederacy enrolled no more pious adherent of slavery and State rights. As Secretary, however, he seemed more absorbed in dignity, ceremonial honor, punctiliousness, than in the organization of an army. "That slow coach, the Secretary of War," Mrs. Chestnut calls him. In early July the prayer arose in Richmond for a Southern "Napoleon." "Not one bit of use!" this lady notes in her Diary. "If Heaven sent one, Walker would not give him a commission." William H. Russell of the London *Times* devotes a few lines to this unimpressive statesman. Unfortunately the gentleman was addicted to a habit exceedingly distasteful to the fastidious Briton — the absence of which in Jefferson Davis he regards as especially praiseworthy. "Mr. Walker is the kind of man generally represented in our types of a 'Yankee' — tall, lean, straight-haired, angular, with fiery, impulsive eyes and manner — a ruminator of tobacco and a profuse spitter — a lawyer, I believe, certainly not a soldier; ardent, devoted to the cause, and confident to the last degree of its speedy success." This overweening faith in a quick triumph, indeed, is the one thing for which Walker is remembered; the only remnant of a Walker biography that survives is his prophecy that soon the Confederate flag would be waving over Fanueil Hall, Boston. Diarist Jones, his chief clerk and office companion, is almost more contemptuous of Walker than of Benjamin. The secretary was almost continuously ill. When sufficiently well to attend to business, he was constantly fretting over the constant mountain of mail, most of it from politicians seeking commissions. A single eccentricity discloses his talents as an executive: he disliked writing brief replies to his correspondents, and would sign no letter, even though the subject was perfunctory, of less than three or four pages.

Naturally such a spirit soon found himself at sea in the details of his department. Davis immediately lost respect for him as a cabinet minister and continuously ignored his existence. In one respect Walker was more unlucky than his colleagues. Davis had served as Secretary of War under Pierce; he well understood the routine of such an office, and appreciated Walker's incapacity from the first. Moreover, as something of a militarist in his own right, this was the department in which the President's interest was most keen and over which he kept the closest watch. Naturally the futility with which it was being conducted alarmed and irritated the chief of state — an attitude which he made little effort to conceal. It did not require a person of Benjamin's shrewdness to anticipate an early vacancy in this branch of the Government. That he hoped from the first to step into Walker's shoes is not an unwarranted assumption. Those who properly interpreted the increasing intimacy between the Attorney General and his chief were already appointing him to the office. What a waste of good material! Here was the ablest member of the Cabinet assigned to a post in which there was practically nothing to do! And here was almost the weakest placed in a post that, at the present moment, called for the greatest abilities.

The extent to which Benjamin had advanced in royal favor

came to the front on that glorious day in Confederate history — July 21, the day of Bull Run. The whole Cabinet, and as much of the populace as could squeeze in, gathered in Walker's headquarters on this hot Sunday. Another centre of excitement was the Spottswood Hotel, Richmond's leading hostelry and the abode of the upper caste of Confederate society. Here President Davis and his family had their temporary home — waiting until the new "White House" could be prepared for their reception. Here lived James Chestnut and his wife, Colonel Wigfall of Texas, Secretary and Mrs. Toombs, Secretary and Mrs. Mallory, and other leaders of society and public affairs. Most of the husbands had already left for the approaching battle; the rumble of the guns had for several days startled the citizenry. President Davis had just departed for Manassas to devote his military talents, if necessary, to what was expected to be a decisive campaign. Mrs. Davis was the centre of all interest to this exclusive company. She was really the headquarters for news, for it was known that the President was in communication with his wife by telegram. At the War Department Secretary Walker was cursing the fortune which kept him prisoner in a civilian office, thus depriving him of the chance of winning glory in battle; Hunter, the recently appointed Secretary of State, was scanning attentively the messages as they came in, but making no comments; Howell Cobb, President of Congress, not too pleased with uncertain, contradictory news, offended patriotic friends by declaring that the battle was evidently a drawn one. Benjamin was present, most unperturbed of all, but perhaps also the most solicitous.

In the midst of the disturbance Benjamin slipped out of the room and started toward the Spottswood Hotel. Here he sought out Mrs. Davis who, telegram in hand, was surrounded by a crowd of jubilant women. She handed the paper to Benjamin, who read it and rushed back to his colleagues. His message brought the news that ended all argument. "We have

"THE BRAINS OF THE CONFEDERACY" 181

gained a glorious but dear-bought victory," so ran the President's brief telegram to his wife, which Benjamin now relayed to the crowd. "Night closed upon the enemy in full flight and closely pursued." The last two words, as events disclosed, were inaccurate. Their appearance in the President's brief telegram in itself gives some notion of the confusion that followed the engagement. But the one overwhelming fact was true — the Southern army had met the Federals and had not only defeated, but routed them. The reporters, having taken down from Benjamin's dictation this, the first authentic report of the result, rushed off to their newspapers, which, next morning, broke out into paeans of exultation. In the minds of Benjamin's little audience, as well as in that of the Southern people in general, that laconic despatch meant the end of the war and the permanent establishment of the Confederate Republic. Beauregard, it was taken for granted, was at the moment pursuing the Federal troops to Washington. The Confederate flag would in a day or two be waving over the Federal capitol! For once even Benjamin's composure forsook him. "Joy ruled the hour!" writes Diarist Jones. "The city seemed lifted up and everyone appeared to walk on air. Mr. Hunter's face grew shorter; Mr. Reagan's eyes subsided into their natural size, and Mr. Benjamin's glowed something like Daniel Webster's after taking a pint of brandy."

4
Benjamin in the War Office

Bull Run, however, brought no glory to the man who, above all, would seem to have some claim to sharing in it — the Secretary of War. In the general acclaim the head of the War Department was more than ever neglected. Indeed, the very triumph itself further discredited that incumbent. The South had won a smashing victory, but from it had reaped no military advantage. Soon everybody — civilians, politicians, and military men — was discussing the all-absorbing topic: Why had the Confederates not pursued the fleeing Federals, assailed the city of Washington, and captured the Northern capital? Did not the road lie open for them? Little mystery to-day enshrouds this point. The army so hastily assembled by the South was as much of a mob as that which had been scrambled together by McDowell. Obviously, it could not follow up its success when there were food supplies for only a day or two, and when in all the *matériel* for formidable war-making it was terribly deficient. Not the lack of military valor and generalship forced the Confederates to withdraw to their camps, but the lack of military organization. For this defect, inevitably, the War Department itself was held responsible. It is doubtful whether an abler man than Walker could have properly equipped and organized an army in that brief time, but naturally popular fury, as well as executive disapproval, focused on the poor man's head. In September his resignation was promptly accepted and Judah P. Benjamin was elevated to the vacant post. "Just as I expected," notes Jones. "Mr. Benjamin is to be Mr. Walker's successor." "Mr. Benjamin's hitherto perennial smile faded almost away as he realized the fact that he was now the most important member of the Cabinet."

Benjamin filled his arduous post for seven months, until March, 1862. His career in that office was hardly more glorious than Walker's. The army itself disliked him because he was a civilian; politicians and newspapers turned fiercely upon him for the most logical of reasons: he headed the War Department at a time of humiliation for Confederate arms. In such misfortunes the public always requires a scapegoat and this distant, always smiling, nonchalant Jewish Secretary most acceptably filled the rôle. The South's spectacular success at Manassas has obscured the historic sequence of the next few months. A popular impression still prevails that for the first year of the war, Southern arms were generally victorious.

The opposite is the truth. Despite the wild retreat of Federal troops into Washington after Bull Run, the Federal army piled up far more victories to its credit in the first twelvemonth than did its opponent. Even more important, its victories had a quality of military substance that was lacking in those achieved by the South. The Davis policy, at the beginning, was defensive; the cries of men like Toombs for an invasion of the North, and the capture of Washington, Philadelphia, even New York, were ignored; Southern strategy was not to win the war by decisive, offensive measures, but to prevent the enemy from accomplishing its purpose. This it did brilliantly on several occasions, but these successes had no particular military effect. The Northern soldiers might be thrown back, but they came on again in greater numbers than before. In the first year, however, the Federal Government made progress in its military objectives. Its grand plan was gradually to seize Southern territory and Southern cities, and reduce these areas to Federal control. This plan steadily advanced during 1861 and the spring of 1862; the tragic year for the North, in a military sense, was the last half of 1862 — the Peninsular campaign — and the early part of 1863.

For all the period that Benjamin filled his new office, the Federal forces seemed to be succeeding in their task of crushing the South. Three great border states, Maryland, Kentucky, Missouri, which Davis confidently expected would join the Confederacy, Lincoln's statesmanship and the Northern armies kept in the Union. McClellan's brilliant campaigns in the western part of Virginia redeemed this great area for the Federal Union and resulted in the creation of a new state, famous for its loyalty to the Washington government. Grant's campaigns in the West — Fort Henry, Donelson, Shiloh, and the rest — cleared all the Southern armies out of Kentucky and western Tennessee, and did much toward opening the Mississippi River to the north and splitting the Confederate country into two parts, inaccessible to each other. Along the coasts of Virginia and North and South Carolina the mixed military and naval Federal forces won a succession of victories that contributed further to the Confederacy's isolation from the sea. Burnside's capture of Roanoke Island off the coast of North Carolina gave the North dominance in the waters of that region and led to the capture of New Bern and adjacent territory. Finally came the greatest blow of all, the capture of the Confederacy's largest and richest city, New Orleans, which had the vast military importance of all but completing Federal control of the Mississippi, the very life artery of the South. Only by reading the Southern diaries of that time can the full significance of these disasters be understood. Even the most strong-hearted thought that this doomed the Southern States. "Down to the very depths of despair are we," records Mrs. Chestnut, when news came that Farragut had passed the forts of New Orleans. "New Orleans gone and with it the Confederacy! That Mississippi ruins us if lost. The Confederacy has been done to death by the politicians."

That last sentence succinctly gives the reasons for Benjamin's downfall as Secretary of War. Probably any man who had been Secretary of War at this time would have suffered the same fate. During the period of most of these disasters he was the head of the department that should, in popular estimation, have made them impossible. Therefore curbstone orators and press turned ferociously against him. And Congress also, full of his enemies, placed the blame upon his shoulders. The immediate cause of the onslaught was Burnside's capture of Roanoke Island. That important place had fallen, it was asserted, because of its failure to receive ammunition. Who was responsible for this failure? A Congressional committee investigated this lapse and definitely fixed the blame. "The committee, from the testimony, are constrained to report that whatever of blame and responsibility is justly attributable to any one for the defeat of our troops at Roanoke on February 8, 1862, should attach to Major-General Benjamin Huger and the late Secretary of War, Judah P. Benjamin."

Benjamin was "late" Secretary because, a few days before this report appeared, President Davis had transferred his favorite from the War to the State Department. Davis displayed certain qualities that were subsequently marked in Woodrow Wilson. One of these was loyalty to his chosen appointees. Perhaps vanity has something to do with this fidelity. To discredit a Cabinet member would obviously be a criticism of the President's own judgment; the surest way to cement the Presidential devotion to such a man was intemperate criticism. But there was another reason why Davis stood firmly by Benjamin in this crisis. This was his sense of justice. He knew — something of which the public was unaware — why Benjamin had not sent powder and other munitions to Roanoke. That was because he had none to send. The Confederate storehouses were empty. Unfortunately this was a circumstance that, at the time, could not be publicly avowed. Such a disclosure would have injured the already lowered morale of the South and strengthened that of the North. Davis therefore saw something commendable, if not indeed heroic, in Benjamin's refusal to defend himself when his only possible defense would reveal a situation dangerous to the country. Probably this explanation, had it been publicly given, would not have satisfied critics in that depressing moment. Was it not the business of the War Secretary always to have supplies of munitions on hand? If he could not send materials of war to the protection of Roanoke — and this indeed would have been a valid criticism — should Benjamin not have withdrawn the troops from such an indefensible post and thus have prevented their capture?

    But Davis for some time had had different plans for his favorite Cabinet member. From the beginning the State Department had posed a serious problem. The career of the brilliant but erratic Toombs in that post ended July 21, 1861. His successor, Robert M. T. Hunter, of Virginia, brought to the office a man who had served alongside Davis in the United States Senate, representing, for the most part, the Davis ideas on national questions, and who, in 1860, had been Virginia's favorite son for the Presidency of the United States. Toombs's retirement gave Davis the chance of "recognizing" Virginia in his Cabinet, and for this purpose no one seemed so fitting as Mr. Hunter. Not that he was a statesman of genius; in fact, he was a person of lumbering temperament and not too energetic mental processes; but he belonged to the "old Virginia aristocracy," was a man of great wealth, orthodox in his Southern principles, impressive in person, and respectable in character. In the celebrated gathering of "conspirators" in the Washington Capitol, January 5, 1861, Hunter was at first marked out for the Presidency of the impending Confederacy, the expectation at that time evidently being that Virginia would at once join the Secession movement. That Davis should have selected this high-standing Virginian for Secretary of State on Toombs's departure seemed inevitable. Hunter's social and political status in pre-Confederacy days perhaps explain the brevity of his tenure. He really was a Southern "aristocrat," Davis was not. Difficulties political and personal soon arose between the two men. As a Southern character this Virginian rated himself considerably above the Mississippian who was officially his superior. He insisted on actually being Secretary of State, "not the clerk of Mr. Davis," as he himself told his friends. Bad feeling reached a climax one day when Hunter, in a general Cabinet discussion of the military situation, ventured to utter a few words on that subject. "Mr. Hunter," Davis replied, "you are Secretary of State, and when information is wished of that department it will be time for you to speak." [12]

The next day Hunter's resignation dropped on the President's desk. It was probably not an unwelcome missive. It enabled Davis to solve his Benjamin problem — among other things. He deferred to popular anger to the extent of easing Benjamin from the War Department, but still retained him

[12] Edward A. Pollard relates the episode in his *Jefferson Davis*, p. 151.

in the Cabinet — and in a position that was rapidly assuming far-flung importance. This new department for Benjamin — the third he filled in four years of war — was the one for which he had real qualifications. The Southern public was quite content when a man of such subtle intellect and diplomatic temper took up this office at its most critical period. In that sphere Benjamin and his perpetual smile might find themselves at home.

VII

CONFEDERATE FINANCE

1

CHRISTOPHER MEMMINGER

LIKE Benjamin, the Secretary of the Treasury, Christopher Gustavus Memminger, was foreign-born. Like Benjamin also, he suffered suspicion and revilement at times for his European origin. One of his recommendations for the career of statesman was more highly esteemed in the North than in the South. Memminger's origin was extremely humble. The difference in the way the two sections regarded such a beginning appears in an anecdote related by Dr. John Joseph Craven, the Federal army doctor who attended Jefferson Davis in his prison cell in Fortress Monroe. One day the two men began discussing Memminger and Confederate finance. "I asked," records Dr. Craven, "how Mr. Memminger had obtained prominence in so aristocratic a state as South Carolina, the report being that he was a foundling, born with little claim to either wealth or fame. Mr. Davis said he knew nothing of the matter, and immediately turned away the conversation, appearing displeased."[1]

Memminger's father was a casualty of the Napoleonic wars; he served the Prince Elector of Wurttemberg as quartermaster in the battalion of foot jägers stationed at Heilbronn, twenty miles from Naylingen. In this latter town the future Confederate statesman was born, January 9, 1803. His father was killed a month afterward, leaving the young widow in distress. Struggling for a time against unfavorable circumstances, she left Germany with her father, mother, and infant, landing at Charleston, after a long, arduous voyage. In 1808 she, too, succumbed, and the five-year-old boy became the

[1] *The Prison Life of Jefferson Davis*, by John J. Craven, p. 159 (edition 1905)

JUDAH PHILIP BENJAMIN (1811-1884)
Courtesy of the New York Historical Society, New York City

George W. Randolph of Virginia (1818–1867)
Courtesy of the New York Historical Society, New York City

Christopher Gustavus Memminger of South Carolina (1803–1888)
Brown Bros

care of her father and mother. No details are forthcoming concerning these grandparents; all that is known is that they entered the child in a Charleston orphanage, departed for Philadelphia, and never saw him again. The story reads like a rather callous one; it is that of a parentless, poverty-stricken, friendless, and neglected child. The experience, however, apparently left no bitterness; Memminger, as a successful Charleston lawyer, became a trustee of the institution in which he had been reared, and devoted a large part of his time to works intended to improve the condition of children. If his early life left any scar at all, it was in making Memminger an exceedingly serious, industrious man, with almost no lighter side to his nature, no humor, no talent for the relaxations that made existence so tolerable to a Benjamin or a Toombs. His mind also lacked the brilliancy of the first and the penetration of the other. Education, law, finance, above all religion, had exclusively occupied Memminger's days. As child, boy, and man the church provided abundant consolation. Abstruse theology and ecclesiastical history claimed most of the man's spare time. Charlestonians, informed, in 1861, that Memminger had acceded to the Treasury, recalled not so much the able lawyer and advocate of Southern rights as the familiar gray-haired, slightly bent figure, browsing in secondhand bookstores, seeking out ancient shabby tomes that dealt with the doctrinal mysteries of the Christian church. Memminger displayed a precocious mind from the first, entering the University of South Carolina at eleven and graduating at fourteen, second in his class, and this taste for theology, as well as others similarly recondite, marked him at an early age.

The precocious boy had attracted the attention of a trustee of the orphanage, Thomas Bennett, who took him into his own home and provided for his education. In a few years Memminger attained distinction at the Charleston bar, specializing in commerce and finance. And that, in the Charleston law courts, was the day of legal giants, John C. Calhoun,

James Hamilton, Robert Young Hayne, Langdon Cheeves, and William Drayton. Memminger never quite ranked with these figures, but he was an advocate of sound learning, lucid forensic skill, and tested integrity, a man who commanded universal respect and attracted a most substantial clientele. On one occasion Memminger did rise to a height that even these celebrated jurists seldom scaled. This was the "Bank case," as it was known then, and is known in South Carolina history. The issue involved was the one known to-day as "sound money." The Bank of South Carolina, disregarding the state law, had suspended specie payments and was redeeming its notes only in paper money. The state instituted suit to vacate its charter, engaging Memminger as counsel. The case, which absorbed public attention for several months, had the most momentous effect upon the financial policy of the state. For Memminger won, and won gloriously; as a result, from that date until the Civil War, South Carolina enjoyed a national fame for the honesty of its banks and the soundness of its standing in matters of finance. Lord Morpeth, afterward the Earl of Carlisle, a visitor in South Carolina at the time, constantly attended the Memminger pleadings. He pronounced the argument the finest he had ever heard in a court of law. "In his forcible style of delivery and directness of method, he compared Mr. Memminger to Sir Robert Peel."[2] The case made the South Carolinian's reputation as a lawyer and opened new possibilities for him in public life.

Yet he was a public man in a restricted sense. Gustavus Memminger played only a minor part on the national stage. First and last he was a Carolinian. He never served in Congress or the Senate and never held office under the Federal Government. He was a parochial statesman, a man who gave his best efforts to his locality. Alderman in Charleston, member of the Board of Education, delegate to the Assembly for twenty years — such were the restricted arenas in which he

[2] Quoted by Henry D. Capers, *Life of Memminger*.

fulfilled the rôle of useful citizen. So far as he showed interest in the great question of the day, it was on the liberal side. But Memminger was not one of the great statesmen of the decade preceding 1860. He possessed no strong appeal for the populace. Stern, matter-of-fact, rigidly Germanic in devotion to detail and statistics, undistinguished in appearance, his name had hardly extended beyond South Carolina when he entered the Davis Cabinet. His one departure on a larger scene came in 1860; in that year he went to the Virginia Legislature as a delegate from South Carolina. The purpose was to persuade Virginia to join in the Secession campaign of South Carolina. He was not exactly the man for that job. His nature lacked passion and his oratory in Richmond left the Old Dominion cold; that commonwealth, in January, 1860, was still a good Union state. From now on Memminger grew steadily in favor of withdrawal from the Union, though his previous attitude still made him a person suspect in strong Secession quarters. He took a leading position as member of the South Carolina Convention. For this he wrote a majority report, so much of which was copied in the Ordinance of Secession that he is sometimes called the author of that historic document.

He went as a delegate to the Montgomery Convention and here served as chairman of the Committee that drew up the provisional Constitution. Despite all this, his appointment as Secretary of the Treasury was not widely applauded. In particular it infuriated R. B. Rhett and his following. For years Memminger had fought that firebrand and his secession plans. As the life-long advocate of the Southern Confederacy which had now come to life, Rhett believed that he was entitled to such "recognition" in the new Government as might be parceled out to South Carolina. He thought himself entitled even to the Presidency; since that had gone elsewhere, however, he was willing to become Secretary of State or representative to Great Britain — for Rhett fancied himself as having a real talent for foreign affairs. But Davis, with that icy disdain which was one of his conspicuous — and, at times such as this, not unattractive qualities — ignored all Rhett's ambitions. For the favored son of South Carolina he chose Robert Barnwell. Since Toombs had been marked out for the Treasury, Barnwell was offered the Department of State. His declination of the "premiership" upset the whole programme. Barnwell, stepping aside, called Davis's attention to Memminger. He described the German's fine record in banking, and proposed him for South Carolina's representative in the Cabinet as Secretary of the Treasury. Davis accepted the suggestion, and transferred Toombs to the State Department, leaving Rhett entirely outside the breastwork. This made the irascible South Carolinian Davis's deadly enemy. For the present — but for only a short time — Rhett's paper, the influential Charleston *Mercury,* spared the President, but the attack on Memminger started at once. Memminger's career, as already outlined, left certain openings. The man's record showed — so ran these journalistic bombardments — that, like Davis himself, he was a "reconstructionist" at heart. Robert Bunch, British Consul at Charleston, notes this suspicion. "Even now it is believed that his [Memminger's] feelings are not enlisted in the movement, the possibility of which he openly ridiculed six months ago" — so Bunch reported to his Government. Edward A. Pollard of the Richmond *Examiner* joined Rhett in this campaign, describing Memminger as the most inept member in a cabinet of "intellectual pigmies." Davis "added to his own deficiencies [in finance] by an almost inexplicable choice of his Secretary of the Treasury." Memminger was chiefly known as a lawyer, said Pollard, and "he had the hard, unsympathizing face of that profession." He pictured the man as "an unpleasant eccentricity" and "a zealot in religion, who had a strange passion for controversial theology."[3] The amiable Jones reflects these disrespectful

[3] Pollard's *Jefferson Davis,* pp 174–175.

judgments in his Diary. "Mr. Memminger came in the other day with a proposition to cease from labor on Sunday, but our secretary made war on it." Jones quoted another caller as saying that "Mr. Memminger's head is as worthless as a pin's head."[4] Explosive Senator Wigfall of Texas made the Secretary a butt. He declared that Memminger had proposed to finance the Confederacy by leaving collection bags in the churches. Others assailed him for his foreign birth. The term "Hessian" was freely used; at any rate, the man was no "Carolinian."

Memminger's real misfortune, however, was not the abuse showered by the Rhett-Pollard combination. In a sense he was the one logical appointment in the Cabinet, for he did have a knowledge of banking. And in that consisted his bad luck. Memminger's reputation had been made as an enemy of paper money. For years anything suggesting wild-cat currency or inflation had riled him. His efforts, more than those of any other man, had lifted South Carolina from the financial morass in which most Southern and Western states were sunk in the fifties, and had made its banks a name of honor throughout the Union. The Pollard and Rhett attacks on him as a man ignorant of finance thus flew in the face of facts. The man was a "gold Democrat" long before that term passed into political speech. But the tragedy of his new fate was that sound finance was the last thing he would be able to practice. The man who thought that only gold and silver were money would be called upon to pay the bills of his Government with endless issues of paper. Had William McKinley, in 1897, appointed to the Treasury the most conservative banker in the nation, and then instructed him to carry out the policies of William Jennings Bryan, he would have done precisely what Jefferson Davis did when, in 1861, he placed Christopher Gustavus Memminger at the head of this department.

[4] *A Rebel War Clerk's Diary*, Vol. I, pp. 54, 211. (Edition 1935.)

2
WHITE GOLD

The headquarters of the Confederate Treasury scarcely emblazoned the sovereign power of nearly nine million people. The office that was eventually to dispense not far from a billion dollars — money of a kind — found its first abiding place in a modest-sized room of the commercial building in Montgomery which sheltered the Confederate Government. This room, when Memminger moved in, was bare of furniture; a rough matting hastily tacked on the floor, a desk, and a few chairs quickly transported from a near-by shop, finally gave it a faint air of human occupancy. A scribbled card attached to the door informed inquirers that this was the sanctum of the Confederate Treasury Department. Within there reigned only one employee — Henry D. Capers, afterward Memminger's biographer. Capers always liked to describe the modest beginnings of this, the financial bulwark of the improvised Government. For the first days Memminger was busy with Congressional duties, and his secretary maintained the shabby little empire. Capers not only managed its financial concerns during this interim, but swept and cleaned the place. Hardly had the office opened, when a smartly attired, energetic Confederate colonel appeared, with an order from President Davis, instructing the Treasury Department to provide the wherewithal for fitting out one hundred men. "I want the money, sir," he peremptorily informed Memminger's trusty subordinate, "to carry out the instructions of the President." Capers dove his hands into his trousers' pockets, eventually pulling forth five or ten dollars of Federal currency. "This is all the money there is in the Confederate Treasury at present," he said. Memminger came to the rescue, arranging a small credit at the local bank on his personal guarantee. With this the petty-cash requirements of the first few days were met. "At the beginning," Memminger himself said afterward, "the Confederacy did not have money enough to buy the desk on which the Secretary wrote."

Probably no Government ever started life so handicapped in the mere mechanics of the office. For decades the South had depended on the North for all the materials of business and finance. It had obtained its paper and stationery from the area with which it was now at war; all its bank notes and bonds had been engraved and printed in New York. Thus when the new Government began to plan the issue of all those promises to pay that inevitably finance an insurrectionary movement, it made a startling discovery. Not an engraver could be found to prepare its notes; there was not a sheet of banknote paper on which to print them and no printer experienced in this kind of work. It is a curious commentary on the confused situation existing in those early weeks that the American Bank Note Company of New York — a company still in flourishing condition — printed the first bonds and treasury notes of a government which its fellow citizens called "rebel." These were all ready for shipping to Richmond when the Washington authorities seized the assignment as contraband of war. Not until the Confederate capital was moved to Richmond did it discover the means of turning out the crudely engraved pieces of paper that served as the first currency. An old German lithographer was found, who, in a fashion, executed the plates, and Maryland sympathizers smuggled enough bank-note paper from New York to satisfy a temporary demand. For office stationery the departments were dependent chiefly on shipments from England, and one of the duties of the new ambassadorial force was to obtain such supplies in London.

The methods adopted by Memminger to finance the war have a perennial interest, not only for the student of economics, but for the statesman. Military operations to-day involve such enormous expenditures that it seems impossible for any power to withstand the strain for a protracted period. The

Confederacy throws considerable light upon this problem. For money, as that substance is understood in conservative quarters, was practically unknown in that region during the war. Pieces of printed paper in vast sheaves inundated a suffering people, but coins of gold or silver were rarely seen. At the start, indeed, the Treasury did assemble a certain quantity of metal, and Mr. Memminger, in four years of office, scraped together a total of this liquid capital reaching perhaps $25,000,000. That figure represents all the hard cash with which the Confederate States were kept going for four years. In that quadrennium the Government maintained an army of hundreds of thousands of men, kept employed a great force of civil servants, provided the circulating medium for the economic life of 9,000,000 people, having at its disposal only this minute store of that kind of money which is recognized as valid in the markets of the world. That is at the rate of about $6,250,000 a year — only twice what the Federal Government was spending in a single day.

Mr. Memminger accumulated this modest supply of gold and silver by several devices. About $6,000,000 was confiscated from Federal customhouses and mints, a little less than $3,000,000 was realized from the one gold loan negotiated in Paris and London, an undetermined sum from the sale of so-called cotton bonds in Europe, and the rest was the product of the one successful financial measure adopted by the Confederacy. This was the $15,000,000 domestic loan floated in the first months of the war. The spirit of patriotism was then running high; the average Southerner was aflame to make heavy personal sacrifices; the atmosphere was favorable for obtaining subscriptions to a loan. In these early days considerable reserves of gold and silver coin were resting in private possession or in the vaults of banks. The purpose of the loan which was offered in May, 1861, was to draw all this money from its personal owners into the Confederate Treasury.

The plan succeeded with a completeness that cheered the heart of Secretary Memminger and enhanced general confidence in the loyalty and steadfastness of the Southern people. Individuals brought to the Treasury their stocks of metallic money, receiving in return the promises of their Government to pay in ten years; and banks extended all kinds of facilities to encourage subscriptions. For most of the subscribers this was to be a final glimpse at gold or silver. Not for many years did they gaze upon the precious object again. Appropriately this transaction was called the "specie loan." "Specie" was indispensáble to the Davis forces in these early days, and the only places — except the sequestrations noted above — from which it could be obtained were the strongboxes of citizens. The bonds offered could be purchased only for specie; they bore eight per cent interest, payable in gold; to service them a small tax was laid on cotton exports, also payable exclusively in hard money. Thus most of the coin in the Southern States started in rivulets in the direction of Richmond, and, in a comparatively brief period, it was concentrated in Mr. Memminger's vaults. The money so obtained, added to the $5,000,000 or $6,000,000 seized in Federal mints and customhouses, immediately gave Memminger about $20,000,000 cash. Most of it at once found its way to Europe. It was sorely needed on that continent, for there the Confederacy was obliged to acquire war supplies. European merchants, a hard-fisted lot, declined to do business with the new sovereignty except upon a cash basis. When Confederate agents first appeared in British shipyards and munition plants to place orders, the hardy Britisher looked at them skeptically. Where was the money forthcoming to pay for this war material? The agents first suggested Confederate bonds, only to be met with laughter. Shipmasters declined to lay a keel until advance payments were put down in good England pounds. The first Confederate gold loan, plus the money seized in Uncle Sam's mints and customhouses, solved this problem. Part of this gold and silver hoard went to build the *Alabama,* the *Shenandoah,* and other ships whose exploits become historic.

For the Southern people themselves — the soldiers in the army, the civil workers, the merchants, wage earners, and the like — an entirely different kind of circulating medium was provided. While constructors of *Alabamas* and munition makers received compensation in the coin of their respective realms, the Southern citizen himself was forced to accept the paper evidences of debt which the Richmond printing presses began to manufacture in vast amounts. If the Confederate Government exemplifies the possibility of conducting extensive military operations with a minimum of cash resources, it also illustrates, in bewildering detail, all the vices of inflation. It is not necessary to rehearse the dreary story again. No need once more to tell the wearisome annals of bonds redeemable in notes, of notes exchangeable for bonds, of paper money issued in hundreds of millions, of the lightninglike enhancement in prices, of crazy speculation and ruined fortunes. The Confederate story is always profitably rehearsed when modern economists wish to picture the folly of the belief, evidently ingrained in the human mind, that the mere fiat of a government can give value to something which has no value, that calling a slip of paper a dollar or a franc or a pound makes it one. While the experience of the Confederacy duplicated that of other historic attempts of similar kind — the assignats of the French Revolution, the paper issues of the Continental Congress, and more recent but identical experiments following the World War — it is doubtful if any of these, unless it is the last, reached such grotesque depths as did the expedients of the Davis Government. Issues of paper money commonly succeed for a period, and that period can be pretty well defined. The people will accept such currencies at face value as long as public confidence survives in the ability of the government to redeem them in gold. The varying fortunes of

Federal greenbacks and Confederate Treasury notes from 1861 to 1865 illustrate this truism. Secretary Chase's paper money suffered its ups and downs, as did Secretary Memminger's, though it never attained such unfathomable depths as did that produced in Richmond. No better way of tracing the variations of popular expectation of the outcome could be devised than the daily quotations for the two currencies.

During 1861 Confederate fiat dollars stood the strain pretty well; this reflected the patriotic fervor of that early day, upheld by such a military triumph as Bull Run. Federal greenbacks, at their first issue in 1862, soon acquired a similar respectability; they symbolized a mighty cause; they appeared in Northern eyes instruments of victory, and they aroused the same loyal devotion as did the Union flag itself. The last years of the conflict told a different story. At the end, Federal paper dollars retained a value of about fifty cents in gold; after four years of exceedingly expensive war, in which the Federal credit had been strained to the utmost, this can hardly be regarded as an extravagant loss of value. Confederate dollars, on the other hand, completely mirrored the sinking fortunes of the Government that had issued them. In the last quarter of 1865 their value was about one cent in gold; after Appomattox, one dollar in gold would purchase $6000 in Confederate money. One thing that particularly annoyed the Davis Government in the latter years was the increasing popularity of Federal greenbacks in the Confederacy itself. As the Union armies penetrated the South, large amounts of this currency seeped into Southern hands. Richmond passed laws making its circulation illegal, all to no purpose. The eagerness with which Southerners reached for this money, at the same time rejecting their own, told the story. In their heart the people knew that their cause was lost, that some day Yankee greenbacks would attain the value of gold, and that their own paper dollars would be worthless.

Even as early as 1862 the Confederacy was committed to

this paper basis. By the end of that year it was hopelessly mired in the morass. The horror with which Memminger had always looked upon such a circulating medium availed him nothing. Month after month he kept sending forth the kind of money which he had constantly denounced as unworthy of an honest people. The familiar cycle of inflation, in all its stages, ran the inevitable course. Paper money inevitably increases prices; increased prices necessitate more paper money; so issue after issue followed, as it always does when the process is once begun. How irretrievably the Confederacy ran this financial rake's progress a few figures make plain. Inflation here, as always, started gingerly, deprecatingly; thus the first issue. in June, 1861, was a paltry $1,000,000. By the fall of 1863, the last date for which trustworthy statistics are available, $700,000,000 of Treasury notes had flooded the Southern States. Beyond that all is darkness and confusion. It may safely be estimated, however, that by 1865, Richmond had put forth at least a billion of this currency.[5] Compared to this the North should have marveled at its moderation. Despite its superiority in resources and population, it had issued fiat money only to the extent of $450,000,000.

But these comparative data picture the situation only in part. The printed paper of the Confederacy, enormous as its total was, represented only a fraction of the worthless currency in circulation. The doctrine of State rights, as a principle of politics, is fairly debatable, but there is no question that it exercises a fatal spell in finance. The Federal Constitution of 1787 prohibited the states from coining money or emitting bills of credit. Not so the Montgomery Constitution of 1861. Such prerogatives were then regarded as the sovereign rights of states, of which they could not justly be deprived. Soon after the war started, individual commonwealths began acting on this theory. They added their paper currencies to those of

---

[5] See *The Confederate States of America*, by John Christopher Schwab (Yale Bicentennial Publications, 1901), p. 165.

the Richmond Government. Counties followed states in contributing to this flood. Cities followed counties, and towns followed cities. Finally private corporations added to the ever-increasing stock. Not only banks, but railroad companies, turnpike companies, factories, and insurance corporations joined in the mad competition. The need for money in small denominations flooded the country with a variety of odds and ends — little tokens valued at five cents, ten cents, a quarter, and a half dollar. "Shin plasters" were not unknown in the North, but no such deluge swept that region as the one which now burst upon Dixie. A miscellaneous horde of private persons — tobacconists, grocers, milk dealers, innkeepers, barbers, and bartenders — emitted these tiny bills to an extent that sorely taxed the paper supplies of the eleven seceded states. To all this enterprise must be added the unremitting industry of counterfeiters. Theirs presently became one of the most thriving of occupations; the legal money was so crude in printing that this army of criminals had no difficulty in reproducing it. The prevailing demoralization is exemplified by the defense that these unofficial gentlemen would put up when arrested: they would claim that they were bankers, engaged in a recognized business.

3

WHITE GOLD, CONTINUED

This financial debacle was particularly tragic because, in the opinion of most students, it was unnecessary. All the time that the Confederacy was frantically seeking to strengthen its money position by endless emissions of worthless currency, it had ready to hand the materials on which a splendid financial structure could have been built. The most obvious fact in Southern life held the solution of its problem. Mr. Memminger lacked the kind of gold that the geological past has secreted in mines, but he did possess the kind that was waving in thousands of Southern fields. Cotton, the mainspring of Southern history for seventy-five years, the cause of the political conflicts that had separated the sections for four decades, and that had finally precipitated war, would, wisely handled, have furnished abundant power. "White gold," the Southern people called it, and never was a name more appropriately applied. It dotted almost every acre in the lower Southern states, it filled to overflowing every steamboat that glided down the rivers, it stood piled on a thousand wharves and stored in a thousand warehouses. Here was money, in vast quantities, just as real as was the specie that Memminger was frantically abstracting from the banks and the coffers of private citizens. No alchemist's art was needed to transmute this inert substance into the most precious of metals. Six months after Sumter was fired upon, a thousand factories in Great Britain and France were stretching beseeching hands across the Atlantic. "Cotton! Cotton!" became the universal cry. On these white bolls, glittering over an ocean of American plantations, depended their very existence. Without a steady supply whole English counties would close their spinning mills and millions of workers would be thrown upon the streets. Herein lay the key to successful Southern finance. As long as this cotton wealth lay inert in field or warehouse, it possessed practically no value. Once landed on European shores, it would instantaneously change to liquid credits and become an abundant store of that capital without which the Confederacy could not survive. With the metal obtained from its sale, deposited in London and Paris banks, the Confederacy would construct a stronger financial foundation than that of the Federal Government. Mr. Davis would quickly become a richer President than Mr. Lincoln. With these teeming reserves, not only could he have financed Confederate purchases in Europe to an enormous extent but he could have given Confederate currency a gold basis that would have made the badly printed Confederate notes as valuable as the British pound.

When Benjamin Franklin crossed the Atlantic in 1776 to establish a diplomatic home in Paris and negotiate a treaty with France, the ship that transported him also carried, in its bowels, a cargo of fine American tobacco. This he was expected to sell, using the proceeds to pay the expenses of his mission. As a financial measure the plan was perfect, for tobacco, once deposited in French storehouses, was the same as money. The Confederacy should have profited from this example. The financial scheme available to its statesmen, in retrospect, seems simplicity itself. Cotton planters, in the fall of 1861, had millions of bales on hand for which they were despairingly seeking a market. They would gladly have exchanged these for Confederate bonds. The Treasury could have given out its obligations, bonds or notes, for a sufficient quantity of this cotton to finance its needs, shipped the product to Europe, and, on the great cash balances thus acquired, established its fiscal security. Only one member of the Confederate Cabinet saw the problem in these elementary terms. Leroy P. Walker, the Alabamian who for a brief period filled the war office, afterward bore testimony to this fact. At the first Cabinet meeting, he related, "there was only one man there who had any sense and this man was Benjamin. Mr. Benjamin proposed that the Government purchase as much cotton as it could hold, at least 100,000 bales, and ship it at once to England. With the proceeds of a part of it he advised the immediate purchase of at least 150,000 stands of arms, and guns and munitions in corresponding amount. The residue of the cotton to be held as a basis for credit. For, said Benjamin, we are entering on a contest that may be long and costly. All the rest of us fairly ridiculed the idea of a serious war. Well, you know what happened." [6]

One of the Cabinet members who ridiculed the proposal was Christopher G. Memminger, Secretary of the Treasury. He regarded the idea as both unconstitutional and economically

[6] *Life of Judah P. Benjamin*, by Pierce Butler, p. 234.

unwise. The cotton-buying scheme was advocated on two grounds: it would heap up credits for the Confederacy in Europe and would bring relief to the planters, then burdened with great crops for which there was no market. "Soup house legislation," Memminger called the plan, referring to this eleemosynary phase of the proposed transaction. The opposition he displayed rose to plague him in subsequent years. Of all the sorrows of Confederate statesmen and generals, after Lee's surrender, none were quite so acute as their ruminations on this disregarded advice. In every post-mortem on the reason for defeat, the failure to use their strength in cotton took a leading place. A prisoner in Fortress Monroe, Jefferson Davis mourned this fatal oversight. And his references to his Minister of Finance were not overgenerous. "South Carolina placed Mr. Memminger in the Treasury," Dr. Craven quotes him as saying, "and while he respected the man, the utter failure of Confederate finance was the failure of the cause. Had Mr. Memminger acted favorably on the proposition of depositing cotton in Europe and holding it there for two years as a basis for their currency, their circulating medium might have maintained itself at par to the closing day of the struggle; and that in itself would have ensured victory." More than 3,000,000 bales of cotton rested unused in the South at the time of secession; if these had been rushed to Europe before the blockade had attained any efficiency, said the reminiscent President, they would have ultimately brought a billion dollars in gold. "Such a sum," Dr. Craven quotes Davis as estimating, "would have more than sufficed all the needs of the Confederacy during the war; would have sufficed, with economic management, for a war of twice the actual duration; and this evidence of southern prosperity and ability could not but have acted powerfully upon the minds, the securities and the avarice of the New England rulers of the North. He was far from reproaching Mr. Memminger. The situation was new. No one could have foreseen the course of events. When too late the wisdom of the proposed measure was realized, but the inevitable 'too late' was interposed. The blockade had become too stringent, for one reason, and the planters had lost their pristine confidence in the Confederate currency. When we might have put silver in the purse we did not put it there. When we had only silver on the tongue, our promises were forced to become excessive." [7] From his prison cell at Fort Warren, Boston, Vice President Alexander Stephens put forth a similar wail.[8] General Joseph E. Johnston, in his memoirs, published in 1874, attributed the downfall of the cause to this blunder. The Confederacy collapsed, General Johnston insisted, not because of military weakness, but of financial.[9]

Memminger was living when his former colleagues, civil and military, poured forth these complaints in books, letters, and private conversation. The criticism stung him deeply. He refrained from replying to Davis, out of consideration for that statesman's misfortunes; but all the fierceness of his German heart was expended on Johnston and other revilers. His rejoinders, on the whole, were not convincing. He could not have purchased Southern cotton with Treasury notes or bonds, he said, because the Confederacy had no facilities, in this early period, to print such instruments of exchange! That was a rather childish argument; certainly an ingenious statesman would have found some way of devising temporary expedients to meet this difficulty. His next objection was more to the point. The entire crop of 1860–1861, continued Memminger, had been gathered and shipped before February, 1861, when the Confederacy was organized; therefore the critics were mistaken who insisted that the Government had 3,000,000 bales at its service, when war broke out. So far as this crop, of 1860, is concerned, Memminger's explanation is unanswerable; but most of the critics, like Johnston, were referring not to the cotton that had been gathered before

[7] *The Prison Life of Jefferson Davis*, by John Joseph Craven, pp. 155, 158.
[8] *Recollections*, pp. 64, 65.
[9] *Narrative of Military Operations*, pp. 421–422.

February 1, 1861, but to the new crop planted in the spring of 1861, and all ready for shipment in the autumn of that year. This was, in size, a normal crop — the last one grown in the South until after the war. It was the wealth that was then so embarrassing to the planters. In previous years practically all of it had gone to the Northern states and to Europe. The North obviously was no longer a customer, but how about the European markets? Memminger found his explanation of the failure to export this supply in the Federal blockade. This had now become so stringent, he said, that all the ships of the world had fled from Southern waters. The blockade, it was true, had not succeeded in making completely inaccessible Southern ports, but it had succeeded in monstrously increasing insurance rates and frightening vessels from the Confederacy. The South had no tonnage of its own; for the shipping of its main source of wealth it had always depended upon the North and on England. But all these vessels had vanished from the Southern coast by the time the new cotton crop became ready for export. To send to Europe 4,000,000 bales would require 4,000 ships at the average rate of 1,000 bales to the hold; where were these ships to be obtained?

Such figures make the apologia preposterous. No one proposed to load 4,000 ships and launch this crop across the ocean in one gigantic armada. The proceeding would have taken at least a year, each steamer making ten or a dozen voyages; thus, even were the whole 4,000,000 bales landed in Europe, it would not have needed one tenth the number of vessels the angry Secretary imagined. More important still, it was not necessary for the salvation of Confederate finance that 4,000,000 bales be exported. The amount suggested by Benjamin, according to Mr. Walker's recollection, 100,000 bales, would have netted not far from $50,000,000. That would have given the Confederacy great strength in the early critical months. It seems a fair conclusion that not only could this much cotton but far more — 500,000 bales is the favorite estimate — have been shipped, a good deal of it before waiting for a new crop, had the Confederate Cabinet proceeded with energy.

But most discussions of this failure, before and since, overlook the significant point. Benjamin, despite Mr. Walker's statement, was not the only Southerner who, at the time, saw the possibilities of cotton finance. It was not the failure to detect the opportunity, not the Federal blockade or lack of shipping, that kept the Confederacy's greatest economic weapon uselessly locked up within its own borders. The all-important fact is that the South really did not desire to export its cotton. Memminger was not the only one at fault; Davis, though free enough of criticism in retrospect, cannot escape his share of blame. The Confederacy in 1861–1862 not only was not shipping cotton, but was taking all precautions to prevent it from being shipped. To these statesmen the Federal blockade, in those early days, came almost as a godsend. "Mr. Davis," says his contemporary Southern biographer, "actually welcomed the blockade and vaunted it as a blessing in disguise."[10] It was assisting the Confederacy in its great objective, for it was aiding in keeping the darling staple from the markets of Europe. Such was the policy of Confederate leaders in this early time. There is therefore no need to discuss the question that so agitated Southern statesmen after the war — whether they could have transported cotton to England and France and so have saved the day. They were determined, at the outset, that no such attempt should be made. Long before Lincoln laid his blockade on Southern ports, the South had tacitly declared one of their own. This brings us again face to face with the greatest single delusion of Confederate statesmanship — that conviction that "Cotton is King" which remained its watchword throughout the war. The experience of Yancey and his companions in the Foreign offices of Britain and France had not taught the folly of this unreasoning faith.

[10] Edward A. Pollard, *Jefferson Davis*, p. 169.

Even after these humiliating failures, the Richmond leaders continued to base their hopes on this evangel. The fact is that Cotton actually was "King," though in a sense that the Confederate Government apparently never grasped. It could have been made the supreme support of the cause as a rock of financial and economic power. The mere cessation of cotton imports never moved the British and French Governments, so far as recognition was concerned, but the statesmanlike handling of the strength provided by its cotton crop would have built a mighty fortress of financial credit. Whether this in itself would have saved the Confederacy cannot be proved, but it would have enormously added to the problems of the North. Instead of making the best use of this resource, the Davis Government deliberately did all in its power to make it useless. Lincoln with his blockade, Davis with his embargo — here were two forces, outwardly enemies, working successfully to a common end, the destruction of the South as an economic and financial power.

4

The Cotton Famine

Thomas Jefferson was the inventor of that policy of "peaceable coercion" which presently became the diplomatic weapon of the South. He believed that he could settle the American problems arising from the Napoleonic wars by closing American ports to European commerce. Europe, he maintained, stood in such vital need of American products that to withdraw them would soon bring the enemy to their knees. He tried this plan, and, of course, tragically failed. Despite this historic example, this same scheme of "coercion" was gospel in the plans of the Davis Government in 1861. The idea at this time was not a wholesale Jeffersonian cessation of commerce. To bring Great Britain and France to terms — that is, to force them to recognize the South as an independent nation

— all that was required was to keep cotton from reaching foreign ports. A "cotton famine" in Europe was the one certain way to victory. Like most daring military offensives, it should be precipitated quickly, almost instantaneously, bringing the foe to immediate surrender by one fierce, concentrated attack. To understand this policy, one fact must be kept in mind. With a few exceptions all Southern statesmen expected a short decisive war. Few imagined that the struggle, started in April, would last longer than the succeeding Christmas. All plans in this early day were based upon this conviction. The "cotton famine" in England and France should therefore come quickly, remorselessly, if it was to accomplish its purpose.

At that time one fifth of Great Britain's population — about 5,000,000 — was dependent upon the spinning industry. The extent to which this aggregate was hostage to a raw material produced three thousand miles away had been a gloomy foreboding in England for years. Consequently most English economists accepted as true the picture gloatingly drawn by Southern writers of the desolation that would ravage the favored isle with the sudden end of this supply. What would be the result, political and economic, should 5,000,000 men, women and children suddenly be deprived of their livelihood? That revolution would ensue was a common prophecy; certainly British foreign trade would face ruin and British preeminence in industry and finance be endangered. To threaten its greatest customer with this "cotton famine," to start such a "famine" as quickly as possible, now became the mainspring of Southern statecraft. The mere prospect, it was thought, would strike terror into English hearts and make the world's greatest power an ally of the South. It was to be a stroke of "frightfulness" in the economic field.

Thus all means were taken to prevent this commodity from reaching Europe. When Yancey and Mann were protesting against the Lincoln blockade, denouncing it as "ineffective" and a violation of international law, they were really playing a hypocritical part. The more "effective" that blockade became, the better the Davis Administration would be pleased. All this time, indeed, Davis was instituting obstructions of his own. For the first year of the war, Confederate and Federal policy in the matter of cotton kept pursuing an identical end — to stop its shipment. The rival Governments were actuated, of course, by different motives. Lincoln wished to keep Southern cotton at home because he knew that, once placed on English docks, it would give the South impregnable financial strength. Davis believed a cotton famine in Europe was the one way speedily to end the war. Lincoln's preventive measure was known as the "blockade," that of Davis as the "embargo." Lincoln's procedure was open, acknowledged; the Davis methods were unofficial, not proclaimed from the housetops. This caution was diplomatically inevitable. The Confederate Government could not brazenly lay an interdict on the transportation of its staple. But many bills were introduced in the Confederate Congress establishing such a prohibition. Debates on this subject, unlike most proceedings in this secret assembly, were ostentatiously printed in the newspapers, and these accounts — of course by intention — found their way into the English press. Such proposed legislation was useful as a threat, but the bills never were passed — Davis and his Cabinet saw to that. Nevertheless the embargo that followed would have been scarcely more effective if it had been ordered and enforced by the Government.[11] The whole South — planters, cotton factors, city and state governments, and especially organized Committees of Safety — joined in a concerted movement, from April, 1861, until April, 1862, to prevent cotton from embarking on the sea.

Not a bale for Europe, so long as Europe refused to recognize Southern independence! Such was the battle cry. Planters

[11] The authority on cotton, blockades, and the like is *King Cotton Diplomacy*, by Frank Lawrence Owsley (1931). To this exhaustive study all writers on the subject, including the present one, are profoundly indebted.

kept their cotton stored on the plantations, declining to send it down the rivers to Southern ports, fearful, once it reached places of shipment, it might be smuggled across the ocean. Vigilance committees constantly stood guard, day and night, in such great ports as New Orleans, Mobile, Savannah, and Charleston, to see that no supplies were transferred to blockade runners. Some, of course, did slip through, for the business was enormously lucrative, but in the main the work of these illegal censors was successful. The warehousemen of New Orleans, in August, 1861, issued a circular to planters, telling them to send no cotton to that port; it would not be accepted for shipment.[12] Other leading cities followed this example. Southern governors issued proclamations enjoining planters to send no cotton to the seaboard. Governor Milton of Florida called such attempts to ship through the blockade "an infamous traffic."[13] Memminger afterward said, as noted above, that cotton was not sent to Europe in these early days because no ships could be obtained. Yet many times British ships, loaded with this much desired cargo, were prevented from sailing by these self-appointed committees. On one occasion six large British cotton ships, all ready to depart from Wilmington, North Carolina, were thus forcibly held in port. The disappearance of English vessels from the South in the fall and winter of 1861-1862 is thus easily explained. They were not scared away by the Federal blockade, as Memminger afterward declared. Foreign carriers abandoned Southern ports for the best of commercial reasons — there were no cargoes to be obtained. Blockade running in 1862 and afterward became one of the most profitable industries. So rich were the rewards that plenty of captains took the risk of Federal capture — and this when such risks were much greater than in 1861. It would have been similarly profitable in that fateful year, and vessels would have swarmed in Southern

[12] *King Cotton Diplomacy*, p. 30.
[13] *The same*, p. 37.

ports, had not the efforts of the Confederacy, official and non-official, been concentrated on preventing exports.

The mania presently reached insane proportions. In the winter of 1861–1862 a new watchword swept the South. The discourteous treatment of Confederate Commissioners in London, the strange obstinacy of Great Britain in refusing diplomatic relations with the new Government, further infuriated the people. Now was the time really to turn the screws! Europe had large reserve supplies of cotton when war broke out, but these, by the fall of 1861, were rapidly diminishing, and the winter promised to be a severe one in the textile areas — as in fact it proved to be. Southern newspapers, governors, chambers of commerce, factors, and planters all joined in a new plan of coercion. Plant no cotton in 1862! Burn the present supply! Amazing as it seems, both these proposals in considerable measure were carried out. A normal cotton crop was between 4,000,000 and 5,000,000 bales; in 1862 only 500,000 bales were grown. As a result, the terrible cotton famine which had been predicted for England came to pass, with all the unemployment and starvation that had been foretold — only, most exasperating to Southern statesmen, it did not bring that recognition on which they had staked their cause. The burning of cotton that lighted the South with thousands of bonfires in 1862 had its direct consequence in millions of English and French workmen walking the streets and highways in the search for bread. Still no recognition came. One of the most unrestrained of cotton restrictionists was Albert Gallatin Brown of Mississippi, long the rival of Davis in that state. In the Confederate Senate Brown called upon the Government to purchase all outstanding cotton, and burn the entire stock in one magnificent holocaust. That was the way to get European intervention! The Government did not adopt the suggestion, but in practice the people accomplished much in that direction. The advancing Federal armies in Tennessee, Mississippi, Louisiana, and other states gave these wholesale burnings some military excuse. But the necessity of war was not the only incentive, probably not the most important one. The way in which Confederate publicity agents in England broadcast the news showed that the Government wished to impress on British public opinion the direct interest England had in the incineration of a material indispensable to its existence.

And meanwhile, what of Father Abraham's blockade in this first year, 1861–1862? Lincoln, whose sense of humor was his prevailing characteristic, must have kept his tongue in cheek in those first few months, as his sparse and ramshackle navy paraded, at long intervals, up and down the Southern coast. Lord John Russell, in London, also must have smiled secretly as he solemnly assured the world that this blockade was an "effective one," entitled to general respect. In all the history of naval warfare, probably no such gigantic bluff was inflicted on the world. Just consider two facts — potent ones, in 1861, when Lincoln proclaimed the whole Southern coast line under interdict and forbade all ships under pain of capture and confiscation from attempting to enter Southern ports. One of them was that this coast line, suddenly closed to commerce, was about 3,500 miles long. The other was that the United States Navy, at that moment, had just three ships available for enforcing its decree — less than one ship to each 1,000 miles. The Navy, as a whole, possessed between forty and fifty war vessels more or less useful for the purpose, but they were scattered all over the globe — in North and South America, China, and other inaccessible ports. It was impossible to convince Union men in 1861 that this scattering of America's armada had not been deliberate, intended to cripple the Government in its dealings with Secession. Whether this was the case or not, it took several months to bring the Navy home and engage it on the blockade. Even then it was pitifully inadequate to the task. By December 1, Secretary Welles had scraped together about 120 steam vessels — a nondescript lot, ranging from warships to ferryboats — but this flotilla was absurdly inadequate for the greatest blockading task any nation had ever attempted. It is not necessary to set forth the situation in statistical detail.[14] The fact is that, for the first year and part of the second, all the great ports of the South and practically its entire coast line were accessible to the shipping of the world; after the spring of 1862 the blockade began to tighten, the Federals ultimately having 600 war vessels stationed at the several strategic points. But for the first year no actual blockade existed, except on paper. Ships could leave and enter Southern ports almost at will. In fact, they repeatedly did so. Southern privateers went out unmolested and returned unhindered with their prizes. Numerous ships, defying both the Lincoln blockade and the Davis embargo, stole in and presently emerged with cargoes of cotton. Despite Memminger's defense, that there were no ships available for this purpose, between 500 and 700 vessels ran the blockade in 1861. It may thus be said that, in this, the most critical year of the Confederacy, a practically unimpeded sea highway extended from the Southern States to Europe. Professor Owsley, the foremost authority on the subject, estimates that the Confederates could have transported one half of the 4,000,000 bales of cotton raised in 1861 had Davis made any serious effort to do so.[15]

In failing to take advantage of this superb opportunity, the Confederacy made the mistake that spelled destruction. In any review of Southern finance this fact must be kept foremost in mind. Because of this lapse, the Government, by January, 1862, after ten months of existence, was a ruined financial structure, struggling under a mass of paper money, crippled in its credit abroad, its brave soldiers walking barefoot in the snow, its munitions supplies constantly inadequate to the task, its people hungry for food, the whole extent

[14] For a complete statistical survey of the subject see Chapter VII of Professor Owsley's *King Cotton Diplomacy*.
[15] *The same*, p. 289.

of its territory wracked by poverty. The resources that would have secured all those things and many more were wasted in the pursuit of an impossible foreign policy. The statesmanship of all history discloses few blunders so monstrous.

VIII

FRENCH BANKERS FLEECE THE CONFEDERACY

1

THE ERLANGER LOAN

IN THE field of international finance Memminger's activities were limited to a single transaction — the negotiation of a loan for $15,000,000 in the Paris and London markets. Like practically everything pertaining to the Confederacy, these Confederate bonds revolved around the subject of cotton. By the summer of 1862 the Government understood its great initial blunder, the failure to transport this most desired staple to Europe and thus establish a huge reservoir of foreign credits. Unfortunately, the opportunity had now passed. The supply of cotton had greatly decreased. Vast quantities had gone up in flames or fallen to the Federal armies, and little new seed had been planted in the spring of 1862. The difficulties of shipping had increased. The Federal blockade, while even now not "effective" in the strictest sense, was becoming more so every day. No longer did a practically unimpeded ocean stretch between the South and its European customers. Another circumstance, probably more hindering than the blockade, was keeping ships from the sea. The greatest cotton port, New Orleans, since April, 1862, had been in possession of the Federal forces. The loss crippled the Confederacy in more than a military sense. For years the great plantations, those bordering the Mississippi itself, and the scarcely smaller areas drained by the Red River, the Arkansas, and many others, had sent their cotton to New Orleans, making it by far the greatest shipping point of the South. The city's capture completely shut off these territories from access to the sea. Farragut's fleet had sealed it with a finality that a dozen blockades could never have accomplished. The Federal

Government wasted thousands of lives and limitless treasure in efforts to capture Richmond; but, in its effect on winning the contest, New Orleans was infinitely more valuable to the Federal cause. Its surrender meant that none of the cotton raised in this Mississippi watershed could get to market, but must lie uselessly on the plantations or be committed to the flames.

Thus there were several reasons why the opportunity which lay open in the previous year of shipping cotton to England and France and purchasing with it the supplies indispensable to war had now been lost forever. Still the hope persisted that this staple might be used to strengthen the Confederacy. In 1861 and 1862 the Government acquired about 450,000 bales in subscriptions to a so-called produce loan. Little likelihood prevailed of sending this to Europe in appreciable amounts; but could it not still be used in some way to obtain European credits? Was there no possibility that Europeans would accept this substance as collateral for loans, even though it could not be bodily transported overseas? Cotton on Southern plantations or in Southern warehouses hardly possessed the value that inhered in the same material deposited in Europe — that fact was recognized; yet the proffered security was very real and, at a sufficiently low price, might tempt adventurous foreigners. On this basis arose the so-called cotton bonds. The plan was simply one to borrow money, giving as mortgage cotton lying untransported in Southern states, owned by the Confederate Government. The plan met with indifferent success. Cotton resting on the soil of the Confederacy made no great appeal, as surety for loans. It was subject to too many vicissitudes. The enemy might capture or burn it; every day, in fact, European papers emblazoned accounts of such "vandalism." Should the war end unfavorably to the South, the Federal Government would take care that no cotton to redeem "rebel bonds" be shipped to Europe. Thus, while some money was raised on this tenuous guarantee, it soon became obvious that no dealings on a large scale were possible.

Still, this distant cotton, — distant, that is, in European eyes, — even though it found little favor with conservative investors, presently made a strong appeal to the speculator. Widows and orphans could not be enticed into buying cotton bonds; but enterprising gentlemen might be persuaded to take a flyer on this inert material, even though it was stored three thousand miles away. A combination of events in the fall and winter of 1862–1863 gave zest to this gambling instinct. The first of these was the high price of cotton in Europe and the comparatively low price in the Confederacy. The cotton famine on which Southern diplomatic policy rested had now become a reality. Textile areas in Lancashire and in the northern region of France had reached an appalling depth of unemployment and misery, and millions of English workers were encumbering the highways, in a state of impending or actual starvation. Those who think unemployment relief is some modern device should study European conditions in 1862–1863, when the British and French Governments were carrying armies of textile workers on the poor rolls. The "famine" had forced cotton up to fifty cents a pound, or $200 a bale in the European market. Yet in the Southern States this same product was offered at ten or twelve cents a pound. Such possible profits would obviously justify great risks. One preeminent fact, in the winter of 1862–1863, made purchases of cotton at these low figures a tempting gamble. Europe confidently believed that the war was approaching its end. The military events of 1862, successful as they had been to Federal armies, in the beginning, soon turned the balance in favor of the South. The collapse of McClellan's Peninsular campaign, the second battle of Bull Run, and the tragedy of Fredericksburg indicated to the average Englishman and Frenchman a quick Confederate victory. Lord Palmerston openly joked about the discomfiture of the Yankees; Gladstone made his famous speech, declaring that Jefferson Davis had "created a nation"; and now, for the first and, as it proved, the only time, Great Britain seemed to be planning to recognize the Davis Government. The intrigues of Napoleon III were evidently bearing fruit; he was in constant communication not only with the British Government, but with the pro-Confederate forces in the British Parliament; and these influences, combined with the distress of the English industrial areas, the apparently shattered forces of the Federal Government, and the generally accepted belief that the Union could never be restored, were clearly counterbalancing the nonintervention policy of Lord John Russell. At this crisis — 1862 and the early part of 1863 — the Confederacy stood at its peak. If money was to be made in a cotton speculation, the time to act had come.

If the Union, as English observers said, was as dead as the Anglo-Saxon Heptarchy, its end would bring to the lucky holders of cotton a great increase of wealth. The eyes of European speculators were dazzled at the prospect. Cotton that could now be purchased at ten or twelve cents a pound would jump to fifty cents and more if war came to a close with a final Southern victory. Since little cotton had been planted in 1862, these high prices would prevail for a long time. Out of this combination of circumstances — Federal defeats, the impending recognition of the Confederacy by Great Britain and France, the anticipated early end to the war, the low price of cotton in the South, and its extremely high price in Europe — came into being the celebrated Erlanger loan. For the important fact to be kept in mind is that this was not a loan, as such governmental transactions are usually understood, but a huge speculation in cotton.

Significantly the first approaches to this transaction did not come from the Confederate agents in Europe, but from the bankers themselves. At that time John Slidell had secured an excellent personal position as Confederate commissioner in

Paris. His ancestry contained perhaps a Jewish strain; at any rate, in Paris he became an intimate of leading Jewish families. One to whom he was especially close was Emile Erlanger, head of the great French banking house of Erlanger et Cie. Presently closer ties bound this wealthy family and the Confederate commissioner. Erlanger's son, afterward created Baron, quickly fell in love with Slidell's daughter, the *spirituelle* Matilda; and, from that moment, Confederate and French relations present a romantic association of Hymen and *Haute Finance*. Erlanger was made the French intermediary in all Confederate transactions. He busied himself day and night in the Confederate cause; exerted all his influence, which was powerful, upon the Emperor in its behalf; bestirred himself in the schemes of Maximilian for the Mexican throne; caused books and magazine articles to be published presenting the Confederacy in most attractive guise; and acted as agent in the construction, in French shipyards, of ironclads and corvettes for the Confederate Navy.

It was in September of 1862, at the height of Confederate military success, that Erlanger first broached the subject of a loan to Slidell. He was prepared to raise $25,000,000 in gold in exchange for Confederate bonds. Mr. Memminger's bank balances in Europe at that moment were reaching a low ebb, and such a windfall as Erlanger now proposed to Slidell would clearly establish new credits, thus making possible purchases that would speed the expected Southern triumph. M. Erlanger was so confident of this that his banking house offered to underwrite the entire issue — that is, to purchase the bonds outright — and thus at once put the Confederacy in funds. The terms, it must be agreed, were a little severe. The bonds were to bear 8 per cent interest; they were to be delivered to Erlanger et Cie at 70 — any price received above that amount in the open market was to go to the bankers. Numerous stipulations for commissions also seemed likely to enhance the Erlanger profit. And another condition was attached, unusual in the case of solvent governments; security was to be exacted. This provision changed the whole character of the transaction. Ostensibly a loan, it became really a speculation in cotton. For every dollar received the Davis Government was to pledge its only source of wealth. Each bond was made exchangeable at its face value — that is, at 100, although the Erlangers were to obtain it at 70 — for New Orleans middling cotton, at twelve cents a pound, not later than six months after the ratification of a treaty of peace between North and South. Just as soon as the sounds of battle ceased, that is, — and this event was regarded as certain to take place within a few months, — the Erlanger bonds were to be transmuted into cotton at twelve cents a pound — cotton that was marketable in Europe at five times that figure. Should any holder be tempted to realize before the expected treaty was signed, he could demand his share of the much-desired staple at the rate of twelve cents a pound; at this demand the material was to be moved from the plantations to within ten miles of a railroad or a navigable river, transportation from that point being at the risk of the bondholders. Thus Erlanger and his clients pictured themselves, at the end of the war, the possessors of not far from $100,000,000 worth of cotton, acquired at one fifth its value. In particular the prospect was one that would hold spellbound the adventurous group surrounding Napoleon III. Emile Erlanger was close to the imperial favor and confidence and not improbably Napoleon himself had a finger in this promising pie. At least, his interest in the success of the "loan," which reached a point that violated all the proprieties of international intercourse, and the notorious unscrupulousness of his own character, warrant such a suspicion.

2

SLIDELL AND BENJAMIN

Mr. Slidell informed Erlanger that he had no authority to conclude such a contract and suggested that the banker go in person to Richmond or send representatives. But his correspondence shows that the proposal entranced him. He was greatly flattered because the initiative came from the bankers. "These gentlemen presented themselves to me," he wrote Benjamin, October 28, 1862, "without any suggestion on my part, of a desire to borrow money for the Confederate states."[1] He used one word in this same letter which discloses that he may have glimpsed the real motive impelling the Frenchmen. "Messrs. Erlanger & Co. proposed to embark on the speculation on a much more extended scale." Agents of Erlanger were already on their way to Richmond, he added, and "will arrive before this despatch." The Erlanger companions, who landed in due course, caused no excitement in the Confederate capital. In fact, very few people knew anything of their presence. Mrs. Chestnut, who met all visitors worth meeting, made no entry concerning these gentlemen; the curious Jones, who would have been unusually garrulous had he known that great French bankers, bearing large quantities of gold credits to a sadly depleted Treasury, had invaded Richmond, maintained a portentous silence. The fact is that the negotiation was put through with the utmost secrecy. Congress ratified the loan behind closed doors; not a word concerning it appeared in the local press, and the people of the Confederate States heard nothing of it until the subscription books were opened in London and Paris. Though Memminger was not entirely ignored — his signature necessarily appeared in the contracts — the chief intermediary for the Confederate Government was Benjamin. It proved to have been a wise substitution. The conflict of these two Jewish

[1] *Official Records of Union and Confederate Navies*, Vol. 3, Series II, p. 568.

brains — Benjamin and Erlanger — caused modification very beneficial to the Confederate Government. Benjamin at once saw through the whole scheme; it was a cotton speculation, he declared, not a bona fide loan, and rather astonished his compatriots at first by opposing it. He denounced the interest rate and finally screwed Erlanger down from 8 to 7 per cent. He objected to 70 as the price at which Erlanger was to purchase the bonds, and succeeded in elevating this to 77. Benjamin also declared that an issue of $25,000,000 was too large, and disappointed Erlanger by cutting it down to $15,000,000.

The truth is that Benjamin was opposed to the whole business, even with these amendments. On its own merits, he insisted, he would have advised a rejection. Except for one consideration, advanced by Slidell, he would have sent Erlanger back to Paris, his mission unfulfilled. "We would have declined it altogether," he wrote, "but for the political considerations indicated by Mr. Slidell, on whose judgment in such matters we are disposed to place very great confidence." What he evidently meant was that this loan would stimulate the campaign for recognition, then at high tide. He believed that the crowd of government speculators always surrounding Napoleon would be stirred to new zeal in behalf of the Confederacy. Much as the French Government favored this loan, there was one thing that it refused to do. Despite their pro-Confederate sentiments, the fact remained that France and the United States still maintained diplomatic relations, and financial activity on behalf of "rebels" clearly contravened international comity. Drouyn de Lluys, French Foreign Secretary, therefore warned Slidell that the loan must not be advertised in the newspapers; all his publicity efforts must be limited to circulars. Erlanger took the issue directly to the Emperor, who overruled his Foreign Minister. Thus, in violation of law, advertisements of the Confederate loan appeared in the Paris press. "I mention this," wrote Slidell to Benjamin, "as offering renewed evidence of the friendly feeling of the Emperor." [2] It did indeed, and it also lent color to certain suspicions of Napoleon's motives, already intimated. Indeed, that his private secretary, Mocquard, had subscribed to the loan was a matter of general report in Paris.[3]

Almost simultaneously with the opening of subscription books, the younger Erlanger led Miss Matilda Slidell to the altar. One of the most cheering features of the marriage celebration was the "brilliant success" of the offering. In London especially investors hastened to the bankers to enter their names. Many did so in order to display their sympathy with the Confederate cause; in fact, several of the leading Tories and noblemen of Great Britain testified in this way — and, as it turned out, to their pecuniary loss — to their hopes for the speedy collapse of the great Republic. Others, regarding the destruction of Federal power as assured, feverishly seized this opportunity to acquire marketable cotton at bargain rates. Hardly had the subscription books closed, when another great military triumph apparently justified their optimism. The subscription books were opened to investors on March 18; about five weeks afterward came the battle of Chancellorsville, a crowning humiliation to Federal arms. By the evening of the first day the loan was oversubscribed; in a week the demand reached $80,000,000 though only $15,000,000 had been put on sale. Purchasers appeared not only in England and France, but in all parts of Europe. Mason, Confederate agent in London, announced that one subscription came "even from Trieste"; as this Adriatic port was the home of Maximilian, then meditating his attack on the Mexican throne, this was perhaps a guarded way of including him among the bondholders. Naturally an atmosphere of jubilation enveloped Confederate headquarters in Paris and London. "You will, before this despatch can reach you," wrote Slidell to Benjamin, "have seen by the newspapers the brilliant success of Erlanger

---

[2] *Official Records of Union and Confederate Navies*, Vol. 3, Series II, p. 719.
[3] See *Lest We Forget* by John Bigelow, Jr, p. 7.

and his loan. The affair has been admirably managed, and cannot fail to exercise a most salutary influence on both sides of the Atlantic. It is a financial recognition of our independence, emanating from a class proverbially cautious and little given to be influenced by sentiment or sympathy."[4] "I think I may congratulate you," wrote Mason, March 30, "on the triumphant success of our infant credit; it shows, malgré all detraction and calumny, that cotton is King at last."[5]

Erlanger issued the bonds to the public at 90; as he had underwritten them at 77, his "spread," as modern bankers would say, gave him a profit of thirteen points. When quotations presently rose to 95½ — the highest ever attained — great riches seemed to have fallen into his lap. But soon something happened. The Mason and Slidell reports to Benjamin presently lose a little of their triumphant ring. Their confidence in the outcome is still expressed, but not so exultingly. The distressing fact was that prices for Confederate bonds, soon after this auspicious beginning, began to fall. On April 9 Mason recorded that the loan was fluctuating from day to day "with a depressing tendency, until in a single day it dropped 2 to 2½ per cent, closing that day from 4 to 4½ per cent discount." M. Emile Erlanger appeared somewhat disconsolately in his office. The Frenchman had an explanation for this unexpected turn. "The Erlangers, with their advisers in London, came to me and represented that it was very manifest that agents of the Federal government here and those connected with them by sympathy and interest were making concerted movements covertly to discredit the loan by large purchases at low rates, and, succeeding to some extent, had thus invited the formation of a 'bear' party, whose operations, unless checked by an exhibition of confidence strongly displayed might and probably would bring down the stock before settlement day (April 24) to such low rates

[4] *Official Records of Union and Confederate Navies*, Vol. 3, Series II, p. 721.
[5] *Ibid*, p. 730.

as would alarm holders and might in the end lead a large portion of them to abandon their subscriptions by a forfeiture of the instalments (15 per cent) so far paid." [6] The Erlanger accusation proved to be not entirely groundless. Naturally Mr. Adams in London and Mr. Dayton and John Bigelow in Paris had not been uninterested observers of this attempt to bolster Confederate credit in Europe. Anything they could do to circumvent this effort was clearly regarded as their duty as representatives of the United States. There is a pointed passage in a letter written about this time by Mr. Bigelow, then consul general in Paris, subsequently Minister to France. Mr. Bigelow's duties as consul general were merely a cloak to hide his real activities — which were to act as a kind of "publicity man" for the Federal Government, to guide the French press in an accurate understanding of the American crisis, to serve as a foil to Henry Hotze, who was fulfilling this task most ably for the Confederates. Mr. Bigelow's comments on this fiscal enterprise were not over-complimentary. He denounced the whole thing as a "swindling transaction" and his opinion of the Erlangers, whom he called "the midwives of the loan," were not more flattering. In a communication to Seward, April 17, 1863, he put his finger on one possibly vulnerable joint in the finance of Mr. Jefferson Davis. "I am surprised that no one ever thought of collecting the evidence of J. Davis' counsel in favor of repudiating the Mississippi debt. Slidell has contradicted the statement and there is no means on this side of the Atlantic of proving it. I think it will be worth whatever trouble it may involve to accumulate all the evidence and lay it before the public with as little delay as possible." [7]

Mr. Seward was not slow in adopting Bigelow's suggestion. Soon Robert J. Walker, an ex-Secretary of the Treasury of the United States, and an accomplished student of economics

---

[6] *Official Records of Union and Confederate Navies*, Vol 3, Series II, p. 736.
[7] *Recollections of an Active Life*, by John Bigelow, Vol. I, p. 642.

and finance, began flooding the London newspapers with letters on "Davis, the Repudiator" — setting forth how the President of the Confederacy, as a Senator from Mississippi, had publicly defended the action of that state in defaulting on its bonds, and described those who bewailed their losses as guilty of "crocodile tears." As most of the sufferers were English investors, the airing of this episode hardly helped the Erlanger loan. Seldom has a press campaign proved so effective. Events were also facilitating Walker's campaign. That recognition of Southern independence on which the Erlangers had rested hopes of a speedy end of the war had not been forthcoming. The military situation, after the terrible reverse at Chancellorsville, again suddenly changed in favor of the North. Grant, who for several months had been pounding away vainly at Vicksburg, was now actually making progress. Lee was beginning preparations for his disastrous invasion of Pennsylvania, much to the misgivings of his admirers. These circumstances, and above all the Walker revelations, had reduced Erlanger to panic. Drastic measures, he pleaded, must be adopted to save the rapidly dwindling Confederate credit. And now ensued the most picturesque chapter in the history of this ill-fated loan.

3

International Finance

The plight of Erlanger et Cie can be readily understood. They had pledged themselves to take the entire $15,000,000 at 77 — a speculation of something more than $11,000,000. So long as the bonds were being quoted at 90 and more, and so long as the fortunes of the Confederacy were smoothly sailing, this contract was all very well. When the issue began to fall on the stock exchange, with the likelihood that it would drop far below 77, the prospect of great profit was not so glittering. Financiers have discovered only one way of checking the debacle when securities like these start on the decline. That is to speculate in their own stocks. A huge buying campaign is the one possible method of stemming the downward rush. Such expedients are hazardous and expensive and Erlanger had no stomach for risking his own property in such an adventure. But there were certain bank deposits that might be used. Subscribers to the Confederate bonds had paid considerable installments on their subscriptions and the money was lying in foreign banks to the credit of Mr. Memminger's department. Could this not be advantageously used to counteract the machinations of unscrupulous Yankees? It was true that trusting Englishmen — for most of the purchasing had taken place in London — had paid this hard cash largely out of sympathy with the Southern cause and might be shocked at its being used to boost artificially their investment on the Stock Exchange. But there was no reason why they should know anything about it. "All this thing," Mr. Mason wrote Benjamin, describing the buying campaign, "is, of course, done in confidence." There are evidences that, at Erlanger's blunt suggestion, Mason was a little shocked. "I confess I was at first," he wrote Benjamin, "exceedingly averse to it." He called in Slidell and expressed his reluctance to use Confederate money — and his Government had so little! — in market operations of the kind. But presently the Erlanger group began to use other than soothing arguments. Mr. Shroeder, the Erlanger representative in London, observing this delicacy about using subscribers' funds to "strengthen" their own securities, resorted to threats. If the Confederate agents declined to enter into this scheme, then Erlanger et Cie would withdraw from the whole proceeding, and close the subscription books. At that time the first installment, about $2,000,000 already paid in, did not belong to the Confederacy, — so Mason and Slidell were informed — but to the bankers; it represented part of the commissions they had been guaranteed. If, as the firm now intimated, the enterprise should be abandoned, naturally the money already in bank would become the property of the Paris bankers.

A meeting took place, those present being Erlanger, Mason, Slidell, and James Spence, an English adviser of the Confederacy, who hated the Frenchmen and denounced them as little better than swindlers. Spence put up a heroic fight, but Mason and Slidell gave way to their exactions. An understanding was reached, under which it was agreed that "if the market opened after the Easter recess under the same depression, the government [that is, the Confederate government] should buy through Erlanger and Company, but of course without disclosing the real party in the market, in the manner indicated." [8] This written contract, signed by J. M. Mason, for the Confederacy, and Emile Erlanger & Company and H. Hamberger, may be read to-day in the official records of the Confederacy, published by the United States.[9] The "Whereases" are uncommonly piquant. They recite that "various parties have set themselves to depressing the loan in the market by circulating rumors, by selling large amounts for future delivery and by other machinations in order to alarm the holders and if possible to drive them to abandon the loan," and that this plot has succeeded so well "that, if unresisted, it may have a disastrous effect on the interest of the government and the bondholders." Therefore Erlanger et Cie are empowered to expend $5,000,000 of Confederate money in an attempt to rig the market.

In two days Erlanger paid out $2,000,000 to "strengthen" the bonds. This succeeded in advancing the issue one or two points. Ultimately about $6,000,000 was poured into the buying campaign. It all came from the subscribers who bought the bonds. The result should have been foreseen in advance. Through several weeks the experience was the same. The

[8] Mason to Benjamin, *Official Records of Union and Confederate Navies*, Vol. 3, Series II, p. 736.
[9] Mason to Benjamin, *Official Records of Union and Confederate Navies*, Vol. 3, Series II, p. 738.

days when the Confederacy was purchasing its own bonds, those securities remained "firm," and even went up a trifle; the moment this support was withdrawn, they went down. Had "the government" possessed an inexhaustible supply of cash, it could have kept prices up indefinitely. But its "stabilization fund" was limited. And, about the time this golden fountain dried up, other circumstances, more destructive than Walker's contributions to the press, or the "raids" of Federal "bears," dealt Confederate finance a terrible blow. These were the battles of Gettysburg, Vicksburg, and Port Hudson. Henry Hotze, the very clever and very frank Confederate publicity man in London, described the effect of these Southern disasters. "When the last lingering doubts about the events on the Mississippi were removed," he wrote to Benjamin,[10] "and no hope remained of Lee again turning upon the enemy, the loan, despite the utmost exertions of its friends, fell with accelerating velocity, until it touched the unprecedented depth of 36, though only for a moment. . . . You may be sure that Federal agents did not fail to avail themselves of this trepidation, and it is stated positively by those who have means of knowing that large sums of money are freely exercised to injure the credit of the Confederacy. You have here, in the tremulous condition of the loan, a sufficiently accurate description of the state of public opinion." We know now that the Federal victories of 1863 destroyed the Confederacy. They also annihilated what was left of Confederate credit. In particular they cast the Erlanger loan into a disrepute from which it never emerged.

Scholars in Confederate finance have little difficulty in uncovering the real facts in the Erlanger loan and the stock market operations associated with it. Erlanger was not so simple as to believe that a purchasing campaign of a few million dollars would restore permanently Confederate credit. This was not his real motive for browbeating Mason and

[10] *Official Records of Union and Confederate Navies*, Vol. 3, Series II, p. 875.

Slidell into embarking on such an enterprise. At bottom his interest did not lie with the Confederacy and the solidifying of its standing was not the cause nearest his heart. John Christopher Schwab, for many years Professor of Economics at Yale, the most authoritative student of Confederate finance, discovered, after a painstaking study of the Erlanger loan, only one party who found it profitable. That was the banking house of Erlanger et Cie. Matilda Slidell's father-in-law emerged from the transaction with gains not far from $2,700,000.[11] Of the total receipts, according to Professor Schwab, "about $6,000,000" was "squandered in bulling the London market with no lasting effect upon the standing of the bonds."[12] Yet certain speculators did profit from these essays on the Exchange. Erlanger et Cie again! For Professor Schwab was convinced that the bonds they were exchanging for what was left of the Confederate gold supply were their own. The real motive for the famous contract with the gullible Mason and the shrewder Slidell was to sell back to the Confederacy a good proportion of the securities they had underwritten at 77. "They are certainly open to the grave suspicion," says Professor Schwab, "of having themselves been large holders of the bonds in question, especially in view of the presumably large amount of lapsed subscriptions, and of having quietly unloaded them on the unsuspecting Confederate agents when the market showed signs of collapsing."[13] Thus $6,000,000 of the Confederacy's receipts vanished in this desperate attempt to "strengthen" the issue. That left Mr. Memminger about $5,500,000 in gold, but large amounts of this disappeared in the shape of a bewildering array of bankers' commissions and other contractual perquisites — and the bankers, of course, were Erlanger et Cie. It is a fair estimate that the Confederate Treasury obtained about $2,500,000 from a bond issue for which it had pledged payment to the extent

[11] *The Confederate States of America*, John Christopher Schwab, p. 36.
[12] *The same*, p 35.
[13] *The same*, p. 35.

of $15,000,000 in capital and seven per cent in interest. On this basis the French bankers and the Confederate Government realized almost the same cash returns, which must be regarded as an historic curiosity in international finance.

The real losers were the purchasers of the bonds, mostly English sympathizers with the Confederacy. In the treasure chests of many of the greatest English families Confederate bonds repose to-day, souvenirs of a curious episode in British-American relations. Their many attempts to realize on these securities — at times going to such grotesque extremes as appeals to the Federal Government to redeem them — form one of the minor tragedies of the Civil War.

IX

JAMES MURRAY MASON

1

A Virginian in the Making

THE respective rôles played by Mason and Slidell in this stockjobbing operation — one the dupe and the other the wire puller — were thoroughly in character. They accord well with the description of these gentlemen current at the time. Mason was honest, obtuse, and blundering, Slidell shrewd, able, and unscrupulous — such seems to have been the opinion of both friend and foe. "Mason was the personification of insolence, Slidell of craft" — so ran a newspaper comment of the time. "Mason was ardent, impetuous and arrogant," remarked that Connecticut Yankee, Gideon Welles, "Slidell crafty and designing." The writings of the Adams family, during the Civil War and afterward, are sprinkled with adjectives of similar tenor. Mason "lacked the finesse of Slidell," according to Charles Francis, American Minister to England; according to his son and namesake, Mason was "a dull-witted Virginian" and Slidell "an acute, intriguing Louisianan," while Henry Adams, his father's secretary, expresses his astonishment, in his *Education*, that Mr. Davis "chose Mr. Mason as his agent in London at the same time that he made so good a choice as Mr. Slidell in Paris."[1]

These are the opinions of enemies, but the appraisement of friends does not greatly differ. Mrs. Chestnut treats the eminent Virginian with contempt. "My wildest imagination will not picture Mr. Mason as a diplomat," she recorded, when news of the appointment reached Richmond. "He will

[1] *Education of Henry Adams*, p. 184.

say 'chaw' for 'chew' and he will call himself 'Jeems' and he will wear a dress coat to breakfast. Over here whatever a Mason does is right in his own eyes. He is above law. Someone asked him how he pronounced his wife's maiden name; she was a Miss Chew from Philadelphia. They say the English will like Mr. Mason; he is so manly, so straightforward, so truthful and bold."[2]

The spiteful but entertaining lady tells of an argument with Russell, of the London *Times*, who insisted that Mason and his colleague in the United States Senate, Hunter, were the most admirable of the Southern leaders. "Now you just listen to me," Mrs. Chestnut retorted. "Is Mrs. Davis in hearing? No? Well, this sending Mr. Mason to London is the maddest thing yet. Worse in some points of view than Yancey and that was a catastrophe."[3]

"A fine old English gentleman," Russell insisted, "but for tobacco." This reservation concerns that free rumination of the quid quite general with Southern statesmen — and by no means unknown at the North. Mason's tobacco-chewing, indeed, has passed into legend. Anecdotes from malicious Yankees floated across the Atlantic describing ambassadorial expectorations on the floor of the House of Commons, and other inappropriate shrines.

Clearly, these disjointed vignettes do not comprise the complete picture. Russell was as vindictive in his comments on Southerners as on Northern men, and his judgment of Mason must be placed alongside these unfriendly sketches. The *Times* man discussed the new-made diplomat with William Porcher Miles of South Carolina. "We agreed perfectly. In the first place, he has a noble presence — really a handsome man; is a manly old Virginian, straightforward, brave, truthful, clever, the very beau ideal of an independent high-spirited F. F. V. If the English value a genuine man they will have

[2] *Dairy from Dixie*, p. 116.
[3] *The same*, 117.

one here. In every particular he is the exact opposite of Talleyrand. He has some peculiarities."

Yet Russell was not consistent in his treatment of Mason. He greeted the appointment of Mason and Slidell with comments in the London *Times* that made unpleasant reading for the friends of both of these statesmen. He had his own solution for the problem that puzzled Mrs. Chestnut and her coterie. Why had Davis selected this not overtactful gentleman as his envoy to England? Mainly, wrote the journalist, to get rid of him. "It is not too much to suppose that he sent them [Mason and Slidell] on their mission because they were in his way. Mr. Mason is a man of considerable belief in himself; he is a proud, well-bred, not unambitious gentleman, whose position gave him the right to expect high office, for which in some respects he was unfitted at home, where his manners, his accomplishments and his knowledge of society, as well as his moderation of opinion in reference to the merits of other systems of government, were well suited for a foreign mission. Mr. Slidell, whom I had the pleasure of meeting in New Orleans, is a man of more tact and is not inferior to his colleague in other respects. He far excels him in subtlety and depth and is one of the most consummate masters of political manoeuvre in the States. He is a man who unseen moves the puppets on the public stage as he lists, a man of iron will and strong passions, who loves the excitement of combinations and who in his dungeon, or whatever else it may be, would conspire with the mice against the cat rather than not conspire at all." [4]

Most references to James Murray Mason describe him as "an old-fashioned Virginian," a kind of eighteenth-century survival, the embodiment of the qualities and manners that made the word "Virginian" a distinctive force in the American evolution. The fact is that Mason was an "old-fashioned Virginian" in an even more authentic sense. He was one of

[4] London *Times*, December 10, 1861.

those rare phenomena in "cavalier Virginia" — a veracious "cavalier." Modern Virginia historians have destroyed the "cavalier" tradition in its most extravagant form. The idea once widely prevalent in the Old Dominion that Virginia was chiefly "Anglo-Norman" in its population and New England more rustically "Anglo-Saxon" — one derived from ruling lords of the old country, the other from their conquered churls — no longer prevails. Agreement is general now that the settlers of both North and South represented, in the main, the same social classes; they were city merchants, even artisans and landless country folk looking for acres of their own. While this general statement is true, it is true also that a small number of "cavaliers" in the proper understanding of that term — followers of the King in the civil wars, and well-born officers in the Royal army — did flee for safety to Virginia after the triumph of Cromwell and establish families on the Potomac and the James. One of them was that John Washington whose name is not inconspicuous in American history; another was Colonel George Mason, member of Parliament in the reign of Charles I and commander of a regiment of the Royal army at the battle of Worcester. Here we apparently have a genuine "cavalier." Honors in plenty came to this George Mason in colonial Virginia, but his chief glory is that he was grandfather of the celebrated George Mason of Gunston Hall. Virginians have long regarded this philosopher — author of the Fairfax Resolves, of the first Virginia constitution, and of that immortal Bill of Rights, incorporated in large part in the first ten amendments to the Federal Constitution — as one of their three or four leading publicists. He has gained an almost ambiguous fame for his work in the Philadelphia Convention; after playing a determinative rôle in framing the Constitution Mason refused to sign it and exerted all his influence in the Virginia Convention to prevent its adoption.

The reasons for this independent behavior have considerable interest in viewing the career of his grandson, the Confederate envoy to Great Britain. The Federal Constitution, in the opinion of the master of Gunston, sinned in two ways. It recognized slavery and (for a stipulated period) the slave trade. Nothing seemed quite so evil, in the estimation of this Virginian, as the enslavement of the black man. He declined to put his name to an instrument that condoned it. In the second place, the Constitution flouted his fundamental gospel of the supremacy of the states. He wanted no "consolidated" union to take the place of those little republics which he regarded as the guardians of supreme sovereign power. His grandson, James Murray Mason, companion of Slidell in Confederate diplomacy, loyally adopted the second article in this ancestral creed, but abandoned the first. He proved true to his grandfather's teaching by becoming one of the strictest of strict constructionists, but sadly departed from George Mason's humanitarianism by adopting, in its extremest form, the new Southern gospel of slavery extension. Those two ideas comprised the basis of a political life extending over more than thirty years. The fierceness with which Mason sponsored them transformed him into a hero of the advanced school of Southern rights, and at the same time made him in Northern circles almost the most odious figure in American public life. Probably his relationship to George Mason intensified his unpopularity in New England. The orator of slavery, the author of the fugitive-slave law, the foe of the Compromise of 1850, the advocate of slavery extension to Oregon and California, the preacher of Secession at a time when most Southerners rejected it and when most Virginians recoiled from the proposal in horror, the apologist of Bully Brooks for his assault on Sumner, the leader of Virginia disruption in 1861 — such was James M. Mason's record in part, and New England moralists felt an eloquent disgust that this man should be the grandson of the gentle spokesman of liberty, human equality, and freedom for the blacks in 1787. Mason had added the vice of apostasy to doctrines in themselves detestable! This feeling explains the hosanna of joy that swept the country north of the Potomac when Mason, with his confreres, was seized on board the British packet *Trent* and taken to Fort Warren, Boston, as prisoner of war. The Union had bagged the most abhorrent of its enemies! The emotions described by Charles Francis Adams, Jr., in his *Autobiography* were felt in every Northern breast. He tells of a freezing walk in November, soon after the historic seizure. "In sleet and snow, in chilling winds and under cheerless skies, my spirits rose as I walked to and from the railroad station (for we were still at Quincy, and my walk to the train was over the hill and commanded a full view of Boston Bay) and looked at the low, distant walls of Fort Warren, surrounded by the steel blue sea, and reflected that those amiable gentlemen were there, and there they would remain! I remembered the last exhibition I saw Mason make of himself in the Senate Chamber, and I smacked my lips with joy."[5]

As prophecy, this outburst proved unfortunate — for Mason and Slidell suffered durance for only a brief period — but the passage is priceless as a picture of the New England resentment at a grandson of George Mason who had proved faithless to that statesman's great ideal. Mason spent many boisterous years in public life before he attained this eminence of hatred. His early Virginia existence flowed quietly in the most charming Virginia tradition. Born in 1792, at Georgetown, he alternated his winters at that pleasant suburb with his summers at Analostan Island in the Potomac, not far from Gunston Hall. The "island," as it always affectionately figured in his recollections, formed part of the patrimony which his father had inherited from the illustrious George. It was a complete plantation on the most approved eighteenth-century model. Like all of the Potomac "manors," it made an

[5] Charles Francis Adams, *Autobiography*, pp. 127–128.

economic entity in itself. Across the water stood Gunston with all its varied intimations of democracy and the ancient regime — a favorite rendezvous of Washington, birthplace of many of the impulses and concepts that found lodgment in the Constitution. James Mason's father, fourth son of the great colonial thinker, inherited not only this splendid estate but the love of country life that formed so large a part of the Virginia character. George Mason, the father, in manners, tastes, and associations was no Democrat — any more than was his fellow philosopher, Thomas Jefferson. He believed in books, in tobacco planting, in friendship, in genial companionship with his equals; and he also believed in birth and landed estates. He had complete confidence in Virginia and assumed that his beloved state had qualities of leadership not discernible elsewhere. It was in this conviction that James Murray Mason was born and nurtured.

Despite this loyalty to everything lying south of the Potomac, James Murray went north of that boundary for the two most important things in any man's existence, his education and his wife. Both he obtained in Philadelphia. The University of Pennsylvania endowed him with one, conferring its bachelor's degree in 1818; the important Philadelphia family of Chew gave him the other. In selecting his sphere of action, Mason showed independence again; first of his line to abandon Tidewater, he migrated, soon after marriage and an apprenticeship in law, to the distant city of Winchester, in western Virginia. This town, of which much was to be heard in Civil War days, was then standing guard at the head of the Shenandoah, almost a frontier outpost; this fact opened a promising prospect to a young man who, abandoning the family habit of tobacco growing — the Potomac soil was rapidly thinning — tempted fortune in the practice of law. In his profession Mason had considerable success; his modest home, Selma, presently became a social center; an accomplished wife and a large family of children provided the domestic delight, which, for several years, seemed to be his chief interest. But Mason, though he had abandoned the family environment, did not prove false to its traditions. Even in this new country the political prerogatives of certain clans was unquestioned. Masons for generations had represented their counties in the Virginia House of Burgesses — now House of Delegates — and James Murray was fond of reading the Congressional *Globe* and following the ups and downs of state concerns in the Legislature. In this latter body, in his thirtieth year, he appeared as member for Frederick County. His career as lawmaker was independent and creditable, but brief. In 1829 Mason appropriately appeared as a member of the Virginia Constitutional Convention called to modernize the document which his grandfather had put together in 1776. From that day he was one of the reigning political favorites of a large part of the state. He served one term in Congress, and when, in 1847, Senator Pennypacker died, the Governor appointed him to the vacancy. And with his entrance in the Federal Senate, Mason's real career began.

2

The Virginia Claim to Superiority

At this time he was forty-nine years old; he remained in continuous service in the upper chamber until his expulsion by the angry brethren amid the disturbances of 1861. In this body Mason upheld for fourteen years, at times unpleasantly, the cherished Virginia pretension. He was the most arrogant embodiment of the Virginia claim to superiority in the science and amenities of government. The man was really a throwback from the eighteenth century; he revivified the "barons" of the Potomac and the James, enemies of the "levelers" who took seriously the Declaration of Independence. James Murray Mason and his confreres were arrayed against the proletarian tide, especially that which was rising in the large cities of the North. Trade and manufacturing they regarded as unworthy the interest of gentlemen; even agriculture in general they looked down upon, unless it involved so distinguished a product as tobacco; recently they had condescended to include cotton as fairly respectable, but they still regarded the word "planter" as only properly applied to the grower of the noble weed. Aristocracies may lose wealth, prestige, and influence, but there is one thing that they do not lose, or do so only gradually and protestingly. That is pride. And pride, even "hauteur," burned as fiercely in the breast of Virginia statesmen in 1850 as in 1789. The political power which they had lost remained a pretension to which they persistently clung. Their leaders regarded Northerners as presumptuous upstarts, usurpers of the lofty heights that belonged in justice south of the Potomac. To those who take psychology as a potent force in history, the influence of this insulted dignity on developments preceding the Civil War should be a most suggestive study. Someone has said that Virginia, in the decades from 1830 to 1860, had two choices — to become the tail of the North or the head of the South; and it would be a simple matter to show how, in culture, intellect, manners, and statesmanship the best classes in Virginia had more in keeping with the Brahmins of New England than with that uncouth Southwest with which, after much hesitation, it cast its fortunes. But logic did not exclusively direct sectional policy in this era. Ordinary human emotions — grief at vanished glory, anger at the refusal of North and West to concede cavalier precedence, and fear of ultimate submergence — played an important part. The mental state of political Virginia was one of insistence on its capacity to lead and protest against a growing national tendency to ignore that claim. The mere fact that Mason became a Senator evidences this state of mind. The magic of his name, rather than inherent ability, explains his election. That name symbolized Virginia's past and the yearning of

Virginians for a revival. James Murray well embodied this pride and hope. Physically he looked the part. Tall, large-framed, dignified, if slightly pompous in bearing, with a fine leonine head, from which, on the sides, reached out huge billows of gray hair; a face half questioning, half friendly; kindly though almost suspicious blue eyes; a tight slit of a mouth and a small feminine chin — the expansive features well accorded with the old Potomac background. Even as cordial a hater as Charles Francis Adams, Jr., conceded this. "Mason, of Virginia," he writes of a visit to Congress in 1860, "afterwards my father's vanquished opponent in London, also attracted my attention from the first, — a large, handsome man, not unpleasant to look at, as dressed ostentatiously in Virginia homespun, he appeared to own the Senate Chamber." But Adams also found him "overbearing to the last degree, self-sufficient and self-assertive."[6] Very serious he was — his daughter lists among the books, gifts of Bishop Meade, which Mason used to read to his wife, such tomes as *The Philosophy of True Religion, The Power of Religion on the Mind;* his lighter gifts included a small talent at playing the flute; like a good Virginian he loved horses and was a skillful rider, and he loved to work in his garden and chop down trees. But, despite occasional references to a "hearty laugh," humor and gayety did not much disturb his sober thought.

The new Senator's debut was most Masonian. His reverence for the Constitution immediately appeared. What more natural? Was not his grandfather to a considerable degree its author? But his allegiance was especially unyielding to the first ten amendments. These were the revered articles that had prevented the Constitution from being the "consolidated" despotism that Hamilton and Madison had planned, and had made it a compact of sovereign states. And of all the life-saving amendments Mason hugged most closely to his

[6] *Autobiography*, p. 47.

bosom immortal Article X. "The powers not delegated to the United States by the Constitution, nor prohibited by it to the States, are reserved to the States respectively, or to the people." On that rock rested the whole doctrine of State rights.

But it was Mason's slavery worship that explained the odium which his name quickly acquired in other sections. For there was nothing gentle in his advocacy. The epithets most frequently attached to him in the literature of the time are "arrogant," "presumptuous," "overbearing." Mason held few slaves himself, but that was because he lived in the western section of Virginia. His devotion to the idea grew intenser as years went on. Here again his motives were not strictly philosophic. He adopted the new slavery dogma because it was Southern and because it aroused hostility in the North. He wished to see the nation expand on the basis of Southern, not Northern culture. In every situation that arose from 1847 to 1861 his proslaveryism, hypersensitive to every whiff of public opinion, immediately sprang into life. The visit of Louis Kossuth inspired from him a flood of vituperation. Most Senators — even Southern Senators — left their cards when that patriot came to Washington. Mason was one of the few exceptions. Congress gave the Revolutionary leader a banquet, but Mason refused to attend. What was the great man's sin? Merely that he had expressed an opinion that slavery was an evil. Mason was one of the most intemperate advocates of "the positive good" in Kansas, his Kansas speech proving to be about the most ferocious which that bleeding territory called forth. In 1850, the year of the Compromise, Mason did not ally himself with Toombs, Yancey, Stephens, Howell Cobb, and many more of the great Southern chieftains. He joined the Rhetts and other obscurantists in fighting the bills. He would not surrender an inch on slavery extension in order to save the Union, and contemptuously uttered his "disgust" with fellow Southerners who showed a more complaisant mood. The real reason was that Mason, even at this early day, cared nothing for a Union that had repudiated the leadership of Virginia. He was ready for Secession in 1850; six years afterward he openly advocated it. In case of Fremont's election, Mason's programme, loudly proclaimed, was "secession immediate, absolute and eternal."

Naturally these sentiments received even more emphatic expression during the Lincoln campaign. Mason was one of the first to hail South Carolina's defection, declaring that that act made the United States of America a thing of the past. His most conspicuous act of legislation proved an embarrassment in his career as ambassador. He was the author of the Fugitive Slave Law. In view of these activities, his personal associations in Washington caused no surprise. He became a member of Calhoun's "mess" soon after reaching Washington, and one of the numerous candidates for that great man's "mantle" after his decline. James Murray was the disciple Calhoun selected to speak this final allocution. In the presence of that spectral figure the Virginian sonorously intoned this testament of Southern protest and foreboding. But the younger man had characteristics not derived from his high-minded preceptor. He embellished Calhoun's doctrines of sectionalism and secession with a bitterness that was all his own. This appears especially in his dislike of New England. He was a follower of Robert Young Hayne in his feeling on this score — without Hayne's ability and oratorical power. This despite the fact that New England now and then made a tender of good feeling. Thus, in 1857, on the dedication of a monument to Joseph Warren at Bunker Hill, Mason was invited to be one of the speakers. His appearance on that occasion aroused dissonant emotions. He spoke appreciatively of Warren and Revolutionary New England, but he also used this rostrum as the scene for delivering a eulogy on State rights. Those disgruntled natives who thought it "sycophantic" to invite the author of the Fugitive Slave Law to grace this festival insisted that their worst apprehensions had been justified. But the cordiality of his reception in Boston did not increase Mason's love for Yankee-land. New Englanders, in his view, had no political principles and no political talents; their leaders he looked upon as hucksters, concerned only with trade; their more modest citizens were mere artificers, engaged in manual labor. To such a community statesmanship was alien; it needed Southerners — above all, Virginians — to show it the ways of government. This was Mason's first visit to New England and his last. An invitation that came some years afterward led him to indulge in the strangest of prophecies. No, he said, he would not go to New England a second time; he would never visit that country again except in the guise of an ambassador. No forecast was ever more grotesquely fulfilled. A few months after making it Mason was a prisoner in Fort Warren on an island in Boston Harbor; and he was an ambassador, too, in a sense — not, as he anticipated, from the Southern Confederacy to the Northern Republic, but from the Davis Government to the Court of St. James's.

This New England antagonism came into high relief when Mason, in the middle fifties, found himself in close Senatorial propinquity to Charles Sumner. Their personal relations, at first civil enough, soon became torrid. Neither was governed by a compromising temperament and when Sumner, in his omniscient way, started to discuss the black man, immediate signs of discontent were audible from a station not far from his own. Sumner, soon after arrival, announced his intention of introducing an amendment that would repeal the Fugitive Slave Law. When he declared that he would soon speak on this explosive theme the haughty author of that measure, scowling at the foe, shouted, "By God, you shan't!" and, indeed, by the clever manipulation of parliamentary rules, he did prevent the avalanche. But only for a time. This passage served as preliminary to the speeches that preceded the onslaught of Bully Brooks. Reading this debate in the sober light of the present day convinces one that the honors, in the matter of name-calling and invective, were fairly even. The phrases did not materially differ from those that had been cheerfully bandied in the same chamber for several years. Sumner's reference to a drooling impediment in Senator Butler's utterance as "the loose expectoration of his speech," and his criticisms of that statesman for assiduously courting "the harlot slavery" were quite matched by Mason's description of Sumner as "a common artificer and forger"; but the palm for literary expression really must go to the Massachusetts man. Sumner analyzed the defects of the Virginia statesman in more seemly detail. "Among these hostile Senators," he said, "there is yet another, with all the prejudices of the Senator from South Carolina, but without his generous impulses, who, on account of his character before the country and the rancour of his opposition, deserves to be named. I mean the Senator from Virginia [Mr. Mason] who, as author of the Fugitive Slave Bill, has associated himself with a special act of inhumanity and tyranny. Of him I shall say little, for he has said little in this debate, though within that little was compressed the bitterness of a life absorbed in the support of slavery. He holds the Commission of Virginia, but he does not represent that early Virginia, so dear to our hearts, which gave us the pen of Jefferson, by which the equality of men was declared, the sword of Washington, by which independence was secured; but he represents that other Virginia from which Washington and Jefferson now avert their faces, where human beings are held as cattle for the shambles, and where a dungeon awards the pious matron who teaches little children to relieve their bondage by reading the word of life. It is proper that such a Senator, representing such a state, should rail against free Kansas." Mason, in his reply, referred to certain inconveniences of the Senatorial life. One was that "they bring us into relations and associations which, beyond the walls of this chamber, we are enabled to avoid; associations here whose presence elsewhere is dishonor and the touch of whose hand would be a disgrace."

The episode to which these compliments served as prologue — the bludgeoning of Sumner, almost his murder, by the South's avenging angel, Preston Brooks — elicited loud rejoicings south of the Potomac. Many voices subsequently prominent in the Confederacy — Toombs, Jefferson Davis, Mallory, Secretary of the Navy, Slidell, Mason's twin in the foreign field — shouted ululations of praise. Among the most approving was Mason himself. He wrote a widely circulated letter, eulogizing the assailant; when Brooks appeared in court to answer the charge of felonious assault, Mason accompanied him, as friend and moral support. All these details obtained wide circulation in the English press, which, then as now, delighted to report the more barbarous aspects of life in the Great Republic. Perhaps this was one of the reasons why Mrs. Chestnut, on the ground of diplomatic expediency, regarded his appointment as a blunder. It was one of the reasons that made Richard Cobden, when Mason reached London, stigmatize him as "that old slave dealer."

3

ENGLAND AND THE UNITED STATES

In the minds of contemporary Americans, Mason and Slidell signify chiefly one of the most celebrated events in the diplomacy of the nineteenth century. The story is so familiar that it need not detain us long. Sailing, one dark and rainy night, from Charleston, their ship successfully ran the blockade and landed in Cuba in late October. Two weeks afterward they embarked on the *Trent,* a British steam packet bound for Southampton, England. It so happened that Captain Charles Wilkes, of the United States Navy, who was bringing home from Africa one of those Federal warships which the Buchanan Administration had stationed far away from the American coast line, put into a Cuban port at the very time that Mason and Slidell were sojourning in that friendly country. Entirely on his own initiative, Captain Wilkes conceived a bold plan. Stationing his ship in the Bahama Channel, athwart the course of the *Trent,* he stopped that vessel, firing two shots across her bow, sent a searching party aboard, and seized Mason and Slidell as prisoners of war, ultimately depositing them in Fort Warren, Boston Harbor. Seldom has a naval exploit caused such world-wide excitement. Naturally the whole British Empire was ablaze. Lord Palmerston, then in one of his most imperialistic moods, proposed to demand the immediate release of the captives and a groveling apology. The British Navy was mobilized for action and large military forces sent to Canada. The proceeding involved many curious, almost amusing, circumstances. One was that Captain Wilkes, in invading this British ship and seizing these distinguished passengers, had violated international law as always interpreted by the United States. The other was that his act was authorized by British precedents. It was for depredations resembling this, perpetrated by the British Navy against Americans, that the United States declared war on Great Britain in 1812. Again, had Wilkes slightly varied his procedure, England would have had little ground for action. Had he seized the ship itself, instead of violently ripping from it four [7] civilians, and taken it, with all its cargo, human and material, to the nearest American port and handed it over to a prize court, there is little doubt that this would have been regular. For the *Trent* was carrying Confederate despatches, and these, according to the Queen's recent proclamation, were contraband of war. A ship carrying such contraband is subject to search and seizure and adjudication by a prize court. Captain Wilkes's foolhardy behavior brought the United States to the

[7] The other two were the Secretaries to Messrs. Mason and Slidell.

verge of war at a moment when, in the Confederate States, it had about as much trouble of that kind as it could conveniently handle.

Inherently the position of the American Government was not a difficult one. Captain Wilkes had acted entirely on his own responsibility, without orders or the slightest intimation from his Government. Instead of being widely acclaimed as a hero, he should really have been court-martialed. Washington, with no loss of dignity, could have disavowed the seizure and surrendered the prisoners. But the attitude of the British Government at first made this almost impossible. Its demand for restitution, as first framed, was couched in insulting terms, such as no proud nation could accept. Happily that despatch never went beyond the British Foreign Office. Before being sent it was submitted for approval to the Queen. Much fanciful history had been conceived about Her Majesty's intervention. So far no one has unearthed a scrap of evidence showing that Victoria sympathized with the Federals or had the slightest interest in democracy.[8] But that her husband, the Prince Consort, did intervene, and that she acted in accordance with his persuasion, is the fact. Albert spent several hours going over the preliminary draft, blue-penciling its offensive phrases, introducing here and there a conciliatory sentence; the episode derives pathos from his own condition at the time, for the illness from which he died two weeks afterward was already upon him. He himself told the Queen he could barely hold the pen while writing the paper. Instead, therefore, of a browbeating demand, the Lincoln Government received a most friendly message, expressing the British conviction that Captain Wilkes had acted without the knowledge and authority of his Government — which, in truth, was the case — and that therefore the United States would not refuse to release the

---

[8] See the chapter, "Queen Victoria and the Civil War," in *Studies Military and Diplomatic*, by Charles Francis Adams, 2nd (1911). The most authentic account of the rewriting of the *Trent* despatch is found in *The Life of the Prince Consort*, by Sir Theodore Martin, Vol. V, p. 347 *et seq.*

prisoners and give adequate apology. Mr. Lincoln met this request in the same spirit; Mason and Slidell were freed from their "dungeon" in Boston Harbor, delivered to a British warship, and safely transported to their diplomatic posts. The most superb piece of editing in history had prevented a senseless war between Great Britain and the United States, and the gratitude of both nations to the Prince Consort has always been profound. That the outcome was satisfactory to Lord Russell and Palmerston was also true. Both statesmen wished to avoid war with the United States; their policy from the first excluded such a drastic programme and only an open defiance and "insult" from Uncle Sam, such as the seizure of the *Trent*, could move them to hostile action. In that day the "*civis Romanus sum*" principle was the brightest jewel in Britain's diplomatic diadem, and only the violation of this by the United States could produce a menacing gesture from the Foreign Office.

This kidnapping and imprisonment represented the nearest approach Mason and Slidell made to a diplomatic triumph. They had been sent abroad to embroil the United States in war with Great Britain and France; and, without any effort on their part, they came within an inch of succeeding. Locked in their cells in Boston Harbor, they were a terrible menace to the American nation; once landed in London and Paris, their capacity for mischief-making was greatly curtailed. This was evidenced on their arrival in London. They stepped upon the railroad platform unwelcomed and unnoticed, like the most obscure travelers; although their names had filled the press of the world for nearly three months, no one paid the slightest attention to their advent. The whole transaction had left the British people with a sense of irritation. Mason and Slidell were about the most expensive guests who ever crossed the British threshold; their recapture and the military preparations involved had cost the British Exchequer not far from $20,000,000. Possibly this explains the one editorial greeting extended by the British press. The London *Times*, until then an unfailing assailant of the Federal Government, now suddenly veered and vented its loudest thunder against the Confederate envoys.

"How are we to receive these illustrious visitors?" it asked. "Of course they will be stared at and followed and photographed and made the subject of paragraphs. There is no help for that. Messrs. Mason and Slidell, though not so handsome and graceful as their countryman Blondin,[9] would certainly fill the Crystal Palace if they proposed to address the visitors there on the merits of their cause. But we may as well observe that Messrs. Mason and Slidell are about the most worthless booty it would be possible to extract from the jaws of the American lion. They have long been known as the blind haters and revilers of this country. They have done more than any other men to get up the insane prejudice against England which disgraces the morality and disorders the policy of the Union. The hatred of this country has been their stock in trade. In this they have earned their political livelihood and won their position, just as there are others who pander to the lowest passions of humanity. A diligent use of this bad capital has made them what they are and raised them to the rank of commissioners. It is through their lifelong hatred and abuse of England that they come here in their present conspicuous capacity. The nation under whose flag they sought a safe passage across the Atlantic, the nation that has now rescued them with all her might from the certainty of a dungeon, and the chance of retaliating murder, is that against which they have always done their best to exasperate their countrymen. Had they perished in the cell or on the scaffold amid the triumphant yells of the multitude, memory would have suggested that their own bitter tirades had raised the storm and that their death was only the natural and logical conclusion of

---

[9] The famous tight-rope walker, at the time one of the sensations of London. He was a Frenchman, not an American, as the extract implies.

their own calumnies and sophistries. So we sincerely hope that our countrymen will not give these fellows anything in the shape of an ovation. The civility that is due to a foe in distress is all that they can claim. The only reason for their presence in London is to draw us into their own quarrel. The British public has no prejudice in favor of slavery, which these gentlemen represent. What they and their secretaries are to do here passes our experience. They are personally nothing to us. They must not suppose, because we have gone to the verge of a great war to rescue them, that they are precious in our eyes."[10]

This diatribe was not accidental; it unquestionably was inspired by the Government, and represented the official attitude toward two unwished-for guests. Lord Palmerston and Delane, editor of the *Times,* were close friends and confidants, and that paper was frequently used to express informally the real emotions and sentiments of the Cabinet. Mason was unpopular because he stood for something most distasteful to British officialdom. He wished to drag Great Britain into war with the United States. But war was something that Britain did not desire, especially in behalf of a people fighting for slavery. Not that the Government, as a Government, or the ruling classes felt kindly to the American Union. In fact, the inmost sentiments of the governing classes and the aristocracy, as well as those of European royalty, were hostile to the United States. These elements applauded the secession in 1861; in their minds it had freed them of a great international nuisance. Nothing could exceed the jubilation of Tory journals — *Blackwoods,* the *Quarterly Review,* the London *Times,* the *Morning Post* — over the collapse of the greatest experiment in democracy the world had ever known. For the general conviction prevailed that the Confederate guns aimed at Fort Sumter had not only doomed that fortress, but had ended definitely this presumptuous attempt of men to govern themselves.

[10] The London *Times,* January 11, 1862.

This belief that the Union was forever destroyed was that not only of enemies, but of friends. All classes accepted the great American schism as permanent. Unless one grasps the wide extent to which this conviction prevailed, at least until the latter part of 1863, British policy cannot be understood. Those who rejoiced at — or at least were not discomfited by — the debacle of the Union, like Palmerston and Gladstone, and those who bewailed it, like Cobden and John Bright, were agreed on this point. The broken fragments of the United States could never be put together again. In the judgment of most well-wishers to the British empire, it was better so. Voices were indeed raised, such as Cobden's and Bright's, insisting on such fantastic considerations as justice, liberty, enlightened human progress; but these new statesmen did not administer governmental programmes. The attitude of the forces in command was well expressed in a letter written November 20, 1861, by Uncle Leopold, King of Belgium, to his niece, Queen Victoria. He regarded it "as of vital importance to England that there should be two great Republics instead of one, the more so as the South can never be manufacturing and the North, on the contrary, is so already to a great extent and actually in many markets a rival." [11] He had already expressed horror that the Comte de Paris and the Duc de Chartres, grandsons of Louis Philippe, had entered the Federal army and thus exposed themselves "to the chance of being shot for Abraham Lincoln and the most rank radicalism." [12] Here are the two reasons why the aristocracy hailed the American war; it would kill a British business rival and give a blow to popular rule.

The King's commercial view was echoed by Gladstone, who, however, preferred four republics to two, and liked to amuse himself with a map of the United States, drawing the boundaries of his projected new nations. In one respect the United

---

[11] *The Letters of Queen Victoria*, Second Series, Vol. I, p. 48.
[12] *The same*, p. 453.

States was a greater rival to Great Britain in 1861 than it is now. After the Civil War the American flag disappeared so completely from the seas, and Britain's became so preeminent, — as it still is, — that Americans have fairly forgotten the days when their mercantile marine was almost as large as England's. In particular the greater part of the rich transatlantic trade was in the hands of American vessels, and American ships, in beauty and in speed, were the envy of mankind. The extent to which, as a consequence of war, the carrying trade was being shifted to the Union Jack did not displease those Englishmen who took a materialistic view of the contest. A weakened United States meant — or so they thought — an economically stronger England; therefore, from the standpoint of "enlightened egoism," the spectacle of America tearing itself to shreds was not without its compensations.

To-day the world properly regards Great Britain as a great political democracy. But in 1861 it was not a democracy at all. It was not a nation in which the masses possessed and wielded political power. That is to say, they did not vote. So far as the ballot was concerned, England had advanced little beyond the standards of George III. The "great Reform Bill" of 1832 had not widely extended the franchise; it had abolished rotten boroughs and given populous regions representation in Parliament, but the English people, as before, remained without the vote. The ruling powers fought doggedly all movements intended to give city workmen or agricultural laborers any voice in electing members of Parliament. Until 1867, at least 20,000,000 Britons had no representation in the House of Commons; of 7,500,000 men twenty-one years old, less than 1,000,000 could take part in elections. In 1861, great discontent prevailed among the disfranchised majority; it was regarded as a danger that might lead to revolution. The propertied and aristocratic classes looked upon the American Republic as the greatest menace to their power. The "American example" was an ogre that haunted their dreams. For the tremendous success of the United States, its growth in population and territory, in wealth, in general happiness and enlightenment, provided the reformers with a powerful argument for the spread of the same democratic system in England. John Bright, the leader of the rising masses, constantly pointed across the Atlantic. Give Englishmen the vote, and they would correct existing abuses and march side by side with their American brothers in everything that made life worth living! Bright and his associates were even accused of desiring to discard the British Constitution and adopt the Philadelphia instrument of 1787 in its place.

There was only one way of meeting these arguments, and that was by discrediting the American experiment. The travelers' literature published in the half century preceding the Civil War, picturing and exaggerating the faults of the United States and minimizing its virtues, was a part of this campaign. And now, at last, all these dire prophecies had been fulfilled; America had been destroyed by its own vices! No longer would it be heralded as a model for democracy in England. Now Englishmen could see what fate had in store for them should they transform their nation into a republic or even give the people the ballot. Educated Englishmen, wrote Charles Francis Adams, really cared nothing for the South; their "true motive is the fear of the spread of democratic feeling at home in the event of our success." "The real secret of the exultation which manifests itself in the *Times* and other organs over our troubles and disasters," said John Lothrop Motley, "is their hatred, not of America, as much as of democracy in England." The *Morning Post,* Lord Palmerston's favorite organ, struck a similar note, declaring that the triumph of the Union would be the greatest triumph democracy had ever won, while Matthew Arnold echoed the fear that Britain, in case of a Federal victory, would be "Americanized." It was freely foretold at country houses that the success of the North would mean a republic in their own country. That prophecy was not so absurd as it seems; in a modified sense it came true. After Appomattox the demand for the vote became so determined that British Torydom was forced to yield, and, by the law of 1867, began that extension of the franchise which has made Britain as responsive a democracy as is the United States. When Joseph Chamberlain and Sir Charles Dilke, in the seventies, raised the banner of the English Republic, their main argument was the United States which, they declared, had met successfully the greatest test to which any nation can be subjected — that of civil war.

Despite all this, even royalty did not wish intervention. In the first place, this was not necessary to that Federal defeat which the aristocracy so desired. What was to be gained by war with the United States? Indeed, the longer the war went on, the better for Europe, for the longer it lasted, the more would the great transatlantic rival be weakened. There was thus no sense in tempting the dangers that intercession involved. Palmerston, falling back on cheap doggerel, echoed this fear. "Those who in quarrels interpose, are apt to get a bloody nose," he chanted, and he likewise called attention to the proverbial risk one ran in interfering in a fight between husband and wife — that the combatants may temporarily lay aside their differences and jointly pitch upon the interloper. Perhaps Seward was right; an attack by England on America might start such an outburst of national feeling that the Old Country would confront a much larger enemy than she had bargained for. Then there was the British merchant marine. At the first sound of battle, the United States would let loose hundreds of privateers against British commercial ships; Americans had no fears of a counterattack from Britain, for their commerce had already disappeared from the seas. Lord Palmerston had been Secretary at War from 1812 to 1815, the period of America's second war with England; in those three years American privateers had sunk about 2,500 English ships, almost England's entire marine. Palmerston did not care to go through such an experience again; neither did British shipmasters. Canada also represented a formidable hostage to fortune. In 1862, when the question of intervention was uppermost, the United States had a splendidly equipped and trained army of more than 600,000 men; should it detach say 100,000 from Southern camps, and march them across the border, the conquest of Canada, utterly unprepared for war, would have been a simple matter. Gladstone saw this so clearly that he imagined a unique solution for the problem. He meditated a plan of recognizing the Confederacy, and, as appeasement and "compensation" to the Federal Government, offering it the annexation of Canada!

Why run all these dangers when the one thing British Toryism desired above all — the practical destruction of the United States — Americans were themselves so successfully bringing to pass?

X

QUEEN VICTORIA'S "TWO BAD BOYS"

1

Lord Palmerston

THIS purely egoistic conception of foreign policy was well embodied in the two men then dominant in the British Cabinet. Both these statesmen — Lord Palmerston, Prime Minister, and Lord John Russell, Foreign Secretary — were products of the eighteenth century. Palmerston was born in 1784, three years after Yorktown; he was himself five years older than the American Government, if that Government is dated from the inauguration of Washington in 1789. John Russell was born in 1792, and looked upon himself as the inheritor of the political ideas of Pitt, Charles James Fox, and George Canning. Both men derived from the upper aristocracy; Palmerston fell heir to an Irish viscounty at eighteen years of age, while Russell was a cadet of the great ducal house of Bedford. Though frequently antagonistic and unfriendly, Palmerston and Russell stand out in the history of their epoch as political twins. "Pam and Johnny" — so were they known in popular parlance. Queen Victoria, who intensely disliked them both, — for they had a way of disregarding that good lady's desires and thwarting her most cherished plans, — called them her "two bad boys" and delighted in quoting a characterization of the time, which pictured them as "Robin Hood and his Little John." For Russell was as diminutive in size as Palmerston was large; when the former married a widow, London paragraphers began to refer to him as "the widow's mite." To write the lives of these two men would be to relate the history of England for the half century preceding the Civil War. They had the habit of alternating in high position, and this sequence, individualistic as they were, gave them a kind of identity in

James Murray Mason of Virginia
(1798–1871)

John Slidell (1793–1871)

Brown Bros

LORD JOHN RUSSELL (1792–1878)

Brown Photos

VISCOUNT PALMERSTON (1784–1865)

the management of Britain. Both were Prime Minister twice; when Russell held the Premiership, Palmerston was Foreign Secretary; when Palmerston ascended to that post, Russell went to the Foreign Office. Thus, foreign policy, in 1861, was the thing that had always chiefly interested both men; and in reality Mason had to conciliate two Foreign Secretaries instead of one.

Palmerston's absorption was Europe. He knew little about America and cared less. All his associations with American problems, for the previous thirty years, had stimulated this Tory aversion — for Palmerston, in opinions and prejudices, was always an eighteenth-century Tory, despite his party affiliation with the Whigs. As noted above, he retained vivid recollections of the unpleasantness of 1812; and the many disputes between England and America that had followed since had strengthened his view that Americans were bumptious, bad-mannered, persistently insulting to England, overbearing in maintaining their rights, undisposed to yield an inch or to stand in the slightest awe of Britain's power, where their interests were concerned — evincing many of the qualities, indeed, for which Palmerston himself was distinguished. Similarly, he abhorred Seward for a pro-Americanism that could be matched only by his own truculent devotion to the interests of Britain. "The Yankees," he complained, "are most disagreeable fellows to have to do with about any American question." Their land-grabbing propensities — another quality in which "Pam" himself was not deficient — he found irritating. "I have long felt inwardly convinced that the Anglo-Saxon race will in process of time become masters of the whole American continent, North and South. It is not for us to assist such a consummation, but, on the contrary, we ought to delay it as much as possible." He fumed over the Ashburton treaty, denouncing it as the "Ashburton capitulation." Oregon and the disputes that followed — "fifty-four forty or fight," American intrigues in Cuba and Central America — led him to denounce his transatlantic cousins as "swaggering bullies" and to meditate a military campaign against them; the British fleet was to capture Southern ports, conquer the Southern States, and free all the slaves! This meditated John Brown raid, under British auspices, suggests the most praiseworthy explanation for Palmerston's anti-Americanism. It is possible, in this flippant, jovial, reckless statesman to discover at least two passions that burned hotly. One was his worship of the British Empire. His greatest ambition, he once declared, was "to be a good Englishman" and to thwart all attempts to humiliate his country. The other was his hatred of African slavery. One of Palmerston's first acts, as a young Member of Parliament from Cambridge, was to introduce a petition against the slave trade; he championed the movement which, in 1833, led to the emancipation of slaves in British possessions; and, with Lincolnian fervor, he never missed an opportunity "to hit that thing" whenever and wherever it showed its head.

One might think that this would have made Palmerston think kindly of the Federal Government in the pending contest. Such, however, was not the case. Yet his unfriendliness can be easily exaggerated. In fact, it has been. Americans, at that time and afterward, transformed this good-natured opportunist into a kind of monster, spending his nights and days weaving plots for the destruction of the United States. Some of his jibes at the Union army, and especially his characterization of Bull Run as "Yankee's Run," did not increase his popularity in the North. But the facts do not support the once accepted picture of Palmerston as a force constantly intriguing against the Lincoln Government. The most important of them was that, fundamentally, Palmerston had no great interest in the drama. His thoughts were fixed elsewhere. His eyes were cast eastward, not westward; there was plenty to engage his attention in Europe, and America concerned him only as it helped, or hindered, his plans in that direction. Students of the everlasting problem — "why did England not intervene in the American Civil War?" — devote too much attention to the United States; what they should study, above all, is the situation in Europe. It was because a war with the United States would disarrange and probably frustrate Britain's purposes in this, Palmerston's real world, that he had no wish for such an adventure. Southern statesmen, in 1861-1863, were accustomed to rail at England's "pusillanimity"; Benjamin, himself British-born, found the keynote of British behavior to his Confederacy "fear of a war with the United States." This word "fear" may be disregarded, but certainly Palmerston, in 1861, regarded such a conflict as bad policy. Europe, at that moment, was about as unstable a place as it is at the present time. Nationalities were in flux then, as they are now. New nations and new empires — Italy and Germany — were coming to life; ancient states — Turkey, Austria, the Papacy — were dissolving. The ambitions and animosities engendered by these phenomena were quite enough to keep sleepless the nights of a statesman who was guiding the British Empire. Above all there was the constant threat of that pinchbeck emperor, Napoleon III. Palmerston had the most vivid memories of the imperial uncle who had given this usurper his power and his name. He still remembered the time when, as a Cambridge student, he had drilled daily with his fellows as preparedness against the expected invasion; he was thirty-one when the Battle of Waterloo was fought, and, as Secretary at War, had done his part in equipping Wellington's army. This Napoleonic era had left Palmerston with an implacable distrust of everything French. He turned an icy shoulder against the efforts of Napoleon III to enlist his coöperation in the Maximilian folly in Mexico. The mere fact that Napoleon wished to entice England into a joint intervention in the American Civil War was itself a sufficient reason, in Palmerston's mind, why England should refrain.

Indeed, to find a parallel to the conservative attitude toward France in 1860, we must go to the British feeling toward the

German Kaiser from 1900 to 1914. The parallel is almost exact. The prime necessity of Napoleon's being, as of the Kaiser's, was aggression. Every day Napoleon was increasing his armament. He was building a fleet that, in armor clads, was growing more powerful than Great Britain's. He was hourly drawing closer to Russia, England's historic enemy. He was seeking an alliance — again the Kaiser repeated this exploit — with the Sultan. The Napoleonic plan, Englishmen believed, was the establishment of a new Frankish empire in the east; a foreshadowing of the future *Drang nach Osten*. Napoleon's work for Italian unity aroused suspicion; when finally completed, so it was believed, a Bonapartist king would be placed on the Italian throne. That Suez Canal, then being constructed by the French, was manifestly aimed at the British Empire in India. Above all, the fear of invasion disturbed Palmerston in 1861, as it had in the days of the great Napoleon. Much is heard to-day of aircraft as having deprived England of its advantage as an island. The same talk was voluble in the fifties and sixties about steam. The new steamship had made England an easy victim of attack from the Continent. "Steam has bridged the channel," said Sidney Herbert. In a couple of hours a fleet of side-paddlers could spring from French harbors and land on the British coast — quite a different problem from an approach by sailing ships, subject to caprices of wind and tide. Endless rumors reached Palmerston's ears of Napoleon's flotilla of flat-bottomed boats, which could have been constructed for only one purpose — the invasion of England.

2

Lord John Russell

War with the United States would have meant the despatching of a considerable part of Britain's fleet across the Atlantic and leaving her sacred soil naked to a multitude of enemies. Palmerston, whose mainspring was the protection of his own country, was not the man to run such unnecessary risk. Lord John Russell was similarly reluctant. And America was peculiarly Lord John's problem. His memories, like his colleague's, encompassed the first Napoleon; indeed, one of his most lively anecdotes was the description of a visit that he had made, as a young man of twenty-two, to Napoleon in exile on Elba. This recollection shows how much Lord John was a part of the old England. He had met most of the notabilities, literary, political, and social, of the Napoleonic time; he knew Byron, — was one of the few permitted to read that poet's subsequently incinerated *Memoirs,* — Walter Scott, and was the close friend of Tom Moore. In politics Russell's own career illustrates, as did Palmerston's, the extent to which opportunities, in the first quarter of the nineteenth century, went by favor and privilege. Any son of the Duke of Bedford, in 1813, had merely to desire to add a seat in the House of Commons to his social and literary diversions; an obsequious borough — this one, of Tavistock, a family possession — dutifully sent the young man, not quite twenty-one, to Westminster. Despite his aristocratic introduction, this "formal, bloodless, fishy little man" presently became a popular hero. The Russells had always been Whigs, and naturally the latest sprig aligned himself with that party; but this traditional Whiggery quickly assumed, in young Russell's hands, a dangerous approach to Liberalism. His speech on the Reform Bill, in 1831, brought the little man world-wide fame. Its aura never left him. His attitude was important in the present connection, for, in addition to his other liberal tendencies, Little John cherished an admiration for America. As time went on, his zeal for democracy considerably cooled; but his friendliness to its foremost exponent still flickered feebly. His nature had withstood more successfully than Palmerston's Britain's many diplomatic conflicts with the lusty American Republic; in 1861, he was generally regarded as one of the few aristocrats who wished well to the Federal cause — though, like all the British world, he looked upon it as hopeless. Personally, he was famous for his genial manners with his social equals and his distant, haughty treatment of the rest of the world; for his sharp and witty tongue, frequently exercised against low-born intruders in the British Parliament; for a mighty independence of thought and behavior, sometimes shown, as indicated above, to royalty itself. His daring and self-confidence has passed into a proverb. "I believe Lord John Russell," said Sydney Smith, "would perform the operation for the stone, build St. Peter's, or assume — with or without ten minutes' notice — the command of the Channel fleet." The man's personal appearance hardly suggested such masterful qualities, though a discriminating American observer found him not without distinction. Charles Sumner got a good view of Russell one day in 1838 from the floor of the House of Commons. "In person diminutive and rickety," he wrote, "he reminded me of a pettifogging attorney who lives near Letchmere Point. He wriggled around, played with his hat, and seemed unable to dispose of his hands and feet; his voice was small and thin, but, notwithstanding all this, a house of five hundred members was hushed to catch his smallest accent. You listened and you felt that you heard a man of mind and of moral elevation."[1]

There were only two things, it is said, for which Lord John had any respect: high birth and great intellect. He greatly admired two contemporaries of lowly origin, John Bright and Charles Dickens, and, when proposed for the Lord Rectorship of Glasgow University, withdrew his name, because Wordsworth was the opposing candidate. Whether he regarded his latest diplomatic problem, James Murray Mason of Virginia, as falling within either of these classifications, is not disclosed. He never gave utterance to any admiration and treated that envoy in a manner that roused to fury all his Virginian pride. His personal relations with Mason is a story that is quickly told. It is the Yancey episode over again. The

[1] *Memoir and Letters of Charles Sumner*, by Edward L. Pierce, Vol. II, p. 316.

attention Mason received from British officialdom was precisely the one forecast by the *Times* editorial. Lord Palmerston gave Mason no interview until two years after he had ceased to represent the Confederate Government; Lord John, following the established custom in such situations, received him only once. As in the case of Yancey this meeting took place, not in the Foreign Office, but in Russell's London home in Chesham Place. The conversation, lasting an hour or so, was a somewhat constrained experience for both men. Physically they were symbolic types — one embodying the stiff conservatism of an ancient land, the other just as proudly upholding the eighteenth-century standards of a new world. In personal bearing, Mason must have had the advantage. The large-framed Virginian, with the finely shaped head, made rather insignificant the minute Englishman, clad sombrely in a black coat and a black stock, sitting stiffly with his arms crossed, one leg thrown over the other, his head, closely adjusted to the body, leaning forward to catch fully the unfamiliar Southern accents. Henry Adams writes that Lord Russell bore "a droll resemblance to John Quincy Adams," his grandfather, and there was indeed something in this aging funereal figure, with his wizened face, pointed and protruding nose, high, slanting, partially bald forehead, his cold, unfriendly pale blue eyes, that suggested not only the physical attributes of the famous New England clan but its acrid disposition. Lord Russell, in interviews of this time, was seldom at ease. Dudley Mann, who had gone through the harrowing experience a few months before, found the great statesman about as approachable as an iceberg, and he also reëchoed Sumner's impressions of his lack of quietude. "The Earl was as restless as if he had been seated upon a cushion of thorns. . . . In the interest of long cherished prejudices, perhaps, he seemed determined not to be convinced."

Almost the first words Russell spoke were disconcerting. After the preliminary greeting, Mason reached for a document he had brought, saying that he would like to read to the Foreign Secretary his credentials as Commissioner of the Confederate States to Great Britain.

"That is unnecessary," replied his Lordship, "since our relations are unofficial."

However, he did patiently listen while Mason read part of his instructions. This document was an exceedingly lengthy one, going deeply into the merits of the dispute, setting forth the classic Southern view of State rights, meticulously explaining that Secession was not Rebellion, and that the Confederacy was therefore a legally established independent nation, which Great Britain could recognize without committing a hostile act against the Federal Government. Only those paragraphs of this dissertation referring to recognition and the illegality of the blockade were read to the impassive Briton. At the conclusion, silence reigned again. Mason resumed the conversation — in fact, he was forced to do practically all the talking — enlarging on the valiant spirit of the Southern people in their determination never to unite again with the North, and the certainty of their success. At this Russell showed a little interest. How about Kentucky and Missouri and Tennessee? he asked. Apparently he knew enough about what was going on to understand that the border states were the crux of the problem. These three states, replied Mason, were now members of the Southern Confederation. This was the usual Southern contention of the time — certain forces in Kentucky and Missouri having gone through the form of joining the Davis Government. How about the alienation of northwestern Virginia? asked Russell. The people of those counties had recently withdrawn from the old Dominion and organized the state of West Virginia.

"The pretense of a separate state there," replied Mason, "is an empty pageant. It is credited by the government at Washington, and by it alone, for purposes of delusion."

This about completed the interview. The record when read

to-day intimates no warmth on Russell's part, but the experience was not so disheartening as Mason had anticipated. "I had been told on all hands," he reported to Benjamin, "that his usual manner was cold and repulsive, yet I did not find it so." "He received me in a civil and kind manner." Still Mason drew no encouragement from the meeting. "On the whole it was manifest enough that his personal sympathies were not with us." Earl Russell seemed utterly disinclined to enter into conversation at all as to the policy of his government, and only said in substance that they must wait events. At the close he hoped that Mason would find his residence in London "agreeable," but expressed no desire to see him again. In fact, he never did. This audience comprised all the personal intercourse that took place between the two men. Mason makes the best of it in his despatch to the State Department, but this disinclination to treat him with respect, combined with the studied disregard that ensued, made Russell the chief object of his hatred. We must not forget that he was a Mason of Virginia, always treated from birth as one of the elect; not only the welfare of his new country was injured, but he personally was assailed in that spot, which, from the beginning, had been the most sensitive one, his pride. From now on Mason's despatches disclose the bitterest comment on Russell, whom he regarded as the greatest enemy of the South. When his Lordship, in his occasional references to the new Government, insisted on describing it as "the so-called Confederate states" and Mason himself as a "pseudo-Commissioner," the English statesman became a more odious figure in Mason's eyes than Charles Sumner himself.

3
LONDON SOCIETY

But Mason found consolation elsewhere. "In London society," wrote Henry Adams, "he counted for one eccentric more," and all the Adams tribe take delight in picturing what they regarded as his awkwardness, his mistakes, and the general neglect in which he was held. Adams and his son give instances of Mason's breaks with convention. In the course of a debate in the House of Commons, the Confederate envoy, occupying a preferred seat, began to cry "Hear! Hear!" thus infringing the agelong law prohibiting spectators in that august chamber from applauding. Charles Francis Adams reports, with understandable glee, that Mason at one famous dinner party entertained the guests by describing how, at the very moment he was talking, General Lee had captured Washington and Baltimore — the moment in question being several days after the battle of Gettysburg. These anecdotes do not tell the whole story. The fact remains that Mason did receive much social attention in England, and that a majority of Members of Parliament, and almost all the propertied and upper social classes, sympathized with his cause. And they made a good deal of him. He was a frequent guest at the big houses in London — not, of course, those identified with the Government; and at many of the most pretentious country homes his position was an agreeable one. He did not grace Lady Palmerston's famous receptions, and not a single member of the Ministry, he wrote Mrs. Mason, had expressed the slightest desire of forming his acquaintance, but he had many charming, aristocratic friends. The Anglican Church was profuse in attention. A really impressive list of notables flits across the pages of his correspondence. There were dinners at Stafford House with the Duke and Duchess of Sutherland, and visits to Bedgebury Park, the seat of Beresford-Hope, Member of Parliament for Cambridge University, one of the richest and most powerful men in England, an extremist in Toryism and opposition to popular rule. The Marquis of Bath freely extended the hospitality of Longleat. Mason dined repeatedly with Lord Donoughmore, President of the Board of Trade in the late Derby Government. Lord Malmesbury, Foreign Secretary in the same Administration, showed him unremitting kindness and sympathy. Lord Robert Cecil, afterward, as Marquis of Salisbury, Prime Minister of England; Lord Eustace Cecil; Lord Campbell; Sir Coutts Lindsay — such are only a few of the lofty British names of the day who treated Mason with consideration, and frequently with hospitality. That he reveled in associations of this kind is plain. "I have been kindly received by society in London," he writes soon after arrival. He likes to note "the courtesies received from ladies most distinguished by their rank and their position in society." Mason pays British country life the highest compliment at his disposal. The "best in England" constantly calls to mind the "best in Virginia." His letters to his wife in particular are replete with such comparisons. "I have found the larger portion of the elite but the best type of our Virginia circles." He spends the Christmas holidays at a well-known English country house. "I found their Christmas usages very much like those on the island or at Claremont, according to my early recollections of the better days in the Old Dominion"; the "island," of course, was that Analostan in the Potomac where he had spent his childhood. Occasionally a jarring note interrupted this idyl. Richard Cobden entertained Mason at breakfast, and spent most of the time expressing his strong sympathy with the North. Even Mason's aristocratic devotees would now and then ask questions about the Fugitive Slave Law. They had not forgotten Mrs. Beecher Stowe's harrowing descriptions of Eliza on the ice, and could not quite see in this kindly Virginian the author of the law that had made such cruelties legal. The most knowing also insisted that Mason tell them all about Dred Scott. Whenever the question of slavery came up — as it insistently did — Mason brushed it aside with the statement that it was something only a Southerner could understand and that the fate of the black men could be safely left in the hands of a people so warm-hearted and civilized as that of the Southern States.

Less distinguished folk — Members of Parliament and the

like — used to crowd Mason's headquarters, first at Fenton's Hotel, St. James's, and afterward in his home on Upper Seymour Street. Here he held almost daily levees, unfolding to his guests the true facts about the Confederacy, its present and its future. He has himself preserved little digests of these talks, which have historic value to-day as picturing the territorial ambitions of his country. Thus the empire of Jefferson Davis, as Mason described it, always consisted of thirteen states; it embraced Kentucky and Missouri; long after these commonwealths had been definitely won for the Union, Mason pictured them as loyal members of the Richmond Government. Perhaps the reminiscent aspect of that sacred number — thirteen — made Mason so tenacious on this point. And the Confederacy was to have territories also. He liked to point on his map to the region acquired in the Mexican War. No treaty of peace would be signed with the United States, Mason informed his auditors, that did not assign New Mexico to the Confederacy. New Mexico was the domain out of which the present state of that name, as well as Arizona, Nevada, Utah, and parts of Colorado, have been carved. The end of the war, Mason declared, would see the Confederacy with a larger area than that of the United States, and the time was not far distant when it would have a larger population.

4

The Blockade

All this was very well, but, after all, the Confederate envoy had come to London for a fixed purpose. That purpose had changed somewhat from the one which had prompted the Yancey mission. If we read Secretary Hunter's instructions to Yancey, Rost, and Mann, it will appear that recognition of Southern independence was the point on which emphasis was laid. As the Federal blockade had not then been declared, naturally not much was said on this point. And Yancey, all during the futile ten months he spent in England, made his plea chiefly for recognition. Under the new Secretary of State, however, the blockade became the chief object of Mason's abjurations. By March and April of 1862, the Southern mind had changed on this question. For the first year, as already explained, the South almost welcomed the Lincoln interdict on shipping to Southern ports; it was regarded as a kind of auxiliary to the Davis embargo. It served the South in preventing the export of cotton and so aided in precipitating that cotton famine which would compel England to intervene. Mr. Davis and Mr. Benjamin had recovered from that folly. They now saw that the sale of cotton in Europe was the one way of preserving the economic structure of the South and of assuring the sinews for waging its war. The Confederacy presently became as desirous of moving cotton to Europe as it had previously been reluctant. But this decision, as so many Southern decisions, came too late. Precious years had been lost. Meanwhile the "Yankee blockade" had stiffened. From May, 1861, to April, 1862, the blockade had been so ineffective that merchant ships, in almost any number, could have gone through it like a sieve. After that date the cordon of Federal ships, though by no means impregnable, offered fewer loopholes. And now its destruction seemed indispensable to Confederate success. Almost the first letter Secretary Benjamin sent to Mason insisted that he bring this matter to the attention of Lord John Russell. The Lincoln interdict, as established, he argued — and argued ably — was illegal; it contravened established international law and specific treaties; England should so declare and proceed to disregard it. In a later instruction Benjamin described — not inaccurately — the so-called blockade "as a predatory cruise against the commerce of Europe on 3,000 miles of our coast by the ships of the United States under pretense of a blockade of our ports."

On the basis of facts and of law, Benjamin had the best of this debate. The Declaration of Paris, to which Great Britain and the United States subscribed, had declared that a blockade, to be respected, must be "effective." What did "effective" mean? There seemed little difficulty; British jurists had themselves succinctly explained the significance of the term. The definition given by Lord Stowell, the great British admiralty judge, had become the accepted one. "A blockade *de facto* should be effected by stationing a number of ships, and effecting, as it were, an arc of circumvallation round the mouth of the prohibited port, where, if the arc fail in any one part, the blockade itself fails altogether." Of course the Federal Navy held no Southern port beleaguered in this stone-wall fashion. Neutral ships were slipping in or out all the time. Yet Russell persisted in regarding this blockade as a legal one. He not only shoved aside the doctrines of great British admiralty experts, but invented a new, previously unheard-of principle of his own. Quietly, frigidly, without consulting one of the seven powers that had accepted the Declaration of Paris, he proceeded to amend that solemn instrument. That Declaration had asserted that "blockades, in order to be binding, must be effective, — that is to say, maintained by a force sufficient really to prevent access to the coast of the enemy." But Russell, though ostensibly maintaining allegiance to this principle, now inserted a clause, of his own manufacture, which completely negatived this restriction. A blockade had closed a port, and was therefore "effective," if, he asserted, the enemy power had stationed at the entrance "a sufficient number of ships" "to prevent access to it, or to create an evident danger of entering it or leaving it." That is, a port should be considered closed, when entering it or leaving it was a risky business. Those who denounced most vigorously the inadequacy and therefore illegality of Mr. Lincoln's measure did not deny that any vessel defying it ran "the danger" of capture. The mere existence of such a danger, Lord John Russell stoically maintained, made the blockade one which all neutrals must recognize as effective and binding. Nothing like this had ever been heard before.

Nor did Russell stop here in meeting the wishes of the Federal Government. The American Navy, Benjamin angrily pointed out, was blockading not only enemy, but neutral ports as well. It stationed warships at the mouth of the Rio Grande and seized English ships and cargoes consigned to Mexican ports — especially Matamoros. It kept vigilance off Nassau, in the Bahamas, and similarly seized British vessels attempting to negotiate that harbor. The reason for this stretch of international law, Mr. Seward explained, was that the cargoes so taken consisted of guns, ammunition, and other warlike stores intended for the Confederate Army. As to the truth of this statement there was no dissent. American admiralty lawyers, as ingenious as the British, invented a new principle of their own. This was the now world-famous one of "continuous voyage" and "ultimate destination." When a cargo of contraband, sailing ostensibly from one neutral port to another, had, as its "ultimate destination," the armed forces of an enemy, it was subject to seizure. As quickly as these "neutral" firearms were landed in the Bahamas, they were at once transshipped to a Confederate port — everybody knew that; the whole proceeding, from a British harbor to the Confederate Army, made up a single "continuous voyage" and was therefore in danger of interception. Again Earl Russell obediently accepted this American contention. He sat quietly and made no protest while British shipload after British shipload engaged in such a "continuous voyage" was seized by American cruisers, and consigned to the prize courts.

Mason engaged in a fusillade of objections to these innovations. His protests were met with silent contempt. When he asked for an interview with Lord Russell, that gentleman "presented his compliments," but thought that no advantage would accrue from a meeting. When Mason bombarded his lordship with statistics showing the extent to which the blockade was "ineffective" that statesman again "presented his compliments" and found the material "very interesting." That the unsolicited information bored him was not concealed, and he finally ended the discussion by a cruel blow. He ceased to acknowledge Mason's letters, but had his undersecretary, Layard, do so. This was a subtle snub. By this procedure Russell intimated to Mason that, as a Commissioner who had never been received, he had no right to address communications to Her Majesty's Principal Secretary of State for Foreign Affairs. Mason took the hint and desisted — though not gracefully.

What was the reason for this British acquiescence in Yankee pretension, this "cowardice," as Benjamin called it, "this morbid fear of offending" Uncle Sam? There was a more substantial explanation than these excited phrases imply. Russell was an historic British statesman, and, like others of his breed, saw in British policy not an improvisation to meet a particular crisis but a set of principles that were to endure for all time. He was thinking not only of the existing American war, but of future conflicts in which England itself might be engaged. And he accepted the new rules of blockade introduced by the United States not because he was overfriendly to that nation and not because he feared American anger, but because they were the principles Britain wished to see enshrined as international law. The Declaration of Paris, though accepted perforce by Great Britain, had always been exceedingly unpopular with gentlemen whose chief interest was the greatness of the British Empire. That Declaration, they believed, had robbed Great Britain of the most powerful engine it possessed for protecting England's destiny — the British fleet. To weaken Britain in maritime warfare had indeed been the purpose of the Continental statesmen who had at length succeeded in foisting it upon their great rival. Russell, in 1862, was looking forward to a possible, even probable war with some European enemy; he, like Palmerston, had the aggression of France constantly before his eyes. The Paris rules of blockade would interfere with England's effective use of its fleet in such a contest. Any blockade it would declare would necessarily be a loose one, like Uncle Abraham's; the British fleet could no more blockade the whole coast of France — Atlantic and Mediterranean — than could the American Navy the 3,000 miles of Confederate coast line.

That is, the British fleet would be hopelessly shackled, if compelled, in a European contest, to observe the rules laid down by the Treaty of Paris. How to reduce this instrument to a dead letter had long been the preoccupation of British statesmen. Uncle Sam now providentially showed the way. Though itself a party to the unpopular Declaration, the Federal Government serenely ignored it, and established the kind of naval warfare best adapted to the pending problem. The British Government secretly rejoiced at this turn of affairs. Lord Russell saw in it that thing most precious to the British mind — a "precedent." If acquiesced in by the European powers it would become valid international law and, to all intents and purposes, repeal the Declaration of 1856. Russell therefore paid no attention to Mason's protests or to the carefully reasoned arguments of Benjamin — though doubtless he recognized these as able lawyers' briefs and, from a strictly legal standpoint, unassailable. He quietly accepted the Federal blockade, and all Europe, by following the British example, gave it their approval. The only Englishmen who complained were the British merchants whose cargoes Uncle Sam summarily seized and confiscated. But their complaints did not disturb the Foreign Office. They were not to be pitied especially after all. They were mostly munitions profiteers on a huge scale; they were doing so thriving a business with the North and so many of their vessels destined to the South slipped through the blockade that the balance in their favor was enormous. An occasional loss of a British ship was a small price to pay for establishing new principles of sea warfare indispensable to the future of Britain.

The London *Times*, in the course of the excitement, let the cat out of the bag. "You will see," wrote Henry Hotze to Benjamin, September 5, 1863, that "the *Times*, with characteristic duplicity, while summing up against the Federals, always concludes with the broad hint that the northern interpretation of all these maritime questions is one which England is interested to see pass into a precedent." British policy looks a long way ahead, and not until the outbreak of the Great War, in 1914, did Britain reap the full fruits of "Johnny Russell's" foresight in 1861–1865. But then it reaped them to the full. The interdict on German ports laid in that conflict was constructed on the American model of 1861. Lord Stowell's description, his "arc of circumvallation," never showed its head. The ghost of Lord John, if it hovered over the British performance of 1914, must have smiled with satisfaction at the silent pigeonholing of James Mason's protests fifty years before. For Britain, in 1914, made no attempt to station "arcs of circumvallation" before German ports; its so-called blockade became, to quote again Judah P. Benjamin's vivid description of the Federal one, "a predatory cruise" against the commerce of the world. Britain in 1914–1918 seized neutral ships on the high seas, just as the Americans had done in 1861, and conducted them into her own waters for search and adjudication. And, just as the United States, in 1861–1865, laid violent hands on neutral cargoes bound for Nassau and Mexico, when the "ultimate destination" was indubitably the Confederate States, so England, in 1914–1918, intercepted American ships, whose cargoes were officially consigned to Holland, Denmark, and Sweden, but in reality were bound for Germany. When Ambassador Walter Page, in obedience to instructions, protested such captures, Sir Edward Grey smilingly pointed to the

American practice in the Civil War.[2] The lesson America had taught her Britain was now putting to use. The principles upon which the British Navy was acting, he said, were those established by the admiralty courts of the United States. The United States Supreme Court was the final authority according to which Britain was regulating its warfare on German commerce! This logic left the American State Department helpless, for such was the fact. And when the United States entered the Great War, it acted upon its own precedent with a thoroughness that even its British ally hardly presumed to emulate.

5

THE MOVEMENT FOR RECOGNITION

Any notion that Russell's approval of the Federal blockade was an expression of friendship for the North receives a severe shock when we view his American attitude in the late summer and fall of 1862. Those months — from August to November — represented the only period when the Confederate Government made a near approach to European recognition. And the leader in this new British attitude was Lord John Russell. Just what were his real motives in these tortuous negotiations has been the subject of much discussion. Charles Francis Adams, the American Minister, went to his grave with a kindly feeling for Lord John; he regarded him as an honest man and, at bottom, a friend to the Northern cause. Mason and all Southern agents intensely hated this impassive aristocrat, for the same reason that Adams liked him. It was their belief that the British Foreign Minister was constantly contriving dark plots against the South. Henry Adams echoed, for many years after his father's death, the same friendly sentiments. But all the fury of Henry Adams's nature was aroused by the publication of Spencer Walpole's *Life of Lord John Russell*

[2] See *Life and Letters of Walter H. Page*, Vol. II, Chap. XV.

in 1889. This made clear a hitherto unknown fact: that Lord John Russell was the prime mover for recognition of Southern independence in August–November, 1862. Letters of Russell to Palmerston published in this work left no doubt about the matter. More recently, the papers of Gladstone and Palmerston, made available to American historians, have added a multitude of details.[3] An interesting result of these disclosures is that they completely reverse the parts which Palmerston and Russell, in the American mind, had played in this momentous crisis. For many years after the Civil War it was generally believed that Palmerston was the pitiless enemy of America and that Russell was an influence steadily holding him in check. The facts were exactly the opposite. Russell was, at the time in question, the force working steadily for a European coalition in favor of the South; Palmerston was the moderating voice, holding Russell in restraint and finally wrecking his plans.

No man was more startled and disillusioned by this discovery than Henry Adams, son and private secretary of the American Minister. His *Education* records the bitterness against Lord John produced by this revelation of that statesman's calculated "villainy." Adams completely reconstructed his views of Russell; instead of the distant diplomat, favorable on the whole to the North, we now have a portrait of a coldblooded Foreign Secretary working for three years for the destruction of the Federal Union. Every act of this insidious foe, Henry Adams insisted, fitted into a consistent programme. From the first days of Secession, Lord John had seen in the American war England's great chance. The future of his country demanded that America's progress should be checked. Russell, according to this analysis, laid the basis of this policy when he recognized the belligerency of the Confederate States in May, 1861. His frustrated effort to use the *Trent* affair as a *casus belli* in January, 1862, was another manifestation of the

---

[3] For example, see *Great Britain and the American Civil War*, by Ephraim D. Adams, and *The Life of Lord Palmerston*, by Herbert C. F Bell.

same desire. The escape of the Confederate cruisers — especially of "No. 290," the *Alabama* — clearly was another item in the general plot. Finally came those secret proceedings of the late summer and autumn of 1862, when Russell conducted a vigorous campaign in the Cabinet for the recognition of Southern independence. What particularly enraged Henry Adams, as he surveyed in retrospect these hostile moves, was Russell's duplicity. Adams uses a more specific word. All English statesmen of the time, Adams insists, were irreclaimable "liars," but in this brilliant constellation of mendacity Lord John Russell shone with a glory all his own. In secret the Foreign Secretary was working upon his colleagues in behalf of Jefferson Davis, but, at the same moment, was displaying the most friendly and neutral face to Adams's father, the American Minister. Alarmed at Gladstone's fatuous speech, that Jefferson Davis "had made a nation," the senior Adams rushed to the Foreign Office for explanations. Russell assured him that that oration was not to be taken as signifying any change in British policy. The Government intended to maintain indefinitely its policy of neutrality. The intense animosity Henry Adams ever afterward felt for England was explained, in considerable part, by the deceit with which Lord John Russell had abused his father's confidence.

Another Adams, not of the same family, — Ephraim D., the leading authority on British-American diplomacy in the Civil War, — does not think that Russell's motive in all this double-dealing was a desire to destroy the United States. Of the deception there can be no question; the record speaks for itself. Professor Adams insists that Russell's "sympathies were unquestionably with the North," while Palmerston's were just as emphatically with the South. But Russell, from the firing of the first gun, looked upon the American Union as a thing of the past. In 1862 it was, he sincerely believed, definitely extinct. England would presently be called upon to recognize Southern independence; the facts of the situation, irrespective of right or wrong, or of one's sympathies in the contest, would, he believed, compel such recognition. To bring the struggle to a close as quickly as possible and end the useless shedding of blood, as well as to end the suffering in England directly caused by it, was, in Russell's mind, his chief duty as a statesman. There is no need of going into his lordship's moral considerations in this place. In fact, the long and tangled story of British policy in 1862 has no part in any description of the diplomatic activities of James Murray Mason. For Mason cut no figure in these transactions. Had he never crossed the ocean, the history of that summer and fall would have been the same. Russell naturally — for the Commissioner had no official status — did not consult the Confederate envoy and Mason's correspondence shows that he did not have the slightest inkling of what was going on. In his attitude during this most hopeful period in the history of the Confederacy — the one time, indeed, in which it approached a successful outcome — as well as in that of Henry Hotze, his "publicity agent," editor of the *Index*, the Confederate organ in London, there is a good deal of humor. For it was this juncture that the Southern envoys selected for a vitriolic attack on Lord John Russell, completely ignorant of the fact that that statesman was working day and night for Confederate success.

That Mason should have gone astray is not surprising, for he was not a keen observer, and his attitude toward Russell was warped by that statesman's refusal to treat him "civilly" — the word is Mason's own. Henry Hotze, the Confederate press agent in London, was a much shrewder man. Yet Hotze was as ignorant of Cabinet workings as Mason himself. His hatred of Russell was just as intense. In his letters to Benjamin, Hotze seldom refers to Russell except in hostile terms. "There are but two men of weight in both houses of Parliament," so Hotze wrote in one of his communications, "who are our declared foes, — Earl Russell, who has lately made himself the apologist of the Federal government in the House of Lords,[4] and Mr. Bright in the Commons, who, I am happy to say, represents or leads no party but himself." Hotze kept on in this strain, even in that period when Russell was leading the pro-Confederate bloc in the British Cabinet. For several months Hotze confined these uncomplimentary views to his personal correspondence, but in the fall of 1862 he launched an open press campaign against the statesman who was then almost his only friend. "You will see from the editorial columns of the *Index*," Hotze writes Benjamin, October 24, 1862, "that I feel myself strong enough to attack the Cabinet, though I have not ventured upon doing so since the paper was established, despite the urgent advice of Mr. Slidell, and less important counsellors. The same prudential motives which then restrained me no longer exist, and I shall continue the attacks without fear of prejudicing our cause with the public at large." If Earl Russell had the habit of reading the *Index*, some of its comments at this time must have tickled his sense of humor. For he is here pictured as the foe of the Confederacy, struggling against its recognition by Great Britain! Russell's action in this crisis, so said the *Index*, had made him "the laughing-stock of Europe." "The nominal control of foreign affairs is in the hands of a diplomatic Malaprop, who has never shown vigor, activity or determination, except where the display of these qualities was singularly unneeded, or even worse than useless." Of course, to a realistic, unruffled diplomat like Russell denunciations of this kind had no effect one way or the other. Whatever Confederate agents might say or do had no bearing upon his problem. That problem was one exclusively of Britain's interests, and Britain's position in the world.

Russell, finally, in December, 1862, abandoned his efforts at mediation, recognition, or an armistice — for, at several times, his efforts assumed these several guises — and abandoned

---

[4] Lord John had recently become an earl and transferred himself to the hereditary chamber.

them, it proved, for ever. As a politician, he discovered that persistence in this policy would cause the break-up of his Cabinet and the fall of his Ministry. Out of its fifteen members only three, it appeared, favored mediation or recognition — Lord Russell himself, Lord Westbury, and that unaccountable combination of idealism and practicality, William Ewart Gladstone — the one inveterate and persistent advocate of the recognition of that "nation" which he thought Jefferson Davis had created. So far as Great Britain was concerned, the movement for recognition was dead. From other sources it still remained alive. And that concerns the story of John Slidell.

XI

FRIENDS OF THE SECOND EMPIRE

1

JOHN SLIDELL

ONE grievance rested heavily on the proud Virginian spirit of James Murray Mason. That was the high consideration shown Slidell in Paris compared with the indifference accorded him in London. "I see and hear nothing from the British government, officially or unofficially," Mason wrote Benjamin, November 7, 1862, ten months after his arrival. "Mr. Slidell has an advantage over me in this, as he sees the ministers frequently, as well as the Emperor. I have sometimes thought it might be due to the dignity of the government under such circumstances that I should terminate the mission here."[1]

The contrast in the standing of the two men at their respective courts was startling indeed. While one chilly interview with Lord John Russell constituted Mason's relations with the British Government, Slidell saw constantly the French Foreign Ministers, first Thouvenel and afterward Drouyn de Lhuys, as well as the other entertaining characters who governed the Second Empire — De Morny, Walewski, Persigny, Rouher, and the Emperor's private secretary and intimate friend, Jean François Mocquard. One can imagine the rage that would have swept the United States had Queen Victoria received Mason at Buckingham Palace or Balmoral. Yet Napoleon III held lengthy and most cordial interviews with Slidell at the Tuileries, Saint-Cloud, Vichy, and Biarritz. At the latter place Slidell and his wife and daughters became members of the Imperial social set. The Empress not only treated the Confederate envoy with great courtesy, but showered attentions upon Mrs. Slidell and the Misses Matilda and Rosina. "I was

[1] *Official Records of the Union and Confederate Navies*, Series II, Vol. 3, p. 607.

invited, with my family, by the Empress to a ball at the 'Villa Eugénie' on the 7th," Slidell writes Benjamin from Biarritz, September 22, 1863. "We were most kindly received; the Empress conversed with me for nearly half an hour and expressed the warmest sympathy for our cause. I was surprised to find how thoroughly she was acquainted with the question, not only in its political aspects but with all the incidents of the war and the position of our armies. . . . I mention these circumstances because I consider them as not without significance in a political point of view, especially as the Empress is thought by those who have the best means of judging to exercise no inconsiderable influence in public affairs." [2]

The gentleman so distinguished by the most beautiful and most powerful woman in Continental Europe had personal qualifications, aside from his political status, entitling him to such honors. Slidell spoke French with reasonable fluency — as well as Spanish, Eugénie's native tongue; he was a man of intelligence, good manners, and handsome and imposing presence. Charles Francis Adams, hearing of the appointment, at once perceived his fitness for the Court of Napoleon III. "There he'll find a man of his own sort who'll be delighted to see him," Adams commented. The remark was not intended to compliment either man. Neither the career of Louis Napoleon nor that of John Slidell had fulfilled those rigid standards of private and public rectitude upheld by Puritan New England. Both men had led rather adventurous lives; both in politics were cynical opportunists: neither, in accomplishing his ends, had ever shown much squeamishness about methods. The imprecations which Victor Hugo, from his exile in Jersey, was hurling at "Napoleon le petit" could be matched, on a smaller and less heroic scale, by the epithets that had followed Slidell in his progress from obscurity to political power. Even so practical a politician as Martin Van Buren had looked upon the youthful Slidell as a man who would bear watching. In

[2] *Official Records of the Union and Confederate Navies*, Series II, Vol. 3, p. 905.

his political heyday opposition newspapers in New Orleans cried "Cataline" at his handsome figure, accusing him of political ruffianism in every shape — "Plaquemine frauds," "cab-votes," "Gallatin street assassinations and thuggery." The *True Delta* used to refer to "the vulpine eye of Houmas Slidell" — an epithet that recalled the most famous of the political jobs with which his name had been connected. Henry S. Foote, Senator from Mississippi, stigmatized him as "John Slidell, well known in Louisiana for many years as a corrupt tamperer with popular elections in the interest of the Democracy." Going further into details Foote depicted Slidell as a man of "vivacity of temperament, exceedingly astute and dexterous in dealing with men of all classes, and strongly suspected of being not over scrupulous in the use of means adapted to the attainment of his coveted objects. He conversed with ease and sprightliness, made no professions of special political purity, evinced the utmost pertinacity in the pursuit of his various objects and often avowed in connection with public affairs, motives of action such as many politicians, if swayed by them, deem it expedient to conceal."[3] Murat Halstead, in his account of the Charleston Convention of 1860, describes Slidell as prepared to "buy up" all followers of Douglas whose political virtues could not resist cash arguments. It remained for the rigorous powers of Charles Sumner, as always, to cap these contemporary allusions. This characterization appeared in December, 1863, about the time that Slidell was basking in the smiles of Eugénie at Biarritz. "The present struggle is characteristically represented by John Slidell, whose great fame is from electioneering frauds to control a Presidential election; so that his character is fitly drawn when it is said that he thrust fraudulent votes into the ballot box, and whips into the hands of task-masters."

Here, to the possibly jaundiced Northern mind, seemed to be a diplomat especially contrived by nature to deal with the

[3] *Bench and Bar of the South and Southwest*, by Henry S. Foote, p. 202.

dictators of France — the makers of *coup d'états*, the suppressors of liberty, and the disturbing meddlers in foreign affairs, who, with an illustrious name as their only stock in trade, had usurped the destinies of a great country. Yet had one of these critics dropped in on an Imperial party at Biarritz, the view of Mr. Slidell would hardly have suggested the evil fame he had left in America. All contemporary accounts pay tribute to his charm and dignity. A man of large stature, with strong, broad shoulders, a massive, finely-shaped cranium, enveloped in silky, snow-white hair, so thin that through it the top of his head, to quote Murat Halstead, "blushed like the shell of a boiled lobster"; symmetrically chiseled, well-placed features; eyes set closely together; a long, straight nose and small mouth, bearing just the trace of a smile; decisive chin, lofty, rectangular brow — here there were few intimations of geniality or gentleness; the outward person rather emphasized Slidell's description of himself as "a man of strong will, with some tact and discretion." Under it all there lay indications of reserve, possibly of ruthlessness; one feels that this urbane presentment masks those more impassioned qualities that made Slidell, commonly the polished gentleman of the world, also the leader of political gangs. A portrait that survives of Slidell in his early days suggests these more aggressive, defiant attributes. This picture reminds one of nothing so much as contemporary paintings of Lord Byron. There is the same erect, well-poised torso, the same challenging head, thrown backward, and Byron's chestnut, curly hair; the expression is not so scornful as that of his poetical counterpart, but it is full of determination and fire. It is not surprising to discover certain romantic episodes in Slidell's early life that harmonize with this youthful delineation.

In origin, it is true, Slidell could hardly be called a pattern of chivalry. The man stationed by the Confederate Government in Paris, to repeat there the feat of Benjamin Franklin eighty-five years before, — entangle the French monarchy into alliance with a revolutionary republic, — had a beginning in life not unlike that of his famous predecessor. Like Poor Richard, Slidell was the son of a candlemaker. One evening, at a fashionable dinner party in New York, after Slidell had attained fortune and some fame, a sprightly lady sitting next to him remarked, "You have been dipped, not moulded, into society." Other less witty but equally cutting jibes at the ancestral occupation frequently found their way into public print. And it was all true. Anyone passing down lower Broadway, New York, in the first decade of the nineteenth century would have encountered a modest establishment at No. 50, over the door of which was displayed the sign, "John Slidell, soap-boiler and tallow chandler." This was the father of the future envoy. For the irreconcilable statesman of the South was, in origin, a New Yorker — born in 1793, of a family that had been established in that city for a considerable period. Scoville's *Old Merchants of New York* lists many Slidells, besides the one recorded above, all of them men of modest vocation; they were tailors, measurers of grain, shoemakers. Their origin is not precisely known. When the most famous Slidell became a national figure, it was commonly said that the stock was originally Jewish. Slidell's niece married the most prominent American Jew of the time, the great New York banker, August Belmont; his daughter — as already recorded — married another, Baron d'Erlanger, and all his life Slidell himself was the political and business intimate of Judah P. Benjamin; these facts perhaps explain a prevailing belief in this genealogy. On his mother's side Slidell certainly was not Jewish. She was a Mackenzie, descended from a Jacobite member of the famous Highland clan who emigrated to America after the battle of Culloden. That Slidell's father married into this highly placed New York family indicates a considerable rise in the social and business scale. That his sister married Matthew Calbraith Perry, who "opened" Japan, is evidence to the same effect.

The fact is that the elder Slidell, in addition to his tallow business, became president of the Mechanics Bank and of the Tradesmen's Insurance Company, and was sufficiently prosperous to give his son what few Slidells had ever had — an academic education. He received his A.M. degree from Columbia in 1810. Of Slidell's mercantile and professional career in New York little has been handed down. Despite his education, he too became a tallow chandler, besides engaging in a commission business that came to grief in the War of 1812. The Jefferson embargo ruined Slidell, as it did countless others, yet this misfortune did not deter him, in his first venture in politics, from casting his fortunes on the Democratic side. Only his debts and a certain romantic episode remained in the memory of old New Yorkers as reminders of Slidell's adolescent days. Strangely enough, his favorite boyhood friend in the old First Ward was that Charles Wilkes, who, half a century afterward, as commander of the *San Jacinto*, stopped the *Trent*, and, by seizing its conspicuous passengers, almost caused war between the United States and England. But Slidell and Wilkes had parted as enemies long before this, for they had quarreled over the affections of a girl of their neighborhood. A few years later, Slidell had another similar adventure of which the consequences were more portentous. The artistic glory of New York from 1800 to 1820 was the old Park Theatre. Here Slidell was a frequent attendant, interested not only in the plays but in one of the most popular ladies of the cast. In this romance again the adventurous young man met opposition — this time in the person of the celebrated Stephen Price, manager of the Park. One morning on the city's outskirts the two rivals met at pistol point in the most approved Hamilton-Aaron Burr manner; the theatrical manager was seriously wounded, and this, as well as his multitudinous debts, made desirable for Slidell a residence in some distant region.

In the early nineteenth century one friendly paradise, above all others, opened its arms to young Northerners in need of rehabilitation. In this same place Judah P. Benjamin had found asylum after his unseemly departure from Yale. Edward Livingston, one of the idols of the youthful Slidell, had discovered, in the emerging metropolis of New Orleans, the beginning of a new existence that ultimately made him Secretary of State and Minister to France. A lively rush of exuberant New York blades southwestward was an established phenomenon of the day. These young men all cultivated the same ambition: to practice law, plant sugar on the side, ascend the rungs of political fame, capping all by marriage with the inevitable "beautiful Creole." This prospect had already lured countless metropolitans to the mouth of the Mississippi and in 1819 John Slidell, ruined financially, socially ostracized for dueling, betook himself to this hospitable shore. And here he quickly realized all the most alluring promises of the enterprise — professional success, fortune, political triumph, even the Creole bride.

2

Exile in New Orleans

Of all the Yankees who sought this sanctuary from their more frigid natal soil, probably none underwent so complete a transformation as John Slidell. For mercurial natures like Benjamin, adaptation to new surroundings was not difficult; he started life as a Southerner, unaffected by the thoughts and *mores* of the North. The most successful of the *émigrés*, Edward Livingston, never really joined his fortunes to those of Louisiana; he used the new home as a springboard to political office, but, as soon as this ambition was achieved, contentedly returned to his native New York, to die and be buried there. Slidell, more chameleonlike, quickly laid aside his old existence and became part and parcel of the new country. The French and "American" communities in New Orleans then held themselves distinct, both in geography and in spirit; Canal

Street strictly divided the two allegiances: on one side lay the *ancien régime,* on the other the bustling, robustious, and — as the old French residents superciliously believed — vulgar new English-speaking generation. Slidell identified himself with the descendants of the era of Louis XV; in all important concerns of life, he "went native." With his career in New Orleans came a new profession; in New York, while engaged unsuccessfully in commerce, he had studied law on the side; the requirements for admission to practice were not rigid, and soon this industrious exile accumulated a practice worth $10,-000 a year — a large sum in those days. The prudential side of his character had apparently developed since his gusty New York days; for it was not until he had thus been solidly established that he married. He was forty-two at the time — 1835; his bride, barely twenty, was Mathilde Deslonde, daughter of one of the leading French families. Until her fifteenth year this girl knew no English; all her ancestry was pure-blooded French; she was a devout Catholic, a feminine representative of that irreconcilable Gallic instinct which resisted the modernizing tendencies of the Anglo-Saxon. The new household that grew up in the Creole quarter and at Slidell's plantation was exclusively French. William H. Russell, who met the Slidells on the outbreak of war, was impressed by this foreign atmosphere. "In the evening I visited Mr. Slidell, whom I found at home with his family, Mrs. Slidell and her sister, Madame Beauregard, wife of the general, two very charming young ladies, daughters of the house, and a parlour full of fair companions. . . . The conversation, as is the case in most Creole domestic circumstances, was carried on in French." In one of his meetings with Napoleon III, Slidell pleased the Emperor by saying that the language of his Louisiana home was the Emperor's own and was able to give a description of French life on the lower Mississippi that at once put the two men on companionable grounds.

And any Northern principles Slidell may have imbibed in

his New York birthplace similarly disappeared. "Mr. Slidell," said Russell, "though born in a northern state, is perhaps one of the most determined disunionists in the southern Confederacy." Thirty years before, President Andrew Jackson had stigmatized him on the same grounds. Significantly, this early reference emphasized the failing which seems persistent throughout Slidell's career — his lack of high character as a public man. "From testimonials submitted," writes President Jackson to Vice President Van Buren, November 19, 1833, in that rough-and-ready style that makes his correspondence so diverting, "Mr. Slidell has imposed on the Secretary of the Treasury and myself in his recommendation of an appraiser of the Port of New Orleans, — the man had been suspended as inspector for intemperance twice and then permitted to resign . . . it is stated further by Mr. Gordon that Slidell, Nicholson and Grimes are all calhoun men and nullifiers. . . . Knowing that you had a favorable opinion of Mr. Slidell as well as myself this letter is written to put you on your guard of this man, that you may not break your shins over stools not in your way and that you may be guarded in any communication you may happen to make with him."[4]

Slidell's emotions on slavery and disunion never reached extravagant expression; but that was rather because, where principles were concerned, his nature lacked fervor. He cheerfully accepted the ideas of his environment, for that composed the material with which he had to work. In reviewing the lives of such Confederate leaders as Davis, Stephens, Toombs, and most of the others, questions of conviction loom large, for they were vital matters; but, in developing the great issue of the prewar era, Slidell was an unimportant figure. He made no contributions to the discussion, one way or the other. He performed only one important public service: an abortive mission to Mexico, in 1845; for all the rest of his days, Slidell's activities were purely political. In this less ex-

[4] *Correspondence of Andrew Jackson*, Vol. V, p. 227.

alted field, his career was rapid and triumphant. His progress was that of a great political Boss — first of New Orleans, then of Louisiana, finally, in 1856, of the Democratic party in the nation. Beginning as herder of election mobs in best Tammany style, he ended, in this latter year, as President maker and national patronage bestower of the Buchanan Administration. And his methods were the coarsest of a rugged period: they included ballot-box stuffing, the manipulation of "floaters" and "repeaters," the brokerage of offices, and pork-barrel legislation. Slidell served one term in Congress and nearly two terms in the United States Senate, but his record comprises scarcely a speech, and no serious piece of legislation. His first party coup, in the Polk election of 1844, gave him national reputation — of a kind. In this contest he "swung" Louisiana for the Democratic candidate. Chartering two steamboats in New Orleans, Slidell loaded them with purchased roughs, sailed down to Plaquemines parish, stopping at several landings while his mercenaries cast a succession of ballots for James K. Polk, thereby giving him the electoral vote of Louisiana.

Long before Slidell attained the Senate, therefore, — in 1853, — the word "Slidellian" had taken on a well-defined meaning. The complicated Houmas scandal had added to this doubtful fame. In this proceeding Judah P. Benjamin was his associate, as in politics generally; and, justly or unjustly, the standing of both men suffered severely. Slidell and others had acquired an old land claim of uncertain validity; Benjamin introduced a bill in Congress intended to give these grantees a legal title. The man who most severely denounced this transaction, and caused it to be undone, was Robert Toombs, of Georgia. The *New York Times* charged that Benjamin had received a fee of $10,000 for putting through the bill. Benjamin and Slidell's biographers have been unable to discover the truth or falsity of these accusations, any more than they have proved, or disproved, similar scandals involving the Tehuantepec

Railway, in which both Benjamin and Slidell were concerned. But that Slidell was a machine politician of an extreme type is true. His enemies accused him of transplanting at least one institution of his abandoned New York to the bayou country — the methods of Tammany Hall; yet it is not certain that this honor is his, for floaters, repeaters, and thuggery at polling booths were not unknown even before Slidell's arrival; significantly one of the largest parishes of Louisiana rejoiced in the name of St. Tammany.

And Slidell's more expansive nature rapidly advanced beyond the narrow sphere of parochial politics. He had two ambitions; one was to become a Senator from Louisiana, the other to make James Buchanan President of the United States. He realized the first in 1853, the second three years afterward. His enthusiasm for Buchanan was not entirely selfish; it involved, indeed, a real belief in the man and even a personal affection. Among the posts the grateful Buchanan proffered was that of Minister to France. But Slidell refused at the hands of his dearest friend the job that he afterwards accepted from Jefferson Davis, a President to whom he was not friendly at all. There is something almost fatalistic in the way Slidell's career skirted diplomacy. He occupied two positions in this field — that to Mexico in 1845, and that to France, for the Confederacy, in 1862. In both cases he failed of an official reception. Mexico declined to recognize any American Minister in 1845 — the two nations were on the brink of war over Texas — and Slidell was forced to view the revolutionary scene from Vera Cruz and Jalapa. Yet his brief Mexican experience had an important bearing on his existence in France from 1862 to 1865. For Mexico was the pivot about which his diplomatic efforts for the Confederacy were to revolve and the three months' furtive glimpse Slidell obtained of that Republic and the forces, revolutionary, social, and ecclesiastical, that ruled its life, proved a most enlightening preparative to his subsequent career near the Quai d'Orsay.

3

INTRIGUE IN PARIS

Even Mexico, in 1845, hardly presented such a scene of personal intrigue and complicated politics as France in 1862. Napoleon III himself once described this period as the "apogee of the Second Empire." This potentate, who, only a few years before, had been the laughingstock of Europe, came now close to being its dictator. In alliance with Britain, he had won the Crimean War and humbled Russia; almost singlehanded he had driven the Austrians from Lombardy and created an independent Italian nation. The glories of Magenta and Solferino were still resplendent when this emissary of the South, with his French wife and Frenchified daughters, began his gingerly approach to the Tuileries. It was a curious group of statesmen with whom Slidell had to deal. Louis Napoleon, with all his failings, had one pronounced virtue; he was loyally devoted to old friends and fellow conspirators. Thus nearly all the *"brigands triomphants"* who, in December, 1851, had precipitated the *coup d'état*, abolished the short-lived second Republic, and almost overnight transformed Napoleon from a bourgeois President into a tinsel Emperor, still held chief posts in the Government. Everywhere Slidell confronted personal reminders of the first Napoleon. Walewski, son of the greatest of the Bonapartes and his famous Polish mistress, Countess Walewska, had recently left the Foreign Department, but still, in his post of Minister of State, remained one of the closest of advisers. He bore a striking physical resemblance to the victor of Austerlitz, and had inherited at least a suggestion of his ability; he was the closest confidant of Eugénie, and champion of that lady's extreme views on church and state. One of the most amazing of all the amazing characters even France has generated was the predominant force in governing the Empire. This was that Count — afterward Duke — De Morny, who, as supreme artificer of the *coup d'état,* had been instrumental in placing Napoleon on his throne.

This man maintained a sumptuous life at the Palais Bourbon, only second in splendor to that of the Tuileries itself. And, indeed, with some justification, for both royal and imperial blood liberally flowed in Morny's veins. He was half brother to Napoleon III, for he was the illegitimate son of Napoleon's mother, Queen Hortense, and the Count de Flahaut — who, strange to relate, was serving, at the time of Slidell's arrival, as French Ambassador to London. Morny's habit of conspicuously advertising this blood connection greatly annoyed the Emperor, but, on grounds of descent, irregular as it was, Morny was far more illustrious than the brother he had seated on his throne. Not only was he the son of the fragile Queen Hortense, but the grandson of Talleyrand and the great-great grandson of Louis XV, all, of course, irregularly.[5] He thus forms a fascinating problem in heredity. It is not fanciful to perceive in this new friend of Slidell — for he speedily became such — traits of all these distinguished ancestors. He possessed much of the social grace of Hortense, the cunning, adroitness, and audacity of Talleyrand, and the utter moral worthlessness, public and private, of Louis XV. A man of many-sided talents — a leader of fashion, one of the most sought-for wits at the salons, a collaborator with Offenbach in operettas and vaudevilles, an inveterate gambler at the clubs, an entrepreneur who, at the age of twenty-seven, created the sugar industry of France, an able statesman — De Morny was all these things, and at the same time he was colossally corrupt. Alphonse Daudet has drawn his character in the de Mora of *Le Nabab.* The thing above all that gained De Morny infamy was the extravagance of his life. This demanded a huge income, which he obtained chiefly by using state secrets on the stock exchange.

---

[5] The recently published *Diary of the French Revolution,* by Gouverneur Morris, contains much about the Countess Adelaide (or Adéle) de Flahaut, the mother of De Morny's father. She was herself supposed to be the granddaughter (irregularly) of Louis XV.

This practice, as will appear, had an important bearing on Franco-American relations in the Civil War.

Both Walewski and Morny received Slidell with the greatest cordiality. "The Duc de Morny, whom I frequently see, is now and has been for some months a warm sympathizer with our cause" — such passages are common in Slidell's letters to Benjamin, though, characteristically enough, Morny was at the same time confiding to John Bigelow his unswerving devotion to the Union. Soon after arrival Slidell had a most satisfactory interview with Walewski, and found him also "decidedly favorable" to the Southern side. From the beginning, however, Slidell dealt chiefly with another of the old companions of Napoleon's vagabond days, his fellow conspirator at Strassburg and Boulogne, and, next to Morny, the main engineer of the *coup d'état*. This was the Count de Persigny, Minister of the Interior. John Bigelow described Morny and Persigny as "the two most conspicuous and reckless adventurers in Europe," yet there was a difference between the two men. One was as sincere in his devotion to the new empire as the other was opportunist. Morny, in his early time, was an Orleanist; even his affection for his half brother did not propel him into the Bonapartist camp until indications safely pointed to triumph. When the fortunes of Louis Napoleon had reached their lowest ebb, however, Persigny was a devoted follower. Victor Hugo, in his poetic imprecations on the new regime, pictured Morny as a jackal; he might just as appositely have described Persigny as a Newfoundland dog. For Persigny, in the darkest days, lived only to advocate the Bonapartist cause. Having shared all Napoleon's misfortunes — poverty, prison, exile — Persigny also shared his triumphs; and, by the time Slidell appeared on the scene, was the closest imperial confidant. By the outside world Persigny was looked upon as the Emperor's spokesman. His speeches and conversation were regarded as echoing Napoleon's thoughts and programmes. This gave significance to Persigny's friendliness with Slidell. His newspaper, the *Constitutionel,* fervidly championed the Confederate cause. In personal meetings he treated the Confederate envoy with more than official courtesy. He was, as Slidell reports to Benjamin, "an ardent and steadfast friend." Within a week of his arrival, Slidell had seen this Cabinet officer twice. "He is with us, heart and soul," Slidell wrote Benjamin. "He said that our cause was just, and that every dictate of humanity, the well established principles of international law, and the true policy of France all called for our recognition and the declaration of the inefficiency of the blockade. He said that the Emperor entertained this opinion." "M. Persigny has invited me to call upon him frequently and has directed his huissier [door-keeper] to admit me at any time." [6]

Quite a contrast, this, to the icy treatment Mason was receiving in London! Yet Persigny did not direct foreign affairs; he was Minister of the Interior, not exactly the official with whom one might suppose a foreign diplomat should be holding secret sessions. Where, meanwhile, was the Secretary for Foreign Affairs, the statesman who filled the same position in France that Russell did in England? Slidell had met this functionary also; in this case, however, the experience had proved less satisfactory than the other conversations. Édouard Antoine Thouvenel, in February, 1862, Foreign Secretary of France, little resembled his brother statesmen of the Second Empire. In manner of life, in morals, in personal and political history, in international ideals, he stood quite apart from his imperial associates. Thouvenel was the only member of the group who had not figured in the conspiracies that had placed Napoleon on the throne. In his existence barricades, backstairs plottings, *coup d'états* had played no part. The more sedate career of lawyer and diplomat had been his training ground; ability as a negotiator of commercial treaties and

[6] Slidell to Benjamin, February 11, 1862. *Official Records of Union and Confederate Navies,* Series II, Vol. 3, p. 341.

Balkan alliances, as well as a most modern attitude on the Italian question, had been his chief recommendations for his exalted post. Younger than most of his companions, concerned with statecraft rather than politics, the trade of revolutionist was alien to his nature, and the exciting days of December, 1851, found Thouvenel quietly serving his country as Minister in Munich. In this office Thouvenel had served with a single-hearted devotion to the new liberalism of France that had won the approbation of patriotic Frenchmen and the undying hatred of Eugénie. For years the Empress and her favorite Minister, Walewski, had championed the extreme temporal power of the church, and when Thouvenel, the exponent of Italian unity, displaced this ultramontane statesman, the lady's resentment burned with a real Spanish fury. Historians have estimated Thouvenel in a more admiring spirit. He is almost the only one of Napoleon's advisers for whom they have a friendly word. Thouvenel and De Tocqueville, wrote John Bigelow, were the "two Ministers of Louis Napoleon in whom France has most reason to take pride and whose displacement she has most reason to deplore." Possibly Bigelow — Federal consul general in Paris, afterward Minister — was not an impartial critic. He could hardly help feeling kindly toward the man, who, almost alone of Napoleon's Ministers, showed a favorable disposition to the cause that so occupied Bigelow's heart.

For this unimpassioned diplomat steadily repulsed the blandishments of Slidell. The Davis Government never aroused in him any enthusiasm. Nonrecognition, nonintervention, neutrality in word and deed, acceptance of the Federal blockade — even Lord John Russell himself was hardly more inflexible in resisting Confederate arguments. This aloofness proved a constant irritation to Slidell. His letters to Benjamin bristle with complaints. The Foreign Minister, he writes, is no friend of the South. "He is decidedly hostile to our cause." "He is the only member of the Ministry whose sympathies are not with us." Slidell even carried his complaints to Persigny, and the friendly Frenchman with difficulty soothed his ruffled feelings. Do not take too seriously Thouvenel's coolness, Persigny said. Remember that he is a diplomat and that diplomats must move cautiously. "His reserve and coldness are habitual" — they arose partly from his temperament, always quiet, uncommunicative, noncommittal, and also from his lifelong training in diplomatic posts. "Above all," cautioned Persigny, "keep in mind the restraints imposed by his position!" After all, Thouvenel was Foreign Minister of France; what he said committed his country; Persigny, Rouher, Baroche, and others could discuss the American question more or less informally, but Thouvenel had to weigh his words. Slidell may have been persuaded, but he was not consoled.

Persigny might have been more successful in soothing Slidell had not that envoy's first meeting with Thouvenel left him with a sense of chill. Not that it failed in courtesy. Thouvenel, however indisposed to grow sentimental over the Confederacy, was still a Frenchman, to whom the blunt rudeness of an Earl Russell was alien. Perhaps this icy politeness made the experience a more trying one. Thouvenel, for instance, quite contentedly let Slidell do most of the talking. On purely personal matters — experiences on the *Trent,* Fort Warren, the release, the general satisfaction of France that Great Britain had avoided war with the United States — the Frenchman waxed conversational. When the talk touched foreign policy, however, he lapsed into a silence that would have done credit to Lord John Russell himself. "Finding him indisposed to open a new subject of conversation," reported Slidell, he himself most diplomatically broached the delicate topic. Before granting Slidell's request for an interview, Thouvenel had insisted that the question of recognition should not be brought forward. Slidell now cautiously mentioned this prohibited topic.

"I shall not refer to the subject of recognition until I have reason to believe that the French government is better prepared to entertain it."

M. Thouvenel received this observation in silence. "The Minister was determined to say as little as possible himself," Slidell reported to Benjamin, "but was not unwilling to hear me."

So Slidell now delivered a lengthy discourse on the Federal blockade, making the usual objections; that it contravened the Treaty of Paris, that it was ineffective, and that Confederate vessels were disregarding it at will. He produced a long array of statistics to substantiate the last point. But then M. Thouvenel interrupted with almost the only question addressed to Slidell in the interview. It was a penetrating one and clearly annoyed the Confederate.

"If so many vessels have broken the blockade, how is it that so little cotton has reached neutral ports?"

The whole of Europe at the time was asking this same question. Slidell explained that most ships slipping through the blockade were small ones, engaged in transporting turpentine to the West Indies. Larger vessels refrained from commerce through fear; in most cases they could get through, but the danger of capture deterred them from making the attempt.

Then Slidell posed another delicate question. He had been informed that Great Britain had approached France on blockade matters and other infractions of the Federal fleet, and had received a response that the blockade was an ineffective one and not entitled to recognition.

"If my question is not indiscreet," he said, "I should like to know whether my information is correct?"

Thouvenel replied in words which his visitor described as "categorical and unqualified."

"No communication of the sort has been received by France from the British government." He was also certain that no exchange of views on the subject had been held with other powers. "If there had been I could scarcely have failed to know it. I have heard nothing of the kind."

Thouvenel explained once more that a practical alliance existed between France and Great Britain on the American question. Neither would take action except in coöperation with the other. This agreement had been made on the outbreak of the Civil War, and it was still in force. But the French Minister, reticent in this as in all matters, did not definitely describe the nature of this understanding, though Slidell learned the facts in the next few weeks. It was far more unfavorable to the Confederate cause than had been supposed. It was not an agreement on equal terms, for by it France had given the initiative in American affairs to Great Britain. "Take the lead, we follow!" — this was the basis of the one-sided *entente.* Thus France had already accepted Russell's attitude on the blockade, much as that contravened her own policy, and great as was the danger that such a ruling held for her in future wars. But the European situation was then acute; a good understanding with Great Britain was indispensable to Napoleon's foreign policy; thus he had no wish to quarrel with England over anything, above all, America.

"Finding M. Thouvenel very decidedly reticent and unwilling to say anything which could possibly commit himself or his government," wrote Slidell, "I took my leave of him without waiting for any intimation that the interview had been sufficiently prolonged." [7]

[7] For this episode, see Slidell to Mason, with enclosures, February 11, 1862, and March 26, 1862. *Official Records of Union and Confederate Navies,* Series II, Vol. 3, pp. 341–372.

XII

NAPOLEON III AND THE CONFEDERACY

1

A Cautious Friend

HERE was hardly an auspicious beginning for Slidell's mission, nor did his relations with Thouvenel improve in the succeeding months. This Foreign Minister, like most Frenchmen, detested slavery; he was far more interested in Europe than in America, was concerned more with Italian unity than with a new republic rising three thousand miles away, and was determined, in the furtherance of his foreign policy, to keep on the best of terms with Great Britain. He was disposed, therefore, to give the British Government precedence in American affairs, and to support whatever attitude British statesmen might adopt. In taking this stand, Thouvenel better represented French public opinion than did Napoleon and his other Ministers. Practically all classes in France inclined in sympathy to the North. This held as true of the upper social orders and the bourgeoisie as of more humble Frenchmen. With the aristocracy, indeed, precisely the opposite situation prevailed in France from that which Mason had found in England. Both Orleanists and Legitimists early manifested their sympathy for the Union. This was not owing entirely to enthusiasm for the Federal cause. Hostility to Napoleon III largely directed the attitude of Royalists on all public questions. The mere fact that the man these elements looked upon as a vulgar usurper favored the Confederacy automatically placed them on the other side. Orleanist cordiality to the North was sufficiently displayed when the Comte de Paris, pretender to the throne of France, his brother, the Duc de Chartres, and his uncle, the Prince de Joinville, joined the Federal army and served on McClellan's staff; the Count afterward wrote a history of the Civil War so friendly to the Federal cause that it aroused great anger in the South. The royal family of France had historic reasons for making the Union cause their own. The Bourbons had always regarded the United States as their own creation in part. In its progress they took dynastic pride. Had not their ancestor, Louis XVI, supported the Revolutionary cause of 1776, first surreptitiously and afterward openly, and thus greatly contributed to its success?

Moreover, the true interests of France demanded the triumph of the Lincoln Government. The same reasoning which made it good national policy for France in the eighteenth century to favor the establishment of an independent united America made it wise statesmanship to prevent its disruption in 1861. France had helped the new republic in order to weaken the British Empire. A strong unified power in the western Atlantic was needed to act as a counterpoise to maritime England. That principle held just as true in 1861 as in 1776. A disintegrated America would enormously strengthen England and increase her power against France and the Continent. Thus political and dynastic France evinced a disposition toward America diametrically opposed to that of similar forces in England. For a century the Federal Union and monarchical France had lived on terms of intimate friendship. French writers, unlike British, had not been busy for a century heaping ridicule and abuse upon a raw, undeveloped nation; French travelers, in the main, had made agreeable reports of life beyond the Atlantic and a great French philosopher, De Tocqueville, had given the world its most understanding analysis of American institutions. To the British aristocracy and propertied classes, the United States, in 1861, was despised as a faithless, ungrateful child that had left the parental roof and was now being properly punished for its sins; to France, it was an adopted son, whose misfortunes were a matter of sympathetic concern to the foster parent. This sentiment found its appropriate symbol in the attitude of the descendants of that Bourbon king who had done so much to bring the new nation into being.

Many Bonapartists, despite the behavior of their head, followed the royal example. The house of Prince Napoleon — "Plon-Plon" — himself second in line to the Imperial throne, served as gathering place for French adherents of the North. Such leaders of French literature and statesmanship as Thiers, Henri Martin, Laboulaye, and Louis Blanc openly espoused the Washington Government. The most influential French newspapers, unlike their principal counterparts in London — *Le Temps, Le Journal des Debats, La Presse,* — advocated daily the Northern interest. The greatest French periodicals, in particular *La Revue des Deux Mondes,* devoted large space to defending the Union, and the mercantile and working classes, in large part, accepted this leadership. The cotton famine was not so acute a problem in France as in England. Cotton spinning was not such a supreme industry in France as on the other side of the Channel. Britain, in normal times, took 5,000,000 bales from the South and France 500,000. Thousands of French artisans lost their occupation, it is true, but the extreme miseries of Lancashire had not descended on northern France. Indeed, the scarcity of cotton brought compensations, for it stimulated the French linen, silk, and woolen industries. But the thing that chiefly influenced the French masses was their aversion to slavery. Mason found this hostility a serious matter in England but nowhere in the world, except perhaps New England, did this system arouse such hostility as in France. These several considerations explain Napoleon's hesitation in the American crisis. This is the reason why he dared not make warfare on the North, especially without England as partner. It was freely declared at the time that such action on his part would have precipitated a revolution and driven him from his unsteady throne.

On the merits of the case, therefore, Napoleon III should

have supported the Federal Government. Had he truly reflected French opinion, such would have been his course. He understood clearly the true welfare of his nation and the prevailing state of public sentiment; in his first interview with Slidell, the Emperor frankly said that French interest demanded that he support the North; its break-up would be a misfortune for France. A powerful America was desirable as a *contrepoids* to Britain. Why, therefore, did he adopt his pro-Southern course? The explanation was purely Napoleonic and dynastic. It had no relation to the vital concerns of the French people themselves. The underlying motive of his plan has been set forth in a preceding chapter. It was all comprised in the single word Mexico. That imperial scheme, in its formative stage in 1861, had grown in proportions in the succeeding twelvemonth. At first a tentative, hesitating enterprise, it had now become a determined policy. By the time John Slidell reached Paris, Napoleon was so deeply enmeshed that he could hardly withdraw. The tripartite expedition of 1861 — France, England, and Spain — had collapsed. Neither England nor Spain had shown any interest in establishing a Hapsburg Mexican empire that would grow into an appanage of France. But the departure of British and Spanish ships caused consternation in French official circles.

Some of these statesmen, especially De Morny, had personal reasons for regretting the defection. This speculator, one of the first movers in the Mexican expedition, probably did not feel great enthusiasm for Maximilian, nor for French imperial designs on the American continent. But he had one substantial reason for wishing the advancing armies well. John Bigelow tells of a charming visit he made, in September, 1863, to M. Berryer, one of the most eloquent of French advocates. The old aristocrat spoke scathingly of the Mexican business. "What good will that do France?" he asked. Bigelow suggested that possibly French creditors might collect their debts. "Yes," replied Berryer, "to fill the pockets of Morny and his speculators."[1] This ancient Frenchman — a fine old Royalist whose American policy, he informed Bigelow in 1863, was that "of Louis XVI" — had better information than most of his contemporaries; not until the collapse of the French Empire did the secret origin of the first invasion of Mexico become known. The French Commune, ransacking and burning the Tuileries, uncovered documents which laid the whole thing bare. De Morny's avarice, it then appeared, had been the incentive that made him, next to Eugénie, the chief supporter of this fatal intervention. A Swiss banker, J. B. Jecker, in 1859 advanced Miramon, one of the many short-lived clerical Presidents of Mexico, 3,750,000 francs, taking in exchange Mexican bonds to the face value of 75,000,000. His attempt to collect this monstrous bill started the train of Mexico's misfortunes, for, failing by ordinary means, Jecker entered into a bargain with Morny. In consideration for using the military and naval forces of France to extort payment, Morny was to receive one third of the profits. At about the time that Jecker and Morny concluded this secret agreement, a group of Mexican exiles in Paris, extremely monarchical in politics and ultramontane in religion, were ingratiating themselves into the confidence of the pious Eugénie. The joint expedition of France, Spain, and England had followed. This demonstration was dissolved by the withdrawal of Spain and England, soon after Slidell's arrival.

But Napoleon's soldiers remained, for the reason that debt collection was only one of the purposes of their invasion. The larger aim — the overthrow of the Mexican republic, and the creation of a Hapsburg empire in its place — now hung by a single thread, the fate of the Confederacy. The new foreign policy of Napoleon III was thus linked to the fortunes of Jefferson Davis. Herein we have the explanation of Napoleon's genial interest in Slidell; this is the reason why Eugénie began to invite Mrs. Slidell and her charming daughters to exclusive

[1] *Retrospections of an Active Life*, by John Bigelow, Vol. II, p. 66.

imperial functions. They needed the Confederacy to carry through their Mexican plan. The triumph of the North would spell the doom of the projected empire. It is an interesting study to review the ups and downs of the Mexican adventure, and to observe how each vacillation in attitude depended on events in the American Civil War. Not until the Federal armies met disastrous defeat at Bull Run did Napoleon despatch his forces to Vera Cruz. Not until Lee triumphed in the campaign before Richmond did he decide, despite the withdrawal of Great Britain and Spain, to pursue his Mexican campaign alone, and gave General Forey orders to march his troops to the City of Mexico. By the time Slidell reached the imperial court, the possible restitution of the Union was a nightmare that haunted Napoleon's dreams. From the beginning Washington had frowned upon his project. Congress had passed a resolution of most unfriendly tenor and Lincoln had announced that the Monroe Doctrine still embodied the American aspiration for the Western Hemisphere. If the Civil War should come to a victorious end, the United States would possess an army of not far from one million men — perfectly equipped, well led, and with several years' active experience in warfare. What opposition could the few French divisions Napoleon might safely send to Mexico present to such a force? Especially as, at this moment, a multitude of enemies were rising against Napoleon in Europe itself, ready to pounce should he become involved in a transatlantic struggle? The result would have been defeat, humiliation, national bankruptcy, and the end of the Napoleonic empire. The debaclé that came in 1871, after a terrible military disaster, would have simply been antedated by five or six years.

French policy for nearly a hundred years should therefore have placed Napoleon on the side of the Union; public opinion in France strongly supported the North; but these considerations gave way to the pursuit of a purely dynastic end. Napoleon's position was particularly difficult because, for reasons already explained, he could do nothing in American affairs without the assistance of Great Britain. And Great Britain had no immediate reason for burning her fingers in that particular fire. Yet the Emperor did not entirely lack allies. Judah P. Benjamin and John Slidell clearly saw the value to the South of the Maximilian scheme. Not that it aroused much enthusiasm in either breast, especially when it was learned that the Napoleonic plan contemplated the reestablishment of Texas as an independent republic, to serve as a buffer between Maximilian Mexico and the domain of Jefferson Davis. Still Mexico could be useful in obtaining French recognition. At the famous consortings in Biarritz in the autumn of 1863, this matter reached a crisis. Maximilian's fortunes were then in critical state. After preliminary reverses, the French had finally captured the City of Mexico. French agents in the capital had gone through the form of abolishing the Republic and setting up the Empire. A Mexican delegation, headed by Guitterez de Estrada, had visited his prospective Majesty at Miramar and offered him the "crown of Montezuma." Still the Hapsburg hesitated. Would he accept the dangerous dignity? Such was the question disturbing the imperial group at Biarritz. Wherever the Slidells went this topic held chief place in conversation. Here Slidell saw much of Hidalgo and Guitterez, who, like himself, were members of the imperial set. As to acceptance, Guitterez declared, there was no doubt. According to reports from Miramar, however, one difficulty still stood in the way. The future Emperor was keeping a close eye on the Confederate armies. His cause, he had recently informed a visitor, and that of the Confederacy were one![2] Why were France and Britain so slow, he complained, in recognizing Davis? Until they did so, he seemed unwilling to move. "My friend at the Foreign Office," Slidell wrote Benjamin, December 3, 1863, "confirms what is said

---

[2] Slidell to Benjamin, December 3, 1863. *Official Records of Union and Confederate Navies*, Series II, Vol. 3, p. 969

of the value that the Archduke attaches to our recognition. He has seen the paper in which the Archduke set forth the different measures which he considers essential to the successful establishment of his government. The recognition of the Confederacy headed the list." [3]

2

A LARGE BRIBE OFFERED FRANCE

What made the situation so trying was the unyielding attitude of Great Britain. France could take no step except at the initiative of Queen Victoria, a monarch who seemed to grow more stubborn every day. By this time — September, 1863 — Slidell had spent more than a year seeking to change the Napoleonic attitude. But nothing could be done so long as the Franco-British understanding on "the American question" prevailed. As a shrewd diplomat Slidell could find only one solution to the impasse. That understanding itself must be broken. Some inducement must be offered France to persuade her to forsake her British ally and take independent action on the Confederacy. Would England ever change her policy? Never, said Slidell. France must act therefore alone or his Southern cause was at an end. The friendly disposition of French statesmen, even of the Emperor, counted for nothing in itself. To Slidell's constant pleadings that the Southern enterprise was just, the answer of Cabinet Ministers was always forthcoming: *"Oui, oui, Monsieur!"* Then why did not France take action? A shrug of the shoulders gave the only reply. There was England, so obstinate, so determined to let the Americans fight it out by themselves! *Que faire?*

Clearly, so long as this *entente* prevailed, no progress could be made. Evidently Slidell's job as negotiator was to drive what diplomats call a "wedge" between the two powers. For

[3] Slidell to Benjamin, December 3, 1863 *Official Records of Union and Confederate Navies*, Series II, Vol. 3, p. 969.

Britain both Benjamin and Slidell felt the utmost dislike and contempt. The relations of the United States and England, Benjamin declared, in a letter to Slidell, "have now become settled on the established basis of insulting aggression on one side and tame submission on the other." Benjamin even expresses a surreptitious admiration for Seward, who had so completely subdued the British lion. Slidell was just as hostile. Russell's American policy he pilloried as cold, callous, inhuman. It had no sympathetic interest in either side; it was using both as pawns to advance the political and material concerns of its own empire. The purpose — Slidell summed up the whole thing in a talk with Napoleon — was "the destruction of the agricultural industry of the South and the bankruptcy and disintegration of the North." The hard cynicism innate in Slidell's own character was attributed — probably not unjustly — to the British Cabinet. "I have no hope from England," he wrote his "dear Benjamin," August 24, 1862, "because I am satisfied that she desires an indefinite prolongation of the war, until the North shall be entirely exhausted and broken down. Nothing can exceed the selfishness of British statesmen except their wretched hypocrisy. They are continually boasting about their disinterested magnanimity and objection of all other considerations than those dictated by a high toned morality, while their entire policy is marked by egotism and duplicity."[4] The South foolishly imagines, Slidell declared, that its military victories will bring English recognition. It does not see that these very triumphs make such recognition impossible. Had the Confederacy lost the Battle of Bull Run — such was Slidell's conviction — Great Britain would probably have rushed to its aid. All that this and other successes accomplished was to convince British statesmen that the South could win without their help. Why therefore should it risk the dangers of intervention?

To break the Franco-British agreement on American af-

[4] *Official Records of Union and Confederate Navies*, Series II, Vol. 3, pp. 520–521.

fairs, and to bring about separate French action now became the single goal of Slidell's diplomacy. He went about the matter ably and intelligently. The fundamental facts in the situation strongly favored his argument. The most important of them was that the interests of Great Britain and France in this neutral position were not the same. The policy which Britain had adopted and France had obediently followed was, Slidell pointed out, a very good thing for England but a very bad thing for her associate nation. For instance, there was Britain's recognition of the blockade. Such recognition might, in the long run, bring advantage to England, but it might easily spell the ruin of France. Why should the latter country pave the way to her own eventual economic strangling by accepting the Lincoln interdict as legal — as she was doing by the simple process of not repudiating it? Lord John Russell had always in mind a possible, even probable war with France; he planned, in such a very probable contingency, to blockade French coasts in precisely the same way that the Federal Navy was now closing Southern ports. Again, the prolongation of the war would strengthen England, but would it not, at the same time, weaken France? England welcomed the American war, even the distressful cotton famine, because that would help her carry out a scheme she had long been contemplating, the establishment of cotton culture in India. Would not that mean death to the cotton-spinning industry of northern France? The British plan of nonrecognition and nonintervention was thus, from whatever point of view regarded, opposed to the real interests of the Empire, whatever, benefit it might bring to England.

Benjamin now came to Slidell's aid with an inducement of his own. This clever statesman evolved a "wedge-driving" device of most practical nature. This was little less than a proposal to purchase French support. "Bribery" is not an inapt word to describe his programme. Benjamin would use this kind of persuasion in two ways. One was an offer of special trade facilities, and the other essentially an outright money *douceur*. Not inaccurately had these shrewd gentlemen assessed the calibre of the gambler then occupying the French imperial throne. Give trade and financial aid to the sadly depleted Imperial treasury and withhold them from Albion the abhorred — here was Benjamin's way of separating the two Governments. Almost the new secretary's first act was to confide this ingenious secret to Slidell. His letter bore several injunctions as to its extremely "confidential" character; it was a matter, indeed, in which silent action was desirable. Had France accepted this offer, the Anglo-French agreement would have been undone, and that, of course, was the purpose. On his part Napoleon was to defy the Federal blockade and despatch his merchant ships to Southern ports. In return French products were to be admitted to the Confederacy, duty free, for a "certain defined period." Thus France was to enjoy free trade with the Confederacy, to the exclusion of Great Britain and other nations. And there was another even more tempting consideration. France, Benjamin informed Slidell, was known to be short of funds. Mexico and other imperial schemes were proving a terrible strain. Perhaps the Confederacy could ease this situation a little! To-day the spectacle of Mr. Davis's Government, itself living mainly on paper money, offering financial aid to this, greatest of Continental powers, has its humorous aspect. Yet the resourceful Benjamin had devised a plan by which it might be done. King Cotton again! The reward of France for defying the Federal blockade was to be a large gift of this indispensable "white gold." Benjamin's first offer was 100,000 bales, but Slidell could increase the amount to almost any extent in case the French manifested a bargaining spirit. Another trading advantage was suggested. The French ships coming for this cotton would bring large quantities of French products, which the Southern states desperately needed. On the mere basis of 100,000 bales, and the profits on imported (duty free) articles, Benjamin estimated a net increment to the French treasury of $25,000,000. "If it should be your good fortune to succeed in this delicate and difficult negotiation," Benjamin informed Slidell, "you might well consider that practically our struggle would have been brought to a successful termination, for you would, of course, not fail to make provision for the necessary supply of small arms and powder (especially cannon powder) which alone are required to enable us to confront our foes triumphantly."[5] The real objective was to entangle France in the Civil War. Napoleon could break the blockade only by sending warships to accompany his merchant fleet and warships off the American coast could have had only one result.

Significantly, Slidell did not lay this proposal to purchase intervention before Thouvenel, the proper intermediary for his communications to the French Government. Thouvenel was not only friendly to the North, but he had the reputation of being a high-minded gentleman, and it would have taken a bold spirit to suggest to him the purchase of French support. Instead Slidell consulted Persigny, now almost become a familiar crony, and probably the closest of all Frenchmen, except De Morny, to the Emperor. No record exists of Persigny's response, but there are indications that the idea was not unpleasing. "I communicated to him confidentially the substance of my new instructions," Slidell wrote Benjamin, July 25, 1862 — a delay of several weeks was caused by this Minister's absence in England. Persigny's reply was immediate. "Go to Vichy and see the Emperor." Count Persigny "gave me a very warm letter to General Fleury, who is a great favorite of the Emperor and constantly accompanies him, urging him to procure an audience for me. I went accordingly to Vichy on Tuesday, arriving there in the evening. The next morning I sent a note to General Fleury, enclosing that of M. de Persigny soliciting his good offices to procure me 'une

[5] Benjamin to Slidell, April 12, 1862. *Official Records of Union and Confederate Navies*, Series II, Vol. 3, p. 327.

audience *officieuse'* [6] with the Emperor. I very soon received a reply saying that the Emperor would receive me at two o'clock."

3
THE COLD SHOULDER

Little in the appearance of the gentleman who welcomed the Confederate envoy suggested a Napoleonic origin. Most visitors confronting the Emperor for the first time felt keen disappointment. The squat figure, the dull eyes, the hesitant speech, the exceedingly awkward carriage hardly seemed appropriately to embody the man then generally acclaimed the master of Europe. It is true that Madame Récamier found the youthful Louis Napoleon *poli, distingué, et taciturne,* but the latter quality was the only one that impressed Americans who met the unsuccessful conspirator in New York in 1837. To Charles Greville, who encountered the Prince at Lady Blessington's, soon afterward, he was "a short, thickish, vulgar-looking man, without the slightest resemblance to his Imperial uncle, or any intelligence in his countenance." Judging from succeeding commentators, maturer years and lofty station had not greatly dignified the imperial presence. Two Americans, meeting Napoleon III at about the same time as Slidell, have left vivid and pungent pen portraits, which may serve as adequate introduction to the monarch who now pleasantly advanced, with outstretched palm, to greet his transatlantic guest. Neither the Emperor nor Empress had favorably impressed John Bigelow, who was presented for the first time at a ball in the Tuileries, in January, 1860. Eugénie was "a pretty woman; had a graceful figure; beautiful sloping shoulders and drooping eyelids; and yet there seemed to be nothing regal or sovereign in her appearance, nothing that indicated any comprehension of the part she and her husband

[6] Semiofficial.

were playing in the history of the world." "The Emperor also disappointed me. He is short, with broad shoulders, large chest, and barrel tapering off into two legs, so short as to seem very, very small. His head, too, seemed rather too large for his legs, and he looked, too, as the sailors say, 'all by the bows,' like a cat-fish. . . . Owing to the shortness of his legs, his walk is not graceful. He seems to advance first on one side and then the other as on a pivot, his head moving from side to side as if trying to keep time with his legs."[7] Two years afterward John Hay, Secretary of Legation at Paris, painted a corroborative, but even more uncomplimentary picture. "Short and stocky, he moves with a queer, side-long gait, like a gouty crab; a man so wooden-looking that you would expect his voice to come rasping out like a watchman's rattle. A complexion like crude tallow — marked for Death whenever Death wants him — to be taken sometime in half an hour, or left neglected by the Skeleton King for years, perhaps, if properly coddled. The moustache and imperial which the world knows, but ragged and bristly, concealing the mouth entirely, is moving a little nervously as the lips twitch. Eyes sleepily watchful — furtive, stealthy, rather ignoble; like servants looking out of dirty windows and saying 'nobody at home' and lying as they say it. He stands there as still and passive as if carved in oak for a ship's figurehead."[8]

Slidell, lacking the literary talents of Bigelow and John Hay, has left no personal description of Napoleon III; had he done so, it would probably have been less acid than these brief but illuminating sketches. Slidell had the same reason for admiring the Emperor that the two Yankees had for detesting him: he was a friend and champion of the South and never more so than on this afternoon when, with an effervescence unusual with him, he greeted the Confederate envoy. Napoleon began speaking in rapid French; though Slidell could

[7] *Retrospections of an Active Life*, by John Bigelow, Vol. 1, p. 246.
[8] *The Life of John Hay*, by William Roscoe Thayer, Vol. 1, pp. 235–236

handle this language for most colloquial purposes, probably his ear was not acute enough to detect what was obvious to true Parisians, that the Emperor spoke with a slight German accent, the result of his boyhood passed in Arenenberg. In cordiality the greeting left nothing to be desired. How sorry he was not to have met Slidell before! Splendid news that in last evening's papers — the Federal defeats before Richmond! His sympathies, Napoleon told Slidell, had always been with the South. Was not the South struggling for self-government and had that not been the great end to which his own life had been dedicated? He had always desired to show this sympathy in some practical way, but there was England, always unwilling to coöperate! Several times France had approached the British Government in hope of joint action, never meeting with a favorable response. Still France could not act alone, though doubtless England would like to have her "draw the chestnuts from the fire for her benefit." But what were Mr. Slidell's views? What could France do to help the Confederate cause?

Slidell, having reached this critical point, requested leave to continue the interview in English; a request partly intended as a compliment, for Napoleon spoke excellent English and was extremely proud of his facility in that tongue. The Confederate plunged at once into the subject of Benjamin's latest instructions. He delicately outlined the reward that would come to the French treasury for acceding to his views. Break the blockade, urged Slidell, and the South would quickly win the war. He described the great mistake France had made in following the English attitude in this matter. The blockade was illegal, contravened the Treaty of Paris, and held untold mischief for France in the future.

"I committed a great error," Napoleon replied, "and I now deeply regret it. France should never have respected the blockade. And she should have recognized the Confederacy." The time for such action was the preceding year, when all the Confederate ports were open and Southern armies were menacing Washington.

"But what," he asked, almost in despair, "can now be done? To open the ports forcibly would be an act of war."

There was no reason to fear the Yankees, Slidell protested; they were always making threats, which seldom materialized. See how they had backed down in the *Trent* affair! And now he unfolded Benjamin's scheme for financing the French Navy, and filling the French treasury with money, in case the appearance of French war vessels at blockaded ports brought about war with the United States.

"This proposition," Slidell concluded, "is made exclusively to France. My colleague in London knows nothing about it."

"How am I to get the cotton?" Napoleon asked.

Then Slidell touched upon one of the weakest spots in the Emperor's abundant vanity. Of all his war machines there was nothing of which he was so proud as of his new ironclad vessels, the *Gloire,* the *Couronne,* and the *Normandie.* The building of these ships had strained to the breaking point French relations with England. Certainly the ramshackle American Navy, Slidell insisted, could not stand up against their guns. He drew a picture for Napoleon's benefit of these men-of-war reducing to ashes New York, — Slidell's native city, — Boston, and Fortress Monroe — a picture which the Emperor keenly enjoyed. He agreed with Slidell that the *Gloire* and her sisters, all by themselves, could end the blockade and with it the war. But again — there was England!

Though Slidell does not record the Emperor's comment on his financial plan, he says that "it did not seem disagreeable" to him. But he made no commitment. Over this as over every phase of the conversation rose the shadow of English opposition. Slidell and the Emperor discussed all phases of the situation — mediation, recognition, a six months' armistice — but the outcome was most unsatisfactory to the Confederate, despite imperial sympathy and personal kindness, for the fact that stood uppermost in his mind, as he left the presence, was that France would make no independent move, was still determined to leave the initiative to the British Government, and would acquiesce in whatever that Cabinet decided. His favorite policy of driving a wedge between France and Britain, even when reenforced by a huge money bribe, stood little chance of success.

"All that you say is true," concluded His Majesty, "but the policy of nations is controlled by their interests and not by their sentiments. It ought to be so." And the sad fact was that the interests of France demanded that, in American affairs, she should not act independently of Great Britain. All Slidell's denunciations of Britain and her lowered prestige in the world — the periodical collapse of British prestige, it will be observed, is nothing new — did not budge the imperial purpose.

"Your Majesty," pleaded Slidell, "has now an opportunity of securing a faithful ally, bound to you not only by ties of gratitude, but by those more reliable — a common interest and congenial habits."

"Yes," replied the Emperor, "you have many families of French descent in Louisiana who yet preserve their habits and language."

Pleasant personally as may have been this interview at Vichy in July, 1862, it was barren of results. Much as Napoleon would have welcomed the proffered subsidy, the price demanded of him was too great. His wily mind must have quickly detected the motive that really animated Benjamin and Slidell. He was not prepared to jettison the *entente* with Great Britain on American affairs, and thereby cast himself adrift in a world of European enemies. Slidell's further consultations with the Emperor had no more satisfactory results. Cordial interviews followed at Saint-Cloud in October and at the Tuileries the following June; on these and other occasions Napoleon announced his willingness to recognize the Confederacy — provided Great Britain should do so first. By this time one change, auspicious for Slidell, had taken place in the French Cabinet. Thouvenel, friend of the North and enemy to all Southern arguments, had been forced out of the Government. Slidell reported that Thouvenel's attitude toward the Confederacy was, at least in part, the cause of his dismissal, but in this he was mistaken. Thouvenel's opposition to Eugénie's Papal policy — for he was strongly anti-clerical — had brought the two into conflict for a considerable time; one violent scene over this issue had recently taken place in the Council, which the Empress regularly attended. In this meeting Eugénie, after denouncing Thouvenel, had rushed out of the room in a rage, leaving her imperial husband white and speechless. No Foreign Minister could long retain his office after such a scene.

Thouvenel's successor, Drouyn de Lhuys, was sufficiently pro-Southern even for Slidell. But he could do nothing. Lord John Russell's move for recognition, already described, reached its crisis at the moment of this change. Thouvenel's opposition was one reason why it had failed, but his successor arrived on the scene too late to revive the expiring negotiations. A year later — in the summer of 1863 — Napoleon and De Lhuys attempted again to enlist England in a similar *démarche*. This episode, known in England as the Roebuck resolution, fills many pages in Parliamentary debates and usually occupies much space in histories of Confederate diplomacy, but it was not important. The fact that soon after negotiations began, the battles of Gettysburg and Vicksburg were fought, gave no hope of success. And the whole controversy soon degenerated into a farce. Roebuck, an eccentric character, crossed to Paris and had an intimate talk with Napoleon. Then, a few days afterward, he rose in Parliament and told the story, many of the details being most confidential, and damaging to the prestige of France. The Emperor, in an understandable anger, denied the truth of Roebuck's narrative and berated him for violating his confidence. As a result the famous debate was concerned not so much with recognition of the Confederacy as with the question — not yet settled — whether Napoleon or Roebuck was a liar. The proceeding did not enhance the imperial dignity, and Napoleon III became more cautious than formerly in his approaches to the difficult American question.

By this time, likewise, Slidell's usefulness as a diplomat had reached an end. Sympathetic as he was to the Confederate cause, the official attitude of Drouyn de Lhuys differed little from that of Thouvenel. France, he repeatedly told Slidell, would recognize the Confederacy and defy the blockade whenever England set the example. New European complications — the insurrection in Poland, the menacing encroachment of Prussia — were daily adding to Napoleon's troubles and making him more and more dependent on cooperation with Britain. And, more important than all, the Federal military position was changing in almost startling fashion; its armies were now everywhere in the ascendant; for the first time, European statesmen began to realize that the Confederacy was fighting a losing cause. After the summer of 1863, Slidell's prestige in Paris consequently declined. He did not follow Mason's example and close his headquarters, but his latter period was full of bitterness and disappointment.

From the beginning the only hope of Confederate success in France had rested on Mexico. His imperial designs in the Western Hemisphere had been the compelling reason for Napoleon's cordiality toward the Confederacy and its representatives. But its failure would spell doom for the fragile Mexican empire. All Europe completely understood this, above all Napoleon himself, but Slidell never saw the issue quite so clearly. This obtuseness brought him his greatest humiliation. The Mexican conspirators in Paris constantly fed his hopes. Guitterez de Estrada, whose unceasing importunities had fired the spirit of Eugénie, was one of the Southern

Charles Louis Napoleon Bonaparte (1808–1873)

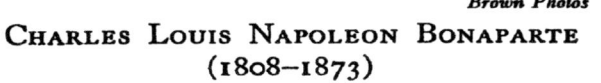

Brown Photos

Eugénie de Montijo (1826–1920)

Brown Photos

MAXIMILIAN (1832–1867)

envoy's confidants. In early 1864, Maximilian, after much vacillation, accepted the Mexican throne, and, in March, on the eve of his departure for Vera Cruz, spent a week in Paris. Slidell naturally expected to be received with open arms. Acting on the advice of Guitterez, he sent the conventional petition for an audience. The reply acceded to the request, but set no time for the meeting. That, as Slidell well understood, was the polite formula of declination. During the week that Maximilian remained in Paris, Slidell kept assiduously pounding his door and demanding the promised interview; but Maximilian did not even answer his notes. The explanation was apparent to most observers. Maximilian now centred his hope of recognition on the Federal Government, not on the enfeebled Confederacy. He had been falsely informed that if he kept clear of the South the Lincoln Government would regard his schemes with a friendly eye, and this bare chance of winning the favor of Washington made him extremely cautious. Not only did he cold-shoulder Slidell, but the French Government followed the same cue. In the autumn of 1864, Slidell could feel an increasing frigidity on every hand. The Tuileries and the "Villa Eugénie" at Biarritz welcomed him no more. Madame Slidell and Mesdemoiselles no longer appeared at imperial balls. Drouyn de Lhuys ignored requests for interviews. In all disputes involving North and South the French now turned a friendly face to the Federal Government. When the *Alabama* appeared in the harbor of Cherbourg the French ordered it to leave, thus forcing that famous vessel into combat — and destruction — with the Federal warship *Kearsarge* waiting outside for its prey. When the *Rappahannock*, a Confederate unarmed vessel, put in at Calais, she was interned. Napoleon had himself furtively instigated the construction of Confederate warships in French shipyards, but, at the demand of the Federal Government, he now vetoed their delivery. If we seek the explanation for this new friendliness to the Federal cause we shall find it in Virginia, where Grant, despite fierce opposition, was progressing in his slow advance on Richmond, and in Georgia and the Carolinas, where Sherman was blasting his way through all the Confederate defenses, every day signaling a new victory, and bringing nearer the inevitable end. Napoleon now knew that Maximilian was doomed and that the withdrawal of the French forces in Mexico was unavoidable. His whole American policy had been based upon a false assumption — the invincibility of the South — and the only course remaining was to extricate himself from a dangerous position as gracefully as he could.

Benjamin now began to rage more bitterly against France than he had against England. Of the two countries, the course of the British, in his eyes, was more honorable toward the South. Slidell, in his resentment, became indiscreet. He informed callers — knowing that the words would be repeated in official quarters — that peace would soon be established between North and South; one of the stipulations of the treaty, he added, would be an alliance between the two previously contending powers to enforce the Monroe Doctrine and expel all European adventurers from American soil. With only two members of the Imperial court did Slidell keep up friendly relations, and these were personal, rather than official. Slidell had found real companions in Persigny and Morny; the three had tastes in common, especially a fondness for cards. Yet this association also came to an end, under conditions that involved the displeasure of Napoleon. John Bigelow tells the story, as he received it, several years after the war, from William Preston who, for a few fleeting weeks, held the purely decorative post of Confederate Minister to the Court of Maximilian. "While playing at the Club one night with Persigny and de Morny, among others, Slidell stated what he had learned through de Haviland about a certain promise and request in high quarters. One of the dukes, — for in those days it was the custom to call both Persigny and de Morny 'duke' — said that ——— had never made any such request. Slidell reaffirmed his statement. The duke repeated in yet more emphatic terms that it was not true. Slidell rose from his seat and with some vehemence, exclaimed, 'By God! No man, whether Duke or Emperor, shall ever say that what John Slidell said was not true!' " [9] Morny, greatly offended, reported the episode to the Emperor. That ended Slidell's standing at the Imperial court. Requests for audiences were denied from this time forward. Only once again did the Confederate meet his Imperial Majesty, and this at a time when he was majesty no more. It was in 1871, when both the Confederacy and the French Empire lay in ruins. In 1871 the two exiles — one representative of the lost cause of France, the other that of America — came together at Chiselhurst, England, the place in which the dethroned Emperor had found peaceful asylum. The angry mood of Slidell's last days in Paris had vanished in a common misfortune, and the two men grasped hands, though they were so affected that it was some time before they could speak. In a little more than a year both were dead. Of all the bitter survivors of the Civil War, Slidell was probably the bitterest. He never saw his native land again, dying at Cowes in 1871. Both daughters married Frenchmen — one, as already related, Baron d'Erlanger, the other the Comte de Saint-Romain, whose daughter is the wife of that Colonel Marchand, who, as commander of the French troops at Fashoda, almost precipitated a war with Great Britain in 1899.

[9] *Retrospections of an Active Life,* Vol. 2, pp. 200–201.

XIII

THE DISCORD OF THE GOVERNORS

1

SECRETARY SEDDON

THE Cabinet post that gave Davis his greatest trouble was the one which, in that military administration, might seem to be the most important of all — the Secretaryship of War. Change, indeed, was the order of the day in all departments. The Cabinet comprised only six portfolios, but seventeen incumbents filled these several offices in four years of war. Stephen R. Mallory, who headed the Navy, was the only Cabinet member to serve the entire Presidential term. Three Secretaries of State, four Attorneys General, two Secretaries of the Treasury, two Postmasters General, and six Secretaries of War — such was the personal record of the Davis Administration. On this basis unfriendly critics have drawn conclusions unfavorable to Davis as a manager of men. According to John A. Wise, there were six Secretaries of War for a paradoxical reason — because there was really "no Secretary of War." The men who nominally filled the place were merely "clerks," "underlings"; the President himself administered the department. These alternating ghosts might flutter through the executive building in Richmond, but it was Jefferson Davis who organized armies, appointed officers, supervised military campaigns, and attended even to the details of the office.

The first War Secretary who succeeded Benjamin, George W. Randolph of Virginia, experienced to the full these assertive qualities in the Chief. Here was a different social type from most of the men who surrounded Davis. The son of Thomas Jefferson's oldest daughter, Martha, Randolph was an "aristocrat." Educated amid his New England relatives — in Cambridge, Massachusetts — and at the University of Virginia, Randolph had gained some first-hand experience with war; a service of six years in the United States Navy, several months' experience in the Confederate Army, had won for him a brigadier-generalship, and the respect of Beauregard and Joseph E. Johnston. Perhaps the favor with which these men regarded Randolph explains the ill fortune into which he quickly fell. Both esteemed Randolph the ablest of the half dozen men who filled the Secretary's seat. Many others, civilian and military, agreed with this judgment. Randolph's troubles with Davis, however, set in immediately. He quickly discovered that his office was an honorary one, that the real war lord of the South resided in the executive mansion. The eight months that Randolph nominally acted were therefore harrowing. To obtain his knowledge of important military decisions after they had been made, to learn of many military appointments for the first time from the press — such surprises were hardly gratifying to a man who really aspired to serve his country. The inevitable parting, which came in November, 1862, was the one exciting event of Randolph's official life. General Grant's menacing approach to Vicksburg in November, 1862, found the Confederate armies in the Mississippi Valley dispersed. Deciding to assert his authority, Randolph instructed General Holmes, then operating in Arkansas, to send ten thousand men across the Mississippi and form a junction with Johnston. No doubt exists to-day that this was the proper military move. But Randolph's initiative angered Davis exceedingly. For his subordinate to make such a vital decision over the President's head could not be endured. From the President's office issued a summary demand to Randolph to rescind his order. Randolph's reply was a tart letter of resignation. President Davis, perhaps taken aback, suggested an interview; could not their differences be discussed? Randolph declined. "As you thus without notice and in terms excluding inquiry retired," Davis wrote, "nothing remains but to give you this formal acceptance of your resignation." Randolph's successor, Brigadier General Gustavus Smith, — a gentleman whom the outbreak of war discovered serving as Street Commissioner of New York City, — occupied the post for three days. Then Mr. Davis elevated James A. Seddon, an accomplished but subservient Secretary who functioned virtually for the rest of the conflict. Seddon, like Randolph, was a Virginian of lofty social origin. It is important to emphasize this point, for Seddon's family and associations had an important bearing upon his work. Davis retrieved him from an environment, in Goochland County on the James, which perfectly symbolized the ideas and traditions that had drawn North and South asunder. At this period the James River grandees claimed the highest eminence in the caste system of their state. Two or three generations previously, the Potomac region might have disputed such an ascendency, but the Northern Neck had long since suffered decline; its once fertile tobacco farms had relapsed to underbrush, but the valley of the James still preserved much of its historic splendor. Here tobacco raising was still a profitable enterprise, and abounding acres of corn also gave it economic strength. Sabot Hill, the country house maintained by the Seddons, was not one of the most pretentious Virginia establishments, but few exceeded it in the graces of Virginia life. Seddon himself was a good linguist, a deep reader, a scholastic advocate of fine-spun Southern doctrine, and a philosopher deriving from the academy of John Taylor of Caroline rather than from that of Jefferson Davis. He was a believer in absolute state sovereignty, in nullification, and in other recondite tenets not especially popular in 1862 even in Richmond. He gave Sabot Hill a quality of classic culture and of the best old-time Virginia statecraft — an atmosphere as far removed from the new-rich ostentation of Alabama and Mississippi as from the stolid intellectualism of New England; it was his wife, the former Sally Bruce, who contributed the grace that made it the rendezvous of the best in the South. Witty, vivacious, a brilliant talker and letter writer, Mrs. Seddon enjoyed a kind of national fame. She was the subject of one of the most popular songs of the day, "The Gay and Charming Sally," written for her by an intimate friend, the Yankee poet, Nathaniel P. Willis. When Sally and her sister, Ellen Bruce, appeared in Richmond, in the early forties, the town, then at the peak of its prestige, at once capitulated; her marriage to Seddon, a Member of Congress representing the Richmond district, in a way foreshadowed the coming Secession, for they made their city home in that austere "mansion" of Clay Street which subsequently became the "White House" of the Confederacy. Seddon's frail health impeded his career as a practical statesman; he retired permanently to his books, his music, and his circle in the Valley of the James, from which polite obscurity Jefferson Davis recalled him abruptly in November, 1862, to take charge of a cantankerous executive department in which four men had already failed.

The selection of a man of position in Virginia for this Secretaryship was not unwelcome to a snobbish group in Richmond that liked to ridicule the middle-class atmosphere of official circles. Davis himself and his wife had not been spared in current gossip. Readers of Mrs. Chestnut's *Diary* will find recorded several of the sharp things whispered of the social failings of the Richmond "White House." Virginia, having entered the Confederacy three months after its establishment, when most of the important offices had been filled, had held only a minor rank in the Administration. This omission detracted — or, at least, so the blue bloods said — not only from its statesmanship, but from its dignity and grace. Davis certainly tried to remedy this defect. His selection of Hunter in the State Department, Mason for the English post, and Randolph for War were all attempts to "recognize" the most famous of Southern states. Though not one of these heavy-handed Virginians had proved a success, Davis was still undiscouraged. His ambition to keep Virginia at his council table, at least in form, probably explains, more than anything else, the surprising elevation of Seddon. For it cannot be said that other qualifications for his disturbing post were preeminent. Two terms in Congress, not notable for achievement, and a moderately successful law practice in Richmond formed his only background. When the fact is added that Seddon's physical and nervous frame lacked vigor, and that he was subject to frequent spells of invalidism, the chances of success seem even less promising. The ascetic portraits of Seddon that survive — the long, well-modeled head, the sharp nose, the thin-featured face, the dark beard, the hair curling over the ears, the whole surmounted by a black skullcap — suggest nothing so much as a Jewish rabbi. Jones, the War clerk and diarist, who delighted in macabre metaphors, paints a forbidding picture. "Secretary Seddon is gaunt and emaciated, with long straggling hair, mingled gray and black. He looks like a dead man galvanized into muscular animation. His eyes are shrunken and his features have the hue of a man who has been in his grave a full month. He is an orator and a man of fine education, but in bad health, being much afflicted with neuralgia."[1]

After this it is not surprising to learn that Seddon, though given to thought, was deficient in humor, not congenial to the ruck of humankind, and not accessible to the chance callers who constantly besieged executive departments. Indeed Seddon had not long been established in Richmond when tirades against his aloofness began to echo in the press and in Congressional orations. Until his incumbency, the Secretary's door had readily swung open to all comers. Seddon introduced a schoolboy's slate, upon which intruders were requested to write their names and the nature of their mission. To modern eyes, some such precaution seems indispensable, but, in those easy-going republican days, the in-

[1] *A Rebel War Clerk's Diary*, Vol. I, p 312.

novation proved a bad beginning for Seddon. Charges of "aristocrat" and "James River exclusiveness" echoed as far as Georgia and Mississippi and created feeling not only against the Secretary, but against the "imperial regime" that was supposed to be rapidly taking shape in Richmond. To one man, however, Seddon was always tactful, always yielding. He amiably accepted the Davis interpretation of that Constitutional provision which made the President commander in chief of the Army and Navy. Any qualities such as those constantly displayed by the arrogant, frequently brutal, but always masterful Stanton in Washington never appeared in the opposite department in Richmond. Seddon, unlike his predecessor Randolph, made no attempt to take a hand in appointing generals, moving troops, or planning campaigns. Soon after his arrival, Joseph E. Johnston asked him to do what Randolph had lost his job for doing — transfer reënforcements from Holmes's army in Arkansas to the threatened Mississippi field. "The suggestion was not adopted or noticed," dryly records that chronicler.[2] Davis treated Seddon just as he had treated his predecessors, though in more courtly fashion. He took important decisions, and sometimes — not always — informed him what had been done in his department; and this sort of thing Seddon quietly accepted. Moreover, he adopted all the Presidential enthusiasms and hatreds. The hostility Davis constantly showed to Beauregard and Joseph E. Johnston Seddon made his own. The strange admiration Davis lavished on Braxton Bragg, Seddon shared. When Davis brought that hapless commander to Richmond, and installed him in the War office as "military adviser," Seddon did not object, although in a sense that action involved his own supersession.

[2] *Battles and Leaders of the Civil War*, Vol. II, p. 203.

2

Pro-Unionism in the South

But, submissively as Seddon accepted the dominance of Davis, there were other persons and groups in the Confederacy whom he did not suffer so complacently. His nearly three years of service, indeed, consisted of a constant battle with an assortment of strange characters as obnoxious to him on social as on administrative grounds. Seddon's struggle with the governors forms one of the most profitable studies in Confederate history. It brings to light one of the greatest weaknesses in the Southern republic and almost in itself gives an explanation for its failure. There are those who believe — and the number is increasing — that the Confederacy collapsed, not through inherent military weakness, but through certain defects that lay at the basis of the structure. These defects were social, political, above all the disintegrating doctrines of government which served as foundation for the experiment. It was a familiar idea with Davis and his compeers that two distinct inharmonious nations existed within the old Union, and that the schism of 1861 was the inevitable outcome of this fact. That may have been the case, but there was another incongruity, equally marked, on which appropriate emphasis was not laid. There were two separate discordant nations within the Confederacy itself. Seddon, Secretary of War, represented one — the rather strange combination of ancient Southern traditionist and get-rich-quick cotton planter that had joined forces against the North; while the sections that made his administration so difficult — the populous, non-slaveholding, and, in the main, poverty-stricken mountain classes — represented the other. These two unsympathetic forces were constantly working at cross purposes in the Confederate organization, and their unceasing conflict, in the end, accomplished almost as much in destroying it as the Federal armies. Herein lies the chief interest of Seddon's career.

THE DISCORD OF THE GOVERNORS 331

The common belief that Mason and Dixon's line formed the boundary between North and South is not precisely true. The actual frontier was far more irregular. To include the region where Union sentiment prevailed, in places overwhelmingly, it would be necessary to indicate a huge peninsula, striking from the Pennsylvania boundary into the heart of the South as far as northern Georgia and Alabama. Here we have a great expanse nearly two hundred miles wide and five hundred deep, with the Blue Ridge mountains forming roughly its eastern boundary and the Cumberland and other continuous ranges its western. In territorial extent it comprises at least a third of the country that lies south of the Ohio and east of the Mississippi. It formed a huge area of discontent, placed in the heart of the Southern Republic. This area comprehended great stretches of western Virginia, eastern Tennessee, western North Carolina, as well as generous territory in northern Georgia and Alabama. This part of the South had never shown much enthusiasm for secession. Had the decision rested with it, there would have been no Civil War. Even after the outbreak, it remained as a whole — though there were oases of Confederate adherence — loyal to the Union. So intensely raged the hostility of the western part of Virginia to the Confederacy that it seceded from the Old Dominion, set up the state of West Virginia, and attached itself to the Federal Union. Only by the barest chance is there to-day not similarly a state of East Tennessee, for a strong movement started, in the early days of the Civil War, to form such a commonwealth, and the loyalty of this region to the Union created great difficulties for the South. The Lincoln party, in 1864, recognized the Federal attachment of East Tennessee by selecting its most illustrious son, Andrew Johnson, as candidate for Vice President — a gesture that had the unlooked-for result of making him seventeenth President of the United States.

The same pro-Unionism prevailed in great stretches of the

other districts outlined above. These regions had voted against secession, when that issue was tested at the ballot box; and this feeling remained a powerful influence during four years of war. In origin, occupation, and manners this peninsula of hostility had little in common with the cotton planters who had brought on the struggle. The largest strain in their racial amalgam was Scotch-Irish; in religion they were Baptists, Methodists, Presbyterians — not Anglicans, the predominating faith of the more polished elements; in occupation they were small-scale farmers, cultivating with their own hands their own plots, seldom owning slaves; in politics they had been, for the most part, Whigs. These "up-country" people disliked their contemporaries of the Piedmont and the coastal plains on both political and personal grounds. Constant efforts had been under way for a century to restrict their political power. Ridiculed as "hillbillies," "crackers," "poor whites," or other opprobious names, they maintained an independent, sturdy life as far removed from the existence of a Seddon or a Lee as from that of a New England farmer. In modern times these people, "our contemporary ancestors," as they have been happily called, have become of great interest to students of folklore and literature; they figure extensively in modern fiction and have even reached the theatre. Their solitary existence, far from cities and railroads, has caused this people to keep alive the language, the songs, the legends, and many of the customs of the settlers of two centuries and more ago. Illiterate and rude, as, until modern times, these mountaineers were, even law-defying and given to family feuds, they still exemplified most of the sturdy British virtues of the race from which they sprang.

For many of the troubles that sapped the Davis Government these forces were responsible. The truth that Southerners were not unanimous in supporting the cause comes at first as a surprise. So glamorous have been the conventional pictures of Southern loyalty that one is hardly prepared to learn that the Confederacy also had its squalid side. It escaped none of the evils that beset a nation engaged in the unlovely business of war. With its ugly phases in the Federal Army — treason, desertion, evasion of duty, profiteering — we have long been familiar; only recently have we realized that all these inevitable accompaniments of war were just as conspicuous in the South.[3] In practice these disrupting phenomena harmed the Confederacy far more than they did the Union, because its men and resources, as compared to those of the Federal States, were limited. The North was afflicted by segments in its population who worked against the cause, but it did not contain a huge, almost homogeneous minority almost unanimously opposing national effort. This mountain country has always been celebrated for secret organizations, lawlessly engaged in forcing their will in defiance of constituted authorities. In pre-Revolutionary days these bands were known as Regulators; in the early times of the Republic there were the Whiskey Boys — moonshiners bound together to fight the tax gatherer; in a more recent period they have been reincarnated as the Ku Klux Klan. In the same way, from 1861 to 1865, several societies flourished whose business it was to fight the Confederacy and do everything in their power to accomplish its destruction. They paraded many high-sounding titles; they called themselves Peace and Constitutional Societies, Heroes of America, and the like; they had a bewildering array of passwords, signs, and grips; the brethren were bound together by most blood-curdling oaths, and their elaborate rituals distilled hatred to the Confederacy and loyalty to the Union. Scarcely a county in the domain of disaffection — southwestern Virginia, eastern Tennessee, western North and South Carolina, northern Georgia and Alabama — was unrepresented in these secret orders. Their object was to obtain enlistments for the Union army, to prevent recruiting for the Confederacy, to oppose tax

---

[3] Two books — *Disloyalty in the Confederacy*, by Georgia Lee Tatum (1934), and *Desertion During the Civil War*, by Ella Lonn (1928), illustrate this condition in great detail.

measures adopted in Richmond, to fight conscription laws, to stimulate desertion, and to agitate peace on the basis of a return to the Union. Their methods were terroristic; the membership was large, many thousands finding their way into the Federal forces. Anyone who studies the pension history of the Civil War is astonished to discover, on the rolls, the great number of ex-Union soldiers living in this Blue Ridge country of the South; and this is only one tangible evidence of the extent to which the "mountain boys" persisted in their old allegiance and testified to it by fighting with Grant and Sherman.

An even greater number showed their aversion to "Jeffy Davis," as they called the Southern President, in less heroic ways. One dark feature of the Confederate army on which the romantic school of writers lays little stress is its record for desertion. Desertion in the Federal forces was just as extensive, perhaps even more so; but somehow this does not seem so unnatural as that the South should likewise have had its large proportion of skulkers, *embusqués,* bounty jumpers, stragglers, and runaways. The brilliant spectacle of nine million people springing to arms in defense of an independent existence is one that does not easily die. In the first year, indeed, there was much in the spontaneous volunteering of the "chivalry of the South" that justifies this exalted picture. Secretary Walker reported that he had more than 200,000 volunteers whom he could not use. In that early day Southerners regarded the war as a few months' holiday; a single battle, it was believed, would settle the matter; and an eagerness seized everybody to get into the fray. After the first few months, however, especially after the victory of Bull Run had been succeeded by Confederate disasters, and the truth dawned that the country was facing a long, bloody war, this popular zeal began to cool. No better proof is necessary than that in April, 1862, about a year after hostilities started, the Confederacy was compelled to resort to conscription. This unexpected method of raising troops gave the "mountain boys" their opportunity. A conscription agent appearing in their region was about as welcome as a press gang in eighteenth-century London. Such emissaries were frequently met with shotguns. More than one left his dead body on the ground. Why, said these sons of the soil, should they sacrifice their lives for Virginia "aristocrats" and wealthy cotton planters? Were there not signs in plenty that it was a "rich man's war and a poor man's fight"? That provision which caused so much dissatisfaction in Yankee-land — the purchase of "substitutes" by rich men — was also a feature of the Confederate conscription law, and was about as popular south of the Potomac as north. The system also exempted owners of twenty slaves or more; and the "twenty-nigger law" similarly seemed discriminatory to the mountain peasantry. Here were the slave owners, the men responsible for the war, living in safety and comfort at home, while the thrifty, nonslaveowning, small farmers were being dragged from their little cabins to fight the battles of the plutocrats.

Back of all this lay the century-old hostility of the "upcountry" to the Piedmont and Tidewater. The mountaineers simply did not like the overlords who were riding high in Richmond and had no intention of promoting their cause by force of arms. Nor was this hostility entirely confined to the mountain region; there were other great blocs of opposition, especially in southern Alabama, the southeastern piney woods of Mississippi, the bayous of Louisiana, the swamps of Florida and great stretches of Arkansas and Texas. Its most demoralizing sign was the high desertion rate in all Southern armies. The evil, marked in the earlier days, proved a constant discouragement to Secretary Randolph, who explained the failure to follow up Southern victories by the large-scale desertion that followed each one. The habit became more pronounced as the contest wore on; after 1863, Confederate soldiers left the armies in droves. Grant said that, in 1864, the enemy lost a regiment a day by desertion; in March, 1865, a whole brigade of Lee's forces decamped, and that general wrote bitterly to the War Department of his losses from this cause. "The condition of things in the mountain districts of North Carolina, South Carolina, Georgia and Alabama" — such was the statement made by Judge Campbell, Assistant Secretary of War, to Seddon in March, 1863 — "menaces the existence of the Confederacy as fatally as either of the armies of the United States." The historian of this subject, Ella Lonn, has collected statistics showing 103,400 desertions [4] from the Confederate army. In a speech delivered at Macon, Georgia, in September, 1864, President Davis estimated the number of deserters from Hood's army as nearly two thirds of all then enrolled. "Two thirds of our men are absent; some sick, some wounded, but most of them absent without leave." [5] After the evacuation of Corinth — and this was as early as May, 1862 — Sherman found several thousand Confederate deserters in the woods around Booneville. Nor were all Confederate deserters craven. Thousands crossed into the Federal lines and "volunteered" for service in the Union army; but a much larger number were impartial, nonbelligerent creatures who refused to fight on either side. They hid in the caves numerous in the mountain country; frequently they carved out dugouts in the sides of hills, betook themselves to the everglades of Florida or the cane brakes of Mississippi. But the time came when they made no pretense at concealment; desertion developed into so popular a practice that the men could be found on most Southern highways, or the streets of cities — they even openly displayed themselves in Richmond.

3

Joseph Emerson Brown

The chief interest of Seddon's labors is his incessant battle with this element. The grander aspect of the secretaryship engaged little of his time; the main tasks left for Seddon

---
[4] *Desertion During the Civil War*, by Ella Lonn, p 231
[5] *Jefferson Davis, Constitutionalist*, Vol. VI, p 343.

therefore — and in these also the presidential oversight was always vigilant — concerned the recruitment, provisioning, and munitioning of the armies. In this routine labor his troubles at once began. Seddon came to his office at a critical time. The war passion which early swept over the Confederacy had subsided by November, 1862. It is true that the year which witnessed his elevation proved to be the most glorious in Confederate history. The Federal victories that had followed Bull Run, culminating in the capture of New Orleans, had given way to even greater successes by Confederate troops. The defeat of McClellan's forces before Richmond signalized also the rise of a great military leader in Robert E. Lee, and the rout of Pope at Second Bull Run heightened expectations of a speedy Confederate triumph. Ordinarily such performances should have rekindled the early fire and made the business of raising and training armies an easy matter. However, they did not have this effect. The first conscription law, of April, 1862, which enrolled all capable men between eighteen and thirty-five in the Confederate army, did not accomplish its purpose; almost simultaneously with Seddon's arrival in the War Office, the second conscription act, raising the military age to forty-five, was adopted. Seddon's official career was engaged in desperate attempts to enforce these laws. The contest has its piquant side, significant of the social and economic distinctions that split the Confederacy in two, and really destroyed its military energies. On one side we have the old "Virginia cavalier," James A. Seddon, the upholder of slavery, the standard-bearer of all traditional influences that made up the revered planter, and, on the other, the fierce, unruly, uncultivated slaveless pioneering stock of the Alleghenies. This latter contingent also had its leaders — far more vigorous, racy, and, in some cases, more able than the Tidewater chieftain; two of these in particular, Joseph Emerson Brown of Georgia and Zebulon Baird Vance of North Carolina, did perhaps as much as Grant and Sherman to destroy the Southern

Republic. At least they — in company with such more scholarly, theoretic statesmen as Alexander H. Stephens, Robert Toombs, and Robert Barnwell Rhett — can be taken as the commanders of disorganization which rendered the Confederacy helpless in the face of the smashing, unified military power of the Federal Government.

"Who the devil is Joe Brown?" asked Robert Toombs, in 1857, first hearing that the Democratic party of Georgia had selected as its candidate for governor an unknown, uncouth "mountain boy" from its western recesses. Toombs and others obtained a complete answer in the next seven years, for Brown was not only elected in this first campaign, but served as Governor until 1865 — all through the Civil War. No more animated, colorful, and obstreperous character ever filled an official chair. Anyone more removed from the cultivated Secretary of War could hardly be imagined. Yet — for Brown's character was a complex of contradictions — he was, himself, in the early period, a prophet of Secession, and no man, in the four years of warfare, was more voluble in asserting his loyalty to the Confederate cause. In spirit, in determination, in wrongheadedness, even in fanaticism, Brown suggests no one so much as a certain Northern character of the same name who frequently came in for his bitterest revilings — the departed incendiary of Osawatomie and Harper's Ferry. Both hark back, for their prototypes, to the Old Testament. For Joseph, like John, found his main inspiration in the old Hebrew worthies; New England never produced a more hidebound devotee of Israel, a more Puritanical adherent of a pleasure-denying daily regimen. Brown did not smoke, drink, or chew — something really unusual in his day; he was the strictest of Sabbatarians, and signalized his first term by a battle waged to prevent Sunday trains and Sunday mails. A fanatic of extremely narrow kind, Brown looked the part. A patriarchal figure, with expansive white beard, the outer strands reposing on his chest; long locks of darker hair sweeping wavelike about the ears; a head and face of classic Anglo-Saxon type — lengthy, narrow, with a high forehead and thin protruding nose; a determined, tightly pressed mouth; an erect slender figure — it is not strange that the "better" classes in Georgia viewed with dismay the sudden leap into prominence of this free-ranging child of the distant "azure hills." This feeling found expression in T. R. R. Cobb's catalogue of possible Confederate Presidential candidates in February, 1861; "even Joe Brown is talked about" he wrote his wife. For Brown's qualities of character, as well as his rough and ready exterior, had by this time made him a dreaded person. The fury of combat gleamed in his fierce blue eye. Nothing delighted him so much as a good row. Stubborn, full of arrogance of opinion, sticking to an idea to the last merely because it was his own; the extremest of egoists; invariably identifying his own prejudices with the supreme welfare of the state; never forgetting his humble origin and always conscious of the contempt it brought him; concerned only for the good opinion of the masses who worshipped him and who repeatedly reëlected him to the governorship in face of the many efforts of the fashionable to relegate him to private life; and with it all vigorous, able, vital, of untiring energy, possessing an easy, vituperative eloquence — Brown was really, beside the pallid figure of the deprecating, ineffective Seddon, a powerful, even magnetic leader of men.

"I was brought up among the working class," Brown once exclaimed in a speech. "I rose from the mass of the people. They took me by the hand and sustained me because they believed I was true to them. I was one of them and they have never forsaken me in any instance, when the popular voice could be heard." Herein we have the key to his character. As Andrew Johnson was always publicly boasting of his "plebeian origin," so Brown never once forgot his own beginnings, and his hostility to men of loftier breed, reminiscent of the great Tennesseean, had much influence on his public policy. He just as scrupulously dressed the part. A broad-brimmed stovepipe hat, a broadcloth shad-belly coat, a gold-headed cane, an enormous fob watch — such was the accepted Georgia garb of statesmanship in antebellum days; but trappings like these the man of the people disclaimed, always appearing in gray homespun, the wool grown on his beloved western hills and woven by the women of the log cabins in which he felt so much at home — in fact, in one of them he had been born.

Brown's speech abounded in those old English survivals which are the joy of modern philologists; Chaucer would have understood these phrases, though many of his contemporaries at Milledgeville found them outside their ken. Not that the man was destitute of education; indeed many of the statesmen who smiled at his homely idiom trailed far behind Brown in mental acquirements. Born in Pickens County, South Carolina, in 1821, carried as a child into the bordering Union County of Georgia, Joseph E. Brown came of the most authentic Anglo-Saxon stock. His earliest opportunities, however, were of the primitive sort to which this region has been limited almost up to the present time. As a boy he cultivated a small patch of land on the side of a hill, carrying his potatoes and cabbages into town each Saturday, snatching a few fugitive hours now and then for brief lessons at a rural school. In 1846 he spent a year studying law at Yale, and, returning to his own country, soon picked up a living practice. But politics from the first became his one interest. Though not a rabble-rouser, Brown's eloquence possessed that intimate, friendly quality that quickly made him a popular leader. His temperance principles proved something of a handicap, for free whiskey, dispensed by rising statesmen, was then the requisite of a successful campaign; but Brown did get into the State Senate, was afterward elected judge, — holding court in mountain log cabins, — and finally, to the astonishment of the blue bloods who had for decades monopolized that office, fought his way into the Governor's chair.

The time of his advent, 1857, was an exciting one. His attitude on the great national issue seems at first incongruous. For Brown, mountain boy that he was, and sympathizer with his people in their conflict with the seaboard, was almost a Tidewater Virginian in his political tenets. The Whig heresies of Stephens and Toombs never affected him. Despite his environment, he cared little for the Federal Union. He stood, above all, for the absolute sovereignty of the state. No slave owner himself, he adopted extremist proslavery opinions. He knew that this agitation would lead to war, and was quite ready to engage in one for his favorite doctrine — the complete, untrammeled independence of each and every state. Thus as Governor, Brown showed main interest in what would be called to-day "preparedness." He believed, in view of the approaching contest, that every Georgian should possess a rifle and learn how to use it. So he devoted his energies to training the state militia — always keeping foremost in mind the defense of Georgia. In the election of 1860, his attitude was uncompromising. Alexander Stephens might declaim against using Lincoln's election as a reason for Secession, but not Brown. After November, 1860, he, foremost among Georgians, demanded that the state follow the example of South Carolina. All attempts to patch up the quarrel Brown regarded as dangerous shilly-shallying. His activities had the greatest influence on the crisis. Had Georgia refused to secede, the Southern movement would probably have failed. And, until late January of 1861, Georgia's attitude was much in doubt. Brown's part in swinging the state for Secession thus had much to do in precipitating the Civil War. In fact, Brown's cantankerous character finds a striking illustration in the contradictory rôle he played in this event. Few statesmen did so much in starting the Confederacy as this stern, unbending orator of the Blue Ridge, and few, after it was organized, did so much to destroy it. In this Brown would have seen no discrepancy. His motive, both in seceding from the Union, and subsequently in seceding from the Confederacy, — for his behavior amounted practically to that, — was the same: an unyielding devotion to that principle of State independence and State individualism which formed almost the only item in his political creed.

4
ZEBULON B. VANCE

Brown's companion Governor in North Carolina was a man of different type. For Zebulon B. Vance had formerly possessed one loyalty that Brown had never shown — a profound devotion to the Federal Union. Brown's insistence on Secession was immediate but it was something to which Vance came most reluctantly. When news of Lincoln's call for troops reached North Carolina in April, 1861, Vance was addressing an angry meeting in Buncombe County, called to protest against the secession of the state. "I was addressing a large and excited crowd," Vance afterwards said,[6] "large numbers of whom were armed, and literally had my arm extended upward in pleading for the Union of the fathers, when the telegraphic news was announced of the firing on Fort Sumter and the President's call for seventy-five thousand volunteers. When my hand came down from that impassioned gesticulation, it fell slowly and sadly by the side of a Secessionist. I immediately, with altered voice and manner, called upon the assembled multitude to volunteer, not to fight against, but for South Carolina. I said, if war must come, I preferred to be with my own people."

Similar as Brown and Vance were in origin — for Vance came from the extreme western region of North Carolina, — in training, in outlook, in human attributes, the men had little

[6] In a speech delivered in Boston in 1886.

in common. In all respects Vance was the more sympathetic character. He had the one quality which his co-worker from Georgia so lamentably lacked: an ever-active sense of humor. It was Vance's rollicking conversation, his repartee and gift for anecdote, that made him the most popular man in his state, and for many years — for he lived three decades after the war, dying in 1894 one of the most powerful members of the United States Senate — the dominant political force in North Carolina. To-day Vance's statue stands in the Capitol rotunda at Washington, as North Carolina's favorite son. This was an eminence which the living Vance enjoyed for more than forty years. Compared with this record, the violent and at times even dubious career of Joseph Emerson Brown seems a rather tame affair. First of all Vance had one gift that Brown never attained: he was a great, substantial man-moving orator, the most eloquent North Carolina has ever known. One day, at a particularly dark hour of the Confederacy, Vance appeared in Virginia and spoke extemporaneously before Lee's army. His appearance and his speech on this occasion, remarked Lee, "were equivalent to reinforcements of 50,000 men." Vance was a most persuasive exhorter because he possessed that attribute of innate character always necessary to convincing declamation. He lived through many crises and many temptations, and his honesty survived them all. Though North Carolina, under his administration, conducted an extensive trading business in cotton, an activity that afforded countless opportunities for private gain, Vance never succumbed, and came out of the war as poverty-stricken as most of his compeers. He had another distinction desirable on the platform, a handsome, even a noble appearance. All these oratorical powers Vance exercised to the last day of his life; just as, when little more than a boy, the news of an impending speech would call North Carolinians in droves, so, in the second Cleveland Administration, an announcement that Vance was to address the United States Senate — perhaps against the McKinley Bill, perhaps in favor of free silver — would pack the galleries to suffocation.

Such a fiery spirit apparently marks out this leader as a fair representative of the ancient statesmanlike South, yet Vance, like Brown, derived from the western "mountain country," and, at least in his early days, was also a typical Elizabethan survival. At least he created this impression on the students of the University of North Carolina on his arrival at Chapel Hill. Clad in the customary homespun, his gangling arms protruding from the sleeves, his trousers lightly uplifted, leaving a wide space of white stocking between the bottom and the shoes, for the first few weeks he was merely the object of good-natured raillery. The mere circumstance that Vance had abandoned his native region and sought these classic halls in itself told much of his native ambition. Very few mountain boys in that age left their hills in search of learning. Yet for books Vance had had a fondness from early days. He not only read good literature, but tried his imitative hand at writing it; he even indited "poetry"; all his life he was a literary dabbler, his most attractive book being a collection of sketches dealing with the scenery and manners of his beloved Blue Ridge. Thus, though at the University Vance was a "milish" — that is, a militia student, not a member of the regular undergraduate body — and made no effort to obtain a degree, his mountain yarns, his skill as a debater, and his engaging companionship soon made him the dominant campus character. Evidently his appearance then did not differ much from that of after life. His distinguishing physical traits were a large body and head — the latter round, with granite features, and a nimbus of waving hair reaching to his shoulders. He was regarded then and afterward as an extremely handsome man, and his soft, drawling mountain accent, redolent, like Brown's, of Allegheny idioms, added to his general magnetism. His professional and political life followed the usual course. He served one term in the House of Commons — such is the name North Carolina gives the lower chamber of her Legislature — and, in 1858, at the age of twenty-eight, found himself in the popular branch of Congress. But his politics rested on different grounds from those of Brown, the unswerving Jeffersonian Democrat. In these early days Vance was not a State-rights man, but a fervent Unionist. Naturally he joined the Whigs, and when that party came to an end in 1856, declined to ally himself with the Democrats. Instead, like thousands of Whigs in the same dubious position, he for a time affiliated with the Know Nothings. Evidently his faith in the principles of this organization was not profound. At least, though, in his campaign for Congress, Vance ran as the candidate of the Know Nothings and such remnants of Whigs as survived, he freely made sport in his election speeches, of Know-Nothing doctrines. The Congress of 1858–1860, of which Vance became a member, sadly needed the cheerful, fun-making qualities he brought to it. It was the Congress of excited slavery discussion, John Brown's raid, Helper's *Impending Crisis,* and other far from humorous themes. In these issues Vance did not adopt an extreme Southern view. Southern-rights men, like Davis, or even Alexander Stephens, found in him no support. His activities were those of a peacemaker; none of these questions, Vance insisted, should be permitted to involve the sections in war. In the campaign of 1860, he declined to endorse either Douglas or Breckinridge, the two Democratic candidates; instead, he took the field for the "Constitutional Union" standard-bearers, Bell and Everett, emerging from the contest with a nationwide reputation as stump speaker.

After Lincoln's triumph, Vance became the foremost advocate of Unionism in North Carolina. At that time the majority of North Carolinians agreed with him. In October, 1860, a great meeting of Whigs and Conservatives was held at Salisbury, to protest the calling of a convention to consider the question of Secession. The speech Vance made on this occasion long remained a tradition of the State. And presently he engaged in a kind of campaign resembling a religious revival, envangelizing the same cause. He appeared in churches, even at street corners, shouting always the same refrain: "Keep North Carolina in the Union! Let it not follow the example of other Southern states!" All that was changed, as already described, by Lincoln's call for troops. Then Vance became more than a platform advocate of the Confederacy. He organized, among the mountain boys of his native country, a company known as "the Rough and Ready Guards." Captained by Vance, this contingent saw lively service in the early fighting in North Carolina, and in the seven days' battle before Richmond in June, 1862.

From the beginning, however, the Davis Administration was disliked in North Carolina. Those bickerings that were to make so much trouble throughout the war had already begun. The chief leader of this anti-Davis sentiment at the time was W. W. Holden, an opportunist newspaper editor who presently adopted an attitude actually anti-Confederate and pro-Union. Looking for a candidate to carry his anti-Davis standard, Holden naturally hit upon the most popular man in the state, Zebulon B. Vance. In accepting the nomination Vance pledged himself to "the prosecution of the war" but his statement was not taken seriously. Everywhere the Confederate party denounced him as the "Yankee candidate." The restoration of North Carolina to the Union, it was charged, would follow his election. The Richmond Administration similarly distrusted Vance; Davis and his group remembered too vividly Vance's cry of two years before — "Keep North Carolina in the Union!" The Northern press smiled most benignly on his campaign; success would mean the return of North Carolina to her old allegiance and the consequent end of the war. An amazing thing now happened. Though the upper classes ridiculed Vance's candidacy and confidently predicted his defeat, the mountain districts turned out in a huge stream, and put in office their beloved leader by a mighty majority. But the inaugural message gave cold comfort to the North. It demanded the rigorous prosecution of the war, and contained no suggestion for undoing the ordinance of Secession. Despite this the suspicious Davis still remained aloof; Richmond was not satisfied that Vance was playing true.

Some ground existed, indeed, for this skeptical attitude. Both Vance and Brown were unpredictable public men, independent to the last degree. At bottom, neither Vance nor Brown were ever strong adherents of the Confederacy. Neither, in the phase of their careers that now began, did they evince much interest in the Union. Unlike in temperament and character, the two men found a common ground in one devotion. Essentially they were not citizens either of the Confederacy or of the Federal Government; they were citizens of their states. By them Georgia and North Carolina were regarded as independent nations, having the flimsiest bonds with the Confederacy. The political principle that Davis was so fond of describing as the groundwork of the Confederacy — state sovereignty — these sons of nature took literally, applying this philosophy to the Confederacy as well as to the Union. And unfortunately for the Southern cause, both Governors adjusted the principle of state sovereignty to the one function of government to which it is most of all ill-suited. That is the making of war, offensive and defensive.

In the management of armies, centralization of authority and effort is indispensable to effective action. A generation that has passed through the great European war needs little instruction on this point, and the principle was just as sound from 1861–1865 as at the present time. Several distinct commands, each working independently and usually at cross purposes, can result only in confusion and demoralization. Most European authorities regard the strategy of the Northern armies as superior to that of the Southern because it recognized this fact. The first year or two the Federals indulged in much fumbling, but the time presently came when the Union armies were operated as units of one strong centralized command, and from that moment they pushed on to success. The South never attained this conception — or at least never acted upon it. But the failure was not the fault of the Richmond Government. Davis, champion of theoretic State rights as he was, never applied that philosophy to the direction of military effort. In this regard he was as much of a Hamiltonian as General Grant. The statesmen to blame for the dispersion of Confederate military energy were the Governors of the states, above all Joe Brown and Zebulon B. Vance. Neither ever grasped the "general staff" conception of warfare. Each considered the war as an enterprise of individual states and each insisted on raising state armies, officered by state-appointed captains and controlled directly by their local governments — really by themselves. Their business was not first of all to protect the Confederacy as a whole, but to fortify their states against invasion. Both North Carolina and Georgia gave many thousand troops to the Confederacy; indeed, if we are to credit claims constantly made by Brown and Vance, their "countries" contributed larger quotas to the fighting forces than any others. But they always did this as states. Governor Brown, for example, looked upon all Georgia troops, even when enrolled in Confederate armies, as subject to his own command. He retained them in Georgia, if he believed the state in danger of invasion; he released them to the Confederate Government when the local "emergency" had passed; and he felt himself free to recall at any moment his "noble, valiant Georgians" from Lee's army when danger of a Yankee incursion threatened the Georgia coast. Arms and ammunition provided by Georgia remained state property, he insisted, even when employed in Virginia campaigns. At times Brown would demand the return of such munitions, if, in his opinion, they could be better used at home. He was constantly complaining of Confederate neglect in "protecting" his state.

He cried out that Lee's legions, sent on invasions of Maryland, should really have been despatched to Georgia to safeguard the coast from Yankee depredations. Neither Brown nor Vance ever acknowledged the fundamental idea that the one way of safeguarding Georgia and North Carolina was to annihilate the military force of the Northern states and that all Confederate energies should be concentrated in this one purpose, even at the cost of sacrificing minor and unstrategic points. The state! The state! That was the one entity these governors had in mind. The Confederacy as itself the important unit was something their sympathies never comprehended.

XIV

"SECESSION" WITHIN THE CONFEDERACY

1

AN ARMY FOR GEORGIA

THUS here we have two forces, working at cross purposes within the Confederacy itself, important not only as a political, but a social study. Seddon represented the traditional South that put fire into the armies of Lee and gave the Confederacy its success and standing in the eyes of the world. Brown and Vance symbolized a very different South, populous and extensive, a South which had been largely submerged for three quarters of a century. This second South was slaveless, agricultural in the general meaning of that term, separated from the cotton belt that had created the new government, Whig in politics, Unionist in allegiance, anti-Secession in the critical year 1860, and to a considerable extent loyal to the Federal power even after the outbreak of hostilities. The issue between these two antagonistic groups was most sharply drawn on Conscription. No greater exercise of the national power could be imagined than for that power to enter the states and enroll its citizens for the business of the battlefield. Yet by this measure the war might be won; without it, the war would certainly be lost. It soon appeared, however, that practically all the states were fighting conscription even more fiercely than they were battling the Yankees. Many of the greatest Southerners were joining in the fray. Alexander H. Stephens, Vice President, the man who, in the not unlikely event of Davis's death, would succeed to the Presidency, and Robert Toombs, probably the ablest public man in the South, were leading the resistance. Most of the Southern Governors, with Brown and Vance at their head, were waxing every day more hostile to the measure. The doctrine of State rights, elabo-

"SECESSION" WITHIN THE CONFEDERACY

rated — in its latest form — to facilitate the extension of slavery, was now being turned against the vitals of the Confederacy itself. It would be difficult to find in all history a more lethal illustration of the well-worn image of Frankenstein.

From the beginning in April, 1861, Brown had followed his particularistic bent. He did not enter into the preparations feverishly made for the expected first Northern invasion, the one that presently culminated at Bull Run. Instead of contributing Georgia's strength to the Confederate Army, Brown kept busily at his job of organizing independent Georgia troops to save his state from possible Federal raids. When, in response to Davis's call for volunteers, Georgians by the thousands offered their services, Brown would not let them take from Georgia arms that belonged to the state or to themselves. When a few companies, more enlightened than their governor, succeeded in smuggling munitions out of Georgia, Brown angrily called upon the Confederate Government to send them back. At Brown's instigation, the Georgia Legislature authorized the raising of 10,000 volunteers "for the defense of the state" — all this in competition with the Confederacy's effort in the same direction. The troops so assembled were, in Brown's own words, a "patriotic, chivalrous band of Georgians," ready for the battlefield; but Brown marooned them in camp from June 11 to August 2, all prepared to start independent operations against any Yankees who should descend on Georgia. Had Brown sent these men, or a fair proportion of them, to Virginia, they might have made Bull Run an even more disastrous rout than it was, and perhaps enabled the Confederates to push on to Washington. "The crisis of our fate," Walker, then Secretary of War, telegraphed Brown, desperately begging for these men, "may depend upon your action"; still the obstinate Governor held his forces under his own command, fearing, as he afterward said, that an "invasion," similar to that then pouring into

Virginia, would be made "by a landing of troops upon our coast." Such was Brown's attitude at the beginning, and such it remained to the end.

2
JOE BROWN NULLIFIES CONSCRIPTION

The story of conscription is a long, complicated one — too complicated for minute exposition in this place. As one conscription act followed its predecessor, the fight against the whole proposal grew in intensity. Brown's first step in resistance was a personal veto; he refused to let the law be enforced in Georgia. One of the bitterest exchanges of letters in American history ensued between Brown and Davis on this subject. It started April 22, 1862, ten days after the passage of the original law, and continued until the following October. Brown's letters are lengthy, garrulous, a complex of Constitutional quibble and bad temper, contemptuous in personal reference, ignorant in all that pertains to military science and statesmanship on a national scale. The conscription act, so he complains, had completely disorganized the military system of Georgia. It was impeding his noble efforts to raise troops for state defense. The men he needed for this purpose Davis was seeking to impress into the Confederate Army. It was clearly the Presidential ambition to consolidate the military strength of the Southern states in the hands of a strong national government. "I cannot consent to commit the state to a policy which is in my judgment subversive of her sovereignty and at war with all the principles for the support of which Georgia entered into this revolution." In public speeches and in messages to the Legislature, Brown became even more inflammatory. Conscription was a "palpable violation of the Constitution"; it bordered on "military despotism"; under this arbitrary system the "free born citizens" of the state were about to be transformed into "chattels" and "vassals of the Central power." Herein we see, said Brown, Richmond's "pompous pretensions to Imperial" sway. At state expense Brown published all these lucubrations in pamphlets, which were hawked at every street corner in Georgia and distributed gratis among the Georgia troops in Lee's armies.

Mere abuse would not have shackled the War Department, but from words Brown presently passed to acts. He advised Georgians to disregard the law and to defy conscription agents. He ordered the arrest of any Confederate emissary who should attempt to enroll a militia officer. In pre-war days Secretary Seddon had adopted Calhoun's principle of Nullification; this now Brown turned against the Confederacy itself. He suspended conscription in Georgia until the Legislature should declare it constitutional. That was precisely the attitude of Jefferson on the Alien and Sedition laws and Calhoun on the tariff of 1828. Not the Confederate Congress, not the courts, but the Legislature of the "sovereign state" was to decide on the legality of measures passed by the Confederate Congress. When the Georgia Legislature decided the point in favor of conscription, Brown refused to accept its verdict; he now — disregarding his own principle of the supremacy of the Legislature — appealed to the Georgia Supreme Court. When that tribunal in turn determined the question in the affirmative Brown indulged in those criticisms of the court which are the usual executive rejoinder on such occasions. These distinguished jurists, he said, had acted from "heavy outside pressure." That is, Jefferson Davis, in Richmond, had issued his ukase to the highest judicial body in Georgia, which had meekly submitted to his dictation.

The conscription law itself contained several serious defects and Brown seized upon one of these to make the whole thing a nullity. Thus the measure gave Governors of states the temporary privilege of making exemptions. Obviously all able-bodied men could not be enrolled in the fighting forces; considerable parts of the population must be left to manage the farms, manufacture munitions, perform the thousands of functions necessary to sustain a community engaged in war. Brown wielded the prerogative of naming these "exempts" in most arbitrary fashion. He used it as an instrument for emasculating conscription itself. He declared free of military duty more than two thousand justices of the peace and one thousand constables; they were needed, the Governor declared, to preserve domestic peace in Georgia! No man but Brown, said Howell Cobb, "ever conceived the idea that justices of the peace who never held court, constables who never served a warrant, and militia officers who had no mess to command, were necessary for the proper administration of the state government." Brown appointed thousands of men of conscription age to all kinds of state offices, merely to make easy for them the avoiding of military service. No state had ever previously been so well supplied with petty officials, most of them on nominal salaries. In Georgia an enormous increase suddenly took place in constables, deputy bailiffs, deputy clerks, and assistant postmasters. Since militia officers — by Brown's decree — were exempt, he made countless new appointments of this class. School teaching became a suddenly popular profession, Brown having exempted these useful citizens from service at the front. Everywhere little schools sprang up merely to keep this type of slacker out of the training camp. Brown exempted one druggist in every drugstore, with the result that at least one pharmacy came into existence at every crossroad. Jefferson Davis declared that Brown, by giving officers' commissions to able-bodied militiamen, had exempted 15,000 from the Confederate Army. According to Howell Cobb, there were more men of conscription age staying at home — thanks to the several devices adopted by Brown to protect them in their "rights" — in Georgia than had gone into the Confederate service in the entire course of the war.

Brown not only blockaded Georgia from Seddon's conscription officers, but gave the Governors of practically all the states in the cotton belt an example which they promptly followed. Vance adopted the same tactics in North Carolina. In 1861, this state, like Georgia, had rushed in thousands to the Confederate colors but from 1862 to the end of the war, its zeal for military service steadily ebbed. North Carolina had a higher desertion record than any Confederate state. Vance attributed this fact to the Conscription act, but others insisted that his own uncooperative attitude did much to create a public sentiment that made desertion a natural habit. With all the energy of his vital nature Vance hated conscription. His hostility rested on the same grounds as that of Brown. He was the spokesman of the plain, homespun Southern farmer, of the nonslaveholding, non-"cavalier" type. Conscription was an evil — in Vance's mind — because it took these simple, hard-working Southern folk from their humble homes, transported them to bloody battlefields in Virginia and Tennessee, and left North Carolina exposed to its enemies. As the war went on Vance grew more and more defiant; he went even further than Brown in withholding conscripts from the War Department by "exemptions" and "furloughs"; at times he showed a strange partiality for deserters; and his whole course exercised a most damaging effect upon the Confederate attempt to organize an army.

Watts, Governor of Alabama, Pettus, Governor of Mississippi, Murrah, Governor of Texas, presently aligned themselves with Georgia and North Carolina in fighting conscription. In the last two years of the war this whole region was fiercely arrayed against the Richmond authorities. Watts had succeeded Benjamin for a brief period as Attorney General, but his association with the general government had apparently inspired no devotion to the Confederacy, in preference to his state. His letters to Seddon breathe not only defiance, but at times actual threats of war. "I have resisted by remonstrance," he wrote in one instance, "the action of the enrolling officers and I may feel myself justified in going further unless some stop is put to the matter by you." "Unless you order the commandant of conscripts to stop interfering with such companies [that is, his own state troops] there will be a conflict between the Confederate General and the state authorities." Confronted in this way with something resembling civil war within the Confederacy itself, Seddon capitulated and acquiesced in Watts's defiance of the Conscription act. He bowed to similar threats from Murrah in far-off Texas. In Mississippi, Davis's own state, Governor Pettus was pursuing the same course. In this region, General Brandon reported to Seddon, "all are rushing into the state organizations merely as a way of escaping conscription in the Confederate army." Governor Clark, who succeeded Pettus in 1863, virtually threatened war against the Confederacy. "I shall be compelled," he wrote Seddon, "to protect my state officers with all the forces of the state at my command. . . . Unless you interfere there will be a conflict between the Confederate and state authorities." And again Seddon gave way.

How did the people of Georgia regard Brown's unceasing war on the central government of Richmond? That is perhaps the saddest part of the whole affair. In Georgia, public sentiment, whenever it could be tested, supported its bellicose chief magistrate. Brown's tactics became an issue in the election of 1863. In contests of this kind several issues usually confuse the situation; that may have been the case in 1863; yet the fact remains that the state, having this opportunity to repudiate its Governor, failed to do so. Instead it elected him by the handsomest of majorities. Among certain elements he was, of course, an object of execration. In Georgia no public man had ever aroused such animosity as Governor Joe Brown. But in this public attitude social cleavage was only too apparent. Those who thought of themselves as "the best" element denounced the man as a public shame, as a "traitor" to a noble cause, the "Judas Iscariot," the "Benedict Arnold" of the Confederacy. B. H. Hill, Confederate Senator, declared that Brown's messages were "first steps to another Revolution." Howell Cobb, the owner of one thousand slaves, railed vehemently against this "cracker" from the mountain country, "this miserable demagogue who now disgraces the executive chair of Georgia." Cobb remarked that he had never attended a hanging and had never felt any desire to do so, but if Governor Brown should be the chief performer in such a ceremony, he would gladly join the spectators. Cobb and his fellow aristocrats attempted to bring about Brown's defeat at the polls, but met a humiliating failure. In this contest practically every newspaper in the state supported Brown's opponent, a "patriotic" candidate who ran on a platform pledging earnest support of the Confederate Government and especially of conscription. Many choice epithets filled their pages. Brown was held forth as a more dangerous enemy to the Confederacy than Grant or Sherman. But all these outbursts the stolid, white-whiskered little man treated with contempt. He knew his mountain folk. He had made them the chief object of his Governorship. In these mountain areas love of the Confederate Government was not deep-seated and Brown's hostility to many of its policies had not alienated devotion to their favorite governor. And so Brown did not make the slightest attempt to obtain a renomination — and secured one unanimously. He took no part in the campaign and was triumphantly reelected. This result proved a rude awakening for Howell Cobb and Jefferson Davis, for it showed that Brown's policy toward conscription and other Confederate matters had the support of the masses of Georgia. By this time Richmond had begun to suspect that Brown's real purpose was to bring the war to a close, and the support he received from his own state looked like an ominous portent.

3

JOE BROWN'S TEN THOUSAND

These anti-administration Governors interfered with the Conscription Act in an even more disastrous way. All these states — North Carolina, Georgia, Alabama, Mississippi, Texas — organized their own state armies, or militia, or reserves, or "troops of war" — they went by several names, but had an identical object in view. This was to enroll the fighting forces of the state under direct state control and keep them out of the clutches of the Confederate Government. A citizen of Georgia, once gathered under the sheltering wing of a militia company or a "reserve," was protected against the approach of a Confederate conscription agent. That the plan had great elements of popularity, and thus added to Brown's political strength, was apparent. Service in state militia made greater appeals to a certain type of Georgian — and as the toilsome war went endlessly on this type grew more numerous — than life in the Confederate entrenchments before Petersburg. Enrolled in the militia the warrior could spend most of his time on his farm, caring for wife and children; only in case of "emergency" would he be called forth to fight the invader. And the judge whether such an "emergency" existed was not General Lee or General Johnston, or Secretary Seddon, or Jefferson Davis, but the constitutional commander in chief, Joseph E. Brown. The real captain of such of Georgia's sons as had been detailed for the front was thus the "mountain boy" who had jealously protected them for two years. Military operations, in Brown's conception, partook something of the nature of a football game. At certain critical dates the two opposing armies lined up against each other and fought their battle. When this particular contest ended, the war was over for the time being. In such crises it was the Governor's duty to send his state army to reënforce the Confederate forces. When the "emergency" passed, irrespective of which side won, Brown could call his paladins home, and set them to cultivating their crops — until another approach of combat made necessary once more their appearance at the front. Why keep good men idling uselessly in camp when everything was quiet? That warfare was a perpetual "emergency" was a point Brown never grasped any more than he understood that a great army, to be of much value, must be subject to a unified command and operated as a grand unit.

Presently Governor Brown found himself confronted with one of those "emergencies" for which he had made such elaborate preparation. This was the "emergency" that has passed into history as Sherman's march to the sea. This was the campaign, it is now well understood, that broke the Confederacy into a thousand pieces and made inevitable Lee's surrender to Grant. But to Brown and his school of strategists it was merely an invasion of Georgia, an attack that should call into action the "valiant Georgians" whom he had scrambled together for just this kind of crisis. These 10,000 men, if properly trained and organized, would naturally have greatly reenforced Johnston's forces. But the fact is that, terrible as was the "emergency," they really formed no inseparable part of Johnston's army. Brown placed them nominally under Johnston's control, but he himself remained their commander. Johnston could not organize the troops, appoint the officers, or incorporate the Georgia militia in his own army. Joe Brown's Ten Thousand — their fame, in Confederate annals, recalls the Ten Thousand Greeks in the pages of Xenophon — were, said Seddon in a letter to Brown himself, "nondescript organizations, not conforming to regulations of the provisional army, scant in men and abounding in officers, with every variety of obligation for local service, generally of the most restricted character. Thus you were enabled to indulge in the vain boast of raising sixteen thousand men for the defense of the state, while in fact scarce a decent division of four thousand men could be mustered for the field and then only for six months' service." Yet these recruits were the raw material of splendid troops; had they been placed under Confederate control, said Seddon, and incorporated as units in the Confederate Army, Sherman's invasion could have been checked and the Confederacy saved.

But Atlanta fell; Hood started on his fatal campaign in eastern Tennessee, and Sherman struck boldly into the heart of Georgia. Brown's foes, including Seddon and Davis, attributed the disaster at Atlanta, and Sherman's subsequent triumphs, directly to the Governor's obstructive tactics. That he certainly facilitated Sherman's operations, even Brown's friends could not deny. Naturally, when Sherman instituted the siege, Seddon began scraping the Southern states for fighting men. In due course he called upon Brown for his valorous Ten Thousand. The Secretary had the Confederate Constitution on his side. Under this the President had the right to requisition the militia of the states to repel invasion. And here certainly was an invasion! The call came to Brown on August 30, 1864. By this time, however, the Confederate Constitution meant little to Joe Brown. The all-important necessity was the protection of his state, and he fatuously believed that this was his responsibility and not that of the Richmond Government. He not only refused to hand over his troops to Hood, who had succeeded Johnston as general in command, but insisted that Seddon return to Georgia all Georgian troops then engaged in Lee's Virginia army. "I demand," Brown wrote Seddon, "that he [President Davis] permit all the sons of Georgia to return to their own state and within her own borders to rally around her glorious flag and as it flutters in the breeze in defiance of the foe, to strike for their wives and their children, their homes and their altars, and the green graves of their kindred and sires."

Brown had another reason for his refusal, which he made no effort to conceal. General Sherman and the Yankee army were not the only foes Georgia might have to meet. He might

"SECESSION" WITHIN THE CONFEDERACY

need his Ten Thousand to fight the Confederacy itself. The Yankee menace was no more dangerous than that of the "Imperialists" in Richmond. This Georgia state army, Brown now informed Seddon, was "an organization of gallant, fearless men, ready to defend the state against usurpation of power as well as invasions of the enemy." They were Georgia's "only remaining protection against the encroachments of centralized power." He therefore refused "to gratify the President's ambition in this particular and to surrender the last vestige of sovereignty of the state." Those who think that Brown ultimately planned the secession of Georgia from the Confederacy apparently have solid grounds for the suspicion. An actual secession could not have done much more harm than his withdrawal of his Ten Thousand at this critical moment.

All the time that Sherman was penetrating deeply into Georgia, burning and destroying, Seddon and Brown were engaged in a most caustic correspondence; while the Yankees were ripping up railroad tracks, burning crops, demilitarizing cities, making "Georgia howl," in Sherman's own words, Brown's pen was busy, writing long dissertations to Seddon on constitutional government, the rights of the states, and the danger of the growing "imperialism" of the Davis Government. In a speech in Columbia, South Carolina, in October, Davis, in veiled language, virtually called him a "traitor," and Seddon, in his angry letters to Brown, declared that his action had led the enemy to believe that they could make a separate peace with Georgia and that the state "could be seduced and betrayed to treachery and desertion." Brown's behavior, indeed, had had precisely this result; the Northern press confidently predicted Georgia's early return to the Union, and General Sherman expected Georgia to secede from the Confederacy. Brown's crowning act of "treachery," as his Southern enemies called it, could carry hardly any other meaning. In early September, in one of the most critical moments of the war, he "furloughed" his Ten Thousand men; that is, he ordered them to drop their arms, disband their organizations, and return home to work their farms. "Governor Brown," wrote the astonished Sherman to General Halleck, "has disbanded his militia, to gather the corn and sorghum of the state." "It would be a magnificent stroke of policy," Sherman wrote to Lincoln, "if we could, without surrendering principles or a foot of ground, arouse the latent enmity of Georgia against Davis." Sherman went so far as to write Brown, inviting him to a meeting for a discussion of the future relation of his state to the Federal Army. The wary Brown did not venture quite so far as that, though Sherman always believed that it had been his original intention to do so, but that he had finally refrained from prudential reasons — perhaps from fear.

Brown's career after the war gave ground for his enemies to believe the worst. In the Reconstruction era he joined the carpet-baggers, became a member of the Republican Party and an advocate of negro suffrage. He was the active force in the infamous, corrupt administration of Governor Bullock. His personal honesty was not above suspicion; he became one of the richest men in Georgia — some say the richest — and that he had been one of the profiteers of Reconstruction was only one of the current charges affecting his financial integrity. "It is impossible for you to think worse of the scoundrel than I do," Toombs, Brown's former supporter, wrote to Stephens. Yet the instructive fact is that, both during the war and subsequently, Brown never lost the support of the masses of Georgia. After Appomattox he became Chief Justice of Georgia's Supreme Court and served two terms in the United States Senate. His hold on the loyalty of Georgia, despite his anti-Davis policy, thus throws light upon the effect of internal dissension in the breakdown of the Confederate Government. And North Carolina, as already intimated, similarly gave cordial support to Vance, almost as violent in his anti-Confederate tendencies as Brown.

Brown Bros

JOSEPH EMERSON BROWN (1821–1894)

Brown Bros

ZEBULON BAIRD VANCE (1830–1894)

Stephen R. Mallory of Florida
(c. 1813–1873)

James A. Seddon of Virginia
(1815–1880)

XV

MALLORY'S FIGHT ON THE BLOCKADE

1

STEPHEN R. MALLORY

ONE man in the Davis Cabinet had a more statesmanlike view of the situation than these short-sighted Governors who so perversely obstructed the military campaign. The Secretary of the Navy, Stephen R. Mallory, saw the Confederacy not as a league of mutually warring states but as a whole. Upon him fell the difficult duty of repairing the initial mistake of Jefferson Davis. That monumental error, as already made plain, was the failure in the first year to break through the loosely-jointed Federal blockade and send great supplies of cotton to England and the Continent. Judah P. Benjamin was not the only Southern statesman who grieved over this wasted opportunity. Another was the Secretary of the Navy. In Mallory's eyes, the Navy Department had one single objective in the war. That was to save the Southern nation from the two forces that were working for its annihilation. One was the Lincoln blockade, the other the Davis embargo. At bottom, Mallory's job was to get cotton to Europe, to open the sea lanes reaching from Southern ports to the markets of the world. By the summer of 1862 one obstacle had been removed. Richmond had recovered from its delusion that a cotton boycott could bring England and France to terms and had consequently abandoned the embargo. From now on Mallory's only labor was to break the Lincoln blockade. The intelligence and energy with which he attacked this almost impossible problem marks him as one of the most farseeing men in the Administration.

Mallory figures little in Confederate histories and has been neglected by biographers. Yet all contemporary witnesses testify to his industry and spirit. True, he stirred up much opposition; his department, after the fall of New Orleans and the capture of Norfolk, was subjected to inquiry by Congress; yet, as noted elsewhere, he was the only Cabinet member who survived four years of war. There is some significance in the fact that Mr. Davis had six Secretaries of War and only one Secretary of the Navy. Mallory's merits are not the only explanation. Davis was enormously interested in the War Department, but had little concern for its companion service. He thought that everything hinged upon his military chieftains; the tremendous influence a navy might play in bringing victory he did not seem to understand. Certain authorities in the Confederacy noted and grieved over this failing in the chief. "It is evidently no part of the plan of the Administration," wrote Matthew Fontaine Maury, the distinguished oceanographer, to William Ballard Preston, — this as late as October 22, 1863, — "to have a navy at present or even to encourage one," and he almost despairingly sketched a plan for a sea force under the control of Virginia, since the central authority seemed so oblivious of its duty.[1] Captain Maury's sense of the inadequacy of Mr. Davis in naval strategy is substantiated by the scant attention the President gives the subject in his massive two-volumed work on Confederate history. Scores of chapters are devoted to describing military campaigns, while only a few perfunctory pages are given to the operations of the other arm. Davis, however, does pay high tribute to Secretary Mallory and defends his administration from the attacks to which it was subjected in war time. His confidence explains in part Mallory's uninterrupted service; more important, however, was the fact that to Davis the Navy was a secondary interest. Thus Mallory was, for the most part, left free to run his own department.

 The man thus left undisturbed as Secretary of the Navy had two qualifications for his office. He was, in 1861, the most prominent citizen of Florida, and Florida, like all the states of

[1] *Official Records of the Union and Confederate Navies*, Series 2, Vol. II, p. 94.

the first Confederacy, had a rightful claim to representation in the Cabinet. Again Mallory enjoyed a general fame as the best informed man in the South on naval warfare, though his only sea experience was derived from sailing his own yacht. His career as United States Senator from 1851 to 1861 — a career not especially distinguished — had been chiefly associated with this branch of the service. For several years he acted as chairman of the Senate Committee on naval affairs; the few Mallory speeches that have been reprinted do not, like those of most of his contemporaries, concern themselves with the compromise measures of 1850 or the Kansas-Nebraska bill, but with such topics as flogging in the Navy, — in which form of discipline, sad to relate, he believed, — the need of large appropriations for warships, and similar nautical matters. Perhaps Mallory's inheritance and lifetime surroundings explain this natural liking for the sea. One account describes his father — the precise facts about Mallory's origin are not clear — as a sea captain of Bridgeport, Connecticut. In early manhood Charles Mallory moved to the island of Trinidad, British West Indies, to engage in some kind of construction work; here he married an Irish girl of sixteen, Ellen Russell, recently arrived from County Waterford, and said to be a member of the family that afterward produced Russell of Killowen, Lord Chief Justice of England. Stephen Russell Mallory was born at Trinidad in 1813. Ellen Russell, his sprightly mother, seems to have played an important part in forming the character of her son, the future Confederate Secretary. All her life she spoke with the richest of Irish brogues; her liveliness and wit made easier the difficult time she had in bringing up her children, for her Connecticut husband died when Stephen was nine years old, leaving her nothing but her two hands to earn their living. Thus the half-Irish Stephen R. Mallory was the only Roman Catholic in the Davis Cabinet; always about him there hung an exotic atmosphere, emphasized by his wife, Angela Moreno, a pure-blooded

Spanish girl, who developed into a woman of intelligence and beauty. Mallory's lack of education appears in such few letters as have been preserved, which are frequently faulty in construction and spelling. He had been limited to a year's instruction at a Moravian school in Nazareth, Pennsylvania, leaving at fifteen. Mallory passed his first thirty years at Key West, and the few preceding the Civil War at Pensacola. Key West and Pensacola added to the saltiness of his fame, for these two towns — one the extreme southern point of the United States, the other exhaling memories of Spanish buccaneers — suggest the free and open water. Mallory's early life in Key West had as its background the Gulf of Mexico. He earned his living at first in miscellaneous fashion. Part of the time was spent helping his mother run a boardinghouse. Tradition reports that Mrs. Mallory was the first white woman to take up residence at Key West and her establishment was naturally the headquarters of sailors and fishermen. In intervals the young man edited a local news sheet, and acted as correspondent for the New York *Herald,* an important post, for Key West gave rise to much marine news, and Mallory's contributions usually comprised descriptions of wrecks, hurricanes, and high adventure on the deep. Thus his interest in the Navy has a natural evolution. There was also a heartiness about the man, a love of robust living, a fondness for good food and wine, and an overflowing good nature that form indispensable ingredients of the sea dog.

In the exciting disputes that led to civil war, Mallory displayed only incidental interest. He did at times discourse in the United States Senate on slavery, indulged in the usual unfriendly remarks on John Brown, Mrs. Beecher Stowe, and Hinton Rowan Helper. He had the inevitable brush with Charles Sumner, but his concern with such momentous issues never attained a fire-eating tension. In fact, when Davis, at Montgomery, named Mallory to the headship of the Navy, there was much in the candidate's prewar record that caused apprehension. He was the only member of the prospective Cabinet who did not meet immediate approval. Two delegates from Florida itself voted against Mallory's confirmation. The truth is that the nominee's record on slavery and Secession was unpopular with Southern die-hards. There was resentment against his origin and early life in the North, and fear that a Yankee father had poisoned his gospel. Before 1861, Mallory had not been a Secessionist. On the great vital issue his convictions were lukewarm. After the war, Mallory, a prisoner in Fort Lafayette, New York, appealed to President Johnson, asking for pardon and restoration to citizenship. This letter clearly substantiates the conviction, general in Montgomery in 1861, that Mallory's position on fundamental matters was unorthodox. The claim on which he laid chief emphasis for Presidential clemency was his lifelong loyalty to the Federal Union. "I was never a member," he declared, "of a convention or a legislature of any state that advised or counselled Secession." His first election to the United States Senate had come without his knowledge or consent; the Whig party had supported him in 1851 — he now informed the President — because of his devotion to the Washington Government. He had served in the Senate from 1851 to 1861, and in that ten years, "no word or sentiment of disloyalty to the Union ever escaped me." True enough, on January 21, 1861, he had withdrawn from the Senate, after Florida's secession, at the command of the Governor of that state; but it was an "act which, in view of its causes and attendant circumstances, was the most painful of my career." "Educated and trained in love and reverence for the Union as the ark of political safety, I dreaded the perils of Secession, and believed that ample remedies of all political wrongs, present and prospective, could be more wisely, justly and advantageously secured in the Union than out of it." "I never could regard it [Secession] as but another name for revolution, and to be justified only as a last resort from intolerable oppression." The Secretaryship of the Navy in the Confederate Cabinet, the almost repentant Mallory now informed President Johnson, had been forced upon him. He had not desired the honor and had done his best to avoid it. Practically coerced into accepting the post in March, 1861, he had again sought an escape on the formation of the permanent government. "In February, 1862, I requested and requested the acceptance of my resignation, which President Davis declined."

Mallory, in this apologia to President Johnson, refers to the incident which had made him suspect in the eyes of the Confederate Congress. Learning, in early January, of 1861, that "armed bands of Alabamians and Floridians" were planning to attack Fort Pickens, in Pensacola Harbor, he had energetically opposed such a manœuvre. The reference is to one of the most celebrated episodes of the crisis, eclipsed in importance only by the greater éclat that subsequently came to Fort Sumter. Except for Mallory and other conciliatory Southern leaders, the Pensacola fort, and not the one that guarded Charleston, might have gained the doubtful eminence of precipitating the war. Why did the Florida troops fail to capture one of the most strategic points in the Gulf? The Secretary's foes always attributed this mistake to Stephen R. Mallory. It was because he had proved a "traitor" to the Confederacy in this crisis that they raised objections to him as a Cabinet member. That Mallory, after the war, exhibited his conduct to President Johnson on the Fort Pickens business as a reason for release from prison and restoration to American citizenship lends some force to this accusation. What is known is that, on January 28, he sent a telegram to Senator John Slidell, instructing him to assure the Washington Government that no attack was being planned against Fort Pickens, and urging that no reënforcements be sent. Mallory always maintained that his purpose was to preserve the peace, at a critical moment when negotiations were under way to settle the Secession dispute; that "firing on Fort Pickens" would have precipitated war in January, just as "firing on Fort Sumter" did afterward in April; an explanation which, in retrospect, seems satisfactory and public-spirited. By some of his contemporaries, however, "the truce of Fort Pickens," as it was derisively called, was assailed as merely the last-minute expression of Mallory's anti-Secession views and a farewell gesture of good feeling toward that Northern land to which he owed his origin.

2

MEN BUT NO SHIPS

That Mallory's act was the sincere expression of his conscience is attested by his subsequent career. No Southern leader more reluctantly took the plunge into Secession, and not one, after the war started, supported the Confederate cause with more energy. In 1861 Captain Mahan and his philosophy of sea power had not made their appearance. That naval historian, thirty years afterward, demonstrated that the determining element in war has always been the control of the sea. It is the power that dominates the ocean, not the one that wins battles on land, which inevitably emerges victor. In 1861 the importance of sea power was not generally understood. Mallory perhaps did not grasp the truth in all its force, but he came pretty close to it. At least on this foundation he based a most intelligent campaign. The impending struggle, he foresaw, was not to be decided definitely by the armies but by the navies. The one road to success was by breaking through the blockade. At this time Benjamin was trying to achieve this objective with lawyers' arguments, and by a huge money bribe to Napoleon III. England pigeon-holed his briefs, lawyer-like and able as they were, and Louis Napoleon, much as his fingers itched for the money, dared not move alone. Mallory from the first saw that there was only one way of accomplishing the great end; if the Confederate Navy could not destroy the Lincolnian cordon, everything was lost.

The difficulty was that there was no Confederate Navy. One of Mallory's first steps was to summon to Montgomery Captain James D. Bullock, formerly an officer in the United States Navy, now, as befitted an "aristocrat" of Georgia, a fervent Confederate partisan.[2] At this first meeting, Mallory, with Irish humor, described the state of the existing Confederate Navy. It consisted of little except the bare, unfurnished room in which their session was being held. One desirable part of a navy Mallory did indeed command. There were practically no sailors, but there was no lack of officers. Uncle Sam had trained up a large personnel for the Confederate Navy at Annapolis, just as he had for the Confederate Army at West Point. Southerners in the Union Navy, it is true, did not resign their commands and cross Mason and Dixon's line to the same extent that their brothers did in the Army; the greatest naval genius of the North, for example, and one of the greatest of all time was a Tennesseean, David Farragut, who remained loyal to the Union. But the Confederate Navy, even in 1861, had an abundance of admirals, commodores, captains, lieutenants, midshipmen; all it lacked, Mallory explained to Bullock, were war vessels and able seamen.

The more philosophic observer would have pictured Mallory's plight in different fashion. The South at that moment, he would have said, illustrated the martial weakness that resulted from a one-sided national economy. For generations that land had devoted its energies to cultivating a few staple crops, for shipment to Europe. In doing this, those industries and that commerce which form the basis of a well-rounded state had been neglected. Old England and New England transported its products to their appointed markets. The factories of the North provided most of its industrial needs. War, even in 1861, was a much mechanized business; manu-

[2] At this time Captain Bullock enjoyed another distinction, of which he was unconscious, he was the uncle of a small boy, three years old, then living in New York City, who was destined to be the twenty-seventh President of the United States His sister Martha had married into a Northern family and her son was Theodore Roosevelt.

facturing plants of all kinds were essential to its prosecution; above all, ships, both mercantile and warlike, were things it could hardly do without. The South possessed neither ships nor shipyards nor heavy industries. Only two naval yards, capable of building war vessels, existed within its limits, the one-time Federal bases at Norfolk and Pensacola. From the beginning of the war to the close the Union held both the fortifications, Pickens and Fortress Monroe, that commanded these strongholds. Not a station could be found in the South where a vessel larger than a yawl could be built. There were no machine shops, no rolling mills, no shipwrights. While, at the time of Fort Sumter, Northern harbors were clogged with vessels of all description — most of which were promptly pressed into Federal service — practically nothing was afloat in Southern waters that could be transformed to the uses of the conflict. "Our present navy," Mallory informed Bullock, "consists of a little steamer of 500 tons, called the *Sumter*, under the command of Raphael Semmes," — the Semmes who afterward won fame with the *Alabama*. The South therefore needed, first of all, not the gold-braided officers who had departed from the Union Navy, but ships, guns, and a few of those ironclads which were now coming into existence in Europe. As far as wooden ships were concerned, the timber of which they would be built was still standing green in the forests. The hemp of which their cordage could be woven was yet unplanted.

There were two ways in which the aim of a Southern navy — the destruction of the blockade — could be accomplished. One was by way of a direct, frontal attack; one by a more indirect, but still effective, approach. If the South could secure ships vastly superior to those of the Union Navy, the blockading fleet could be sunk or dispersed. If such a plan should not prove feasible, sea attacks of another kind might induce Uncle Sam to separate his strongest ships from the cordon that was tightening around Southern ports and pursue the enemy in distant oceans. Mallory's naval strategy comprehended both these methods. For the first — the frontal attack — the Union Navy presented a tempting opportunity. It had one great weakness that easily made it the victim of an aggressive foe. The American sea force was almost entirely a wooden one. But a new portent had suddenly appeared in the navies of the world. That was the ironclad, steam-propelled battleship. In crude form this new weapon demonstrated its power in the Crimean War; but, by 1860 and 1861, its full meaning had startled Great Britain and France with a shock only comparable to the revelation of the dreadnaught half a century afterward. By 1861 all Europe was agreed that the days of wooden navies were finished. The next European war would be won by the nation that possessed the largest fleet of steam ironclads. Already, Napoleon III had his *Gloire* and Great Britain its *Warrior*, practically equal in destructive force. Both countries were engaged in a naval race as intense as those of modern times. Could the Confederacy have gained possession of either the *Gloire* or the *Warrior*, it could have ended the Federal blockade overnight. The North had been backward in building iron ships; "Lincoln's blockade," in the early days, consisted of almost any vessel that could be kept afloat and practically none of this miscellaneous line could have held the water long after a *Gloire* or a *Warrior* had hailed within shooting distance. Ironclads, on the model of these heroic ships, were what constituted the main purpose of Bullock's trip to Europe.

So much for ironclad battleships — for vessels of huge fighting power, that could confront face to face the Federal blockading squadrons, and by destroying them open the seas to Southern commerce. Should this method fail, Mallory had another plan for bringing about the same result. For this huge battleships of the *Gloire* type were not necessary. Not great fighting power, but great speed, was the prime essential. For the second method did not contemplate fighting as that term is commonly understood. The alternative type of vessel was intended to assail, not warships, but those peacefully engaged in commerce. The story of the Southern commerce destroyers is one of the most romantic of the Civil War. Everyone has heard of the *Alabama,* the *Florida,* the *Shenandoah,* and their success in almost completely sweeping Union merchant vessels from the sea. Yet it is doubtful if their real mission is yet comprehended. Desirable as this work of annihilating American shipping might seem in Southern eyes, such depredations did not represent the ultimate strategic purpose. That purpose was to create a naval diversion that would have ended the blockade. In operations on land this is one of the commonest of resources; the European war witnessed a famous illustration in 1914, when the Russian army, by its onslaughts on the Germans in East Prussia, compelled the Kaiser to deplete his forces in France, with the consequence that the German offensive collapsed at the Marne. The Southern cruiser programme in 1861 was undertaken in the hope of an outcome of similar nature. For in only one way could the Union have ended the "piratical" campaign now let loose on Northern commerce. That was by sending its strongest fighters in pursuit of these "highwaymen" of the deep. But the only warships in Federal hands — and the supply was inadequate to the purpose — were blockading Southern ports. If these should be detached from their Atlantic vigil and scattered to all parts of the world in pursuit of Confederate privateers, the blockade would automatically come to an end. That was precisely the object at which Mallory was aiming. He confidently believed that this would be the outcome. The South always insisted that the ruling motive of the North was the materialistic one. "Yankee cupidity" was the phrase constantly on Southern lips. The pride the Northern section took in its beautiful, swift sailing ships — acknowledged to be superior to anything afloat — was notorious. That New England would sit by patiently and witness this noble armada disappear in flames, or sink, vessel by vessel, beneath the waves, no one in the South believed. A universal demand would arise for vengeance and protection; Mr. Lincoln would be compelled to adjourn his blockade, and send his warships in pursuit of the Davis flotilla. The blockade would end; Southern ports would be open to the commerce of the world; cotton would flow out freely to Britain and France, munitions would enter at an enormous rate; and this great show of strength would end in European recognition and the Confederate States would assume their position as one of the nations of the world.

Such was the real purpose of the voyages of that *Alabama*, whose exploits form so stirring a chapter in the history of the Civil War. For Captain Bullock succeeded in his first mission. He did not build six propeller cruisers in British yards — only because his money gave out; but he did, in this first year of the war, lay down the keels of two — that *Oreto* and *No. 290*, which, ultimately christened the *Florida* and the *Alabama*, slipped out of the Laird shipyards and started their murderous slaughter of Yankee ships. Hardly any vessel, ancient or modern, is so famous as the *Alabama*. It not only sailed in every ocean, searching out its prey in the Atlantic, the China seas, the Arctic, the tropics, capturing and destroying about seventy ships and their cargoes; it had a vast influence on international law. For England, in permitting this vessel to be built in an English port, and winking at its escape, committed an error for which it afterward was compelled to pay $15,-000,000 in damages to the American Government. Confederate histories regard its achievements as one of their most brilliant successes. So far as its most obvious triumphs were concerned — the destruction of Northern commerce — it was indeed a mighty victory. But in the ultimate purpose it was a failure. It did not break the blockade in the slightest degree. The kind of conquests achieved by the *Alabama* were the kind that have little effect in winning a war. The Federal Government did not release its warships from their task of watching Southern ports, in order to engage in a wild-goose chase for this marauder. That would have been to fall into the Confederate trap. It displayed far more stoicism in facing the destruction of its commerce than Mr. Mallory and his confreres had anticipated. Whatever might happen to its merchant fleet, Lincoln never had the slightest intention of giving up the blockade, for the blockade meant the strangling of the Confederacy. The time came when the North did build a swift, powerful cruiser for the express purpose of capturing the *Alabama,* and this vessel, the *Kearsarge,* presently caught the enemy off Cherbourg, France, and sent it to the bottom. But by that time the *Alabama* had finished its work, for very little American commerce was left afloat. Its main mission, the ending of Lincoln's wooden wall around the Confederate States, it never attained.

3

The Ironclads

The belief that such depredations would so agonize the commercial spirit of the North that it would sacrifice its great engine of war thus proved to be only another one of those misconceptions of which Confederate history is so full. Secretary Mallory, therefore, was forced to resort to his other manœuvre — the construction of huge battleships for direct attack. Soon after despatching Captain Bullock he sent Lieutenant James H. North to England to purchase or build an ironclad, but North soon developed temperamental difficulties and proved of no great assistance to the Southern cause. The original task laid upon North was, indeed, a fairly staggering one. That French steam frigate *Gloire,* the most powerful warship afloat, not only kept British naval experts awake nights — for its descent on the English coast was a momentary fear — but had completely captured Mallory's imagination. His despatches are full of glowing references to this terrible floating fortress. If the South only possessed a ship like this! Then,

Mallory insisted, — and he was unquestionably right, — the ramshackle Lincoln blockade would vanish. By constantly thinking on the subject Mallory conceived an almost violent scheme. Why should the South wait to build another *Gloire?* Why not acquire that very ship itself or one of its sisters, recently finished? There were difficulties in the way, to be sure. This was not only the most formidable fighting vessel in existence, but the most expensive. Just where the South could raise the money for the purchase, provided the French could be persuaded to sell, was not clear. And it demanded considerable optimism to suppose that Napoleon III would transfer one of his ironclads to Southern waters, much as he loved the Confederacy and hoped for its success. The *Gloire* was the pride of the French nation; already the French people regarded it as the sure avenger of Trafalgar; besides, though Napoleon was a little careless on the subject of neutrality, its sale to the enemy of the American nation — rebellious citizens, President Lincoln insisted — with which France was on terms of friendship would be a stretch of that doctrine before which even he might be expected to hesitate. Despite this Mallory directed North to acquire a "few ships of this description, ships that can receive without material injury the fire of the heaviest frigates and liners at short distances, and whose guns, though few in number, with shell or hot shot, will enable them to destroy the wooden navy of our enemy." As constructing vessels would take considerable time, Lieutenant North was ordered to approach France on the subject of the purchase from the French Navy of "one of the armored frigates of the class of the *Gloire*."[3] In this lofty negotiation North did not succeed; but he did begin the construction of an ironclad in Glasgow, Scotland — only to be forced, as it neared completion, to sell it to Denmark.

The building of these desired monsters presently fell into Bullock's hands. Mallory did indeed attempt the building of

[3] *Official Records of the Union and Confederate Navies*, Series 2, Vol. II, p. 70.

something of the kind in hastily improvised Southern yards. The reconstructed frigate *Merrimac* was his first attempt of the kind. When a combination of events, including the invention of the strange new Federal warship *Monitor,* caused the Confederates to sink this clumsy craft at its Norfolk dock, Mallory centred his energy on two ironclads already begun at New Orleans, the *Louisiana* and the *Mississippi.* Farragut ended the career of these vessels by his capture of New Orleans. One vanished in flames, the other was blown up, and so Mallory's hopes of building ironclads in Confederate ports disappeared. Bullock and British and French shipyards now became his sole resource.

Simply building the ships involved no problem. British yards were eager for sumptuous contracts of this sort — once the money was safely deposited in advance. But to get the completed vessels into the open sea was an entirely different question. The hullabaloo raised by Uncle Sam over the "escape" of the *Alabama* and the *Florida* still echoed in the British Foreign Office, as it was to do for several years to come. With every fresh "outrage," with every capture and sinking of a fine American merchantman, these protests sounded a new din in the ears of Lord John Russell. Mr. Seward, never a gentle soul in his dealings with Governments friendly to the Confederacy, was becoming extremely exacting, or "bumptious" as the English press put it. Captain Bullock had contracted for two ironclad rams of the *Warrior* type with those odious, mercenary Lairds of *Alabama* fame. Their works at Liverpool were overrun by Federal spies; some were actually engaged as workmen on the rams; yet espionage was hardly needed, for little attempt was made — it would have been useless — to conceal the real destination of the vessels.

Bullock, it is true, had "sold" the ships to an obscure Frenchman named Bravay, who in turn was ostensibly the agent of the Khedive of Egypt; but the subterfuge deceived nobody. Above all, it did not deceive the very alert United States Minister at

London, Charles Francis Adams. The persistence with which Mr. Adams haunted the British Foreign Office, the firmness with which he laid down the law to Lord John Russell, form one of the greatest chapters in American diplomacy. His final adjuration to the Foreign Secretary — virtually an ultimatum — is one of those phrases which Americans still love to repeat. "Your Lordship knows that this means war," he quietly wrote Russell, discussing the possibility that the ironclads, like the *Alabama*, should be permitted to "escape" into open waters. And this time the British Government acted with deadly seriousness. On October 9, 1863, just as the rams were nearing completion, British officials stepped upon their decks and seized possession in the name of Her Majesty. The precautions now taken against the chance that in the dark and fog one or both might accidentally slip their moorings testify both to the determination of the British to prevent their sailing and to the high respect they had for their power. Those Confederates were clever and adventurous chaps; a Confederate crew, with officers, was not far away, prepared to convoy their prizes to Southern waters; not impossibly these daring gentlemen might attempt a *coup*, board the ships in the night, overpower the guards, and get them to sea. Powerful British battleships were therefore placed in the Mersey, ready for instant action, and other precautions taken that made unthinkable any such effort. So Mallory and Captain Bullock found themselves in the plight of Robinson Crusoe. That patient exile, it will be recalled, built a large stout boat, to facilitate departure from his solitary home, and, as it neared completion, discovered that he could not launch it. The Confederate crisis was even more disheartening. Eventually Her Majesty's Government purchased the Laird rams and added them to the British Navy.

Captain Bullock's reports to Mallory of these proceedings are bitter and discouraging. All the hopes and efforts of two years crushed at a single blow! His expectations had involved nothing less than victory for the Confederate cause. In the Mississippi the Laird rams, he believed, would restore New Orleans to the South and frustrate Grant's operations against Vicksburg and Port Hudson. In the Atlantic they would scatter such units of the Federal Navy as they did not sink. "The Atlantic coast offers enticing and decisive work in more than one direction," Bullock wrote Mallory, July 9, 1863. "Without a moment's delay after getting their crews aboard off Wilmington our vessels might sail southward, sweep the blockading fleet from the sea front of every harbor from the Capes of Virginia to Sabine Pass, and cruising up and down the coast could prevent anything like permanent, systematic interruption of our foreign trade in the future. Again, should Washington still be held by the enemy our ironclads could ascend the Potomac and after destroying all transports and gunboats falling within their reach could render Washington itself untenable and could thus create a powerful diversion in favor of any operations General Lee might have on foot. Again, Portsmouth, New Hampshire, is a city given over to hatred of our cause and country. It is wealthy in itself and opposite the town is an important national dock and building yard. The whole lies invitingly open to attack and destruction. Suppose our two ironclads should steam unannounced into that harbor some fine October morning and while one proceeds at once to demolish the navy yard and all it contained the other should send a flag of truce to the Mayor to say that if $10,000,000 in gold and $50,000,000 in greenbacks were not sent on board in four hours the city would be destroyed after the manner of Jacksonville and Bluffton. Portsmouth could well afford to pay that sum for its existence. Philadelphia is another point open to such an attack." [4]

John Bigelow, consul general in Paris during the war, and, on Dayton's death in 1864, Minister to France, held the same view. "Had these vessels reached the coast of America,"

[4] *Official Records of the Union and Confederate Navies*, Series 2, Vol. I, p. 456.

he writes, "the territory of the United States might possibly now be under two or more independent governments."[5] And now John Bull, in obsequious deference to Yankee pretensions, snatched away the victory at the very hour of triumph. Disgusted with England, Mallory turned his eyes towards a more friendly direction. "The hostility of the British government," he wrote Bullock, December 3, 1863, "to our country and cause is as unequivocal as is its readiness to respond to every insolent demand which the Federal government may make upon it and neither government nor people here look for a single act or word in aid or sympathy from that quarter. The assurance which Great Britain now has that the Union is destroyed relieves the war of much of the interest which it presented to her statesmen, and mutual exhaustion of the contending parties is the work that now engrosses their attention. From France, we think from the lights before us, we may fairly expect a different course."[6] For this hope Mallory had excellent grounds. In fact the possibility of building Confederate warships in French yards had been raised by Napoleon himself; he had not been pressed in the matter, but had volunteered his coöperation. A letter from Slidell, dated October 28, 1862, had caused great optimism in the Confederate Cabinet. Naturally Mallory had grasped at the suggestion it embodied. In this Slidell had related the story of his second interview with the Emperor, this time at the Palace in Saint-Cloud.

To tell the story of Mallory and his French ironclads means again tracing familiar ground. Once more the figure of Maximilian steps furtively upon the stage; again the shifty fortunes of Napoleon and his tremulous Mexican empire constitute the springs of action. It is impossible, indeed, to touch Confederate diplomacy in any of its phases without uncovering this insane adventure. For the significant thing about French warship building for the Confederacy is that it was undertaken at

---
[5] *France and the Confederate Navy*, p. IV.
[6] *Official Records of the Union and Confederate Navies*, Series 2, Vol. II.

the suggestion of the Emperor himself. It came to a point at the meeting between Slidell and His Majesty at Saint-Cloud in October, 1862. The date is suggestive, as is always the case in the tortuous Napoleonic course towards the Southern States. It was just after Second Bull Run, just two months before Fredericksburg. That is, it virtually marked the high tide of Confederate success. The Emperor's Mexican invasion, however, was not going so smoothly. The first French expedition had suffered a severe reverse at Puebla, and a second, under the command of General Forey, had recently disembarked at Vera Cruz. It was a moment when France needed friends, and when an alliance with a victorious Confederacy might safeguard not only its present but its future. Inevitably, Napoleon, on this occasion, showed his most seductive qualities to Slidell. "My sympathies," he again told the envoy, "are entirely with the South. My only desire is to know how to give them effect." Slidell cautiously hinted at one way in which His Majesty could show his good disposition. If the Confederacy had just one ship like the *Gloire,* the Federal blockade could be destroyed, and the success of the South be assured. He referred to the unsuccessful attempts that had been made to build such warships in England. Napoleon at once picked up the suggestion. "Why could you not have them built as for the Italian government?" he asked. "I do not think it would be difficult, but will consult the Minister of Marine about it."

Thus the offer for constructing Confederate warships in French yards came directly from the Emperor himself. "The attempt," Bullock wrote Mallory, "to build ships in France was undertaken at the instigation of the Imperial government itself. When the construction of the corvettes was in process of negotiation, a draft of the proposed contract was shown to the highest person in the Empire, and it received his sanction; at least I was so informed at the time." Not only did the initiative come from this source, but, as the French situation in Mexico improved, — Puebla and the capital presently capitulated to the French armies, — the Imperial entourage became almost insistent. The Minister of State — the nearest French approach, at the time, to a Premier — conveyed the news secretly to Slidell that the Emperor wished ram-building to begin. Persigny and De Morny were working on Slidell to the same end. Thus Mallory had one great ally in his shipbuilding undertaking. This was not the love of France for the Confederate States, but the desire to split the Union permanently in two, so as to assure the success of French imperialism on the North American continent. How closely the Emperor was involved was evident from the names that ran through the contracts. His favorite banker, Emile Erlanger, — he of the famous loan, father-in-law of Matilda Slidell, — acted as financial agent, incidentally receiving a commission of $50,000 for guaranteeing the payments. His close friend, L. Arman of Bordeaux, chief constructor for the French Navy and member of the Corps Legislatif, contracted for all the ships. All the papers in the case, which are at present in the possession of the United States Government, make entertaining reading. Two ironclads were contracted for, and according to these specifications were to be really frightful ships of war. Each possessed, in addition to other armament, two revolving turrets, which bore a suspicious resemblance to those Mr. Ericsson had placed upon the *Monitor*. Among the other data preserved in our national records are the authorizations issued by M. Rouher, French Minister of Marine, to the builders, for installing heavy armament. According to French law, no fighting instruments could be placed on ships without the written permission of the Government, but this was most cheerfully given. The complicity of the French Empire in this attempt to destroy a friendly nation is thus clearly established.

But these mighty vessels and the four corvettes intended to continue *Alabama* depredations on American commerce, though finished with reasonable despatch, never reached the Confederate Government. Once more the explanation must be found in distant Mexico. Before the time came for transferring the warships to the Davis Government, the situation on the American front had radically changed. For one thing, other personages than Mr. Bullock and M. Arman had come into possession of these contracts, or of accurate copies of them. Mr. Dayton, United States Minister in Paris, had acquired not only the documents, including the Erlanger guarantee, but all the correspondence that had passed between Bullock, Arman, Slidell, Rouher, and other parties to the transaction. When Mr. Dayton laid this entertaining evidence before the French Foreign Office and categorically and not too diplomatically demanded confiscation of the ships, the shock proved a serious one, even for such masters of duplicity as then guided the destinies of France. Other circumstances added contemporaneously to the discomfiture. The most discouraging was the new picture of the American conflict. By March, 1864, the Confederacy was obviously disintegrating. That great triumph on which Napoleon III had based his plans was fading more and more into the distance. Previously, most European statesmen and military chieftains had taken it for granted that the Confederacy would win. In the spring and summer of 1864 it was certain that it would lose. Victory after victory was perching on Northern arms; the man power and economic resources of the South were growing feebler every day. The Emperor Napoleon now discovered, as Lord Salisbury did several years afterward, that he "had put his money on the wrong horse." Moreover, that barometer of Napoleonic policy in the American Civil War, the Mexican situation, indicated a more cautious attitude toward the Federal Union. The friendship of Jefferson Davis, it was now perceived, could not promote French imperialistic plans and the enmity of Abraham Lincoln might easily destroy them. With that charming cynicism so characteristic of the Second Empire, Napoleon began to seek a new ally for Maximilian. Why not the formerly neglected United States itself? A conciliatory, even affectionate attitude towards Uncle Sam might win recognition for the hard-pressed Hapsburg. At least it was the only hope of escape left. The effect of the new policy on John Slidell has already been described. That envoy was still smarting in Paris under the snub administered by "Emperor" Maximilian, who politely refused to receive his call. But worse things were now to come. In future the Americans to be wooed were not those of Richmond, but of Washington.

Presently a distressing scene took place at the Tuileries. Napoleon had summoned his old friend Arman, the builder of the Confederate ships. His Majesty had some time before sent orders that they could not be delivered, but that constructor, well understanding the vacillating temper of his chief, was moving slowly. Work, despite the Imperial command, was still progressing. If Arman had entertained any doubt as to the Imperial determination, a single glance at his master now quickly undeceived him. Napoleon was in a high rage — or affected to be. How about those Confederate ships? Had Arman not received the Imperial command to sell them? Why had he not done so? Why was he still stealthily attempting to finish the vessels? Why was he intriguing for the escape even of one of the rams? Act quickly, shouted His Majesty, or Arman would find himself in prison. And this must not be any pretended sale, said the Emperor. "It must be *bona fide!*" If this were not done at once, the French Government itself would seize the vessels and take them to Rochefort. Arman lost no time in acting on these orders. Without consulting Bullock, all four corvettes and both rams had been disposed of to Prussia and Denmark. A comic touch to the tragedy was an indignant letter from M. Rouher, Minister of Marine, to the constructor of one of the cruisers, expressing his astonishment that the offending shipwright was erecting such a lethal vessel. This was the identical Rouher who, only a year before, had issued his official authorization to arm each of the cor-

vettes with fourteen heavy guns — *"canons rayé de trente."* [7]
"I certainly thought," Bullock wrote Mallory, "that this kind of crooked diplomacy had died out since the last century and would not be ventured upon in these commonsense days. Captain Tessier saw Mr. Slidell in Paris who told him that he had been informed of the sale and was both astonished and indignant." [8] From this time forward the Emperor Napoleon supplanted Lord John Russell as the most conspicuous object of Confederate hatred. England had indeed acted badly, but not so infamously as France. The British Government had not instigated the building of the ships which it subsequently cashiered. That was precisely what France had done. The case, Bullock wrote Mallory, was "one of simple deception. I was, not as a private individual, but as an agent of the Confederate states, invited to build ships of war in France. The Emperor now favors us so far as to tell us frankly to sell out and save our money." [9] "I am prostrated by the intelligence," Mallory wrote Bullock. "Among all the bitter experiences of the war this disappointment stands prominently forth, presenting, as it does, among other sad considerations, a violation of faith which challenged and received our confidence.". . . "The proof that it furnishes that the plighted word of an Emperor is as unreliable as that of princes, in whom we are admonished by high authority to place no trust, does not surprise me, but, though prepared for the violation of his faith, I did not suppose it would be sacrificed in the maintenance of a policy no less false than feeble. The time is not distant when he will realize the extent of his blunder and earnestly seek the good will which he now so recklessly rejects." For, Mallory insisted, the Emperor was miscalculating if he thought that this belated subservience to the United States Government would win its support for the Mexican adventure. "However well informed a few of the leaders of

[7] *Official Records of the Union and Confederate Navies,* Series 2, Vol. II, p. 667.
[8] *The same.*
[9] *The same.*

the French government may be," Mallory wrote Bullock, "as to the light in which the people of the United States regard the establishment of a monarchy in Mexico under an Austrian prince, it is quite certain that the French people are very ignorant. They are soon to learn that whatever doubts New England may entertain on the divinity of Christ or the immortality of the soul or of their own truth and power, she has no hesitation about the Monroe doctrine and that no man or party can reach power in the United States whose platform does not maintain this as a fundamental truth. What the Emperor's course towards our interest may be when he shall discover the universal and determined hostility of the government and people of the United States to his whole Mexican policy I will not venture to surmise, but that this hostility will soon be unmistakably manifested to France I have no doubt. . . . When the Emperor shall become assured of the views of the United States upon this subject and that active opposition to the permanence of Maximilian's government in Mexico must soon be manifested he will at the same time see that the interests of France in Mexico are intimately connected with those of the Confederate States."

The next two years disclosed that Mallory was right. If Napoleon believed that quashing Confederate shipbuilding plans would win American support for Maximilian, that was only one of the numerous mistakes he made in his estimate of the American character. In 1866, at the conclusion of the Civil War, the State Department sent what was virtually an ultimatum to Napoleon, demanding the withdrawal of French troops from Mexico. At the same time a large American army was moved to the Mexican border. Napoleon could do nothing but acquiesce. He withdrew his French troops, leaving Maximilian to the fate which he met at the hands of a Mexican firing squad.

XVI

COMIC RELIEF

1

THE POST OFFICE

SEVERAL distinguished members of the Davis Cabinet played little part in the Southern Government. John C. Breckinridge, Vice President of the United States under Buchanan, candidate for President in 1860 on the regular Democratic ticket, one of the greatest of Southern orators, probably the most beloved Kentuckian since Henry Clay, entered the Davis family as sixth Secretary of War in February, 1865, in time to join the President and his official companions in their flight from Richmond on the approach of the Federal army. George Davis, the able North Carolinian who succeeded Watts as Attorney General in January, 1864, found little opportunity for official distinction. A man of high character and eminent professional talents, an old-line Whig and lifelong opponent of Secession, which he reluctantly accepted in obedience to the dictum of his state, Davis had the misfortune to head a department that existed only on paper. The Confederacy never developed a judicial system, and thus the man who served as Attorney General was almost without occupation.

John H. Reagan, Postmaster General, has his niche in American annals not as a Cabinet officer of the Confederacy, but as a United States Senator from Texas for many years after the Civil War, and chief author of the Interstate Commerce Law. The abilities Reagan subsequently displayed as Federal lawmaker he applied to the administration of his office in Richmond, but the labor was not of a spectacular kind and was considerably removed from the conduct of the war. The Federal Government, in the seventy years preceding Fort Sumter, had constructed a complete postal system in all the eleven seceding states. Strange as it may seem, this organization continued uninterruptedly until June, 1861, four months after the formation of the Confederacy. What could more eloquently indicate than this the belief, still persisting in Federal circles, that the war was merely a temporary disturbance, a riot on a huge scale, the adventure, not of sober, earnest men, but, as Lincoln described it in his proclamation of April 15, of disorderly "combinations"? All during this time of excitement, Southerners kept contentedly affixing United States postage stamps to their mail, confidently trusting that it would be dutifully sent to its destination by a power with which they were actually at war. Since the "rebellion" would be smothered in a brief period, why should Washington destroy a complicated public service which it had taken nearly a century to construct?

On June 6, however, a Federal proclamation declared that mail deliveries in the Confederate states were at an end. Then Postmaster General Reagan stepped into the breach. The change in status was easily made. The postal service, despite the change in its head, still existed in the Southern states; the post offices still stood, the contracts with railroads and other transportation systems were still in force; the same old army of letter carriers could continue making their rounds; the former Federal postmasters and clerks were quite prepared to go on with their work. The only visible change was that Richmond, instead of Washington, became the centre of the organization. One difficulty was the supply of postage stamps and other materials needed in the conduct of mails; these the Confederacy could not at once produce, any more than it could print paper money. Until the early supplies came from Richmond, therefore, customers of Mr. Reagan's department paid cash for the transit of their letters — precisely as they had done in the old days, before the invention of postage stamps.

Reagan, as Postmaster General, was industrious, honest,

and successful. He even scored one triumph for which the Federal post office, before or since, offers no parallel. Under him the postal service exhibited no annual deficit. It not only paid its own way, but yielded a profit. Reagan accomplished this miracle by discharging unnecessary clerks, cutting off costly and unneeded routes, and driving hard bargains with contractors, railroads, and the like, and by increasing rates for postage. Thus, in unostentatious fashion, he may be regarded as the most successful member of the Administration; at least he was the only one who actually performed the task assigned him. The high regard Reagan won as Postmaster General was further heightened by his career from 1865 to 1905, — for he survived the war forty years, — especially by the spirit of reconciliation he displayed to the reëstablished Union, and the loyalty and ability with which he served it.

Efficiently distributing the mails, however, had only the remotest influence upon the fighting of the war. If we seek the causes for the rapid deterioration of the South in 1864 and 1865, we must look elsewhere. In the diplomatic service and internal politics are still to be found the causes of the final rapid collapse. The failure to elicit the support of great foreign nations and the constantly rising predominance of certain political tenets — above all the doctrine of State rights — explain why this bold attempt at independence inevitably failed. Distrust abroad, political chaos and factionalism at home — these defects, rather than weakened military strength, dug the grave of the Confederacy.

2

The Propaganda of the Confederacy

Anyone who thinks that the publicity agent is a modern character should turn to the propaganda service of the Confederacy in Europe from 1861 to 1865. Its labor in this heroic field presents a study in all the crudities and refinements of the art. The North, it is true, did not entirely neglect the influence of public opinion as helpmeet to its Army and Navy; as its cash resources were larger, so were its expenditures on a more lavish scale; but it is doubtful whether its press agents attained quite the skill in reaching foreign sentiment as did at least one of the Davis representatives.

The State Department entrusted this task of spreading the "truth" in Europe to two men. One of them, Henry Hotze, a native of Switzerland, well-educated, shrewdly intelligent, full of youthful fire, had had a brilliant journalistic career on the *Mobile Register*. His companion worker, Edwin de Leon, the Confederacy's spokesman in France, fell far behind Hotze in ability and finesse. De Leon, indeed, ended his career as one of the most entertaining casualties of the time. His prewar experience in the United States consular service and his close personal friendship with Jefferson Davis seemed to provide an exceptional equipment for his delicate task. These very advantages, however, especially his association with Davis and other leaders, inspired in him ambitions far transcending those of maker of public opinion and largely explained his undoing. Certainly he could not complain of niggardly treatment by Richmond. The starved Confederate Treasury gave Hotze $750 as a working fund for publicity in Great Britain and De Leon $25,000, for the same missionary purpose in France. And Hotze's task was a more exacting one than De Leon's. In those days the work of inspiring fervor in the breasts of French journalists was no difficult or complicated labor. The formula was simple to the last degree. Editorial opinion in the joyous days of the Second Empire, especially in the newspapers that had been lukewarm to the Confederate Government, was a matter of bargain and sale. De Leon began distributing his $25,000 in lavish fashion, with fairly magical results. Papers that had violently opposed Jefferson Davis now became his most valiant champions. Only one stumbling block stood in the way of complete success.

French newspaper readers, as cynical as the press itself, recognized the long-familiar mechanism of fabricating public sentiment; and De Leon's efforts added much to the gayety of a capital trained to lively humor by the operas of Offenbach and the comedies of Scribe.

De Leon sounded a less entertaining note when he published a brochure, under his own name, on the rights and wrongs of the Confederacy, the chief feature of which was a fervid defense of slavery. As the French people hated nothing quite so vehemently as this "peculiar institution," De Leon's rhetoric did far more harm than good. On the whole the man's literary adventures did not prove to be a great success. He might have survived these misfortunes, however, except for certain personal failings. For other complications rendered him an odious embarrassment to Davis and Benjamin. On leaving Richmond, the Secretary of State had given De Leon extremely confidential letters from Benjamin to Slidell. One of these was the message in which, as previously described, Benjamin had sought to bribe Napoleon III into recognizing the Confederacy and breaking the blockade. On the voyage to France, De Leon opened and read these communications; when he presented the documents, with broken seals, to Slidell, that diplomat's anger knew no restraint. The experience made him instantaneously De Leon's enemy. Slidell refused to introduce him to French officialdom, or to facilitate his missionary efforts in any way. De Leon retaliated by writing an abusive despatch about Slidell to Secretary Benjamin; at the same time, evidently stung by French ridicule of his journalistic approaches, he expressed most unfavorable opinions of the French people and their Government. Unscrupulous Yankee spies obtained possession of these official papers, and, in due course, published them, with conspicuous emblazonry, in the pages of the *New York Tribune*. Both De Leon and Benjamin were Jews, but no fraternal feelings deflected the Secretary of State from his duty in the premises.

His published correspondence, Benjamin wrote De Leon, was of such a nature "as not only to destroy your own usefulness in the special service entrusted to you, but to render your continuance in your present position incompatible with the retention in the public service of our commissioner to Paris." De Leon dejectedly returned to Richmond, and fame knew him no more.

If the respective sums of money given to De Leon and Hotze measured the value placed upon their respective services, the Government of Richmond made a great error of judgment. For Hotze proved to be as great a success as De Leon had been a failure. In mental and literary equipment, Hotze was by far the superior man. Only twenty-eight years old, he possessed a suavity, a subtlety, and silence in method that would have distinguished an experienced diplomat. As far back as 1862, he introduced into publicity procedures those "psychological methods" upon which so many modern exemplars pride themselves. No bribery for Hotze — at least, no open, flagrant bribery; he approached his problem in far more insinuating guise. No press agent quite so noiseless as Hotze has ever plied his craft. Indeed, it was not until the publication of his official papers as recently as 1922 [1] that many Americans had ever heard his name. In comparison with Hotze's suppleness and comprehension, James Murray Mason appears a slow-witted blunderer and even John Slidell looks like an unscrupulous marplot. Yet Richmond, at the time of Hotze's appointment, knew nothing of the man's deft qualities. Clearly no great results were expected from this youthful propagandist.

Only one point in common did Hotze and De Leon evince; this was a considerable contempt for the nations whose good will it was their duty to conciliate. The difference was that De Leon published his opinion broadcast, while Hotze dis-

---

[1] In Vol. 3, Series II, of the *Official Records of the Union and Confederate Navies in the War of the Rebellion.* On these letters the present account of Hotze's activity is based.

played his only in carefully guarded communications to his Government. His earliest reports — reports that were well-written and disclosed a sure grasp of English politics and European statesmen — disclosed also complete disillusionment on British motives in the American contest. Do not look for help or sympathy, he insists — unless such an attitude will promote British interests! No other than material advantages were guiding British party leaders. The Government, the upper social castes, the merchants, individuals, and professional men — such was his diagnosis — welcomed American strife because it meant the lasting dissolution of the American Union. That would be a good thing for England because it would open a vast profitable market to her manufactures. The North, by insisting on a protective tariff, had closed this field to English goods; it was the avowed intention of the South to prohibit Yankee importations and to adopt free trade with Europe. Here was the only explanation, Hotze wrote Benjamin, for such sympathy as prevailed in England for the Confederate cause. "Intense selfishness," he wrote Benjamin, August 2, 1862, "overshadows all other national characteristics and this selfishness is narrow-minded, because there is not now any truly great individual intelligence to shape the national policy. Lord Palmerston's blood is chilled by extreme old age; Earl Russell thinks procrastination the perfection of statesmanship."[2] "Reconstruction by the triumph of either party over the other is what the government and people of Great Britain would make every sacrifice to prevent."[3]

Of the London press, whose favor it was his duty to conciliate, Hotze's opinion was not much more complimentary. The editors of those staid journals who were quickly swept within his orbit would have been shocked had they read the secret despatches their friend was constantly transmitting to

[2] *Official Records of the Union and Confederate Navies*, Vol. 3, Series II, pp. 505–506.
[3] *The same*, p. 536.

Richmond. "The English press is not so exaltedly pure," Mr. Benjamin was informed soon after Hotze's arrival, "nor is that of any other country, but that a man entering its ranks with purse held up would find himself practically and in no dignified manner illustrating the classic fate of Actæon" — by which he seems to imply that such an attractive victim would be torn to pieces by mercenary journalistic staghounds. From such a fate Hotze was safeguarded by the trifling sum assigned him for purposes of lubrication. As his usefulness dawned upon Benjamin and Davis, Hotze's paltry appropriation was increased to $10,000 a year, but even then he never descended to the vulgar methods that had brought such discredit on De Leon. Nor, with lofty-minded journals like the *Times*, the *Morning Post*, the *Standard*, the *Saturday Review*, and the other organs of public opinion that were ultimately swept within the Confederate influence, would financial approaches have been conceivable. Here a high order of Jesuitry could alone achieve success.

The London of that day supported a trained group of editorial writers, attached to no particular paper. "Professional leader writers," they were called; like other literary journeymen, they wrote their articles and submitted them on the chance of acceptance. At least eight or ten of this brotherhood were sufficiently successful to make a satisfactory living. The pay was not bad as newspaper writing goes — two to ten guineas, $10 to $50, for a contribution of ordinary editorial length. The London press, Hotze informed the department, was "the most fastidious in the world," and would "never accept an editorial without paying for it" — a punctiliousness which facilitated his operations. Hotze had one great advantage for his job. He was a man of culture, well versed in European history and contemporary politics and himself master of an energetic journalistic style. That is, his talents qualified him for the rôle of "professional leader writer," and such he became, in most unobtrusive fashion. He penned most informing interpretations of what was known in England as the "American question," and presented them gratis to chosen favorites among this little fraternity. No one knew the secret except the two parties in question. London leader writers, like all followers of the craft, had weary moments when they liked to avoid exertion, and well-written acceptable essays such as Hotze's proved godsends — especially as all profits accrued to their advantage.

Hotze's lucubrations, quietly promoted in this fashion, sometimes attained the loftiest sanctums in London. He was able to twist comment on the fall of Fort Donelson in a way that made it look almost like a Confederate victory. Among the papers inspired to take this view was the Thunderer itself; "in one at least of the *Times* articles," Hotze reports to Richmond, "almost my very words are reproduced."[4] On February 22, 1862, Jefferson Davis was inaugurated permanent President of the Confederate States; this happening would have passed unnoticed in the British press had not the leading editorial in the *Morning Post* hailed it as a great historic event. The *Morning Post* was the personal organ of Lord Palmerston, Prime Minister, and the medium he constantly used to broadcast unofficially his views and policies. This conspicuously displayed editorial caused a great buzzing in London clubs. It was even hailed as pointing to British recognition of the Confederacy. Whispers went about that Palmerston had written it himself. His lordship had no claim to this distinction, for the only begetter of the famous editorial was Henry Hotze, though the financial reward was reaped by one of the "professional leader writers" whom he had made confidential friends. "I have the honor," Hotze wrote the Secretary of State, "to enclose my first contribution to the English press, the leading editorial in yesterday's issue of Lord Palmerston's organ, the *Morning Post*. In reading it you will make due allowances for the necessity under

[4] *Official Records of the Union and Confederate Navies*, Vol. 3, Series II, p. 361.

which I felt myself of studiously maintaining an English point of view and not advancing too far beyond recognized public opinion." [5]

But this was only a beginning. Soon Hotze discovered an even more ingenious way of utilizing for the Confederate cause his little select company of free-lance journalists. On May 1, 1862, the first number of one of those weekly reviews for which London has always been famous appeared on English newsstands. It bore the title of *The Index,* and, in format, typography, dignified literary style, and general arrangement of contents, seemed to be a fit companion of such influential periodicals as the *Spectator, Saturday Review,* and the like. That it was greatly interested in presenting the Southern viewpoint in the American conflict was obvious — indeed this was its advertised mission; that it was in any way directly promoted by the Confederate Government did not stand so plainly on the surface. As far as one could conclude, the *Index* was an English publication, founded by Englishmen and devoted to the Confederate cause. Yet the *Index* was the creation of Henry Hotze. He financed the venture in part from his private resources; Confederate devotees in the South made contributions, and another gentleman who has already figured in this narrative — Emile Erlanger, who made so comfortable a killing in Confederate bonds — also came to his assistance. Just how much the *Index* accomplished in directing public sentiment and official policy in England is not clear. Necessarily it had a limited circulation, confined largely to a free mailing list. In reality, however, the ostensible purpose of the *Index* concealed an adroit scheme of corruption. It provided subtle machinery for bribing the press — no less palpable because the victims themselves hardly suspected the truth. Hotze attached to the *Index,* as salaried members of the staff, six or eight of the most successful of his beloved "professional leader writers." These employees, now having steady jobs,

[5] *The same,* p. 346.

— salaries may have been small, but they made a welcome regular increment to the journalistic income, — became accomplished students on the issues of the American conflict, and, in a reasonable period, were as competent as Hotze himself to discuss them editorially.

Week after week, for nearly four years, this group turned out leading articles for the *Index*. In his private communications, Hotze frankly declared that their work for his weekly paper itself was not the point at issue. While earning their salaries as Hotze's assistant editors, these writers kept up their work as contributors to the great London dailies. The information and opinions they had absorbed as *Index* workers inevitably formed the groundwork of their contributions to leading London organs of public opinion. Thus they received double payment. Hotze paid them as salaried workers on his staff; the London papers paid them for the same articles when warmed over for their editorial columns. This wider field was the important one; their contributions to the *Index* were a secondary matter. Hotze's real purpose was to "educate" — the word constantly figures in his reports — a group of able writers who had a pecuniary interest in spreading Confederate gospel in England and Europe. Repeatedly in his letters to Hunter and Benjamin he proudly surveys his handiwork. Popular circulation for the *Index?* Frankly, nothing much is expected on that score. "The value of an organ," he writes, "not merely as a means of reaching public opinion but as a channel through which arguments and facts can be conveyed unofficially to the government itself, appears to me difficult to overrate. The value of the paper as an agency through which connections can be established through other journals is scarcely less. . . . Every additional contributor I am able to employ becomes an ally in the columns of some other paper and I frequently employ writers with no other object." "The writers employed by me for the *Index* are among the first in their profession, and through them I inspire the columns of some of the most influential publications in this country."

He instances as an ally of whom he is especially proud "Percy Greg, Esq., one of the most talented leader writers of London, who, besides being a valuable contributor to the *Index,* is one of our most efficient supporters in the columns of the *Saturday Review* and other literary and political periodicals of high standing." "Honourable men might honourably take their customary fee for the labor of their brains performed for me, and the ideas and information thus engrafted would bear fruit many fold and on many different trees." "One writer usually writes for several publications and I have thus the opportunity of multiplying myself, so to speak, to an almost unlimited extent." "Few suspect," writes Hotze to Benjamin, August 27, 1863, "none know, the silent, unobtrusive agency through which it [the *Index*] has operated upon its contemporaries." Occasionally Hotze completely threw off the mask. Thus, in January, 1864, he placed on the *Index* staff, as Paris correspondent, one Felix Aucaigne, at a salary of fifty francs a week. "You will not be required to write for the *Index,*" he informs this new recruit. "Your duty will consist in propagating through the French papers the views and the intelligence published through the *Index.*" The mention of Percy Greg indicates the quality of the men Hotze drew within his net. Greg was no gutter journalist, but one of the most distinguished contributors to the *Manchester Guardian* and the London *Standard,* besides the *Saturday Review.* He was also a novelist, a historian, a religious and political leader. In after life his hatred for America knew no bounds, and his *History of the United States* is one of the most violent polemics ever committed to paper. How much of this lifelong hostility sprang from Hotze's "education" (at the expense of the educator) is not recorded.

Any idea that propaganda in wartime is a modern invention thus rests upon a misapprehension. Just how effective was this attempt to subsidize public sentiment? It did not accomplish its great purpose — recognition by foreign Governments. Hotze, just like Mason and Slidell, had his blind side. None of them successfully handled the one spectre that always rose and thwarted their efforts. The existence of slavery in the South constantly blocked their arguments at the most inauspicious moments. It enraged Hotze as it annoyed his diplomatic confreres. Everywhere he turned this ogre crossed his path. This was one lesson that his salaried writers balked at absorbing. On constitutional grounds they most eloquently pleaded the cause. An oppressed nation struggling to be free always fired their pens. But the spectacle of black men in the South — of property rights in human beings — proved a more difficult subject. If his "leader writers" could swallow this institution, the editors of the journals for which they wrote set up the bars and articles portraying the beauties of the slave system seldom attained publication. Hotze, usually imperturbable, lost patience. Like most Southerners — like Mason and Slidell, who constantly met the same undisguised dislike of slavery — Hotze never understood European aversion to what, in his opinion, was a beneficent institution. The "editorial tyrants," as he called them, who would not admit apologies for slavery in their columns, represented the greatest obstacle to success. Hotze's correspondence illustrates, even more clearly than that of Mason and Slidell, the baleful effect of slavery in defeating the Southern cause in Europe.

3

The Mission to the Vatican

Another engaging character now makes a final appearance, and with his last exploit the story of Southern diplomacy reaches its end. A. Dudley Mann, a member of the first Confederate mission to Europe, lingered on the European scene long after his companions, William L. Yancey and Pierre A.

Rost, had ended their official careers. When Mason and Slidell assumed charge of negotiations with Great Britain and France, Mann, for some reason never explained, still retained the favor of Jefferson Davis, who appointed him Commissioner to Belgium. The post did not lack importance, for the King of the Belgians, Queen Victoria's "Uncle Leopold," and "father-in-law" of Europe, was regarded by some as the pivot of European diplomacy. Charlotte, the consort of Maximilian, "Emperor" of Mexico, was his daughter — a circumstance that, in the early days, made him necessarily benevolent toward the South. Despite official friendliness, Mann found little scope for his expansive gifts; his labors at Brussels were confined to writing wordy letters to the Foreign Office, enlightening that department on all the disputed points of Southern history and the legal complexities involved in the American crisis. Just what effect these dissertations produced on Belgian statesmen is not determined; one experienced man of the world, however, they excessively wearied. Secretary Benjamin, after reading these interminable essays in his Richmond office, would usually reply with a deft intimation that his Commissioner desist. Mann was the most prolific of all Benjamin's correspondents. His literary exercises, published in the Confederate records, fill far more space than those of Mason or Slidell. Day after day his despatches fell on Benjamin's desk, bulky in size, blowsy in expression, full of false prophecies, false hopes, and wild abuse of men whose opinions ran counter to his own. Always the South was on the verge of victory; always that recognition which never came was only a few hours or weeks ahead. Benjamin seldom ever acknowledged these communications, or sometimes would acknowledge a dozen or so in a few perfunctory lines. Mann's repeated requests for service in wider fields — he wished to be accredited to Vienna, St. Petersburg, and several other European capitals — almost never elicited a reply. To Benjamin's alert mentality, this self-satisfied Virginian was simply a fool, to be tolerated only because he enjoyed Presidential favor.

In the latter part of 1863, Mann fixed his ambition on a glorious prospect indeed. His objective now became the Holy See of Rome. All temporal sovereignties had turned a cold shoulder upon the Confederacy; was it not possible that Pius IX, still ruler of the Papal states, might look upon it with a more friendly eye? The Pope had sent pastoral letters to Archbishop Hughes of New York and Archbishop Odin of New Orleans, expressing sorrow at the American conflagration and hope that it might be brought to an end; here there seemed to be an entering wedge. Moreover, one phase might have a particular interest for the head of the Catholic Church. The Federal Government — so the enemy charged — was stimulating "immigration" from certain European countries, especially Ireland and Germany. A large proportion of such "immigrants" were Catholics and many, soon after passing Castle Garden, found their way into Federal armies. Hence rose the story that Uncle Sam was enticing poor Irish and German Catholics from their happy European homes merely to obtain cannon fodder for Grant's and Sherman's armies. These facts, properly presented to his Holiness, might produce results favorable to the Southern cause. At least the prospect held forth temptations to an industrious diplomat wearied of inaction and neglect and keen for distinction. To make the Vatican, under Pio Nono, an ally of the Confederate States — Mann's imagination fairly burned at the glory of such an achievement.

Mann's commission to Rome entrusted him with no such lofty duty. His responsibility, as set forth in that document, was a comparatively simple one. President Davis had written a letter to his Holiness thanking him for his Christian sentiments and earnest desire for peace. Mann had been selected as the bearer of this communication. But he started post-haste to the Eternal City with far more exalted plans in mind. In a few days he found himself seated in the office of Cardinal Antonelli, the famous statesman who was Secretary of State for almost the entire pontificate of Pius IX. Both Antonelli and the gorgeous pageantry of the Vatican fired the excitable Virginian. Soon he was declaiming on the iniquities of "the Lincoln concern," and his Eminence, according to Mann's report, was expressing his sympathy for the Southern cause and his admiration for President Davis. Mann's great opportunity came the next day, when he was accorded an audience with the Pope. Never had the amiable Pius IX given a more cordial exhibition of his benign spirit. He lifted his hands in horror — so Mann reported — at the fierceness of the American struggle and sorrowfully expressed his hopes for an end to the war. Reaching for his scissors, the Pope cut the envelope of the Davis letter, glanced at the writing, and then looked up at Mann rather despairingly.

"I see it is in English, a language that I do not understand."

Mann's son, who was present as secretary, then offered to translate. "The translation" — this is Mann's own report to Benjamin — "was rendered in a slow, solemn and emphatic pronunciation. During its progress I did not cease for an instant to carefully survey the features of the sovereign Pontiff. A sweeter expression of pious affection, of tender benignity, never adorned the face of mortal man. No picture can adequately represent him when exclusively absorbed in Christian contemplation. Every sentence of the letter appeared to sensibly affect him. At the conclusion of each, he would lay his hand down upon the desk and bow his head approvingly. When the passage was reached wherein the President states, in such sublime and affecting language, 'We have offered up at the footstool of our father who is in Heaven prayers inspired by the same feelings which animate your Holiness,' his deep sunken orbs visibly moistened were upward turned towards that throne upon which ever sits the Prince of Peace, indicating that his heart was pleading for our deliverance from that causeless and merciless war which is prosecuted against us. The soul of infidelity — if, indeed, infidelity have a soul — would have melted in view of so sacred a spectacle."

A silence followed the translation. Then the Pope asked: "Is President Davis a Catholic?"

Mann necessarily answered in the negative.

"Are you?" his Holiness queried; and again the reply was, "No."

Satisfactory and conciliatory as the audience seemed to be, it was not without its jarring note. Mann presently found that, like Mason in London, Slidell in Paris, and Hotze in a hundred interviews, he was facing the one ugly fact that made the ways of Southern diplomacy so hard. The successor of St. Peter also had his reservations on slavery. Was not the North fighting for the destruction of that institution? — such was the embarrassing question next propounded to the Southern envoy. Would it not be "judicious" for the Confederacy to consent to a process of "gradual emancipation"? When secular voices raised this point in Mann's presence, it usually enraged that not too gracious defender, and led him to accusations of "insolence," "unwarranted interference" in the South's internal concerns, "ignorance" of the only possible relation between black man and his master. But the solemnity of this occasion precluded the usual truculence. Instead, Mann entertained his Holiness with his favorite dissertation on the American Constitution. Again those nice distinctions between the central organization and the states which formed the basis of classic Calhounism were set forth at length. The Confederacy, Mann informed the Pope, could not abolish slavery if it would; only the states, in their capacity as sovereigns, could do that. Emancipation, by either state or central government, would be little less than a crime. "True philanthropy," Mann informed Pius IX, "would shudder at the thought of liberation of the slave in the manner attempted by 'Lincoln & Co.'"

In that case, "the well-cared-for negro would become a semi-barbarian." Negroes themselves had no longing to be free. Those whom Lincoln had emancipated looked lovingly back to the old life and wished for nothing so much as to return to it. "If African slavery is an evil," thus Mann concluded his address, "there is a power which, in its own good time, will doubtless remove that evil in a more gentle manner than that of causing the earth to be deluged with blood for its southern overthrow."

"His Holiness," recorded Mann, "received these remarks with an approving expression." The Pontiff complimented the South on its spirit of self-sacrifice and devotion. Devoted indeed! responded Mann, picking up the Pope's last word. These Southerners had been this "from the beginning; there they are still, more resolute, if possible, than ever of emulating in devotion, earthly though it is in character, those holy female spirits who were the last at the Cross and the first at the sepulchre."

"His Holiness received this statement with evident satisfaction" — so Mann informed the State Department. He then reverted to the horrible war. What could he do to mitigate it — even to end it? Mann pictured the plight of those Irish Catholics who were enticed to emigrate and then put in the front ranks of the Northern armies. Without these human sacrifices, the war would have ended long ago. The Pope, according to Mann, "repeatedly threw up his hands" at the revelation. But his greatest horror was reserved for those Protestant clergymen in the North who openly approved such methods. "Would your Holiness believe," Mann asked the Pope, "that these pulpit champions have boldly asserted as a sentiment: 'Greek fire for the families and cities of the rebels, and hell-fire for their chiefs'?"

"Certainly no Catholic could reiterate so monstrous a sentiment," rejoined the Pope, startled at this information.

"Certainly not," rejoined the Confederate envoy. "It finds

a place exclusively in the hearts of the fiendish, vagrant, pulpit buffoons whose number is legion and who impiously undertake to teach the doctrines of Christ for ulterior sinister purposes."

"I will write a letter to President Davis," said Pius. He then extended his hand — the usual sign that an audience had reached an end. Mann retired, overcome by the wonder of his achievement. "Thus terminated," he writes Benjamin, "one of the most remarkable conferences ever a foreign representative had with a potentate of the earth. And such a potentate! A potentate who wields the consciences of 175,000,000 of the civilized race, and who is adored by that immense number as the vice regent of Almighty God in this sublunary sphere." How "majestic" had been the conduct of the Supreme Pontiff toward Mann when compared with that of the temporal sovereigns at whose audience chambers he had been pounding in vain for three years! No "sneaking subterfuges" at the Vatican! "Here I was openly received by appointment at court in accordance with established usages and customs and treated from beginning to end with a consideration which might be envied by the envoy of the oldest member of the family of nations." [6]

But even better things were to come. The Pope's promised letter to Jefferson Davis arrived in due course. An unexcited observer would hardly detect in this communication any great encouragement to the Confederate cause. In it the neutrality of the Vatican seemed to be impartially maintained. On the merits of the conflict the Pontiff observed the most discreet silence. He gave expression to the sorrows with which the struggle afflicted him, and evinced the conventional wish that peace might soon be established. The document itself contained nothing from which even an eager Southerner like Mann could derive the slightest comfort. The direction on

[6] For Mann's account of this audience, on which this narrative is based, see *Official Records of the Union and Confederate Navies*, Series II, Vol. 3, pp. 952–955.

the envelope, however, sent him into ecstasies of joy. For this letter was addressed to the "Illustrious and Honorable Jefferson Davis, President of the Confederate States of America, Richmond." No other sovereign had ever addressed Mr. Davis in this fashion. None had even acknowledged the existence of such a nation as the "Confederate States of America." Nothing in the intercourse with foreign Governments had so chagrined Davis as Lord John Russell's description of his "country" as "the so-called Confederate States." Now the venerable sovereign of Rome had hailed his contemporary of Richmond as a brother ruler. And A. Dudley Mann had achieved this great diplomatic triumph! A week after the Pope's letter arrived Mann burst in upon Mason and Slidell in Paris with glorious news. The Confederacy had at last been recognized by a foreign state! Letters started across the Atlantic, conveying the same information. One can imagine the emotions that stirred the realistic Benjamin on reading Mann's startling epistle. "In the very direction of this communication there is a positive recognition of our government. It is addressed to the Illustrious and Honorable Jefferson Davis, President of the Confederate States of America. Thus we are acknowledged, by as high an authority as this world contains, to be an independent power of the earth. I congratulate you. I congratulate the President, I congratulate the cabinet; in short, I congratulate all my true hearted countrymen and countrywomen upon this benign event. The hand of the Lord has been in it, and eternal glory and praise be to His holy and righteous name."[7]

These congratulations met a chilly reception from the Secretary of State. Nor did Davis look upon them much more indulgently. Lyricism in diplomatic intercourse was foreign to the cold nature of both men. Neither accepted the letter as a recognition of Southern independence, even though the superscription courteously adopted the style of address which

[7] *Official Records of the Union and Confederate Navies*, Series II, Vol. 3, p. 973.

Davis had signed to his own communication to the Pope. Mr. Mann's interpretation would have astonished no one so much as the sovereign Pontiff himself, or his Cardinal Secretary of State, one of the most astute of contemporary diplomats. Benjamin treated Mann's jubilations with contempt. "As a recognition of the Confederate States," he wrote Mann, neither he nor the President attached "to it the same value that you do, a mere inferential recognition, unconnected with political action or the regular establishment of diplomatic relations, possessing none of the moral weight required for awakening the people of the United States from their delusion that these states still remain members of the old Union." The Pope's salutation to Davis as "President of the Confederate States" was "a formula of politeness to his correspondent, not a political recognition of a fact. None of our journals treat the letter as a recognition in the sense you attach to it, and Mr. Slidell writes that the Nuncio at Paris had received no instructions to put his official visa on our passports, as he had been led to hope from his correspondence with you."

Moreover, certain things in the Pope's letter had displeased the President. One expression in particular irritated Southerners then, as it does the majority of Southerners to-day. His Holiness had described the great conflict as a "civil war." The very use of that term, Benjamin informed Mann, showed how far this letter departed from formal recognition. "Civil war" indeed! Clearly Mann's painstaking lessons to Antonelli and the Pope himself on the nature of the states had been thrown away. The Pope completely disregarded the constitutional point involved. The South, Benjamin insisted, was fighting no "civil war." Such words described a conflict between contending factions of the same country. But the one-time United States had split into two independent nations. North and South were no more one country than England and France; war between them was no more "civil war" than would be hostilities between these two foreign powers. The point was not a technical one; it involved the very foundation on which the Confederacy rested its case. In calling the prevailing contest a "civil war" the Pope had almost broken neutrality and aligned himself on the Union side, something far from that recognition which Mann had vainly imagined. The expression far discounted the compliment implied in addressing Davis as "President of the Confederate States."

And so Mann's diplomatic career came to an unglorious end. He lingered in Europe for many years. Leaving Richmond, in 1861, this bitterest of envoys registered a vow. He would never return home until the Confederacy had become one of the recognized nations of the world! Mann kept his word. America never saw him again, and he died in Paris, in 1889, solitary, unknown, and neglected.

XVII

END OF THE "DESPOT" DAVIS

1

THE INEVITABLE SCHISM

BY THIS time the work of those Governors who sought to fight the war on the principles of Calhoun was bringing its appropriate fruit. These Governors were successfully impeding enlistments, making impossible a unified command, stimulating desertion, destroying the enthusiasm that had marked the first year of war, and thus laying the country everywhere open to the incursions of Northern invaders. Nor were the obstructive Governors, Brown, Vance, Watts, and the rest, the most formidable dissentients within the Confederacy itself. An early chapter of this volume reviewed the career of Alexander H. Stephens and his work in framing the new government. Stephens played an even more vital part in the last days of the Confederacy and at this time his influence was entirely destructive. By the autumn of 1864 the enterprise which had been so confidently launched in Montgomery nearly four years previously was rapidly on the decline. In finance, in administration, in diplomacy, in military effort, in legislation, in popular support, in the essential coöperation of state and national governments, every day added to the paralysis steadily creeping over the Southern cause. For this demoralization no man was so responsible as the little spectral figure who held second place in the Administration. When Benjamin H. Hill, one of the ablest of Confederate Senators, declared that the Confederacy had perished, not of attacks from the North, but of dissensions within its own ranks, it was Alexander H. Stephens that he had chiefly in mind.

One of the ideas popular with Southerners was that they

were the legitimate successors to the patriots of 1776 and that their Confederacy, not the United States, was the real heir to the government set up in 1789. Not the integrated nation to the North, but the Southern league of Confederate States, embodied the principles of Washington and Madison. In one respect at least the Confederacy followed the historic example. Its annals, brief as they were, witnessed a revival of many of the controversies that racked the United States in its formative era. The administration of Washington had hardly started when the great argument began concerning the nature of the Federal Government. Two parties appeared, Federalist and anti-Federalist, one insisting on a strong central government, the other as vigorously proclaiming the supremacy of the states. A schism somewhat resembling this disturbed the Davis Administration. The two contending factions adopted no official designations; indeed, they would have denied the existence of a divided public sentiment on this age-long issue. The South had staked its whole cause on the sacred doctrine of state sovereignty, and naturally the existence of divergent views of nationalistic centralism could hardly be acknowledged. Yet in practice, if not in theory, two schools arose that were divided on this very question. Davis and his sympathizers never framed their new Southern doctrine in so many words, but in act they became a force making for concentration in government. One will not find in Presidential speeches any evidence of conversion to a once-detested doctrine, but in measures adopted to conduct the war, a nationalistic spirit was the inspiration. Even the familiar vocabulary of the eighteenth century came to life. Richmond, these neo-Jeffersonians cried, had become a "consolidated government"; Davis, like Washington before him, was seeking "dictatorial," even monarchical or "imperial" power; he was as unscrupulous a "Centralist" as Lincoln himself; and the "compact" which had been established between the Richmond Government and the "sovereign states" was being disregarded. In seceding from one "despotism" — so ran the protesting argument — the Southern states had merely created another. Between Lincoln and Davis there was really no choice; "constitutional liberty" existed neither in the Federal Union nor in the Confederacy. Whatever side might prove victorious in war, it was urged, the sacred cause of "state sovereignty," the one great principle at issue, had irrevocably lost. Indeed, in reading the speeches, Governors' messages, and the like which form the literature of the Confederacy, the mind reverts to Jeffersonians and Hamiltonians of the earlier time, and to the days when Washington, in the eyes of the seer of Monticello, was a "monocrat" seeking to destroy the simple Republican virtue of the people and erect a mighty despotism on its ruins.

It was not only the matter of conscription that formed the groundwork of these allegations and aroused conservative anger. Other pretensions of Richmond similarly set at naught the principle on which the Confederacy had come into being. The suspension of the writ of habeas corpus, the setting up of martial law, the impressment of supplies, taxation in kind — here were other encroachments of Confederate power as despotic as any of the measures that had been adopted by the Lincoln Government. As the conflict wore on, indeed, these hostile critics in the South began more and more to call attention to certain similarities in the Lincoln and the Davis Administrations. Both Presidents — the fact has been practically forgotten — were operating under the same Constitution, for Stephens had forced the convention at Montgomery, in February, 1861, to adopt the United States charter as their form of government. And both, despite the difference in their political past, interpreted that instrument in much the same way. In the last three years of the war, at least, Jefferson Davis followed in the footsteps of that statesman whom, above all men, he despised. Lincoln carried centralization — "despotism," if you will — into other than military matters. If the public safety demanded extreme measures, he was prepared to place the freedom and services of every individual at the disposal of the Washington Government. In the very first month he discovered that the ancient safeguard of Anglo-Saxon liberty, the writ of habeas corpus, must, in certain crises, be dispensed with. When Southern sympathizers in eastern Maryland were tearing up bridges, destroying railroads, murdering Federal troops, isolating the American people from their Government, and imperiling the cause, Lincoln ordered his military authorities to seize suspected fomenters of disorder, throw them into jail, and hold them indefinitely without trial.

Chief Justice Taney might thunder, from the Supreme Court bench, that this was a violation of the Constitution, but Lincoln maintained that it was necessary to suspend the writ if the Union was to be saved. When, in the Confederate States, large sections of the populace raised disorderly obstructions to military success, Davis made the same discovery. When a community ran riot with spies, deserters, "peace" associations, Ku Klux Klans — the name had not yet been invented, but the thing had been — organized for the purpose of opposing conscription, weakening the Confederacy, and traitorously dealing with the enemy; when cities and counties had been laid at the mercy of treasonable mobs, Davis found that the usual legal procedures of peace times could not be depended on. Such disaffected individuals, when arrested, were usually discharged by friendly judges and habeas corpus, which required their immediate presence in court for trial, became their safeguard. The only way to restore order was to do precisely what Lincoln had done in a similar state of stress — suspend the writ, seize all prospective domestic foes merely on suspicion, and throw them into jail. In this way Davis became a good Lincolnian, a thoroughgoing nationalist, a "despot," and, at his urging, Congress temporarily forgot Magna Charta. Lincoln also found that public safety sometimes demanded martial law. So did Davis; and consequently many Southerners who had preached State rights all their lives perceived with horror the hand of the central government reaching over from Richmond, temporarily closing their local courts and constabularies, and placing in their stead gray-coated militarists of the Richmond "oligarchy."

The adoption of conscription by the Confederate Government and the hostility the measure aroused have already been described. No procedure could more completely display the "tyranny" of a "consolidated government." The individual citizen belonged to the state, not the central power; for President Davis to seize a Georgian, a South Carolinian, a Virginian, and compel him to shoulder a musket and fight at the command of Confederate generals — no more utter defiance of the rights of the states, so it was urged, could be imagined. It was "nationalism" on a gigantic scale — "federalism," the strict constructionists called it, reviving a word especially odious to the old classic Southern school. The essence of "federalism" was the asserted prerogative of the "nation" to act directly on the citizen; could any example of such a pretension be cited more to the point than conscription? Other extensions of national power, as distinguished from state, similarly set all Dixie-land in a turmoil. Its civilian population behaved much the same as most noncombatants, even when the salvation of the country depended on their loyalty. They objected to paying taxes, they shied away from worthless Confederate currency, and when they sold food to the army they exacted the highest possible prices. Speculators in the necessities of life preyed upon their fellow citizens, just as they did in the North, and as they have done in all wars in all times. Much has been heard of "starvation" in connection with Southern armies. Yet at no time in the four years did a real scarcity of food prevail in the Southern states; the difficulties were those of distribution — and speculation. Farmers declined to supply the armies except at a profit, and the cornering of food and forage was one of the most thriving of occupations.

Only an imperious centralized power could deal with such a situation; "State rights" was a useless reed. Farmers were presently outraged at the appearance on their acres of certain not too tactful gentlemen, agents of the far-distant Richmond Government. These agents gathered in such of the farmers' crops as seemed necessary to military efficiency, at prices fixed by themselves, paying, of course, in Confederate paper. Besides seizing wheat, corn, and the like, they took wagons on the same terms. Any farm horses or mules that looked as though they might prove useful in the distant armies of Lee or Johnston were also driven away. An always pressing need was black manual labor, and the farmer, even though he had only two or three slaves, was constantly chagrined to see them depart with his crops and other of his stock. Southern agriculturists who for years had passed all their spare time reading speeches by Jeff Davis and other Southern orators on the sanctity of state sovereignty and the very limited powers of a federal government — or a confederate one — had never imagined that, in setting up their new authority, they had created a "monster" (such was the popular word) that possessed immediate suzerainty over its humblest citizens. Perhaps a state, the abiding place of all power, might constitutionally do such high-handed acts, but could the Congress and President of the Confederate States? Not if there was any virtue in that gospel for which the South had gone to war.

2

Hostility within the Cabinet

Unfortunately for the Confederate cause the grumbling did not all arise from the innocent victims. The ablest men in Confederate statesmanship, and almost the highest placed in its official hierarchy, began bombarding the Davis stronghold. The ranking officers of the civil administration, in its earliest phase, next to the President, were the Vice President and the Secretary of State, Alexander H. Stephens and Robert Toombs. As political thinkers, and leaders closest to the popular heart, these were unquestionably the foremost men in the Southern Republic. With them must be joined a third, the half brother of the Vice President, Linton Stephens, a man who, in brilliancy of mind, effectiveness as a speaker, and skill as a leader of public opinion, formed a worthy associate of his more famous mentor. Toombs was the orator who, in the mind of Northerners in his own day and our own, most vividly personalized the fierce Southern intransigence that had precipitated war. Jefferson Davis — the words are his own — made Toombs Secretary of State because he wished, by the gift of the highest office at his disposal, to reward him for his services in the organization of the Confederacy. A previous chapter has reviewed the antebellum activities of Georgia's great triumvirate, Stephens, Toombs, and Cobb. Another Georgia triumvirate succeeded this in wartime. Cobb no longer worked in harmony with his old associates, remaining, from 1861 to 1865, a loyal Davis man; but Linton Stephens, more distinguished mentally than Cobb and far better educated, — under his brother's tutelage, he had studied at the University of Georgia, the University of Virginia, and Harvard, — much better read, keener in political dialectic, stepped into the vacant place.

Linton was eleven years younger than Alexander, who, a lifelong bachelor, lavished upon him all the love and care that the normal man bestows on his children; he also possessed many attractive traits lacking in his neurotic elder. Physically he was a large-framed, handsome man, as conspicuous for vigor as was Alexander for feebleness; his massive, Jovelike head, with wavy, bushy hair and large features, also made strange contrast with Alexander's skeleton of a face. Despite this difference in physical frame, the two brothers politically were Siamese twins. Living at a considerable distance, they wrote to each other almost daily for thirty years. Their letters displayed an automatic agreement on all public questions. It was with both a matter of pleasing observation that, as each new topic intruded on the political scene, both Linton and Alexander, in their diurnal epistolary musings, with no opportunity for face-to-face discussion, invariably registered the same judgment. And this new trio of Georgian statesmanship, confronting the new problems of the war, represented a far stronger force, and a far more intellectual one, than the old. No single power existed in the Confederacy that Jefferson Davis so feared.

There were substantial reasons for his apprehensions. The war had been in progress only a few months when a startling situation developed. The two most influential men in the Administration were opposing its policies and its chief. Toombs, after six months' restless service as Secretary of State, resigned that post and entered the Confederate Army. Stephens did not resign as Vice President, but he pursued a course even more disastrous to the cause. He dropped his gavel as presiding officer of the Confederate Senate, — Hunter for the larger part of the time performing his duties, — shook the detested dust of Richmond from his heels, and departed for his Georgia home. Here he remained during most of the war, a bitter spectator of Confederate proceedings, and an open and extremely hostile critic; occasionally he returned for brief visits to his country's capital, not so much in order to attend to the Vice-Presidential task as to make trouble for a harassed Government. Both Toombs and Stephens have left posterity in no doubt concerning their opinion of their chief. Toombs was the more direct and intemperate. His letters to Stephens and others, written from the Confederate battle front, discuss the constitutional commander in chief in his usual robust terms.[1]

---

[1] These can be read in "The Correspondence of Robert Toombs, Alexander H. Stephens and Howell Cobb," edited by Ulrich B. Phillips, and published in the *Report of the American Historical Association for the Year 1911*. Quotations in the present paragraph are from that report, Vol. II.

"That scoundrel Jeff Davis" is a favorite characterization. "He has no capacity to carry on the government." "We shall get our independence, but it will be in spite of him." "Davis' incapacity is lamentable, and the very thought of the baseness of Congress in the impressment act makes me sick. I feel but little like fighting for a people base enough to yield to such despotism from such contemptible sources." "The real control of our affairs is narrowing down constantly into the hands of Davis and the old army and when it gets there entirely the cause will collapse. They have neither the ability nor the honesty to manage the Revolution." He accused Davis of one of the most odious of sins — sanctimonious hypocrisy. He "clothes his naked villainy with old odds and ends stolen from holy writ and seems a saint when he plays the devil." He "has outraged justice and the Constitution." "I shall be justified in any extremity to which the public interest would allow me to go in hostility to his illegal and unconstitutional course." "The tide of despotism [is] daily pouring itself out upon the country."

Stephens had all Toombs's venomous hatred of Davis, but his was a more sinuous character. His wartime letters to Toombs have disappeared — burned by the gentleman to whom they were written at Stephens's own demand. References to his chief, published in Stephens's own lifetime, betray his distrust, but in polite and guarded terms. They appear occasionally in that famous *Constitutional View of the War Between the States*, which engaged Stephens's leisure in the few years following Appomattox. Differences arose between him and his President — so much he admits — but they never assumed a personal character. Stephens's *Recollections*, however, a diary kept during the summer of 1865, while he was a prisoner in Fort Warren, Boston, and never intended for publication,[2] sound a more rasping note. The view that Davis was not primarily a State-rights man, but a Southern nationalist, is the

[2] It was published as late as 1910.

one Stephens sets forth. "He looked to nothing but independence and separate nationality." "The only independence he was looking for was the establishment of an irrepressible despotism of which he was to be the head." "He was no sooner established in office under the permanent constitution than he began to exhibit total disregard for the principles, aims, objects and views of the masses of the people. . . . They were fighting for rights, not for dynasty." "Whatever else may be said of Mr. Davis, it cannot be correctly said that he was, or is a statesman in any exalted sense of that term. It would be difficult to find in the history of the world a man with such resources at his command who made such poor use of them." "Never did a people exhibit higher virtues in patriotism, in courage, in fortitude, and in patience under the severest trials and sacrifices. The disasters attending the Conflict are chargeable to their leaders, to their men in authority, to those to whom the control of public destiny was confided, and to no one is it more duly attributable than to Mr. Davis himself. He proved himself deficient in developing and directing the resources of the country, in finance and in diplomacy, as well as in military affairs. . . . His greatest failure in statesmanship was either in not understanding the popular aim and impulses, or in attempting to direct the movement to different ends from those contemplated by the people who had intrusted him with power. If he did not understand the purpose of the people, he is certainly not entitled to any rank as a statesman. If he did understand them and used position to abuse confidence, then he equally forfeits the title to honest statesmanship." In the early days Stephens regarded the President merely as "weak and imbecile," "vacillating, petulant, obstinate," but in the latter period, he detected more grievous faults. He was becoming a "despot." He was constantly violating the Constitution. Nor did Stephens entertain a high respect for the Confederate Congress. It was indeed at times a tumultuous gathering, excitement reaching its highest points when Ben

Hill hurled an inkstand at Yancey, cutting a deep gash in his cheek, and when a less distinguished member rushed at another colleague with a bowie knife. "Children in politics and statesmanship" — so Stephens described these lawmakers. He dismisses the Davis Government in one characteristic sentence. "The energy I discover now seems to me like that of a turtle after fire has been put upon its back" — Stephens himself presumably supplying this species of incitement.

Such were the opinions of his chief entertained by the second official of the Confederacy, the Vice President, who, in the event of death or resignation, would succeed to the first position. And such a contingency was not impossible, for several times Davis fell seriously ill, and the possibility of Stephens's succession appalled a goodly part of the people. What was the real animus of Toombs and Stephens in their opposition? Many Southerners, including Davis himself, attributed it to unworthy motives. Neither exercised that influence, it was said, to which, in his own estimation, he had an inevitable right. In 1861 Toombs held the foremost place at Montgomery; he was the universal choice, it was urged, for President; only a foolish accident[3] deprived him of that intensely coveted honor. Before anything else, Toombs was a human being, affected by ordinary human passions and failings; obviously this disappointment influenced his attitude toward Davis. His failure as a soldier did not mitigate his chagrin. Davis's hesitation in making him a brigadier general proved a bad beginning. As Toombs had virtually no military experience, the Presidential reluctance in this respect can be understood. Davis explained his reason for finally granting Toombs's request in a letter to a prominent Georgian. "His abilities as a public man were so distinguished and his service in the political contest which has freed us from a Union odious to our people had been so signal, that I could not but feel a hope of his displaying on the field qualities to justify my giving him the post he

[3] See Chapter III, p. 96.

solicited." And then the President drily adds, "This hope was not realized."[4] The failure to obtain promotion — Toombs aspired to a major-generalship — still further embittered the man. But that these and other misadventures completely explained his hostility is too sweeping a conclusion, though undoubtedly they did much to sharpen Toombs's tongue when discussing the President. His real motives he always put on higher ground. Davis had proved a "traitor" to the Constitution, had abandoned the doctrine of State rights, was seeking to construct a huge personal, nationalistic power on the ruin of his country — such was the burden of Toombs's complaint. "I am determined to stand for Congress in this district," he wrote to W. W. Burwell, of Virginia, June 10, 1863. "Mr. Davis' friends talk of opposing me. I am content and would rather prefer it. He has greatly outraged justice and the Constitution, but the public are disinclined to correct abuses when the empire is rocking to its very foundations and would not look favorably upon a volunteer opposition; but if they make it upon me I shall be justified in any extremity to which the public interest would allow me to go in hostility to his illegal and unconstitutional course."[5] Davis did oppose Toombs's ambition for a seat in the Confederate Congress, and did so successfully; the humiliated statesman — the man whom Stephens called "the brains of the whole concern" — was forced, for a time, to retire to his country home, and solace himself reading his favorite economists, Bastiat and Ricardo.

Though the motives of Toombs in fighting Davis are evidently mixed, the case of Stephens presents no great problem. For his mentality had all the simplicity of a fanatic. In temperament, in directness, in concentration on a single purpose, Stephens had all the intensity of a William Lloyd Garrison. Had Stephens been born and trained in New England, he would probably have been an abolitionist him-

---
[4] *Jefferson Davis, Constitutionalist*, Vol. VI, p. 44.
[5] *Annual Report of American Historical Association, 1911.* Vol. II, p. 619.

self and brought to that cause all the fire, all the utter confidence in his own principles, all the contempt for opposing beliefs, which marked the extreme antislavery men, just as they marked the Southern advocates of a radically different gospel. Stephens had the earnestness and the sincerity that make his type so dangerous. Like all emotionalists, he could see only one side, never comprehended that there might be another, never perceived any qualifications of his general thesis, and was always ready to sacrifice the world itself so long as his conviction might prevail. Substitute for abolitionism the objective which the Georgian called "Constitutional liberty" and Stephens and Garrison belong in the same galley. To a problem that was extremely complex both men detected only one glaringly simple solution. To this conviction they would give up everything, even their Government itself. To lay aside temporarily certain principles in order to gain eventually the main end, to give way on details in order to achieve the great essential — statesmanship like this, in the mind of both Garrison and Stephens, was Machiavellian, Jesuitical; just as Garrison would willingly destroy the Constitution if thereby his antislavery crusade could be advanced, so Stephens was ready to jettison the whole Confederacy if thereby "Constitutional liberty" could be preserved. "Better," he writes to his brother Linton in August, 1862, concerning the suspension of habeas corpus and the establishment of martial law by certain Southern generals, "that Richmond should fall and that the enemy's armies should sweep our whole country from Potomac to the Gulf, than that our people should submissively yield obedience to one of these edicts." In other words the people should defy their own Government and deliver the Confederacy to the invading hosts, whenever, in Stephens's own judgment, "Constitutional liberty" should be temporarily threatened. Egotism could go no further, and Stephens, like all uncompromising pursuers of abstract doctrine, was a supreme egotist.

"Constitutional liberty" meant the fine-spun "compact

theory" so painstakingly evolved by Calhoun. That the meaning of the Federal Constitution, whether it concerned a federation of states or a concise system of national government, had been argued continuously from the day it emerged from the Philadelphia convention — all this learned disputation Stephens disregarded; the Constitution meant precisely what Stephens said it meant, and the opinions of such minds as Hamilton, Madison, John Marshall, Webster, and Lincoln were brushed aside as though they had never existed. The Constitution, he declared, forbade conscription in warfare, the suspension of habeas corpus, martial law, the impressment of military supplies; because the Confederacy had resorted to all these and other measures, Davis had become an imperial despot, and "constitutional liberty" had ceased to exist. Better, therefore, that the whole fabric fall in ruins. It is questionable whether Stephens really desired Confederate success after the enforcement of conscription. A note, almost of exultation, is sounded in the post-mortem on his country which Stephens penned while a prisoner in Fort Warren, Boston Harbor.[6] Why had the experiment failed? Because the Davis policy would have led "to a centralized, consolidated, military despotism, as absolute and execrable as that of Russia or Turkey." The Confederacy was doomed — such is the sum of the matter — because it proved faithless to that interpretation of the Constitution that Alexander Stephens insisted was the only tenable one, and the man seems to find a certain recompense in this justification.

3
A Union Man at Heart

Unlike William Lloyd Garrison, Stephens was a powerful public man, the idol of that Georgia which became the pivot of the Confederate cause. Davis had distrusted him from the

[6] *Recollections*, Alexander H. Stephens, pp. 165–170.

earliest days in Richmond. The Stephens policy had been equivocal from the first. Never had the brothers evinced that whole-souled support of the movement without which no revolutionary enterprise can succeed. They joined the Government hesitatingly, protestingly, and this attitude they maintained, with daily increasing recalcitrancy, until the final collapse. On the eve of Secession, the Stephens brothers insisted that all genuine Southern grievances could be adjusted within the Federal Constitution, an attitude that affected their course throughout the four years of war. Alexander shocked extreme Southern men at Montgomery by proposing a clause in the Constitution admitting nonslaveholding states to the Confederacy; his objective, in making this suggestion, was the Northwestern country, but, as time went on, Stephens conceived a more grandiose plan. Having no sympathy with the Davis scheme of Southern nationalism, of a second American Republic, Stephens actually dreamed of restoring the old Union under the sheltering aegis of the Confederate Constitution. Any vagaries from a man capable of such imaginings might be expected.

At the Montgomery convention, Stephens displayed his lack of Southern patriotism in other ways. Elected Vice President, he sulked at the inauguration. From him, one of the greatest Southern orators, the people, then in a mood of exaltation, expected a ringing speech; instead, they got only a few unhearty sentences. At nearly the same time Stephens, infected, it would almost seem, by a perverse spirit, made another speech in which he described slavery as "the cornerstone of the Confederacy." Here was one of those unhappy phrases that frequently dominate history; widely published in England and France, this Vice-Presidential dictum aroused great hostility to the Davis Government and was regarded, by many Southerners, as largely responsible for the failure of Confederate diplomacy. Henry Cleveland, Stephens's close friend and first biographer, declares that from the beginning the

South regarded Stephens as a "union man at heart." "Stephens and Toombs always liked their seats in the old Congress better than anything less than the head of the Confederacy."[7] Naturally relations between President and Vice President took on a certain frigidity. At first, Davis made confidential approaches and sought his colleague's advice; after the removal to Richmond, however, and after the little figure of Stephens was frequently observed on the floor of both houses of Congress, openly lobbying against administration measures, these consultations ceased. The remarks of Linton Stephens and Toombs, intemperately abusing Davis, and the criticisms of Mrs. Toombs, ridiculing the President and his wife, and their social functions, did not improve the situation. From mere coldness the tension rapidly increased to undisguised hostility. All official association ceased; the cold, studied courtesy with which the two men treated each other in public only emphasized the dislike that prevented all cooperation in public work. In time, even routine civilities were abandoned; toward the close of the contest, the President would not even receive personal calls from his second in rank. On one occasion — Stephens afterward told the story himself — the Vice President ascended the Davis doorstep, and pulled the bell three times. Davis, whose presence was known to his caller, declined to admit him.[8] In one moment of exasperation Davis offered to resign the Presidency — provided Stephens would also lay down his office; he would never transfer the Government to a man, he declared, who would at once surrender it to General Grant.[9]

This was probably merely an expression of anger, not a seriously contemplated program; at the time the remark was made the rift between President and Vice President had become too wide to be bridged. The real cause of dissension was more than personal; it had reached a point where Stephens's

[7] Cleveland to Davis, January 4, 1888 *Jefferson Davis, Constitutionalist*, Vol. X, p. 22.
[8] *Jefferson Davis, Constitutionalist*, Vol VIII, p 213.
[9] *The same*, James Lyon (member of Confederate Congress) to W. T. Walthall.

activities were endangering the Confederacy itself. A previous chapter has reviewed the obstructions to military efficiency raised by Governor Joe Brown of Georgia, especially that opposition to conscription which probably explains, more than any single circumstance, the complete breakdown of the Southern army. It is now no secret that Stephens provided the brains and inspiration to this difficult Governor. Herein is found the reason for Stephens's long absences from Richmond. He wished to remain in Georgia, where he could serve as a constant incitement to his friend. For three years the elfin figure of Stephens — an undying spirit of discontent — hovered beside the bucolic statesman from the Georgia mountains. In his frequent trips to Milledgeville, Stephens used the "executive mansion" as his hotel; he spent hours and days at the state capitol mingling with the lawmakers, adding fuel to their hostility to the Davis Administration. All during this period — 1862-1865 — the Georgia Legislature was distinguished above those of other Confederate states for the contempt evinced for the Richmond Government — a contempt expressed in many acts that hampered military success. The real inspirer of this attitude was the best loved Georgian of his time, Alexander H. Stephens. Governor Brown's long and angry correspondence with Davis did much to hamstring the War Department; in these letters the literary style of the craftsman of Liberty Hall, as well as his political tenets, was only too apparent. That Stephens actually wrote the most destructive of Brown's messages — that of March, 1864, which, widely distributed by its putative and its actual authors among Confederate troops at the front, helped to break down military morale — was well known at the time. Benjamin H. Hill wrote sardonic congratulations to Stephens. "I know I must thank you for it," he said. "Governor Brown can never repay you for the great benefit you have bestowed on him. His only trouble can be, the footprints are too plain not to be recognized." Stephens's admiring opinion of Brown and his courses has been incorporated in his printed works. "He is, in every respect, entitled to high rank among our men and statesmen. . . . No truer man to our course lived, while its standard was up, than Governor Brown."[10] He valiantly defended Brown against the charge, generally made in 1864 and since, that the Governor wished to withdraw Georgia from the Confederacy, and make separate terms with Lincoln. Brown opposed a resolution in the Georgia Legislature expressing confidence in Jefferson Davis; in this opposition, Stephens insisted, the Governor's motives had been "pure"; thus had he shown his loyalty to the "cause" — the cause, that is, not of the Confederacy, but of "constitutional liberty," as Stephens understood that term.

It is not strange, therefore, that Georgia, in the spring of 1864, closely approximated that position which Austria reached in the autumn of 1918, when, departing from its alliance with the Central Powers, it sought independent peace with the Allies. The leaders in this Confederate *démarche* — "separate state action," the proponents called it — were the Stephens brothers, Alexander and Linton, Robert Toombs, and Joseph E. Brown. To what extent could their manœuvres at this crisis be described as independent action by the "Republic of Georgia" exercising its own "supreme sovereignty," irrespective of the central government at Richmond? It is a point on which historians are not agreed. Toombs and Stephens spent a good deal of their subsequent careers explaining the falsity of this charge, and Governor Brown always indignantly denied that his statesmanship contemplated disloyalty to the Confederacy. Henry Cleveland, the biographer personally closest to Stephens, insists that his hero was planning something of this description. The Stephens purpose was peace through the "people and the states alone; this," says Cleveland, "was Stephens' and Brown's lifelong craze."[11] In a letter written

---
[10] *Constitutional View*, Vol. II, p 656.
[11] *Jefferson Davis, Constitutionalist*, Vol. IX, p. 603.

to Davis, November 25, 1887, Cleveland tells the aged ex-President how Toombs and Linton Stephens used to visit "my quarters" — Cleveland was editor of the *Daily Constitutionalist* of Augusta, Georgia — "and abuse you by the hour."[12] A more recent student of Stephens's career, Louis Beauregard Pendleton, thinks that Stephens's speech before the Georgia Legislature, March 5, 1864, hinted at the possible secession from the Confederacy of North Carolina and threatened the secession of Georgia.[13] Certainly many loyal Confederates at the time regarded Stephens's pronouncements in this light. Benjamin H. Hill publicly denounced him as a "traitor." Newspapers all over the South echoed the charge; that small section of the Georgia press strongly pro-Davis joined in the general denunciation. Anonymous letters from all over the South fell on Stephens's desk. Should Davis die, these missives declared, Stephens must at once resign — or be assassinated. Loyal upholders of the regime would never tolerate the succession of such a "traitor" to the Presidency.

The resolutions introduced in the Georgia Legislature in March, 1864, by Linton Stephens and the speech of Alexander supporting them were interpreted by these elements as a threat to withdraw from the Confederacy and to imply a separate peace, on the basis of a return to the Union. That the Georgia Legislature passed the measures increased this apprehension. Naturally the Northern press exulted over this show of a new Southern temper. Editors north of the Potomac accepted the Stephens "peace resolutions" as an olive branch extended to the Lincoln Government. General Sherman wrote not only Brown, but Stephens, proposing a friendly consultation. The agitation had a most depressing effect on the stamina of Confederate soldiers. For these resolutions asserted the right of any state to secede from the Confederacy whenever the central government, in its judgment, failed in its duties

---

[12] *The same.*
[13] *Alexander H. Stephens*, by Louis Beauregard Pendleton (1908), p. 314.

to the people. Ostensibly these sections referred to the departure, in 1861, from the Federal Union, but certain clauses hinted broadly that this right extended to any government which a dissatisfied state had joined. For the declarations called for peace "upon the principles of 1776" and though they urged the general government to take steps in this direction they also insinuated that this was not the only method by which this object could be attained. Not only could the Confederacy make peace, but also "the people acting through their state organizations and popular assemblies." It is not strange that the loyal South believed that such expressions concealed a threat; if President Davis did not move for peace, then the proper authorities of the state of Georgia would do so! When other states, especially North Carolina, Alabama, and Davis's own Mississippi, passed similar resolutions, the disintegration of the Confederacy seemed fairly under way.

Meanwhile Georgia's other favorite son plunged into the fray. Toombs hurled a new word into an already sufficiently disintegrating argument. This statesman always liked to call the Southern cause a "revolution." Now he began loudly to demand a "counter-revolution." A speech of Toombs, made in January, 1864, resounded with hostility to Davis and to the Confederacy as then administered. "I am a revolutionist for liberty and I will be one till I get liberty. If the Yankees stand in the way I am their enemy. If domestic traitors stand in the way I am their enemy." The speech rang with references to certain potentates of the past — Charles I, James II, Louis XVI — who had lost their thrones or their heads for ravishing from their people certain safeguards of liberty, such as habeas corpus. Every "villain" who followed in their path should meet a similar fate! The frequent allusions to Jefferson Davis left little doubt as to what particular "villain" Toombs had in mind. "The President has proclaimed to the country and to the Yankees that half of our army has deserted. I hope this is not true; but if they have deserted, what has caused it?" Conscription and the suspension of the sacred writ! "When they put you all under one man and take away the *habeas corpus*, it is time to draw the bayonet. . . . Better die than bear such oppression; die and leave a glorious name like Brutus, the watchword of patriots for all time, or Cromwell, clouded for two centuries, but now shining with lustre. Save your country, your family; above all, save liberty. I address you as citizens, not as soldiers. As citizens defend liberty against Congress [the Confederate Congress], against the President, against whoever assails it. You had liberty before the President was born, and I trust you will have it after he is dead. . . . I look for no mutiny, unless it be necessary in defense of constitutional liberty. If invasion of these rights came by one, resist him; if by many, resist them. How shall you resist? First go to the courts. But if they will not give you justice, still defend your rights. . . . Conscription had never been heard of in the Anglo-Saxon race until the reign of Mr. Davis." [14]

4

THE FAILURE OF STATE SOVEREIGNTY

It is not likely that the Southern cause fell in ruins because Davis was too much of a despot; rather because he was not despot enough. He quickly abandoned his State-rights philosophy when faced with the inexorable realism of war, but the opposition of the Stephens school made him tread the new path warily and prevented the full application of that centralized nationalism that Lincoln so effectively made the basis of the Federal effort. Meanwhile, everywhere in the Confederacy Stephens and his sympathetic Governors, — Brown in Georgia, Watts in Alabama, Bonham in South Carolina, Clark in Mississippi, Murrah in Texas, — by conducting this incessant cam-

[14] The text from which these quotations are taken is that published by Henry Whitney Cleveland in Tom Watson's *Jeffersonian Magazine*, Vol. XIV, No. 1 (1911).

paign against the only measures that could have brought victory, precipitated chaos. Had the Confederacy, at the beginning, husbanded its great material asset — cotton — and thus built a solid financial and economic structure; had it rigidly enforced conscription, overridden opposition by suspending habeas corpus and martial law in such places as the circumstances made necessary; had it regulated its abundant food supplies and intelligently applied them to the support of the army and the civilian population, the war might have reached a different end. It did all these things deprecatingly and piecemeal. The enemy that faced it on every front was more than the armed forces of the Federal Union; it was that doctrine of State rights that led to secession and then, when adapted to the Confederacy itself, destroyed its vitality and made useless the splendid exertions of its ably led military forces.

General Lee saw the inevitable end in the latter part of 1864; then he informed certain friends that the South was doomed. As late as January, 1865, Alexander Stephens was proclaiming that the cause could still be saved. How? By ending conscription and other "imperialistic" measures and fighting the war on the basis of "constitutional liberty" — that is, his extreme form of State rights! Still, he insisted, peace could be arranged with the North, on this everlasting principle. In March, 1865, Davis decided to let him try; it was the best way, he probably thought, of silencing this disruptive influence. A mysterious visit made to Richmond by Francis P. Blair, supposedly a confidant of Abraham Lincoln, had given rise to the belief that a meeting between Confederate and civilian leaders could arrange peace on terms satisfactory to both sides. Davis yielded to urgent demands to participate in such a gathering, and, very shrewdly, appointed Alexander H. Stephens chairman of the Confederate mission. An historic conference took place between Stephens, Hunter, and Judge Campbell representing the South and Abraham Lincoln and William H. Seward representing the North, on board a ship in Hampton Roads. The last sentence of Davis's brief letter of instructions made this consultation a failure before it began; here again Jefferson Davis, the Southern nationalist, comes to the front. Stephens and his companions were to negotiate "for the purpose of securing peace to the two countries." Two countries! The North had never acknowledged the South to be a "country" and had waged terrible war for four years to prove that it was not. That was the very issue of the struggle. Stephens was right when he declared afterward that Davis had shackled his Commissioners and made negotiations impossible. He was himself eager to discuss the return of the South to the Union, so long as his sacred "principle" — "constitutional liberty" — was safeguarded. The result was a pleasant meeting of old companions in Congress, a charming exchange of reminiscences, and a few chatty anecdotes from Mr. Lincoln. But when the Federal President gave his terms for a cessation of fighting a chill fell upon the gathering. When Stephens asked if there was any way of ending the war Lincoln answered: "There is but one way. That is for those who are resisting the laws of the Union to cease that resistance. . . . The restoration of the Union is a *sine qua non* with me." That's all there was to the much-discussed Hampton Roads Conference. Should the South lay down its arms and return to the Union? Lincoln held forth hopes that it might be recompensed for its emancipated slaves, for, of course "the south must now be convinced that slavery is doomed."

Only one man, civilian or soldier, now believed that Southern independence could still be saved. Davis, on the return of the Commissioners from Hampton Roads, prepared for one final rally at the African church in Richmond. In his eloquent speech on this occasion, the President proclaimed that Southern independence could still be achieved: that the Confederacy, indeed, stood on the brink of a great victory. Stephens subsequently recorded his opinion of this oration. "Brilliant though it was, I looked upon it as not much short of dementation."[15] Davis, laying aside his hatred of Stephens personally, appealed to him to appear on this platform in a final attempt to keep the cause alive. The Vice President refused. There was not the slightest possibility, he said, of breathing life into the corpse. It would be a crime to give the people false hopes.

"What are you going to do?" asked Davis.

"I intend to go home and remain there," replied Stephens, abruptly leaving the room.

The next meeting of the President and Vice President took place on a boat in the Savannah River. Both were prisoners of the United States Government. One was on his way to a two-year torturing confinement in Fortress Monroe, awaiting a trial that was never held; the other was destined to Fort Warren in Boston Harbor, whence, after a summer's sojourn, he was pardoned on his own application to Andrew Johnson, and restored to freedom. Stephens survived the war eighteen years, spending part of his new leisure writing books to show the reasons for Southern failure. Chief of them was the obtuseness of the Confederacy in ignoring his own ideas. Had his philosophy prevailed, the Confederacy — so ran his argument — would have prevailed. And what was his philosophy? Nothing less than that doctrine of State rights which really brought it to grief. This was the truth that never penetrated Stephens's mind.

[15] *Recollections*, Alexander H. Stephens, p. 241.

BIBLIOGRAPHY

DOCUMENTS AND MANUSCRIPTS

THE chief documentary materials for the Civil War are the *Official Records of the Union and Confederate Armies in the War of the Rebellion,* 130 volumes, and the *Official Records of the Union and Confederate Navies,* 31 volumes, publications of the United States Government. Though these are military and naval records, they contain also a good deal of information on civil affairs. This is especially true of the third volume of the second series of naval records, which is a reprint (in large part) of the diplomatic correspondence of the Confederate Government, reproduced from the Pickett Papers. The Confederate Congress made no stenographic report of its proceedings, which were, in the main, secret. Its *Journal,* merely a skeletonized record, was published in seven volumes in 1904–1905 by the Government Printing Office in Washington as a Senate Document of the Fifty-eighth Congress, Second Session. All the Presidential messages, reports of Cabinet Secretaries, and the like appear in James D. Richardson's *Compilation of the Messages and Papers of the Confederacy, including the Diplomatic Correspondence,* two volumes (Nashville, 1905).

The records of the Confederate State Department are fairly complete. They exist, in manuscript form, in the Library of Congress, and are known as the Pickett Papers. Their story is briefly related in the preceding text. The Library of Congress contains also the private papers of James Murray Mason, Confederate Envoy to Great Britain, including not only his own correspondence, but many letters from contemporaries, especially fellow diplomats in the Confederate service. Slidell destroyed all his papers, but many of his letters to Mason are in this collection.

Books

Adams, Charles Francis, 2nd. *Autobiography.* Boston, 1916.
Adams, Charles Francis, 2nd. "The Crisis of Foreign Intervention in the War of Secession." *Proceedings Massachusetts Historical Society,* Vol. XLVII. April, 1914.
Adams, Charles Francis 2nd. *Charles Francis Adams,* by his son. Boston, 1900.
Adams, E. D. *Great Britain and the American Civil War.* Two volumes. New York, 1925.
Adams, Henry. *The Education of Henry Adams.* Boston, 1918.
Alfriend, Frank H. *The Life of Jefferson Davis.* Cincinnati and Chicago, 1868.
Ashley, Evelyn. *The Life and Correspondence of Henry John Temple, Viscount Palmerston.* Two volumes. London, 1879.
Bancroft, Frederick. *Life of William H. Seward.* Two volumes. New York, 1900.
Bell, Herbert C. F. *Lord Palmerston.* Two volumes. London, New York, 1936.
Bellet, Paul Pecquet de. *The Diplomacy of the Confederate Cabinet of Richmond and Its Agents Abroad.* Unpublished manuscript in Library of Congress.
Benjamin, Judah P. Speech in the United States Senate on Constitutional Rights of the States. *Congressional Globe.* May 22, 1860.
Benjamin, Judah P. Speech of the Hon. J. P. Benjamin on the Right of Secession in the Senate of the United States. *Congressional Globe.* December 31, 1860.
Bigelow, John. *France and the Confederate Navy.* New York, 1888.
Bigelow, John. *Lest We Forget: Gladstone, Morley and the Confederate Loan of 1863.* New York, 1905.
Bigelow, John. *Retrospections of an Active Life.* Five volumes. New York, 1909–1913.
Boutwell, George S. *Reminiscences.* Two volumes. New York, 1902.
Boykin, Samuel. *Memorial Volume of the Hon. Howell Cobb of Georgia.* Philadelphia, 1870.
Brooks, R. P. "Howell Cobb and the Crisis of 1850." *Mississippi Valley Historical Review.* Vol. IV, No. 3. December, 1917.
Brown, William Garrott. *The Lower South in American History.* New York, 1903.
Buck, Paul H. "The Poor White in the Ante-Bellum South." *American Historical Review,* XXXI, I.

Buckle, George Earle (editor). *The Letters of Queen Victoria.* Second Series, Vol. I. London and New York, 1926.
Buel, C. C., and Johnson, R. U. (editors). *Battles and Leaders of the Civil War.* Four volumes. New York, 1887.
Bullock, James D. *Secret Service of the Confederate States in Europe.* Two volumes. London, 1883.
Butler, Pierce. *Judah P. Benjamin.* Philadelphia, 1907.
Callahan, J. M., *Diplomatic Relations of the Confederate States with England. 1861-1865.* 1898.
Capers, Henry D. *Life and Times of C. G. Memminger.* Richmond, 1893.
Carpenter, Jesse Thomas. *The South as a Conscious Minority.* 1789-1861. New York, 1930.
Chestnut, Mary Boykin. *A Diary from Dixie.* 1905.
Clay, Mrs. Clement. *A Belle of the Fifties.* New York, 1904.
Cleveland, Henry. *Alexander H. Stephens in Public and Private.* Philadelphia and Chicago, 1866.
Cleveland, Henry Whitney. "Robert Toombs." *Watson's Jeffersonian Magazine,* Vol. XIV, No. 3, p. 731. 1912.
Clubbs, Occie. *Stephen Russell Mallory, the Elder.* Unpublished manuscript in the Library of the University of Florida. 1936.
Cobb, T. R. R. Correspondence, edited by A. L. Hull. *Southern Historical Society Papers,* XXVIII, 280-301. Publications of the Southern History Association, XI, 147-185; 233-260; 312-328.
Corti, Egon Caesar, Conte, *Maximilian and Charlotte of Mexico.* Two volumes. London and New York, 1929.
Craven, J. J. *Prison Life of Jefferson Davis.* New York, 1866.
Curry, J. L. M. *Civil History of the Confederate States.* Richmond, 1906.
Curtis, George Ticknor. *Life of James Buchanan.* New York, 1883.
Dana, Richard Henry. "The Trent Affair." *Proceedings Massachusetts Historical Society.* XLV, 35.
Davis, Jefferson. *Rise and Fall of the Confederate Government.* Two volumes. New York, 1881.
Davis, Varina Howell. *Memoir of Jefferson Davis.* Two volumes. New York, 1890.
DeLeon, Thomas C. *Four Years in Confederate Capitals.* Mobile, 1890.
Dodd, William E. *Jefferson Davis.* Philadelphia, 1907.
Dodd, William E. *The Cotton Kingdom.* New Haven, 1921.
Dowd, Clement. *Life of Zebulon B. Vance.* Charlotte, N. C., 1897.

Du Bose, John Witherspoon. *The Life and Times of William Lowndes Yancey.* Birmingham, 1892.

Eckenrode, H. J. *Jefferson Davis, President of the South.* New York, 1923.

Fielder, Herbert. *A Sketch of the Life and Times and Speeches of Joseph E. Brown.* Springfield, Massachusetts, 1883.

Fleming, Walter L. "Jefferson Davis' First Marriage." *Publications Mississippi Historical Society,* Vol. XII, pp. 21–36. 1912.

Fleming, Walter L. "The Early Life of Jefferson Davis." *Proceedings Mississippi Valley Historical Society,* Vol. IX, pp. 151–176. April, 1917.

Ford, Worthington C. (editor). *A Cycle of Adams Letters.* Two volumes. Boston, 1920.

Gerson, Armand J. "The Inception of the Montgomery Convention." *Report of the American Historical Association.* 1910. P. 181.

Greeley, Horace. *The American Conflict.* Two volumes. Hartford, Connecticut, 1864–1866.

Greer, James K. "Louisiana Politics, 1845–1861." *Louisiana Historical Quarterly,* Vols. XII and XIII.

Guedalla, Philip. *Palmerston.* London, 1926.

Guedalla, Philip. *The Second Empire.* London, 1922.

Hanna, A. J. *Flight into Oblivion.* Richmond, Va., 1938.

Harrison, Mrs. Burton. *Recollections Grave and Gay.* New York, 1912.

Hay, Thomas Robson. "Joseph Emerson Brown, Governor of Georgia, 1857–1865." *Georgia Historical Quarterly,* Vol. XIII, pp. 89–109.

Helper, Hinton Rowan. *The Impending Crisis of the South: How to Meet It.* New York, 1857.

Hill, Louise Biles. *Joseph E. Brown and the Confederacy.* Chapel Hill, 1939.

Hunter, Martha T. *A Memoir of Robert M. T. Hunter.* Washington, D. C., 1903.

Jerrold, Blanchard. *The Life of Napoleon III.* Four volumes. London, 1874.

Johnson, Herschel V. "From the Autobiography of." *American Historical Review.* XXX, pp. 311–336.

Johnston, R. M., and Browne, W. H. *Life of Alexander H. Stephens.* Philadelphia, 1878.

Jones, J. B. *A Rebel War Clerk's Diary.* Two volumes. Philadelphia, 1866.

Kohler, Max. *Judah P. Benjamin: Statesman and Jurist.* Baltimore, 1905.

BIBLIOGRAPHY

Lamar, J. R. Article on Howell Cobb in *Men of Mark in Georgia.* Vol. III, p. 566. 1911.
Lonn, Ella. *Desertion During the Civil War.* New York, 1928.
McCarthy, Justin. Article on Earl Russell in *Galaxy.* Vol. XV. 1873.
McElroy, Robert. *Jefferson Davis, the Unreal and the Real.* Two volumes. New York, 1937.
Mallory, Stephen R. "The Last Days of the Confederacy." *McClure's Magazine.* December, 1900–January, 1901.
Martin, Sir Theodore. *Life of the Prince Consort.* Five volumes. London, 1875–1880.
Mason, Virginia. *The Public Life and Diplomatic Correspondence of James M. Mason, with some personal History.* Roanoke, 1903.
Moore, Albert Burton. *Conscription and Conflict in the Confederacy.* New York, 1924.
Moore, Frank (editor). *Rebellion Record.* Twelve volumes. New York, 1861–1868.
Morley, John. *Life of Richard Cobden.* London, 1908.
Morley, John. *Life of William Ewart Gladstone.* Three volumes. London and New York, 1903.
Morrow, Josiah. *Life and Speeches of Thomas Corwin.* 1896.
Olmsted, Frederick Law. *Journeys and Explorations in the Cotton Kingdom.* Two volumes. London and New York, 1861.
Owsley, Frank Lawrence. *King Cotton Diplomacy. Foreign Relations of the Confederate States of America.* Chicago, 1931.
Owsley, Frank Lawrence. *State Rights in the Confederacy.* Chicago, 1925.
Pendleton, Louis. *Alexander H. Stephens.* Philadelphia, 1908.
Phillips, Ulrich B. "The Correspondence of Robert Toombs, Alexander H. Stephens and Howell Cobb." *Annual Report American Historical Association,* 1911. Vol. II.
Phillips, Ulrich B. *Life of Robert Toombs.* New York, 1913.
Pierce, Edward L. *Memoir and Letters of Charles Sumner.* Four volumes. Boston, 1877–1893.
Pollard, Edward A. *A Life of Jefferson Davis. With a secret history of the Southern Confederacy.* Chicago, 1869.
Pryor, Mrs. Roger A. *Reminiscences of Peace and War.* New York, 1904.
Ranck, James Byrne. *Albert Gallatin Brown, Radical Southern Nationalist.* New York, 1937.
Reagan, John H. *Memoirs.* New York and Washington, 1906.

Rhett, R. B., Jr. "The Confederate Government at Montgomery." *Battles and Leaders of the Civil War.* Vol. I, pp. 99–110.
Richardson, E. Rumsay. *Little Aleck: Life of Alexander H. Stephens.* Indianapolis, 1932.
Rippy, J. Fred. *The United States and Mexico.* New York, 1931.
Rowland, Dunbar. *Jefferson Davis' Place in History.* Jackson, Mississippi, 1923.
Rowland, Dunbar (editor). *Jefferson Davis, Constitutionalist. His Letters, papers and speeches.* Ten volumes. Jackson, Mississippi, 1923.
Rowland, Eron. *Varina Howell, wife of Jefferson Davis.* Two volumes. New York, 1931.
Russell, A. P. *Thomas Corwin, a Sketch.* 1882.
Russell, William Howard. *My Diary North and South.* Two volumes. London, 1863.
Russell, William Howard. *Times* of London. December 10, 1861. Article on Mason and Slidell.
Russell, William Howard. "Recollections of the Civil War." *North American Review.* Vol. CLXVI. 1898.
Scharf, J. T. *History of the Confederate States' Navy.* New York, 1887.
Schwab, John Christopher. *The Confederate States of America.* New York, 1901.
Scoville, J. A. *Old Merchants of New York City.* Second Series. New York, 1863.
Sears, L. M. *John Slidell.* 1925.
Sears, L. M. "Slidell and Buchanan." *American Historical Review,* Vol. XXVII, p. 721.
Sherman, William T. *Memoirs of General William T. Sherman.* Two volumes. New York, 1886.
Simms, Henry Harrison. *Life of Robert M. T. Hunter.* Richmond, 1935.
Sioussat, St. George L. "James Buchanan," in Volume V of *American Secretaries of State and their Diplomacy.* New York, 1927–1929.
Smith, Justin H. *The War with Mexico.* Two volumes. New York, 1919.
Soley, James Russell. *The Blockade and Cruisers.* New York, 1883.
Stephens, Alexander Hamilton. *A Constitutional View of the late War Between the States.* Philadelphia, 1868–1870.
Stephens, Alexander H. *Recollections: His Diary, Kept When a Prisoner at Fort Warren, Boston Harbor, 1865.* New York, 1910.
Stephenson, N. W. "A Theory of Jefferson Davis." *American Historical Review.* October, 1915, pp. 73–90.

Stephenson, Nathaniel W. *The Day of the Confederacy.* New Haven, 1919.
Stovall, Pleasant A. *Robert Toombs, Statesman, Speaker, Soldier, Sage.* New York, 1892.
Strohm, Isaac. *Speeches of Thomas Corwin, with a Sketch of his Life.* 1859.
Tatum, Georgia Lee. *Disloyalty in the Confederacy.* Chapel Hill, N. C., 1934.
Thayer, William Roscoe. *Life of John Hay.* Two volumes. Boston, 1915.
Toombs, Robert. Speech delivered in Milledgeville, November 13, 1860, before the Legislature of Georgia. Milledgeville, Georgia, 1860.
Vest, George. Article on Judah P. Benjamin in *Saturday Evening Post* (Reprinted in *American Israelite,* October 11, 1903).
Waddell, James D. (editor). *Biographical Sketch of Linton Stephens.* Atlanta, 1877.
Walker, Robert J. *Jefferson Davis, Repudiator.* London, 1863.
Walpole, Spencer. *Life of Lord John Russell.* Two volumes. London, 1891.
Welles, Gideon. *Galaxy,* May, 1873. Article on Mason and Slidell and the *Trent.*
White, Laura A., Ph.D. *Robert Barnwell Rhett, Father of Secession.* New York, 1931.
Wise, John S. *The End of an Era.* Boston, 1902.
Yates, Richard E. "Zebulon B. Vance, War Governor of North Carolina." *Journal of Southern History.* Vol. III, No. 1.

INDEX

ADAMS, CHARLES FRANCIS, American Minister to Court of St. James's, 146-152, *passim*, 226, on James Murray Mason, 268, on British attitude toward American Civil War, 255, regard for Lord John Russell, 277; on Slidell's appointment to Paris as envoy of Confederacy, 284, and Confederate shipbuilding contracts, 378
Adams, Charles Francis, Jr, on James Murray Mason, quoted, 238, 242
Adams, Ephraim D., on Lord John Russell's motive in effort toward Confederate recognition, 279-280
Adams, Henry, on James Murray Mason, quoted, 233, 267-268; on Lord Russell, quoted, 265; opinion of Lord John Russell, 277-279
Adams, John Quincy, and antislavery petitions, 32
Adams family, on James Murray Mason, quoted, 233
Agricultural crops, comparative values of, in 1850, 55
Agricultural poverty of South, 27
Agriculture, wasteful method in new Southern country, 26-27
Alabama, and new South, 45
Alabama, 321, 373, 374, 375; escape of, 279
Albert, Prince Consort, and *Trent* affair, 249-250
Antonelli, Cardinal, 402
Arkansas, and Confederacy, 8
Arman, L., of Bordeaux, contractor for Confederate shipbuilding, 382, 383, 384
Arnold, Matthew, attitude toward American Civil War, 255
Ashburton treaty, 259

BACON, D. FRANCIS, *re* Benjamin expulsion from Yale, quoted, 160-161, 163
Barnwell, Robert, 95; at Montgomery Convention, 192
Baroche, 299
Bath, Marquis of, 268
Bayard, Thomas F., 162
Beauregard, General, dispute with Davis, 177; 325, 329
Beecher, Henry Ward, 160
Belmont, August, 287

Benjamin, Judah P., 9-10, 94, 95; Toombs and, 73; in Davis Cabinet, 104; Attorney General, 153; birth and forebears, 154; early life, 158-159; in New Orleans, 164-169; marriage, 166-169; characteristics, 156 *et seq*, 171-175; his secretiveness in personal matters, 157-159, devotion to sister, 169; education and accomplishments, 173, "The brains of the Confederacy," 153-187; Yale incident, 159-164; comparison with Disraeli, 155-156; as legal authority, 173; influence with Jefferson Davis, 174-181; in Senate, 169-175; succeeds Walker as Secretary of War, 182-185; transferred to State Department, 185; and proposed transcontinental railroads, 175; and Mexican diplomacy, 110; seeker of Mexican concessions, 118, 119; and cotton in Confederate finance, 203, 207; Slidell and, in Erlanger loan transaction, 222-225, letter from Hotze, *re* Erlanger loan, 230; business intimate of Slidell, 287; and mission of Slidell in Paris, 283 *et seq.;* and Federal blockade in foreign policy, 271; foreign policy, 369; and Federal blockade, 276; and Houmas scandal, 292-293; and French aspirations in Mexico, 308; and British policy, 310; "wedge-driving" method in Franco-British relations, 310 *et seq.;* proposed bribery of France, 311-314; and French policy, 322; letter to, from Henry Hotze, quoted, 281; and Hotze, 393; and De Leon, 391-392; and Mann, 400 *et seq.*
Bennett, Thomas, 189
Beresford-Hope, 268
Berryer, M., 305-306
Bigelow, John: United States Consul General in Paris, on Erlanger loan, 226; letter to Seward, quoted, 226; 296; on Thouvenel and De Tocqueville, quoted, 298; description of Napoleon III and Eugénie, quoted, 314-315; quoted, 322-323; on Mexican schemes of

INDEX

Napoleon III, quoted, 305–306; on Confederate naval policy, quoted, 379–380
Black Hawk War, 20
Blaine, James G., on Judah P. Benjamin, 157, 177
Blair, Francis P., 430
Blanc, Louis, 304
Blessington, Lady, 314
Blockade, Federal: object of Mason's abjurations in London, 271; aspects of international law re, 272; principle of continuous voyage and doctrine of ultimate destination accepted as precedent in international law, 275; France's acceptance of Russell's attitude on, 301; Mallory's fight on, 363–386
Bonapartists, sympathy for Union, 304
Bonham, Governor, of South Carolina, 429
Bourbons, and United States, 303–304
Bragg, Captain, 95
Bragg, Braxton, 329
Breckinridge, John C., in Davis Cabinet, 387
Brierfield, home of Jefferson Davis, 40, 51
Bright, John: belief in debacle of American Union, 253; leader of English masses, 255; Lord John Russell's admiration for, 264
British Navy, 256–257
Brooks, Preston ("Bully"): attack on Charles Sumner, and defense by James Murray Mason, 237, 246–247
Brown, Albert Gallatin, and Nashville Convention, 49; cotton restrictionist, 212
Brown: John Brown's raid, 78
Brown, Joseph Emerson: governor of Georgia, 337–342, contrasted with Vance, 342–343; devotion to state, 347–349; hostility to Confederacy, 350 et seq.; nullifies conscription, 352 et seq.; conscription exemptions, 353 et seq ; and Georgia Militia, 358–362; 409; 429; Stephens and, 425; 426
Bruce, Sally, Mrs. James A. Seddon, 326–327
Buchanan, President James, 79, 387; Slidell's enthusiasm for, 293
Bull Run, Battle of, compared with battle of Valmy, 6; European opinion of, 113; effect in London on Confederate cause, 150; receipt of news of, in Richmond, 180–181, 307
Bull Run, Second Battle of, 218
Bullock, Captain James D., 370 and n., 374, and Confederate shipbuilding contracts, 377–379, 383; quoted, 379–380; French shipbuilding contracts, 381–386
Bunch, Robert, 141; on Memminger, quoted, 192
Burnside, capture of Roanoke Island, 184
Burwell, William M., quoted, 108, 116–117, 120, 121; 420
Byron, Lord, and Lord John Russell, 263

CALHOUN, JOHN C.: Sectional Southern party plan, 74, 77; 189; and James Murray Mason, 244
Campbell, Judge, on mountain districts and Confederacy, 336; at Hampton Roads Conference, 430
Campbell, Lord, 269
Carlisle, Earl of, admiration of Memminger, 190
Cecil, Lord Eustace, 269
Cecil, Lord Robert, 269
Chamberlain, Joseph, and British democracy, 256
Charleston Convention of 1860, 285
Charlotte, consort of Maximilian, 400
Chartres, Duc de, in Federal army, 253, 302
Chase, as Union statesman, 3
Cheeves, Langdon, 190
Chestnut, James, 180
Chestnut, Mrs quoted, 142–143; on Leroy P. Walker, quoted, 178; on capture of New Orleans, quoted, 184; on James Murray Mason, quoted, 233–234, 235; opinion of James Murray Mason, 247
Civil War: emphasis on statesmanship by North and military achievement by South, 3; relative military strength of North and South, 5–6; European opinion on, 4; European belief in debacle of the Union, 252–257; military task of Union, 4–6; slavery and, 54–55; economic grounds of, 55–56; first Battle of Bull Run, 180–181; Peninsular campaign, 183, 218, Montgomery Convention, 100–104; Fort Sumter, 105–106; Davis policy, 183; blockade on Southern ports, 207, 210; cotton in, 207–215; military situation after Chancellorsville, 227; disappearance of United States Navy after, 254;

INDEX

Southern destroyers of Union commerce in, 373–375; Hampton Roads Conference, 430–431
Clark, Governor, of Mississippi, 356, 429
Clay, Henry, 387
Clay's Compromise, 77
Cleveland, Henry, 424, 426–427
Clingman, Thomas L., duel with Yancey, 142
Cobb, Howell: as Georgia leader, 69–70; as Constitutional Unionist, 75 et seq., as Jacksonian Democrat, 77; his love for the Union, 77; resignation from Buchanan's Cabinet, 79; 91; and Confederate Presidency, 96–99; and Joseph E. Brown, 357
Cobb, Thomas R. R., on Montgomery Convention, 91; quoted, 92–95; 98; 339
Cobden, Richard: opinion of James Murray Mason as "old slave dealer," 247; his belief in debacle of the American Union, 253; 269
Confederacy: geographic foundations of, 8; New-South elements of, 8–9; and State rights, 10–11; reasons for failure of, 11, 58, 429–432; the Montgomery Convention, 85 et seq.; meeting in the United States Capitol, 87–89, 96, 159, 186; efforts toward European recognition, 107, 139–152; commission to Mexico, 107, 117–138; Constitution, 100–104; and possibility of European recognition, 218–219; navy, construction of vessels in foreign countries, 220; mission of Mason in Great Britain, 267 et seq.; territorial ambitions of, 270; "Confederacy of the Cotton States," 86; cotton export policy of, 207–215; cotton shortage as basis of European recognition, 208–215; belated desire to move cotton, 271; efforts of Lord John Russell toward recognition of, 277–282; attack of envoys on Lord Russell, 280–281; attitude of French Foreign Secretary toward, 298–301, 302; government of Napoleon III and, 302–323; inherent weaknesses of, 330; state governors and, 330 et seq.; dissentients within, 409; civilian attitude toward central power, 414; Union area within boundaries of, 331 et seq.; cross purposes in, 350 et seq.

Confederacy, finance of: cotton in, 188–215; liquid capital, 196–197; domestic loan, 196–198; Erlanger loan, 216–232. See also Confederate money
Confederate army, desertion in, 335–336
Confederate Congress, 418–419
Confederate Constitution, 100–104
Confederate money, 195–196, 197, 198–201
Conscription, Confederate: Georgia exemptions, 353–355; anti-administration governors and, 352 et seq.; Joe Brown's Ten Thousand, 358–362, effect on civilian population, 413
Constitution, Federal: reverence of Jefferson Davis for, 32; 53; Stephens and, 67–68
Constitutional liberty, 421–422
Constitutional Union: Stephens-Toombs-Cobb Coalition, 69–70, 75, 78
Contraband, principle of, 273
Corwin, Thomas, United States Minister in Mexico, 108; 118–138
Cotton: demand for product, 26; European reliance on Southern, 139–140; determination of Confederacy not to ship, 207; as security for Erlanger loan, 216 et seq.; restriction of supply, 212–213; failure of Confederacy to use crop for financing war, 194, 201–215; industry in France, 304; Mallory's fight on Lincoln blockade, 363–386; failure of Confederacy to regard as asset, 430
Cotton barons, of Georgia and Mississippi delta, 25–26; 55–56
Cotton belt, Southwestern: agricultural methods in, 26–27; slave system, 27; economic and social aspects, 28; progress in statesmanship, 28
Cotton famine in Europe, 208–210; unemployment in Great Britain and France, 218
Cotton speculation, European, 219–232
Couronne, French ironclad, 317
"Crackers," 332 et seq.
Craven, Dr. John Joseph, 188; on Davis's estimate on cotton value, quoted, 204–205
Crimean War, ironclads in, 372
Cushing, Caleb, 52

DAUDET, ALPHONSE, 295
Davis, George, in Davis Cabinet, 387

INDEX

Davis, Jefferson: and enlistment of negroes, 5; forebears, 12; birthplace, 13; early life, 14–18; appearance, 15, 18; education, 16–19; at West Point, 18–19; characteristics, 18, 20; influence of early training on later political views and allegiances, 16–18, 24; description of, by Varina Howell (Mrs. Jefferson Davis), 38–39; his political ideas, 40–44; accomplishments and equipment, 46–47; army life, 19–20; first marriage, 21–23, 31, second marriage, 33–40; quarrel with Joseph E. Johnston, 19; quarrel with Zachary Taylor, 21–23; retirement and study, 24 *et seq.;* retirement at Hurricane, 31–33, 40; and State rights, 41; political campaigns, 40; Member of Congress, 42; in Mexican War, 42; as President, his interference in army matters, 42; not a modern man, 43; his worship of slavery, 43; and Nashville Convention, 49–50; defeat for Governorship of Mississippi, 50–51; Senator from Mississippi, 47; Member of Pierce Cabinet, 47; and Franklin Pierce, 51–52; as Secretary of War, 52; position in Southern nationalism compared to that of Hamilton in development of Union, 25; and Southern nationalism, 45 *et seq,* as representative of new South, 52–56; his worship of Federal Constitution, 53; position of, on public questions, compared with that of Toombs, 74; in Pierce Cabinet, 78; and Unionism in Secession areas, 78; and Montgomery Convention, 85–95, *passim,* qualities for Presidency, 88–89; as military man, 88–89, election as President of the Confederacy, 95–100; and Yancey, 141–142; and Judah P. Benjamin, 174–181; loyalty to appointees, 185, and Benjamin, in Roanoke crisis, 185; and Cabinet appointments, 185–187; at Fortress Monroe, 188, 204; and Brooks attack on Sumner, 247; and Governors of States, 330–349; and the Navy in the Confederacy, 364; notice of inauguration of, in London press, 395; and suspension of writ of habeas corpus, 412–413; hostility from within the Confederacy, 416–432; and failure of Southern cause, 429–432; instructions to Stephens at Hampton Roads Conference, 431; final rally at African Church in Richmond, 431–432; prisoner in Fortress Monroe, 432

Davis, Mrs. Jefferson (Varina Howell) early life, 35–37, appearance, 35; education, 35–36; influence of Judge Winchester, 36–37; meeting with Jefferson Davis, 38; courtship and marriage, 39–40; and Judah P. Benjamin, 172; on friendship of Davis and Benjamin, quoted, 176–177; quoted, 22, 32–33

Davis, Joseph Emory, 14, 15, 17; as obscure maker of history, 33; his wealth, 29; as type of Mississippi planter, 29–30; his guardianship of younger brother Jefferson, 30–31; 31–33; 33–40; and Howell family, 34; and marriage of Jefferson Davis and Varina Howell, 37–40

Davis Cabinet, 3; personnel of, 9; 104–106; ineffectiveness of first, 178; changes in, in four years, 324

Davis embargo. *See* Cotton

Day, Jeremiah, letter from Benjamin to, 163

Dayton, William L, United States Minister to France, 146–147; 226; United States Minister in Paris, 383

"Deadening" trees, 27

Declaration of Paris, 272, 274

Delane, editor of London *Times,* and *Trent* affair, 252

Desertion in Confederate army, 335–336

Deslonde, Mathilde, marriage to John Slidell, 290

Diaz, Porfirio, 131 and *n.*

Dickens, Charles, 264

Dilke, Sir Charles, and British democracy, 256

Disraeli, Benjamin, comparison with Judah P Benjamin, 155–156

Doctrine of continuous voyage, 273

Doctrine of ultimate destination, 272–273

Donoughmore, Lord, 268

Douglas, Stephen A., 78

Drayton, William, 190

ERICSSON, designer of the *Monitor,* 382

Erlanger, Baron, 220, 224, 225, 287, 323

INDEX

Erlanger, Emile, financial agent in Confederate shipbuilding contracts, 382, 383; and *The Index*, 396
Erlanger et Cie, intermediary in Confederate loan transaction, 220-232 *passim*
Erlanger loan, 216-232
Estrada, Guitterez de, 308, 320
Eugénie, Empress. and Mexico, 111-113; attentions to Slidell and his family, 283-284; and the Church, 298; and Mexican schemes, 306; appearance, 314-315; and Thouvenel, 319
Europe: diplomatic policy on "American question," 4
European recognition, efforts of Confederacy toward, 107, 114 *et seq.* See also Confederacy

FARRAGUT, DAVID, 370, 377
Fillmore, President, 120
Flahaut, Count de, 295
Fleury, General, 313
Florida, and Confederacy, 8
Florida, 373, 374
Foote, Henry Stuart, 50-51; on Judah P. Benjamin, 172; opinion of Slidell, 285
Forey, General, 307
Forsyth, John, 108, 110; in Mexico, 118-119; United States Minister in Mexico, 121
Fort Pickens, Mallory and, 368-369
Fort Sumter, 105-106
France. Confederate efforts toward recognition by, 139-152; 302-323; disposition to support British precedence in American policy, 302-303; general sympathy for Union, 304; Napoleon III and Confederacy, 305 *et seq.*
Franklin, Benjamin: sale of tobacco in France, 203; 266-287
Fredericksburg, 218
French press, advocacy of Northern interest, 304
Fugitive Slave Law, 78, 244, 245, 246, 269

GADSDEN, United States Minister in Mexico, 121
Gadsden Purchase, 54
Garrison, William Lloyd, compared with Stephens, 421, 422
Georgia: and Confederacy, 8; as pivotal state, 84; and Secession, 341; conscription exemption in, 353-355
Georgia Legislature: speeches on Union and disruption, by Stephens and Toombs, 80-84
Gettysburg, Battle of, 230
Gladstone, William Ewart: and Confederacy, 219; belief in debacle of American Union, 253; his plan of intervention in American Civil War, 257; 278, 279, 282
Gloire, French ironclad, 317, 372, 375-376
Gorgas, General, on Judah P. Benjamin, quoted, 173
Grant, Ulysses S.: as military leader, 3; on Jefferson Davis, 42; campaigns, 183; military progress, 227; 321-322, 325, 335
Great Britain; Confederate efforts toward recognition by, 139-152; belief in the debacle of the American Union, 252-257; democratic aspects in attitude toward American Civil War, 254-257; advance in democracy since 1861, 254-257
Greeley, Horace, 86, 121
Greg, Percy, London journalist employed on *The Index*, 398
Greville, Charles, on Louis Napoleon, quoted, 314
Grey, Sir Edward, and Civil War precedent in World War conduct, 276-277

HABEAS CORPUS, suspension of writ of, 412, 428-429
Halstead, Murat, on John Slidell, 285
Hamberger, H., and Erlanger loan, 229
Hamilton, Alexander, 25, 58
Hamilton, James, 190
Hampton Roads Conference, 430-431
Harrison, Mrs. Burton, on Judah P Benjamin, quoted, 172
Hay, John, description of Napoleon III, quoted, 315
Hayne, Robert Young, 190
Helper's *Impending Crisis*, 78
Herbert, Sidney, quoted, 262
Herndon, William H., Lincoln to, quoted, 64
Hidalgo, 308
Hill, Benjamin H., 409; quoted, 425, 427
Hill, J. B., Confederate Senator, 356-357
"Hillbillies," 332 *et seq.*
Holden, W. W., 346
Holmes, General, 325, 329
Hood, Campaign in Eastern Tennessee, 360
Hood's army, desertion in, 336

Hortense, Queen, 295
Hotze, Henry: Confederate publicity agent in London, on Erlanger loan, quoted, 226; 230; on British policy re Federal blockade, quoted, 276; attack on Lord John Russell, quoted, 280–281; 390–399
Houmas scandal, Slidell and, 292–293
Howell, Varina. See Davis, Mrs. Jefferson
Howell, William B., 34
Howell, Mrs. William B. (Louisa Kempe), 34
Hugo, Victor, and Napoleon III, 284; on Second Empire, 296
Hunter, Robert M. T., 88; in Davis Cabinet, 186–187; at Hampton Roads Conference, 430
Hurricane, estate of Joseph Davis, 29, 30, 31; retirement of Jefferson Davis at, 31–33; house party at, 37–40

Independent, New York, article re Benjamin, quoted, 160–161
Index, Confederate review in London, 396 *et seq.*
International law: Declaration of Paris, 272, 274; contraband, 273; Federal blockade, 272 *et seq.*, Lord John Russell and, 274–275; principle of continuous voyage and doctrine of ultimate destination accepted as precedent, 275; application in World War, 276

JACKSON, PRESIDENT ANDREW, stigmatization of Slidell, quoted, 291
Jackson, Stonewall, as military leader, 3, 8
James, Valley of the, 326
Jecker, J. B., Swiss banker, and French intervention in Mexico, 306
Jefferson, Thomas, policy of peaceful coercion, 208; 324
Jews, Sephardic, 154–156
Johnson, Andrew, 331, 339, 367, 368
Johnston, Joseph E.: as military leader, 3, 8, quarrel with Jefferson Davis, 19, 177; on Confederate finance, 205; 325, 329; and Joe Brown's Ten Thousand, 359
Johnston, Richard Malcolm, quoted, 59–60
Joinville, Prince de, 302
Jones, J. B., diarist, on Judah P. Benjamin, quoted, 177; on Memminger, quoted, 192–193; on Leroy P. Walker, 179; on news of Bull Run, quoted, 181; on Secretary Seddon, quoted, 328

Juárez, Benito, President of Mexico, 111, 116, 124 *et seq.*

KANSAS-NEBRASKA BILLS, 78
Kearsarge, 321, 375
Kempe, Louisa (Mrs. William B. Howell), 34
Kentucky Resolutions of 1798, 68
Kossuth, 118
Ku Klux Klan, 333

LABOULAYE, 304
Lairds shipyards at Liverpool, 377
Lee, Richard, 30
Lee, Richard Henry, 31
Lee, General Robert E.: as military leader, 3, 8; enlistment of colored troops, 5, ancestors of, 24; at West Point, 19; preparations for invasion of Pennsylvania, 227; on desertion in Confederate army, 335–336; 430
Legitimists, French, sympathy for Union, 302
Leon, Edwin de, Confederate publicity agent in Paris, 390–393
Leopold I of Belgium, 113, 400; letter to Queen Victoria, on dissolution of American Union, quoted, 253
Lhuys, Drouyn de, French Foreign Minister, 283; successor to Thouvenel as French Foreign Minister, 319, 320; 321
Lincoln, Abraham: as civic leader, 3; forebears, 12; birthplace, 13; early life, 16; on Alexander H. Stephens, quoted, 64; to Alexander H. Stephens, quoted, 57–58; and hypocrisy in politics, 64–65; inaugural address, 104–106; and Polk's Mexican policy, 121; and United States foreign policy, 147–148; and blockade of Southern ports, 210–211, 213–214; and French aspirations in Mexico, 307; and suspension of writ of habeas corpus, 412–413; at Hampton Roads Conference, 430–431
Lincoln blockade. See Blockade, Federal
Lincoln-Douglas debates, 78
Lincoln Government, France's interest in, 303
Lindsay, Sir Coutts, 269
Livingston, Edward, 289
Longstreet, General, as military leader, 8
Lopez, Narciso, 118, 119 *n.*
Louis XV, 295

INDEX 447

Louis XVI, and American Revolutionary Cause, 303
Louisiana, and Confederacy, 8
Louisiana, 377
Lyons, Lord, British Minister in Washington, 115; 145, 146, 148

MALLORY, ELLEN RUSSELL, mother of Stephen R. Mallory, 365
Mallory, Stephen R, 9, 95; Secretary of the Navy in Davis Cabinet, 104, 178, 324, 363–386; and Brooks attack on Sumner, 247; his view of Confederacy as a whole, 363; his effort to get cotton to Europe, 363 *et seq;* origin and early life, 365–366; apologia to President Johnson, 367–368; Fort Pickens affair, 368–369; and lack of ships, 370–371, his sea policy, 369, 372; commission for ironclads, 375 *et seq.*
Mallory, Mrs Stephen R. (Angela Moreno), 365–366
Malmesbury, Lord, 268–269
Manchester Guardian, 398
Mann, A. Dudley: Confederate Commissioner in Europe, 107, 140–152, *passim*, 209–210, 270–271; and Lord Russell, 265; Commissioner to Belgium, 400; mission to the Vatican, 399–408
Marchand, Colonel, 323
Marcy, William L., 52
Martin, Henri, 304
Mason and Dixon's line, 331
Mason, George, Virginia "cavalier," 236–237
Mason, James Murray: antecedents, 236–239; family and Virginia career, 239–240; arrogance, 240–241; opinions about, 233–235; contrasted with Slidell, 233; New England antagonism against, 244–247; Charles Sumner's antagonism toward, 245–247; Confederate envoy to England, 134, 233–257; Confederate agent in London, on Erlanger loan subscriptions, 224, 225; in Erlanger loan transaction, 233; defense of Bully Brooks, 237, 246, 247; and Federal Constitution, 242–243; slavery worship, 243–247; author of Fugitive Slave Law, 244, 245, 246; in Senate, 244–247; seizure on the *Trent*, 238, 247–250; effect of *Trent* affair on his mission to Great Britain, 250–251; diatribe against, in London *Times*, 251–252; his unpopularity in Great Britain, 253;
and Lord John Russell, 264–267; hatred of Lord John Russell, 277; and Lord Palmerston, 265; and Erlanger loan, 228–229; in London, 267–270, and Federal blockade, 271–277, contrast between his reception in London and Slidell's in Paris, 283
Maurice, Sir Frederick, quoted, 6
Maury, William Ballard, quoted, 364
Maximilian, and Mexico, 220, 305, 308; and Slidell, 321; 383–384, 386, 400
Memminger, Christopher G., 9, 95; origin and early life, 188–190; Secretary of the Treasury in Davis Cabinet, 104, 178, 188–232; and Bank of South Carolina, 190; political career, 190–193; at Montgomery Convention, 191–193; Pollard and Rhett attacks on, 192–193; impossibility of reconciling his task with his ideas of sound finance, 193; and failure of Confederacy to raise money on cotton, 204–206; and Erlanger loan, 216–232
Mercier, M, French Minister in Washington, 115
Merrimac, 377
Mexican War, new South after, 44 *et seq.;* constitutional effects of, 74
Mexico: European designs upon, 112 *et seq.;* France and, 111–113; Confederate diplomatic relations with, 107 *et seq.,* 117–138; German proposals to, in World War, 132–133; imperialistic designs on, by Napoleon III, 305 *et seq.;* Maximilian Empire in, 320–322
Miles, William Porcher, 234
Miramon, President of Mexico, 306
Mississippi, and Confederacy, 8; a composite of South, 24–25, and new South, 45
Mississippi, 377
Missouri Compromise, repeal of, 78
Mocquard, Jean François, secretary to Napoleon III, 283
Monitor, 377, 382
Monroe Doctrine: and Mexican diplomacy, 110, 111, 112, 113, and French aspirations in Mexico, 307; 322, 386
Montgomery Convention, 85 *et seq.;* as birthplace of Confederacy, 89–90; Presidential Election, 95–100; Constitution, 100–104; effect on North, 105; 423

INDEX

Montgomery Government, states forming, 8
Moore, Tom, 263
Moreno, Angela (Mrs. Stephen R. Mallory), 365–366
Morning Post, London, Confederate propaganda in, 395
Morny, Count de, 283, 294–296; his schemes and avarice, 305–306; 313; and Slidell, 322–323; 382
Motley, John Lothrop, on British attitude toward American Civil War, 255
Murrah, Governor of Texas, against conscription, 355, 356, 429
McClellan, General. campaigns, 183; Peninsular campaign, 218; 302.
McKinley Bill, 344
McLane, United States Minister in Mexico, 121
McPhee, Captain, 23

NAPOLEON I, and battle of Valmy, 6; 261; 263
Napoleon III: 110–111; and Mexico, 111–113; intrigues of, 219; and Erlanger loan, 221, 261; and "apogee of Second Empire," 294; and American Civil War, 302–323; Mexico as influence in attitude toward Confederacy, 305 *et seq.;* appearance and characteristics, 314–315; and John Slidell, 283 *et seq*; interview with Slidell on proffered Confederate subsidy, 314–318; American policy based on false assumption, 322; meeting with Slidell in exile, 323; 369; meeting with Slidell, 381; offer to build ironclads for Confederacy, 381–382; policy in American Civil War, 383, 391
Nashville Convention, 49–50, 74; Cobb and, 77
Navy, displacement of wooden vessels by ironclads, 372
Negroes, in Southern army, 5
New Orleans, capture of, 184; effect of loss of, on Southern shipping, 216–217; as refuge for young Northerners needing rehabilitation, 289–290
New York Tribune, 391
Normandie, French ironclad, 317
North, Lieutenant James H., 375–376
North Carolina, and Confederacy, 8; and New South, 44–45

OFFENBACH, JACQUES, 295
Olmsted, Frederick Law, account of devastation in southwestern cotton belt, 27
Oregon disputes, 259–260
Orleanists, sympathy for Union, 302
Owsley, Prof. Frank L., quoted, 10–11; on cotton export policy of Confederacy, 214

PAGE, WALTER HINES, and capture of American ships in World War, 276
Palmerston, Lord· 218; and *Trent* affair, 248, 250, 252, and Lord Russell, in efforts toward Confederate recognition, 278; and Lord John Russell, in British politics, 258–282; American policy, 259–263; worship of British Empire, 260; hatred of slavery, 260, conservative attitude toward Napoleon III, 261–262; belief in debacle of American Union, 253; and British intervention in American Civil War, 256; and *Morning Post*, 395
Paris, Comte de, in Federal army, 253; 302; history of Civil War, 303
Pendleton, Louis Beauregard, 427
Perry, Matthew Galbraith, 287
Persigny, Count de, 283; 296–297; 299; 313; and Slidell, 322; 382
Pettus, Governor of Mississippi, against conscription, 355, 356
Pickett, Colonel John T., Confederate envoy to Mexico, 107, 117–125, 129–138
Pickett Papers, 137–138
Pierce, Franklin, and Jefferson Davis, 51–52; and Judah P. Benjamin, 173
Pius IX, Pope, audience of A. Dudley Mann with, 402–405; letter to Jefferson Davis, 405–408
Polk, President, and invasion of Mexico, 64–65; and Mexican War, 74; 120
Pollard, Edward A, 86, 88; on Memminger, quoted, 192
"Poor whites," 332 *et seq.*
Port Hudson, Battle of, 230
Postal system during the Civil War, 387–389
"Potsdam Conference," 87–89
Prentiss, Sergeant S, 34
Press, British, Confederate propaganda in, 394–399
Preston, William Ballard, 322, 364
Propaganda during the Civil War, 389–399

INDEX

QUITMAN, JOHN A., 34

RANDOLPH, GEORGE W., Secretary of War in Davis Cabinet, 324–326, 335
Rappahannock, 321
Reagan, John H., Postmaster General in Davis Cabinet, 104, 387–389
Récamier, Madame, and Louis Napoleon, 314
Reconstruction era, Joseph E. Brown in, 362
Reform Bill, British, of 1832, 254
Republican Party, organization of, 78
Rhett, Robert Barnwell, and Nashville Convention, 49; 53; 78; antagonism toward Memminger, 191–192; 338
Richmond Examiner, 87
Riddle, Dr., Postmaster of New Orleans, and Pickett documents, 137
Roebuck Resolution, 319–320
Roosevelt, Theodore, 370 n.
Rost, Pierre A.: Confederate Commissioner in Europe, 107, 140–152, *passim;* Yancey mission to Europe, 270–271, 399–400
Rouher, M., French Minister of Marine, 283, 299; and Confederate shipbuilding contracts, 382, 383, 384
Russell, Lord John: and Confederate Commission, 143–152; and Seward's foreign policy, 144–150; 213; nonintervention policy of, 219; and *Trent* affair, 250; and Lord Palmerston, in British politics, 258–282; American policy, 263–267, 277–282; his Napoleonic recollections, 263; and Byron, 263; and Wordsworth, 264; and James Murray Mason, 264–267; and Federal blockade, 272–273; and doctrine of ultimate destination, 274–275; acceptance of precedent in Federal blockade, 275–277; opinions *re*, 277–278; his efforts toward Confederate recognition, 277–282; foreign policy, 311; and Confederate ship contracts, 377–378; 406
Russell, William H.: of London *Times*, quoted, 119; quoted, 148; *Times* article on Bull Run, 150; on Judah P. Benjamin, quoted, 153–154; on Leroy P. Walker, quoted, 178; on James Murray Mason, quoted, 234–235; description of Slidell's New Orleans home, quoted, 290–291

Russell of Killowen, Lord Chief Justice of England, 365

SAINT-ROMAIN, COMTE DE, 323
San Jacinto, in *Trent* affair, 288
Saturday Review, 398
Schwab, John Christopher, on Erlanger loan, quoted, 231
Scott, Sir Walter, 263
Scott decision, Dred, 78
Secession: Nashville Convention, 49–50; Jefferson Davis and, 50–51, Stephens and, 57–58; and Confederate Constitution, 100–104, Lincoln and, 105
Secret organizations of mountain country, 333–334
Seddon, James A., War Secretary in Davis Cabinet, 10, 326 *et seq.;* struggle with Governors, 330, 349; on Joe Brown's Ten Thousand, quoted, 359–360
Seddon, Mrs. James A., 326–327
Semmes, Raphael, quoted, 86
Seward, William H.: as Union statesman, 3; instructions to Corwin, quoted, 108; 115; 126; Secretary of State in Lincoln Cabinet, characteristics and foreign policy, 144–150; "Thoughts" to Lincoln, 146; and Erlanger loan, 226–227; foreign policy of, 256; and Federal blockade, 273, and building of Confederate ships in British yards, 377; at Hampton Roads Conference, 430
Shenandoah, 373
Sherman, General, as military leader, 3; in Georgia, 359–362; 427
Shipbuilding, Confederate, contracts in Great Britain, 377–380; in France, 380–386
Shroeder, Erlanger representative in London, 228
Slavery: Jefferson Davis and, 53–55; Yancey and, 142; European opinion of, as Civil War factor, 399
Slidell, John: in Mexico, 118; of Louisiana, 169; and Benjamin, 173; and Erlanger loan, 219–232; contrasted with Mason, 233, 235; and Brooks attack on Sumner, 247; seizure from the *Trent*, 247–250; effect of *Trent* affair on his mission abroad, 250–251; diatribe against, in London *Times*, 251–252; Confederate envoy to France, 135; in Paris, 219 *et seq.*, 283 *et seq.;* contrast between his reception in Paris and Mason's in London, 283–284; intrigues in

INDEX

Paris, 294–301; mission to France, 302–323; popularity at court of Second Empire, 283–286; his political power, 284–285; appearance, 286; contemporary opinion re, 284–287; birth and early life, 287–289; marriage, 290; New Orleans home, 290–291; lack of high character as public man, 291; President Jackson's stigmatization of, 291; absence of strong convictions on public issues, 291–292; career as political boss, 292–293; and Houmas scandal, 292–293; in Mexico, 293; and Thouvenel, French Foreign Secretary, 298–301; and schemes of Napoleon III in Mexico, 308, 309; "wedge-driving" policy in Franco-British relations, 310 et seq., and British policy, 310; proposed bribery of France, 311–314; interview with Napoleon III on proffered subsidy, 314–318; end of usefulness as diplomat, 320–323; meeting with Napoleon III in exile, 323; and Fort Pickens, 368; meeting with Napoleon III, 381; and ship contracts, 382, 383; and De Leon, 391–392

Slidell, Matilda, marriage to young Erlanger, afterward Baron, 220, 224

Smith, Brigadier General Gustavus, in Davis Cabinet, 326

Smith, Sydney, quoted, 264

South. and Confederacy, 7; statesmanship in, 7; and constitution of the United States, 7; antebellum, new type in, 25–26, 28; new, after Mexican War, 44 et seq.

South Carolina, and Confederacy, 8; and new South, 44–45

Southern "aristocracy," 8–9

Southern nationalism, Jefferson Davis and, 24–25; 45 et seq.

Southern Pacific Railroad, 54

Spence, James, English adviser of Confederacy, in Erlanger loan transactions, 229

Spinning industry in Great Britain, 209

Spottswood Hotel, Richmond, 180–181

Standard, London, 398

Stanton, as Union statesman, 3

State militia in Confederacy, 358–362

State rights: and failure of Confederacy, 10, 430, 432; Jefferson Davis and, 41, 54; under Federal Constitution, 68–69

State sovereignty, and war, 347–348

States, Governors of, and Confederacy, 330–349

Stephens, Alexander H., 8; life and character, 58 et seq.; opponent of Secession, 57–58; and State sovereignty, 64; and Lincoln, re hypocrisy in politics, 64–65; his inner life, 65–67; his worship of Federal Constitution, 67–68; admiration for Webster, 67–68; and State rights, 68–69; as Georgia leader, 69–70, and Constitutional Union party, 75 et seq.; refutation of Toombs's disunion arguments, 81–84; and Montgomery Convention, 85; 94, 95; and Confederate Presidency, 97–99; and Polk's Mexican policy, 121; on cotton and Confederate finance, 205; 338; his fanaticism, 420–422; compared with Garrison, 421; hostile critic of Davis administration, 409, 415–422; a Union man at heart, 422–423; rift between Davis and, 424–425; the inspiration of Joe Brown, 425; "peace resolutions," 427–428; at Hampton Roads Conference, 430–431; and doctrine of State rights, 432

Stephens, Linton, brother of Alexander H., 415; 426

Stokes, Anson Phelps, re Benjamin expulsion from Yale, 163

Stowell, Lord, and "arc of circumvallation," 276

Stuart, Jeb, as military leader, 3, 8

Sumner, Charles: attack of Bully Brooks on, 237, 246–247; antagonism toward James Murray Mason, 245–246; his invective against Mason, 246–247; description of Lord John Russell, 264; opinion of John Slidell, 285

Sutherland, Duke and Duchess of, 268

TALLEYRAND, 295

Tapia, Don Santiago, 129

Taylor, John, of Caroline, 326

Taylor, Sarah Knox, marriage to Jefferson Davis, 21–23; 30–31

Taylor, Zachary, 30; quarrel with Jefferson Davis, 21–23

Tehantepec Railway, 292–293

Tennessee, and Confederacy, 8

Texas, and Confederacy, 8

Thiers, 304

Thouvenel, Édouard Antoine: French Foreign Secretary, 283, 297–298;

INDEX 451

interview with Slidell, 298–301; detestation of slavery, 302; European policy, 302; 313; opposition to Eugénie's Papal policy, 319

Times, London, Confederate propaganda in, 395

Tocqueville, De, 298, 303

Toombs, Robert, 53; as Georgia leader, 69–70, 71–75; his fatal gift of epigram, 73; position of, on public questions, compared with that of Davis, 74; and Constitutional Union party, 75 *et seq.*; as disruptionist, 79; speech in Georgia Legislature, 80–81; discussion, 81–84; 95; and Confederate Presidency, 96, 103; in Davis Cabinet, 104; and Lincoln's policy, 106; Confederate Secretary of State, 107, and Napoleonic schemes in Mexico, 115 *et seq.*; and Mexico, 132–133; European diplomacy, 139–152, *passim,* as Secretary of State, 185; at Montgomery Convention, 192; and Houmas scandal, 292; and Brooks attack on Sumner, 247; 338; hostile critic of Davis Administration, 416–429

Trent, British steam packet, seizure of Mason and Slidell from, by Captain Wilkes, 247–250

Trent affair, 278–279, 288

Uncle Tom's Cabin, 78

Union, France's interest in, 303–304

United States mercantile marine before the Civil War, 254

United States Navy, in Lincoln blockade of Southern ports, 213–214

"Up-country," hostility of, to Piedmont and Tidewater, 334 *et seq.*

VALMY, battle of, compared with Bull Run, 6

Van Buren, Martin, and Slidell, 284; 291

Vance, Zebulon Baird: Governor of North Carolina, 337; 342; contrasted with Brown, 342–343, devotion to State, 347–349; hostility to Confederacy, 350 *et seq.,* and conscription exemptions, 355; 409

Vicksburg, Battle of, 230

Victoria, Queen: and *Trent* affair, 249; and Lord Palmerston and Lord John Russell, 258; 309

Virginia: and Confederacy, 8; statesmanship in, 26; exhaustion of tobacco lands, 26; and new South, 44–45; in Confederate Administration, 327–328

WADE, BEN, on Judah P. Benjamin, 173

Walewska, Countess, 294

Walewski, Count, 283, 294, 296, 298

Walker, Leroy P.: in Davis Cabinet, 104; as Secretary of War in Davis Cabinet, 178–182; and cotton in Confederate finance, 203, 206, 207; and Joseph E. Brown, 351

Walker, Robert J., and Erlanger loan, 226–227

Walpole, Spencer, and Lord Russell's attitude toward Southern recognition, 277–278

Warrior, British ironclad, 372

Washington, H. A., on friendship of Davis and Benjamin, quoted, 176

Watts, Governor of Alabama, against conscription, 355–356; 409; 429

Webster, Daniel, and Nationalism, 62; Stephens's admiration for, 67–68

Welles, Gideon, as Union statesman, 3; and Lincoln blockade, 213–214; on James Murray Mason, quoted, 233

Wellington, Duke of, 88

Westbury, Lord, 282

West Virginia, secession from Confederacy, 331

Whiskey Boys, 333

Wigfall, Senator, of Texas, at Richmond, 180; on Memminger, 193

Wilkes, Captain Charles, seizure of Mason and Slidell from the *Trent,* 247–250; boyhood friend of Slidell, 288

Wilson, Woodrow, loyalty to appointees, 185

Winchester, George, as friend and teacher of Mrs. Jefferson Davis (Varina Howell), 36–37, 38

Wise, John A., 324

Wordsworth, William, and Lord John Russell, 264

World War: Civil War precedent in international law, 276–277; sea policy in, 373

Wyke, Sir Charles, 129

YALE COLLEGE, Judah P. Benjamin at, 159–164

Yancey, William Lowndes: and Nashville Convention, 49; 53; 95; Confederate Commissioner in Europe, 107; Confederate Commissioner to Great Britain, 140–152, influence in South, 141–142; and slavery, 142–143; as Commissioner, 207, 209–210; opinions *re*, 234; mission to Europe, 270–271; 399

ZAMACOMA, 124
Zimmerman, German Foreign Secretary, and German proposals to Mexico in World War, 132–133
Zuloaga, 111; 116, 117